T0323398

Famine and Scarcity in Late Medieval and Early Modern England

Surveying government and crowd responses ranging from the late middle ages through to the early modern era, Buchanan Sharp's illuminating study examines how the English government responded to one of the most intractable problems of the period: famine and scarcity. The book provides a comprehensive account of famine relief in the late middle ages and evaluates the extent to which traditional market regulations enforced by thirteenth century kings helped shape future responses to famine and scarcity in the sixteenth century. Analyzing some of the oldest surviving archival evidence of public response to famine, Sharp reveals that food riots in England occurred as early as 1347, almost two centuries earlier than was previously thought. Charting the policies, public reactions, and royal regulations to grain shortage, Sharp provides a fascinating contribution to our understanding of the social, economic, cultural, and political make-up of medieval and early modern England.

BUCHANAN SHARP is Emeritus Professor of British and European History at the University of California, Santa Cruz.

Famine and Scarcity in Late Medieval and Early Modern England

The Regulation of Grain Marketing, 1256–1631

Buchanan Sharp

CAMBRIDGE
UNIVERSITY PRESS

CAMBRIDGE
UNIVERSITY PRESS

University Printing House, Cambridge CB2 8BS, United Kingdom

Cambridge University Press is part of the University of Cambridge.

It furthers the University's mission by disseminating knowledge in the pursuit of
education, learning and research at the highest international levels of excellence.

www.cambridge.org
Information on this title: www.cambridge.org/9781107121829

First published 2016

Printed in the United States of America by Sheridan Books, Inc.

A catalogue record for this publication is available from the British Library

Library of Congress Cataloging-in-Publication Data
Names: Sharp, Buchanan, 1942–
Title: Famine and scarcity in late medieval and early modern England :
the regulation of grain marketing, 1256-1631 / Buchanan Sharp.
Description: Cambridge, United Kingdom : Cambridge University Press,
2016. | Includes bibliographical references and index.
Identifiers: LCCN 2016000903 | ISBN 9781107121829 (Hardback :
alkaline paper)
Subjects: LCSH: Famines–England–History–To 1500. | Famines–England–
History–16th century. | Famines–England–History–17th century. | Scarcity–
Political aspects–England–History. | Food riots–England–History. | Grain
trade–Political aspects–England–History. | Marketing–Political aspects–
England–History. | Agriculture and state–England–History. | Great Britain–
History–1066-1687.
Classification: LCC HC260.F3 S53 2016 | DDC 381/.41310942–dc23 LC
record available at http://lccn.loc.gov/2016000903

ISBN 978-1-107-12182-9 Hardback

To the Memory of Thomas Garden Barnes 1930–2010
Teacher, Mentor, and Dear Friend

Contents

Acknowledgments

This book has been a long time in the making due to both the vicissitudes of life and my inability to say no when called upon by colleagues to take on all too many burdensome administrative tasks. It was only in 2010, when I retired after forty years of teaching at the University of California, Santa Cruz, that I had the time to try and make sense of a mountainous collection of research notes accumulated over many years. In writing a book that explores a topic stretching across the period 1256–1631 and beyond, I am well aware of both my temerity and my limitations. I am not a medievalist but an early modernist, although I have always had a deep interest in the middle ages. Moreover, I have never been comfortable with traditional historical periodization of the past, especially the dividing line at the date 1485 that demarks the late medieval period from the early modern in English history. The questions that interest me arise from my early modern focus on social policy and popular protest. My aim in this book is to push back into the late medieval period issues about the regulation of grain marketing that have long interested early modernists. By coming at the medieval period from a different perspective, I believe that I address important questions rarely touched upon by medievalists.

My thanks to Palgrave Macmillan for permission to reuse in Chapter 3 material that I first published in a chapter "The Food Riots of 1347 and the Medieval Moral Economy" in A. Randall and A. Charlesworth (eds.), *Moral Economy and Popular Protest: Crowds, Conflict and Authority* (Macmillan Press Ltd., 2000). My thanks also to Wiley for permission to reuse in Chapter 2 an article "Royal Paternalism and the Moral Economy in the Reign of Edward II: the Response to the Great Famine" that I first published in the *Economic History Review* 66 no. 2 (2013).

Along the way I have incurred a number of other debts. I am grateful to Steve Hindle who read the whole manuscript and provided much sage advice and to Bruce Campbell for his trenchant response to sections of the manuscript. I also want to thank the anonymous Cambridge University readers for their thorough and helpful comments.

Finally, my greatest debt of all is to the late Thomas Garden Barnes to whose memory I have dedicated this book.

In 1961, I was an undergraduate majoring in history at the University of California, Berkeley, when Tom Barnes became my academic advisor. Little did I know then that my first meeting with Tom was the beginning of a transformation of my life. I was eighteen at the time, a recent immigrant from Scotland, and unclear what my academic goals were. Tom took me under his wing, saw things in me I did not see myself, and provided support and encouragement over the next forty-nine years until his death in 2010. Above all, he taught me paleography, diplomatic and how to do historical research, including the navigation of the medieval and early modern archives in the Public Record Office, now The National Archives. For that and much else, including numerous fishing trips west of the Golden Gate, I remain eternally grateful.

Abbreviations

A Medieval Capital	B. M. S. Campbell, J. A. Galloway, D. Keene, and M. Murphy, *A Medieval Capital and Its Grain Supply: Agrarian Production and Distribution in the London Region c.1300* (Historical Geography Research Series no. 39, 1993).
APC	*Acts of the Privy Council of England*, 46 vols. (London: HMSO, 1890–1964).
Book of Orders 1587	*Orders devised by the especiall commandement of the Queenes Maiestie for the reliefe and stay of the present dearth of Graine within the Realme*, 1586/87.
Book of Orders 1594	*The renewing of certaine Orders devised by the speciall commandement of the Queenes Maiestie, for the reliefe and stay of the present dearth of Graine within the Realme: in the yeere of our Lord 1586*, 1594.
Book of Orders 1595	*A New Charge given by the Queenes commandement, to all Justices of Peace, and all Maiors, Shiriffes, and all principall Officers of Cities, Boroughs, and Townes corporate, for execution of sundry orders published the last yeere for staie of dearth of Graine*, 1595.
Book of Orders 1600	*Speciall Orders and directions By the Queenes Maiesties commandement, to all Justices of Peace, and all Maiors, Shiriffes, and all principall Officers of Cities, Boroughs, and Townes corporate, for stay and redresse of dearthe of Graine*, 1600.
Book of Orders 1608	*Orders Appointed by his Maiestie to be straightly observed for the preventing and remedying of the dearth of Graine and other Victuall*, 1608.

Book of Orders 1622	*Orders Appointed by his Maiestie to be straightly observed, for the preventing and remedying of the dearth of Graine and other Victuall*, 1622.
Book of Orders 1630	*Orders Appointed by his Maiestie to be straightly observed, for the preventing and remedying of the dearth of Graine and Victuall*, 1630.
CCR	*Calendar of Close Rolls*, 46 vols. (London: HMSO, 1892–1963).
CFR	*Calendar of Fine Rolls*, 22 vols. (London: HMSO, 1911–63).
Chronica Majora	H. R. Luard, (ed.), *Matthaei Parisiensis, monachi sancti Albani, chronica majora*, 7 vols. (London: Rolls series, 1872–83).
CIM	*Calendar of Inquisitions Miscellaneous*, 8 vols. (London: HMSO, 1916–68 and Woodbridge: Boydell, 2003).
CLB	R. R. Sharpe, (ed.), *Calendar of the Letter-Books of the City of London 1275–1509*, 12 vols. (London: Francis, 1899–1912).
CPR	*Calendar of Patent Rolls*, 54 vols. (London: HMSO, 1891–1916).
Foedera	*Foedera, Conventiones, Litterae, etc.*, 4 vols. (London: Record Commission, 1816–69).
LP	*Letters and Papers, Foreign and Domestic, of the Reign of Henry VIII*, 23 vols. (London: HMSO, 1862–1932).
Parl. Rolls	C. Given-Wilson, P. Brand, S. Phillips, M. Ormrod, G. Martin, A. Curry, and R. Horrox, (eds.), *Parliament Rolls of Medieval England*, www.british-history.ac.uk/report.aspx?pubid=1241.
SR	*Statutes of the Realm*, 11 vols. (London: Record Commission, 1810–28).
TNA	The National Archives, London.

Introduction

The starting point of my interest in the topic of this book was the serendipitous discovery about thirty years ago of a number of English food riots in 1347.[1] This discovery ran counter to prevailing historical opinion that the earliest food riots in England dated from the 1520s.[2] As a consequence, I was prompted to undertake research to determine if there had been other food riots in the later middle ages. Although I did find a few more riots in the fourteenth and fifteenth centuries, I was only able to examine a tiny fraction of the surviving medieval legal records. It may well be that there are other food riots to be found. Along with the interest in food riots, there was a larger question I wanted to answer: did the late medieval state have a policy of regulating the grain market, especially in times of scarcity or famine, that might be considered an ancestor of the extensive paternalistic regulatory apparatus of the early modern state? At the heart of this book is an attempt to answer that question.

This is a question that English medievalists have never raised. There is a rich historiography that has been produced over the years on areas such as agriculture, grain production, prices, estate management, population, famines and scarcity, local markets, and their regulation by local governments. Much of that work has been extraordinarily important for creating a context for this study. It is striking, however, that the crown is largely absent from such studies except for sections of Gras's book on the evolution of the English corn market that was first published in 1915.[3] In his excellent recent book on medieval market morality Davis focusses

---

[1] I was reading Bellamy, *Law of Treason*, pp. 67–8, 218 where he discusses examples of accroaching the royal power, a crime akin to treason. I realized that a number of his examples were food riots, although he did not appear to notice that since his focus was solely on treason and related crimes.

[2] Stevenson, *Popular Disturbances*, p. 91; Slack, *Poverty and Policy*, pp. 116–17; Guy, *Tudor England*, p. 171. Dyer, *Standards of Living*, p. 272, dismisses the possibility that there might have been food riots in the medieval period.

[3] Gras, *The Evolution of the English Corn Market*.

on both the practical and the moral values that permeated economic transactions in local medieval market places in England and on the enforcement of market regulations in towns by local officials and such institutions as borough and manorial courts.[4] In contrast, national institutions such as crown and parliament are only briefly mentioned.[5]

The overall lack of focus on the crown and parliament in the economic and social historiography appears to be the result of an assumption that the enforcement of regulations of the market in foodstuffs, especially grain, was left to local officials and institutions. At best, crown and parliament occasionally passed regulations but left enforcement to others. One striking statement about the lack of any sort of national social policy is to be found in the work of Christopher Dyer: "Medieval governments had no social policy in our understanding of the term."[6] In fact, the crown was active not only in the creation of market regulations, along with parliament when needed, but it was particularly active in enforcing such regulations in times of scarcity and famine in the interest of the common good.

During the reigns of five of the six kings between 1307 and 1440, Edward II, Edward III, Richard II, Henry IV, and Henry VI, when scarcity or famine occurred, the crown's response was consistent. The punishment of forestallers, who were usually blamed for driving up prices by keeping grain off the market, was urged. So too was the enforcement of traditional measures such as the assize of weights and measures and the assizes of ale and bread. Other actions were perhaps more significant. Prohibitions on export of grain were issued and the import of grain from overseas was encouraged by allowing it to enter England custom free. Also efforts were made to stop or reduce the smuggling of grain from England, although is not clear how effective they were.

During the reigns of Edward II's successors new responses were developed. In 1351 parliament passed a new statute of forestallers, which contained a provision that the goods a forestaller purchased could be forfeited to the king. Later, during a scarcity after the harvest of 1370, Edward III enforced the statute and ordered the sheriffs of London and nine counties to imprison those who forestalled grain, confiscate the grain and sell it in the open market. Such actions continued under Richard II and Henry VI. In 1391, Richard II appointed two local commissions (for Winchester and Tamworth) to search for and seize

---

[4] Davis, *Market Morality*.
[5] *Idid.*, pp. 141–4, 189–98, 231–51 contain most of Davis's discussion of crown and parliament.
[6] Dyer, *Standards of Living*, p. 251.

hoarded grain and then sell it in local markets, while during the famine of 1437–9 Henry VI appointed commissions in seven counties to identify forestallers, regrators, and engrossers and discover how much surplus grain they had on hand. The grain would then be forfeited to the crown under the terms of the statute of 1351 renewed in 1378 and probably sold in open market. In addition, during the scarcity years 1391 and 1429, the government of London bought grain in Europe to supply the city population, including the poor.

One major concern of Edward III, Richard II, and Henry VI, was ensuring the grain supply of London in times of scarcity. This meant issuing licenses to allow the movement of grain by sea to the city from other parts of England and occasionally Ireland, as well as encouraging the import of foreign grain. Another concern was the grain supply of Bristol. That supply could be cut off or reduced in two ways. One was neighboring counties, which were suffering from scarcity, could fail to provide normal amounts of grain for the city. The other was blockades of the River Severn by the inhabitants of other communities along the river, including the Forest of Dean.[7]

Governmental action in response to famine and scarcity was justified by the language of the common good. For example, Edward II's proclamation prohibiting the export of grain, issued after the failure of the harvest of 1315, was for the *comodo populi nobis*.[8] In October 1351, after another poor harvest, Edward III's government issued an ordinance *pur commune profit* that renewed the traditional measures that regulated London grain marketing.[9] In 1378 parliament renewed the 1351 statute of forestallers *pur commune profit*.[10] During the scarcity of 1391, Richard II issued a number of mandates to officials in different ports informing them that native and alien merchants could ship grain to England customs free. Those mandates all contained the same justification, *pro rei publice et relevatio populi*.[11] Finally, at the beginning of the famine of 1437–9 Henry VI ordered a prohibition on export of grain for the *commune bonum*.[12]

There can be little doubt that behind such language were religiously based moral values regarding a monarch's responsibility for the welfare of his subjects. This is made clear in Edward II's letter to the English bishops in 1316 during the Great Famine, which the king blamed on

---

[7] See Chapters 3–5.   [8] *CCR, 1313–18*, pp. 308–9; *Foedera*, vol. 1 pt. 1, pp. 276.
[9] *CCR, 1349–50*, 391–2; *Foedera*, vol. 3 pt. 1, pp. 233–4.
[10] *SR*, vol. 2, p. 8, Ric II stat. i c. 2.
[11] TNA, C54/232 m. 10v; *CCR, 1388–92*, pp. 237, 348.
[12] TNA, C54/288 m. 20v;*CCR, 1435–41*, p. 138.

excessive rains brought on by the sins of the people in failing to obey God's laws. The letter then goes on to express his pain and sorrow at the suffering of his subjects.[13] Similar language appears in commissions that Henry VI issued during the famine of 1437–9 to inquire into those who bought large quantities of grain to advance their individual interest without *visceribus pietatis* "bowels of pity" in time of scarcity.[14]

This leads to one other major point about the medieval, as well as the early modern, crown's regulation of the trade in grain. The interests and aims of the crown were not always the same as those of the consumers. In times of scarcity and rising prices, the crown regularly issued licenses to allow the movement of grain from various parts of the kingdom to ensure the supply of London and elsewhere. It also prohibited export of grain to meet the needs of domestic consumers and thereby prevent starvation or disorder and to fulfill the religiously sanctioned social and moral obligations of the ruler towards his subjects. At the same time, the crown retained the power to license overseas shipment of grain. Often such licensing was used to aid foreign allies or to meet other obligations or commitments, such as warfare in Scotland and France, that had to be supported by the shipment of grain and other foodstuffs out of the country, no matter the domestic consequences. Consumers, in contrast, were focussed much more on their own needs and those of their communities. It is clear from the behavior of late medieval food rioters that they believed locally produced grain should be consumed locally and should not be transported elsewhere, which would result in scarcity and high prices in their home areas.

It is not surprising then that, for example, most of the known medieval food riots occurred in ports and aimed to stop movement of grain either overseas or, in one case, to London. Those ports included Boston (1347), Lynn (1347 and 1405), Bristol (1347), unnamed ports in Kent (1347), Yarmouth (1375), and Southwold Haven (1438). Another riot, at Ipswich in 1438, involved the seizure of grain bought by London merchants, who intended to supply the city. The other locus of food riots was rivers down which grain moved. There was one at Thetford on the Little Ouse (1347) and at least three on the Severn close to the Forest of Dean (1401, 1428, and 1429).

After 1440, England entered into a new era of low grain prices, adequate to good harvests, and few scarcities and dearths. Major contributors to this change were population decline and rising real wages. One consequence was that, between 1440 and 1527, dearth measures

---

[13] Hardy (ed.),*Register of Richard de Kellawe*, vol. 2, p. 1119.
[14] TNA, C66/443 m. 27v; C66/445 m. 25v;*CPR, 1436–41*, pp. 266, 369.

were rarely implemented. An indicator of this change is that for most of this period grain appears to have been freely exported without license when the price of a quarter of wheat was below 6s 8d and barley was below 3s as allowed by the statute of 1445. The only major exception to this development was during the deficient harvests of 1481–2 and 1482–3, when the price of wheat and barley rose well beyond the 6s 8d and 3s per quarter base. In response Edward IV's government prohibited export without a license and ensured the shipment of grain to supply London's need. .

In Henry VIII's reign dearth and scarcity returned. Not only were there especially poor harvests years in 1520–1, 1527–33, 1535–7, and 1545–6 but also there were runs of multiple harvest years with above average wheat prices, 1519–22, 1527–33, 1535–7, and 1541–6. In the years 1519–22, town governments appear to have been highly active in responding to the needs of their inhabitants, while there is virtually no evidence of any actions taken by the crown. The magistrates of Coventry and Norwich, for instance, produced new market regulations to ensure that grain supplies coming to the town came to market and were not forestalled. They also bought grain to sell in the town markets to bring down prices, an action that the magistrates of Bristol and London also took.

It was the drastic failure of the harvest of 1527 that compelled the government of Henry VIII, led by Cardinal Wolsey, to action then and in subsequent years. That action mainly involved the revival of medieval precedents. The export of grain was prohibited and forestallers, regrators, and engrossers were to be vigorously pursued and punished. Considerable official efforts were also made to buy grain in foreign parts, especially for the supply of London and the king's possessions in France, first Calais and later Boulogne as well. As part of the campaign against forestalling and other market offences, Wolsey revived the commissions to search for grain that had been first issued in the reigns of Edward III, Richard II, and Henry VI. But there was considerable innovation in Wolsey's commissions, which were established in every county, rather than in a handful of local communities or counties as was the case with their medieval precedents. Also Wolsey's commissions were given wide search powers as well as authority to compel the owners of surplus grain to sell it in the market and authority to send those, who refused to comply with the commissions' orders, to London for punishment. After Wolsey fell and Thomas Cromwell became Henry VIII's chief minister he maintained the Cardinal's policies and added to them a vigorous campaign against illegal export of grain.

In the Henrician response to poor harvest another continuity with the past was the language used in the proclamations and other pronouncements that conveyed royal policy to local officials and the population at large. Frequently, the "common good" was invoked usually in the form of the "commonwealth," along with the needs of the king's loving but poor subjects. At the same time, the covetousness of forestallers and the like, who sought only their private gain and had no thought for the common good, was regularly condemned.

There was a major shift in the grain policy of Henry VIII's government during the period 1544–6. The focus moved from the needs of the consumers to the supply of the king's armies in Calais and Boulogne. In October 1545, after a poor harvest, commissions to search for surplus grain were revived in eight major agricultural counties. The commissioners, who were mainly purveyors, were authorized to search for surplus grain not to compel its sale in local markets but to supply the king's armies in France. Despite the complaints of the Duke of Norfolk that in such a scarcity year there was little surplus, the king, who was directing this policy, pushed on. Proclamations were issued prohibiting the shipment of grain and other victuals except to three places, London, Calais, and Boulogne. It was only the peace with France on June 27, 1546 that ended this particular policy.[15]

With the return of scarcity and dearth in Henry VIII's reign came food riots, although they were few in number. There were riots in London (1527), Norwich (1527, 1529, and 1532), Yarmouth (1527 and 1532), and on the Severn south of Gloucester (1531). Yarmouth was a port through which grain was shipped either to London or to various European destinations. Such exports provoked riots as was the case in the late middle ages. Norwich was an inland city with a sizeable population of textile workers who had a difficult time feeding their families during periods of high grain prices, hence the riots there. The Severn was the lifeline for Bristol and the riot there involved the seizure of grain bound for that city during a period of scarcity and its sale in Gloucester, which was probably also suffering scarcity.

During the period March–June 1528, there were other signs of popular unrest, which sometimes included talk of planned insurrections, in Wiltshire, Somerset, Hampshire, Berkshire, Suffolk, Essex, and Kent. Only in Kent does there appear to have been any likelihood of an actual insurrection. One element in that unrest was the high prices of grain after the failure of the harvest of 1527. Another was a stoppage of trade with the Low Countries between February and June 1528. Since Antwerp was the main market for English cloth, the trade embargo left English

---

[15] See Chapter 6.

clothiers with too much unsold cloth on hand that meant the threat of short time or unemployment for their workers, who were concentrated in the counties where popular unrest was most apparent. The final element, especially in Kent, was the failure of the king to repay the Forced Loan of 1522–3. Repayment was promised for 1524 but it never happened. By April 1528, there were signs of widespread discontent in Kent over the issue. The failure to repay the loan appears to have intensified the sense of impoverishment among some of the county's inhabitants that was originally caused by high food prices and the disruption of the cloth trade. The result was a failed attempt at insurrection in May.[16]

While the main focus of this book is on the crown's regulation of grain marketing in times of scarcity during the period 1256–1547, the final chapter turns briefly to the years 1547–1631 in the main to examine some of the issues raised by the responses of Henry VIII's successors to scarcity and dearth. Those responses were rooted in the policies of Cardinal Wolsey, who in turn, drew heavily on medieval precedents. After harvest failures in the reigns of Edward VI and Mary I, justices of the peace were authorized to conduct searches for grain, while a new parliamentary statute against regrating, engrossing, and forestalling, was passed in 1552. At the beginning of 1587, after the poor harvest of 1586, the Elizabethan government issued a book of orders that contained regulations that justices of the peace in each county should enforce in times of scarcity and dearth. It was reissued, with occasional revisions, during such periods up through 1631.

The book ordered the justices to conduct, with the help of juries, surveys of grain stocks and to compel owners to sell any surplus regularly in the market in order to lower the price for consumers, especially the poorer ones. After the opening of each market only the poor were to be served for the first hour in the 1587 edition or the first two hours in the 1594 and subsequent editions. The justices were also charged to try to persuade those with grain to sell to reduce their prices in the interest of the poor, while the clergy were urged to use their sermons to exhort the richer sort to sell grain to the poor at less than the market price. There were a number of additional measures for the relief of the poor that were included in every edition of the book from 1587 onwards. The only out of market grain sales allowed were to poor craftsmen and laborers in their home parishes. The book also recognized that lack of money made it difficult for the poor or unemployed to pay for food. It advocated supplying raw material to put the poor to work or increasing poor rates to

---

[16] See Chapter 7.

supply them with money to buy food. If a parish had more poor than it could support, neighboring parishes with fewer poor were expected to provide financial help.

In addition to the book of orders, the crown implemented other dearth measures such as prohibitions on the export of grain, while encouraging the import of grain from abroad, especially the Baltic region. Also local officials in London and other towns raised money to buy grain overseas to supply their markets, which included selling grain to the poor at lower prices. Finally, the most traditional dearth measure that the crown marshalled during the age of the book of orders was rhetorical. In privy council letters and proclamations engrossers, forestallers and the like were routinely denounced for their covetousness and their pursuit of their own private gain at the expense of the poor and the common good. They were also condemned as dishonest and unchristian oppressors of the poor.

While the book of orders and the language of the common good represent forms of royal paternalism and appear to have similarities to the moral economy of the poor, they were not identical. In their localism early modern food rioters were much like their predecessors in the fourteenth and fifteenth centuries. It is obvious from the evidence of the behavior of crowds between the fourteenth and seventeenth centuries that they were governed by the set of norms summed up in the idea of moral economy that Thompson explored so memorably in his article on the eighteenth-century crowd.[17] Central to that moral economy was the belief that the market should provide the consumers with food at affordable prices, especially in times of scarcity. To achieve that end it was necessary for local and central authorities to regulate the market in the interest of the consumers. If the authorities failed in that duty, then consumers acting together were justified in direct action to enforce traditional or established regulations. Such actions included preventing the movement of grain by ship, cart or packhorse from a community where scarcity and high prices already existed or were feared. On some occasions, crowds seized grain shipments and returned them to the market where purchased and compelled their sale at less than the prevailing market price. On other occasions, crowds attempted to compel sellers in the market to charge less than the market price for their grain.

While the crown, during the period 1586–1631, displayed marked understanding of the needs of the poor and made every effort to respond to those needs with the book of orders and other remedial measures, its

---

[17] Thompson, "The Moral Economy."

responsibilities were national rather than local. This meant that monarch and privy council had to undertake actions that ran counter to popular moral economy ideas enshrined in the book. The contradictions in crown policy are best illustrated in the necessary movement of grain in order to feed urban areas, especially London and Bristol.

Ensuring the grain supply of London had been a major concern of royal government during poor harvest years from the reign of Edward II through that of Henry VIII. Such concern continued in the period 1585–1631. In 1587, 1595–8, and 1630–1, the privy council regularly wrote to justices in southern and south eastern counties to lift restraints that either prevented properly licensed London dealers from gaining access to local grain markets or prohibited them from shipping grain to the city that they had already purchased in local markets. In some instances, there were riots to stop such movements of grain and keep it in the local community for its own use. One other indicator of the significance that the crown attached to the supply of London occurred in 1597 when the privy council issued warrants to officials in eight counties to allow licensed London buyers to make private, out of market, purchases of grain to meet the city's needs. This was contrary to language in the 1587 and 1594 editions of the book of orders, but in the 1595 and subsequent editions language was added that the privy council intended to issue further instructions on the supply of cities in the future.

Like the grain supply of London, that of Bristol had been an important focus of crown policy since the fourteenth century. In 1586–7 and 1595–7, the privy council wrote a number of letters to justices of the peace and town magistrates in communities along the river Severn to permit the movement of grain down river to Bristol. In 1586, the actions of impoverished cloth workers were a particular concern, when on two occasions they seized grain from river boats bound for Bristol that were moored south of the city of Gloucester, waiting for the ebb tide. Later, in 1597, the privy council's focus turned to Gloucester where the mayor had ordered the chains to be pulled across the Severn to prevent the shipment of grain to Bristol.

The grain needs of London and Bristol are only two among many examples of the problem of urban supply that the privy council had to deal with. On many other occasions in 1586–7, 1594–7, and 1630–1 the council was compelled to write to local justices in various counties to allow licensed dealers from many different towns to buy grain in local markets and carry it to their grain short communities. The local justices in these cases, as well as in the examples of those who resisted the supply of London and Bristol, no doubt justified their actions by claiming that the grain produced locally should be consumed locally, an assumption that appears to lie at the heart of the book of orders and the moral economy. But such actions and opinions reveal that there was not a single, nationwide moral economy but a series of localized, community based moral economies that either attempted to prevent grain from being transported out of a given area or were in competition with one another for the same grain. The privy council was the only institution that had nationwide concerns and acted, as contradictory as it sometimes was, to satisfy or prioritize as many competing interests as it could in times of scarcity and dearth.[18] Finally, at the end there is a brief discussion of the persistence of popular, localized moral economy ideas among poor consumers in the years after 1631, the last year in which the book of orders was enforced.

---

[18] See Chapter 8.

1 Early market regulation to 1327

During the thirteenth-century England experienced important economic and demographic changes, which had significant implications for feeding the population. These clearly interdependent changes included population growth, an increase in agricultural output, the development of a widespread network of markets for the buying and selling of grain and other foodstuffs as well as a range of handicraft products, and a rise in the number of people partially or totally dependent on the market for food, especially bread grains.

While there is no certain evidence for food riots before 1347, there is considerable earlier evidence for the crown's attempts to regulate trade in foodstuffs in a variety of ways. The crown's commitment to a sustained effort to enforce the assizes of bread, ale, and weights and measures along with the statute against forestalling appears to have its origins in the reigns of Henry III and Edward I. During the reign of Edward II (1307–27), the crown continued to enforce these established market regulations generally but with increased vigor in the area of forestalling.

The traditional regulations were not dearth specific but rather represented a growing commitment on the part of the crown to regulate quality and to moderate or limit rises in the price of food that might be caused either by market manipulation such as forestalling and false measures or by the market distorting presence of the royal court within a particular region. Nonetheless, by the late thirteenth century the crown's responsibility for regulation of the food market in the interest of consumers generally, while insuring a reasonable profit for the seller, came to include a particular concern for poorer consumers. In turn that responsibility, under the pressure of the famine of 1315–17 and the generally hard years of 1315–22, led to direct governmental responses to grain scarcity.

Economic change and population growth

At the moment there seems to be no clear consensus among historians about either the rate of population growth in thirteenth-century England or population numbers in the fourteenth century. Over the past sixty years estimates of the fourteenth-century population total at its highest point, either before the Great Famine of 1315–17 or the Black Death of 1348–9, have ranged from 3.75 million by Russell to as high as 6 million or more by Postan.[1] For a time it appeared that historians had reached agreement on 6 million but in recent years, as a result of the work of Campbell, some seem to be moving back toward a figure closer to that of Russell.

Based on his extensive research on demesne agriculture and his calculations of the likely grain production total, Campbell has argued that the fourteenth-century population could never have grown much beyond 4.25 million.[2] In his book on seigniorial agriculture Campbell threw down the gauntlet at the feet of other historians when he wrote: "The onus is therefore on those who wish to argue for a medieval population at peak in excess of 4.5 million to demonstrate by what means, on known patterns of land-use and productivity, it could have been fed."[3] One historian who has picked up the gauntlet is Stone, who reworked Campbell's figures using different crop preferences for peasant producers and higher yields for peasant land, in comparison to the demesne production of secular and clerical lords, to arrive at a population figure of 5.5 million or more.[4] More recently, Clark has argued for a figure just under 6 million based in part on a calculation that Campbell had underestimated the amount of land available for cultivation by around 5.2 million acres.[5] Whatever the actual number, there is no doubt that the English population grew during the twelfth and thirteenth centuries. The 4.25 million figure represents roughly a doubling of the population since 1086 while the estimate of 6 million constitutes a near trebling in size.[6]

As both cause and effect of population growth, English agriculture became increasingly market oriented during the thirteenth century.[7] This orientation included not only the great lay and ecclesiastical seigniorial demesne producers but also more modest peasant producers. Of course, as Bailey cautions, one should not exaggerate the level of production

---

[1] See the survey of the population question in Miller and Hatcher, *Medieval England: Rural Society*, pp. 28–33. See also Smith, "Human Resources," pp. 188–212 and Rigby, "Social Structure and Economic Change," pp. 13–15, 25–7.

[2] *A Medieval Capital*, pp. 45, 77, 172; Campbell, *Seigniorial Agriculture*, pp. 386–410.

[3] Campbell, *Seigniorial Agriculture*, p. 405.

[4] Stone, *Decision Making*, pp. 267–71; Stone, "Consumption of Field Crops," pp. 19–21.

[5] Clark, "The Long March of History," 118–25.

[6] Britnell, "Commercialisation," pp. 11–12.

[7] Davis, *Market Morality*, pp. 9–22 provides a concise overview of modern scholarship on the late medieval English economy.

for the market in the middle ages.[8] Much production went to feed the family and household, whether of the individual peasant, the great lord, or the ecclesiastical institution. Nonetheless, in the London region the food needs of the city greatly affected agricultural production "with perhaps half of the grain produced by the demesne sector (net of seed and fodder) being distributed via the market,"[9] Such estimates do not take into account peasant production, for which there is no reliable figure at present. Britnell has estimated that in the thirteenth century 30–40 percent of all grain harvested in the southeast of England was sold. The southeast, which included London, was undoubtedly the main center of commercially oriented agriculture in the kingdom followed closely by the midlands. In other areas of the country only 5–10 percent of grain output appears to have been sold.[10]

In tandem with the growth in production for the market, there developed a marketing system. Between 1227 and 1350, English kings made 1,200 grants of rights to markets in England and Wales.[11] While all of the places that received such rights did not survive as markets, many did. More importantly, the number of grants indicates a growing demand and need for markets. Many were small and served a local population, within a circumference of 10–12 miles. To such markets peasants as well as landowners brought their surplus for sale and bought manufactured goods or other foodstuffs either produced locally or brought to the market from some distance by merchants. Peasants might also sell their more expensive wheat for cash and then buy cheaper barley, rye, maslin (a mixture of wheat and rye), or dredge (a mixture of barley and oats) to feed their families. In turn, the grain that producers sold in local markets might be bought either by the people of the market town to feed themselves or by dealers who shipped it elsewhere. It should be kept in mind that there were also numerous but immeasurable out of market sales of grain that both large and small producers made to local consumers, so-called farm gate sales, a practice that lasted into the early modern period.[12]

In addition to small, local markets, there were regional urban centers with much larger populations that depended on buying grain, flour, or bread in the market place for their subsistence. These centers, which included ports, drew grain from much wider geographical areas and dealt in larger quantities, some of which was transported overland or coastwise

---

[8] Bailey, "Commercialisation of the English Economy," 297–311.
[9] *A Medieval Capital*, p. 176, see also pp. 72–6.   [10] Britnell, *Britain and Ireland*, p. 198.
[11] Miller and Hatcher, *Medieval England: Rural Society*, p. 77; Farmer, "Marketing the Produce," p. 329; Britnell, "Proliferation of Markets," 209–21; Masschaele, "The Multiplicity of Medieval Markets," 255–71.
[12] Farmer, "Marketing the Produce," pp. 358–67.

within England, or shipped overseas. The premier urban center in England was, of course, London, which was unique in population size and consequently in its demand for foodstuffs. Estimates of the city's pre-plague population vary considerably, largely in proportion to estimates of the population as a whole. These range from a low of 60,000 to a high of 100,000 with many scholars settling for a 72,000–80,000 range.[13]

To supply the food necessary to feed London's population was a large and complex undertaking. In normal years, that is dearth free, London's supplies came from parts of ten counties in its immediate environs. Given the enormous cost differential between water and overland transport, ready access to coastal waters and navigable rivers – such as the Thames, the Lea, and the Medway – was crucial in determining which particular areas within those ten counties could take full advantage of the opportunities that the London market offered.[14] London's normal supply region took in "market towns up to about 20 miles from the city when only land transport to London was available, and up to 60 miles as the crow flies when water transport could be used."[15] In addition, dealers in London and other urban centers, officials in institutions such as Cambridge colleges, and the agents of numerous aristocratic families sometimes avoided local markets and bought grain and other foodstuffs directly from producers.[16]

By the late thirteenth century, not only was English agriculture increasingly market oriented but a sizeable, although difficult to quantify, proportion of the population had become dependent to one degree or another on the market for food. Beyond the urban population there were growing numbers of laborers and smallholders in the countryside, who were at least partially dependent on the market in good times and almost completely dependent during scarcity. Their existence and survival struggles have been well documented in modern studies of manors in Norfolk, Suffolk, Worcestershire, and Somerset. From at least the late thirteenth century onward population growth made such laborers and smallholders and their families vulnerable to the effects of deficient harvests and, finally and most catastrophically, to the Great Famine of 1315–17.[17]

[13] *A Medieval Capital*, pp. 9–11, 44–5; Campbell, *English Seigniorial Agriculture*, p. 405; Nightingale, "The Growth of London," pp. 89–106.

[14] *A Medieval Capital*, pp. 60–9.   [15] *Ibid.*, p. 173.

[16] Farmer, "Marketing the Produce," pp. 358–77; *A Medieval Capital*, pp. 98–9; Dyer, "The Consumer And The Market," 305–27; Lee, "Cambridge's Food and Fuel," 243–64.

[17] Razi, *Life, Marriage and Death*, pp. 36–45, 76–98; Campbell, "Population Pressure," pp. 87–134; Smith, "Families and their Land," pp. 135–95; Fox, "Exploitation of the Landless," pp. 518–39; Smith, "A Periodic Market," pp. 450–81; Schofield, "Dearth, Debt and the Local Land Market," 1–17; Schofield, "The Social Economy," 38–63.

Early market regulations

One striking political development in thirteenth-century England was the growth in royal power that manifested itself in a number of ways, including the development of the common law, the proliferation of courts, especially those that went on circuit round the country to bring the king's justice to the localities, and the demand of the crown for more resources, through taxes, purveyance, and prises to pay for an aggressive and expansionist foreign policy. English population growth and economic development in the thirteenth century provided the means and resources, including able bodied men, that enabled kings from Edward I onward to wage war, first in Wales, then Scotland, and finally France.

Another dimension of the development of royal authority was the crown's assumption of responsibility to regulate the marketing of food, particularly during the reigns of Henry III and Edward I. Regulations included the assizes of bread, ale, and weights and measures and the statute of forestallers plus occasional short-term and geographically limited price controls on a variety of foodstuffs. The origins and early history of the assizes and the statute of forestallers are obscure although it appears that in the twelfth century local regulation of the weight and price of bread, which reflected the prevailing price of grain, may have either preceded or run concurrently with the crown's proclaimed assize of bread.[18] A similar situation appears to have existed in the case of the assize of ale that regulated the price of ale according to the price of the grain used for the making of malt.[19]

The crown's concern with the price and quality of bread and ale probably originated with rules to be enforced within the verge, the twelve-mile radius around the royal household or court where the monarch resided (a regularly moving entity in an age of an itinerant ruler).[20] Such royal involvement may have been moved by self interest in an attempt to keep down the price the court had to pay for its own supplies but it also benefited consumers who happened to live within the verge through the prevention of price gouging stimulated by the presence of the royal household. Eventually, royal market regulations expanded their range and became the basis of statutory laws that could be enforced nationwide in either royal or local courts.

---

[18] Britnell, *Commercialisation of English Society*, pp. 25–6, 94–7; Davis, "Baking for the Common Good," 465–9; Seaborne, "Assize Matters," 31–3.

[19] Britnell, *Commercialisation of English Society*, pp. 94–5; Bennett, *Ale, Beer, and Brewsters*, pp. 99–101.

[20] Britnell, *Commercialisation of English Society*, pp. 94–6; Davis, "Baking for the Common Good," 465, 468.

The first assizes of bread and ale that might have applied to the country as a whole originated in the reign of Henry II, although it is possible that they only applied within the verge of the court. It is more likely, however, that the first "national" assizes were issued in the 1190s during the reign of Richard I. Thereafter revised versions appeared under John and Henry III.[21] In the final form of the assize of bread that acquired statutory authority, "wastel" bread made from white wheat flour was employed for the calculation of the weight and price of bread, another indication "that the assize of bread was first formulated for high-status white bread in the royal household."[22]

The assizes of wine and weights and measures are closely related to the assizes of bread and ale, but are much more clearly associated with royal initiatives alone. The assize of wine, which set the price of wine, dates from around 1176, during the reign of Henry II, and appears to have been enforced with some regularity thereafter. Clearly the royal court as a major consumer had a vested interest in controlling wine prices. Similarly, as a buyer of large quantities of foodstuffs and other goods, the court had an interest in eliminating fraudulent dealings and imposing standardized weights and measures nationwide. Hence the assize of weights and measures of 1196 and the clause in *Magna Carta* that "there be one measure of wine throughout our kingdom, and one measure of ale and one measure of corn namely the London quarter, and one width of cloth .... Let it be the same with weights as with measures."[23]

The years 1255–6 were particularly important in the development of a royal commitment to the enforcement of the various regulatory assizes. The statutory forms of the assizes of bread, ale, wine, and weights and measures that remained in force throughout the middle ages probably date from 1255–6, when Henry III commissioned clerks and serjeants of the market to go around the kingdom enforcing them.[24] In describing the activities of the commissions the chronicler, Matthew Paris is scathing in his denunciation of the corrupt practices that led to extortionate fines imposed on the guilty and the innocent alike.[25] Similar problems were to arise in the 1340s when Edward III attempted a vigorous campaign

[21] Britnell, *Commercialisation of English Society*, pp. 26, 94–6.

[22] Davis, "Baking for the Common Good," 469 nt. 21.

[23] Magna Carta clause 35 in Holt, *Magna Carta*, p. 461.

[24] *SR*, vol. 1, pp. 199–202; *CPR, 1247–58*, pp. 427, 488, 502, 569; *Chronica Majora*, vol. 5, pp. 594–5; Davis, "Baking for the Common Good," 468 nt. 15; Britnell, "Forestalling," 95, 100; Britnell, *Commercialisation of English Society*, pp. 90–1. It is possible that the enforcement of the assizes began somewhat earlier, in 1254–55, *CCR, 1253–4*, p. 256 and *CCR, 1254–6*, pp. 94, 173.

[25] *Chronica Majora*, vol. 5, pp. 594–5.

of enforcement of the assize of weights and measures.[26] Later in his reign, in 1270, Henry III issued a further commission to enforce weights and measures and other market regulations in five western counties.[27] Then in 1273–6 the government of Edward I sent out similar commissions of clerks and serjeants of the market to enforce the various market regulations nationwide.[28] This use of clerks and serjeants of the market (sometimes called clerks of the marshalsea), who held royal household offices closely associated with regulating markets within the verge, to undertake national enforcement of market regulations provides further confirmation of the close connection between the household and such regulations.[29]

The early history of the statute of forestallers follows very much the same pattern as the assizes. In the twelfth and thirteenth centuries forestalling "was a loose term to cover trading regulations of several kinds" that were enforced by the authorities in various towns.[30] The origin of what came to be known in Edward II's reign as the statute of forestallers, with its definition of forestalling as the buying of goods, including grain and other victuals, before they reached market with the intention of reselling them in the market at a higher price, was also closely associated with the royal household.

The definition of forestalling and the punishments of forestallers ranging from a fine and loss of forestalled goods for a first offence, to sentence to the pillory for a second, imprisonment for a third, and

---

[26] *Parl. Rolls,* "Edward III: June 1344," items 47–8.

[27] *CPR, 1258–72,* p. 454. The counties were Somerset, Dorset, Devon, Wiltshire, and Hampshire. See also *CPR, 1258–72,* p. 630, commission to view weights and measures in boroughs and market towns of Bedfordshire and Buckinghamshire, February 23, 1272, and a case of false measures brought before the eyre justices for Cambridgeshire in 1259 in Richardson and Sayles (eds.), *Select Cases,* pp. 117–19.

[28] *CPR, 1272–81,* pp. 16, 31, 73, 136. See also p. 172, order to the bailiffs of Bristol to buy and sell grain only by the London quarter and order to the Constable of Bristol castle to proclaim the same, November 18, 1276 and *CPR, 1292–1301,* p. 99, appointment of Alexander de London as clerk of the market, October 24, 1294.

[29] For the jurisdiction of the clerks of the market in the reign of Edward I see Prestwich, *Edward I,* pp. 165–7, and B. Byerly and C. Byerly (eds.), *Wardrobe and Household,* pp. xxv, 192–3; Richardson and Sayles (eds.), *Fleta,* p. 117, indicates that either a clerk or a layman could be in charge "of the office of clerk of the Marshalcy." The duties included custody "of the king's measures, which are taken as the standard and pattern measures of the realm." The clerk was also to have a full understanding of the assizes of bread, wine, measures, and ale. This legal treatise, from about 1296, also contains versions of the various regulatory assizes on pp. 117–22. One of the two men commissioned in 1270 to enforce the market regulations in five western counties was described as a clerk of the Marshalsea, *CPR, 1258–72,* p. 454. For the continued regulatory role of the clerks of the market that lasted into the fifteenth century see Davis, "Market Regulation," pp. 81–106.

[30] Britnell, "Forestalling," 89.

banishment from the town for a fourth are one part of a document printed in the *Statutes of the Realm* called *Statutum de Pistoribus* or "the rule (*Composicio*) for punishing the infringers of the Assize of Bread and Ale, Forestallers, Cooks etc." In addition to forestalling, the document – as the title indicates – sets out the assizes of bread, ale, wine and weights and measures and rules on selling unwholesome meat as well as the punishments for their violation.[31] Britnell has convincingly demonstrated that the *Composicio* originated around 1274–5 as a series of directions for the clerks of the marshalsea, whom Edward I sent round the country in that period to oversee the enforcement of traditional market regulations.[32]

During the later years of Edward I, the crown continued to enforce the law against forestalling. In June 1293 the king granted to the mayor of Cambridge and the chancellor of the University jurisdiction over forestallers in the town.[33] Later "in October 1304 commissions of oyer and terminer were appointed to examine complaints that forestallers were intercepting victuals and other goods, and consequently raising prices, in Norwich, Great Yarmouth and Ipswich."[34] At the same time, in response to a complaint by "the poor men" of Lynn, a commission of oyer and terminer was authorized to look into forestalling in that town.[35] Finally, another commission of oyer and terminer of July 1306 was charged with investigating forestalling of fish and other goods at Great Yarmouth. Over sixty suspected forestallers were named in the commission.[36]

Although each of the market regulations can be considered as an individual item, contemporaries regularly treated them as closely related entities as in the *Composicio*. Perhaps one of the most comprehensive statements of the regulations is to be found in the York civic ordinances of August 29, 1301 that Edward I's council issued after consultation with the city magistrates.[37] The ordinances were a response to rising prices in York that followed from the move of the king's government to the city in 1298 so that it could be closer to the ongoing military campaigns in Scotland. The surviving text opens with the justification for the regulations, which were designed "for the remedy and relief of those coming to York, both on the king's business and on that of others, who complain of the extortions and oppressions imposed by the citizens, both by failing

---

[31] *SR*, vol. 1, pp. 202–4 (the forestalling section is on pp. 203–4).
[32] Britnell, "Forestalling," 94–6. See also Gairdner (ed.), *Historical Collections*, p. 70 and Nicolas (ed.), *A Chronicle of London*, p. 27.
[33] *CPR, 1293–1301*, p. 18.   [34] *CPR, 1301–7*, p. 284; Britnell, "Forestalling," 99–100.
[35] *CPR, 1301–7*, pp. 287, 325.   [36] *Ibid.*, p. 477.
[37] Prestwich (ed.), *York Civic Ordinances.*

to observe the Assize of Bread and Ale, and by the intolerable costs of other victuals ...."[38] While the message of this opening statement is clearly that the presence of the king's government in York and the consequent influx of officials and suitors was driving up prices, later in the ordinances another culprit was found to be, at least partially, responsible for the price rise. That was the circulation in the city's money supply of pollards and crockards, debased foreign coins.[39]

The ordinances that followed the opening justification were, in substance, a restatement of the traditional regulations such as the assizes of bread, ale, and wine, and the statute on forestallers along with some additional items. The additions included an ordinance against regrating (the purchase of goods in the market with the intention of reselling them later at a profit in the same market or another close by) and ordinances on the sale of raw meat, cooked meat, and fish that dealt with quality and price. The prices of a wide range of foodstuffs were also set including fowl, eggs, herring, rabbits, and onions but not grain. There were also rules establishing prices for the products of tanners and tailors and regulating the size of cloth and quality of skins. Finally rents were set for rooms let by hostelers and landlords.[40]

The justification for the York ordinances probably originated in the regulations governing the verge of the royal household. Just as market regulations within the verge aimed to control the price and quality of food stuffs within the twelve mile radius around the royal household, the York ordinances had the same aim within the boundaries of the city of York where the king's government was temporarily located, whether the king and his household were actually present or not. In attempting to control prices within the locality where government institutions and personnel were located, the York ordinances were hardly unique. Other examples include the regulations governing marketing in London in the years 1285–98 that the crown issued during a period when it had assumed direct authority over the city and the proclamation that Edward I issued in 1305 on the eve of a meeting of parliament in London against the enhancement of the price of victuals, including the sale of bread, ale, and wine at prices above those set by the assizes.[41]

---

[38] *Ibid.*, p. 9.   [39] *Ibid.*, pp. 14–15.

[40] *Ibid.*, pp. 10–17; there are also ordinances covering the keeping of pigs, expelling prostitutes from the city, and regulating the professional activities of physicians.

[41] *Ibid.*, 4; *CLB*, vol. C, pp. 145, 147; Riley (ed.), *Memorials*, pp. 56–7. For an example of the kinds of demands for food and fodder that a meeting of parliament could make on local markets, see Pelham, "Provisioning of the Lincoln Parliament," 16–32. For the victualling needs of parliaments at Westminster in the period 1312–14 see *CCR, 1307–13*, pp. 463–4, *Foedera*, vol. 2 pt. 1, p. 218, and *CPR, 1313–17*, pp. 194–5.

There is one final indicator of the importance that the government of Edward I attached to the king's authority over market regulations, namely the *quo warranto* proceedings of the reign. Such proceedings were designed to assert royal authority over judicial powers that were in private hands. Starting from the premise that the administration of justice was a royal prerogative, Edward I's government sought, through the *quo warranto* process, to discover the circumstances under which a delegation of such power to a private party had been made, in order to determine whether it was good in law or an illegal usurpation of royal authority. If the private party, who exercised this delegated jurisdiction, could not prove title to it through a royal grant, he was liable to forfeit it or pay a substantial fine to continue to exercise it. In practice, and in the face of noble resistance, Edward I did not push his claims as hard as he may have wanted to; nonetheless, this assertion of royal authority represented another important dimension of the growth in the crown's power in the thirteenth century.[42]

Among the delegated judicial powers challenged through *quo warranto* proceedings was the right of private parties to administer the assizes of bread and ale and impose penalties on bakers and brewers who violated their terms. Masschaele has shown that, in order for private parties to succeed in keeping jurisdiction over the assizes, they had to demonstrate that they had a pillory in which they punished chronic violators of the regulations. Many holders of such jurisdiction apparently had no pillory but only fined assize breakers. The crown sometimes claimed successfully that without a pillory, as required by the assizes, there was no right to the jurisdiction, which was, in effect, forfeit to the king.[43] Early in Edward III's reign, in an opinion on a similar case at the eyre of Northamptonshire, Scrope CJ put it nicely:

The lord of the market must do justice to everyone on the market day for matters, which concern the market. A market cannot be held unless the assize of bread and ale is duly enforced, and that cannot be if the corporal penalties cannot be imposed. So you have claimed a market and disclaimed that which is appendant to a market.[44]

Market regulation in the reign of Edward II

In the early years of his reign, Edward II's government was particularly active in enforcing what was now officially referred to as the statute or

---

[42] The classic work is Sutherland, *Quo Warranto*.

[43] Masschaele, "The Public Space of the Marketplace," 403–5; Davis, "The Cross and the Pillory," pp. 251–9; Richardson and Sayles (eds.), *Fleta*, pp. 121–2; Sutherland, *Quo Warranto*, p. 137.

[44] Sutherland (ed.), *The Eyre of Northamptonshire*, p. 77.

ordinance of forestallers. It may well be the case, as the work of Mate suggests, that the steady rise in prices experienced in the period 1305–10 lay behind the king's campaign against forestalling, which contemporaries frequently blamed as the cause of rising prices.[45] In addition to commissions of oyer and terminer issued to deal with forestallers in Yarmouth, Norwich, and London during his first two years as king, Edward II took a much more significant step against forestallers nationwide on December 24, 1307, when he issued a series of commissions appointing keepers of the peace in each county plus the city of London.[46]

The commissions gave the keepers of the peace and the sheriff of each county power to enforce the statute of forestallers and the statute of Winchester of 1285, designed to maintain the peace. In addition, the keepers were instructed to proclaim that the currency was to remain at the same weight and value as it had in the reign of Edward I and that the prices of goods were to remain as they were in that king's reign. They were also empowered to hear presentments against suspected offenders and to arrest and jail suspects until receipt of the king's special orders, but they were not authorized to conduct trials. On March 17, 1308, the commissions were renewed with some revisions but substantially the same personnel.[47] Bailiffs and constables were to be urged to preserve the peace. If any of them disobeyed the keepers, they were to be arrested and jailed until receipt of the king's further orders. The most significant revision was the grant to the keepers of the power to attach magnates or anyone else who took prises of grain, other foodstuffs, horses, or wagons without the owner's consent. Such offenders were to be committed to jail until delivered by the processes of the law. The new commissions also state that only sheriffs, bailiffs, and other royal officers could take prises on the king's written authority, which they must show to the parties involved.[48]

Only one partial record of the activities of the keepers in one county seems to have survived, that from the hundred of Tendring in Essex. It covers three sessions of early February 1308 held in different communities within the hundred. In addition to jury presentments of disturbers of the peace and offenders against the statute of Winchester, the record

---

[45] Mate, "High Prices," 9–10.

[46] *CPR 1307–13*, pp. 29–31, 37, 42, 130, 241. A full text of the commission is in *Parliamentary Writs*, vol. 2 pt. 2, appendix, pp. 8–9. For a fuller discussion of the early fourteenth-century commissions of the peace see Musson, *Public Order*, pp. 11–33.

[47] Musson, *Public Order*, p. 28 notes that 59 of the 78 keepers appointed in 1307 were reappointed in the new commissions.

[48] *CPR, 1307–13*, pp. 53–5. A full text of the revised commission is in *Parliamentary Writs*, vol. 2 pt. 2, appendix, pp. 11–12.

contains presentments of a total of forty-two forestallers, including one woman.[49] Nonetheless, there is other evidence that provides a better sense of the scope of the work of the keepers and of some unexpected complications that arose before trial. On March 3, 1308, Edward II ordered the sheriff of Derbyshire to release on bail twenty-one accused forestallers (eleven of them women), who had been indicted before the keepers of Derbyshire and imprisoned at Nottingham. The accused were to find "sufficient mainpernors" to appear before the king fifteen days after Easter, no doubt for trial.[50] The next day, the crown issued a mandate in similar terms to the sheriff of Devon to release on bail sixty-one men indicted for various trespasses against the king's peace before the Devon keepers and imprisoned at Exeter. The accused were to appear before the king one month after Easter.[51] Later in March 1308 and scattered over the next eleven months, similar letters were addressed to the sheriffs of Wiltshire, Berkshire, Warwickshire, Yorkshire, Hertfordshire, and Lincolnshire.[52]

By 1310 something appears to have gone wrong with the process for trying the indicted trespassers and forestallers. On April 1, Edward II accused the keepers of negligence and ordered them to enforce the various articles contained in their commissions. The king also indicated that he intended to appoint new commissioners to inquire into the actions of the old ones.[53] More significantly, the plan to try peace breakers and forestallers "before the king," doubtless in the court *coram rege*, had gone awry. Perhaps it was simply that too many suspects were indicted nationwide for that court to handle, so that a backlog of prisoners waiting trial built up. Whatever the reason, a new way of handling the trials was devised. On December 16, 1310, the crown issued new county commissions, each of which included three or four individuals, to conduct trials of indicted peace breakers and forestallers, many of whom were still imprisoned. Although a few of the commissions covered only a single county, in most cases the jurisdiction of each commission included at least two, sometimes three, neighboring counties. It is likely that the consolidation of jurisdiction over two or more counties and the addition of a named quorum to each commission were intended to expedite the work of the commissions.

There were also two significant changes associated with these new commissions of 1310 compared with the earlier ones of 1307 and 1308. One was a significant turnover in the membership of the

---

[49] Cam, "Some Early Inquests," pp. 168–72; Britnell, "Forestalling," 100.
[50] *CCR, 1307–13*, p. 22.   [51] *Ibid.*, pp. 21–2.   [52] *Ibid.*, pp. 23, 39, 73, 92.
[53] *Ibid.*, pp. 204–5.

commissions and the other was the exclusion of sheriffs from their membership. Both undoubtedly reflected the king's discontent with the way the commissions of 1307 and 1308 had proceeded. In 1310, sixty-five commissioners were appointed. Forty-four of them were new, representing a 67 percent change in members. The other twenty-one had served on the 1307 commission of the peace and nineteen of those had also served on that of 1308. The need for the exclusion of sheriffs is spelled out in the text of the new commissions. Since being indicted before the keepers, many of the accused had been kept in prison from which they could not be released except by the king's special order, as specified in the first commissions. Meantime sheriffs and other king's officers were accused of having bailed some suspects on their own authority and taken fines from others for their own use. The charge to the new commissioners was to try the accused for their offences against the peace and the relevant statutes and fine them if found guilty, but beyond that to punish those sheriffs and other officers guilty of taking money from suspects.[54]

Subsequent to the issue of the new commissions, the crown began to issue mandates for the release from prison of suspected forestallers on bail, to appear for trial before the new commissioners. On April 8, 1311, the king ordered eight men accused of forestalling who were imprisoned at Reading, Berkshire to be released on bail to appear before the commissioners, "when they come to those parts."[55] Two royal mandates in identical terms were directed to the sheriff of Kent on May 20, 1311 to release on bail seventeen accused forestallers from Canterbury and Maidstone jails.[56] Finally, on June 1, 1311, a number of mandates were sent to the sheriff of Kent ordering the release on bail of a total of thirty-seven men suspected of forestalling who were held in Canterbury and Rochester jails.[57] What happened to the cases of forestallers indicted before the commissioners for other counties is at this point unknown; so too is the outcome of any trials.

There are, however, indications that some at least of the legal business continued to drag on. On July 20, 1312, new commissions were authorized for Cornwall and Devon to try forestallers and peace breakers and impose punishment on corrupt sheriffs. The implication is that the

---

[54] *CPR, 1307–13*, pp. 327–9. A full text of the commission is in *Parliamentary Writs*, vol. 2 pt. 2, appendix, pp. 32–3. Musson, *Public Order*, p. 30 misdates these commissions to December 1312. As a result, he does not fully connect them to the problems associated with the commissions of the peace of 1307 and 1308. Also it is unclear why these commissions of 1310 were not included in his table of commissions of the peace on pp. 16–17.

[55] *CCR, 1307–13*, p. 305.   [56] Ibid., p. 313.   [57] Ibid., pp. 315–16.

commissioners appointed in 1310 had failed in their task.[58] In Lincolnshire, the death of one commissioner and the frequent absences of another meant that indicted trespassers and forestallers had not been tried as late as July 1313. In fact, this was still the case in November when the king ordered the sheriff of Lincolnshire to release on bail five indicted trespassers, who should have been tried before the commissioners, in order to appear before the king for trial.[59] A similar situation existed in Nottinghamshire, where the death of one commissioner and the absences of a second meant that nothing had been done and a new commission had to be issued in October 1313.[60]

The commissions of 1307 and 1308 certainly seem to confirm Britnell's judgment that "From the beginning of Edward II's reign ... the suppression of forestalling was an obligation of the Crown."[61] At the same time, it appears that in its pursuit of forestallers the government of Edward II was overly ambitious. The evidence leaves the impression that, by summer 1311, the crown was overwhelmed by the magnitude of the task and wished it would all go away. Certainly Edward II's government never again undertook such an ambitious inquiry into forestalling. From 1314 onward new commissions issued to keepers of the peace were stripped of the power to inquire into forestalling or any other economic issues.[62]

Even if after 1314 Edward II's government drew back from its nationwide campaign, it continued to urge action against forestalling. In June 1320, a royal proclamation was issued urging sheriffs to arrest and punish forestallers of victuals and other goods.[63] Much like the government of Edward I, that of Edward II attempted to regulate the activities of forestallers who aimed to profit from the presence of the household or parliament in specific locations. On May 11, 1322 the crown issued a commission of oyer and terminer to investigate a complaint from the magnates attending parliament at York that, as a result of the activities of forestallers from London and York, foodstuffs were now more expensive than before the arrival of the king.[64] Almost three years later, on April 20, 1325, Edward II wrote to the mayor, aldermen, and sheriffs of

---

[58] *CFR, 1307–19*, p. 139.

[59] *CPR, 1313–17*, p. 9; *CCR, 1313–18*, p. 28; see also p. 8, an order to the sheriff of Devon to release on bail two indicted trespassers from Exeter prison to appear before the commissioners for trial, July 8, 1313.

[60] *CFR, 1307–19*, pp. 186–7.   [61] Britnell, "Forestalling," 101.

[62] Musson, *Public Order*, p. 16.   [63] *CFR, 1319–27*, p. 27.

[64] *CPR, 1321–4*, p. 151. See also pp. 43–4 for concern about forestalling in Gloucestershire, Worcestershire, and Wiltshire as a consequence of the king and his magnates visiting Cirencester in December 1321.

London ordering them to act against forestallers who, in anticipation of the arrival of the king and his magnates in the city, would buy grain at reasonable prices in the city and its environs and then sell it "at an excessive profit."[65]

Another effort of Edward II's government, in response to the distortions that a government institution might have on local markets, was to limit the effects of the presence of the eyre. One method of regulation, which appears to date from the early thirteenth century, was for the itinerant justices to issue prohibitions on the holding of other markets within ten miles of the market in the town where the eyre was in session. In the printed yearbook accounts of the three eyres of the reigns of Edward II and Edward III there is one example of such a proclamation being issued, namely at the Kent eyre of 1313–14. At Canterbury in July 1313, the justices issued a proclamation "forbidding fair or market to be holden in the County of Kent during the continuance of the Eyre, and also all trading save in the city of Canterbury only."[66] According to one modern scholar, the prohibition was intended to prevent "the holding of markets in places that would draw people away from the eyre."[67] On the other hand, the legal treatise *Britton,* dating from 1291–2, makes it clear that the prohibition was to be applied only when necessary to ensure sufficient supplies of food in the place where the eyre was sitting: "no market be kept within ten miles, except where our justices shall be, if the town is not able to find sufficient provision for such as shall abide there."[68]

The other, more extensively documented, regulatory measure was much like that which the clerk of the market exercised within the verge. The itinerant justices had the authority to issue proclamations that prohibited forestalling and set prices within any town where the eyre was held. Such proclamations were issued during the preliminaries, before the main legal business was dealt with, and ran for the duration of the session. That was certainly the case with the eyres of Kent 1313–14, London 1321, and Northamptonshire 1329–30.[69] While it is

---

[65] *CCR, 1323–7*, p. 286.

[66] Maitland, Harcourt, and Bolland (eds.), *The Eyre of Kent*, p. 25. See also pp. 49, 55.

[67] Meekings and Crook (eds.), *The 1235 Surrey Eyre*, p. 24.

[68] Nichols (ed.), *Britton*, vol.1, p. 23. The passage is part of item 7 in a list of the preliminaries of the eyre.

[69] There is one other question that cannot be answered from the printed Year Books. The London eyre of 1321 and the Northamptonshire eyre of 1329–30 each sat in only a single town, London and Northampton respectively. Thus in the preliminaries, proclamations on forestalling and prices were issued once for the duration of each covering markets in London and Northampton. The Kent eyre of 1313–14 was held in three towns in

likely that the practice of issuing such proclamations predated 1307, there appears to be little actual surviving evidence for it before the reign of Edward II.[70]

On the second day of the Kent eyre at Canterbury on July 2, 1313, the justices charged the sheriff to choose "two knights and two serjeants, being of the most lawful of the county" to create an assize of wine and food "that the people might by virtue of such assize live as conveniently during the continuance of the Eyre as they had done previously to it."[71] According to another account of the same charge, the "four best knights of the county" were to assess victuals "at a fixed selling price such as should neither cause loss to the dealers nor distress to the people."[72] The next day the four returned to present to the justices the prices they had assessed. On viewing the prices the justices thought they "were higher than they should be" and bid the four assessors to consult among themselves to see if they could alter them. In response, the four asked the justices for their recommendations on what price reductions they should make. The justices "replied that they themselves might assess or abate nothing save [as certified] by the oath of the assessors." As a result, the four assessors consulted among themselves and then submitted the prices to the justices but there is no indication what, if any, changes they may have made. The justices then instructed the sheriff to proclaim the prices "of the assize of food, and that none should dare to sell any manner of food save at such prices as were therein rated." The price fixing covered wheat, oats, livestock, poultry, wine, and ale.[73]

Sometimes the actions of the justices could produce complications, as was the case with the London eyre of 1321. On the first day, January 14, the justices "had it proclaimed that none be so bold as to practice forestalling without or within the town, by which the prices should be forced up in the town, at their own peril."[74] On the fourth day, Saturday,

---

succession, Canterbury, Rochester, and Wye. The printed Year Books contain accounts of the preliminaries at Canterbury including the setting of prices. They do not tell us if the prices applied to Rochester and Wye as well or if the process was repeated at those two other towns. For locations and dates of the three eyres see Crook, *Records of the General Eyre*, pp. 180–1, 183.

[70] Horwood (ed.), *Year Books*, 5 vols. contain reports on cases from a number of eyres. Only one report, on the Cornwall eyre of 1302, contains any information on the preliminaries. It is brief and has no mention of price setting. See Horwood (ed.), *Year Books*, vol. 3, pp. 74–9. Seaborne, *Royal Regulation*, p. 78 nt. 58 has a brief reference to possible price setting at the Northumberland eyre of 1293. See also Meekings and Crook (eds.), *The 1235 Surrey Eyre*, p. 24.

[71] Maitland, Harcourt, and Bolland (eds.), *The Eyre of Kent*, p. 8. There is a misprint in the English translation "awful" instead of "lawful."

[72] *Ibid.*, pp. 15–16.   [73] *Ibid.*, pp. 10–11, 51.

[74] Cam (ed.), *The Eyre of London*, p. 12.

January 17, Hervey Stanton the lead justice ordered six good men chosen by the sheriffs of London to go through the town and assess the price of bread, livestock, poultry, wine, and ale, but not grain "so that the town should not have prices forced up by reason of the Eyre." As part of their charge, the six were to return on Monday, January 19, with a written list of prevailing prices to submit to the judges.[75] On the Monday, the justices ordered the sheriffs to proclaim as fixed the prevailing prices for victuals that the six assessors discovered.[76]

By Saturday, January 24, difficulties had arisen. On that day, the poulterers of London appeared before the justices and were charged with selling their wares at prices higher than those proclaimed, while refusing to sell at the price set by the proclaimed "assize of victuals." The poulterers put themselves on the country and were found not guilty of selling in violation of the assize but guilty of withdrawing themselves from trade and refusing to sell poultry at the fixed price. Rather than imprison them, the justices were willing to bail the poulterers if they would abide by the assize because "the good people of the City cannot be deprived of your services." Immediately, the poulterers petitioned the justices that the prices they paid for poultry were so high that they could not sell them at the fixed price. In response, the justices adjusted the set prices to meet their needs.[77]

Meanwhile, on January 25, Edward II wrote to Hervey Stanton and the other justices of the London eyre with a somewhat different perspective on the problems that their price fixing created. The king instructed the justices to issue a proclamation that merchants and others could sell foodstuffs in London "at a reasonable price without forestalling as they were wont to do." According to the king, a large number of people had come to London on legal business because of the presence "of the king and his pleas." As a result of the price fixing "as usually proclaimed in other eyres" many, who would normally come to sell provisions in London, stayed away, thereby producing "a great want of victuals." What, if any, response the justices made is not recorded.[78]

Although by Edward II's reign eyres were becoming more infrequent, they did linger on into the reign of Edward III. The yearbook account of the eyre of Northamptonshire of 1329–30 indicates that the justices followed the same practices as they did in both of Edward II's eyres. On the first day, November 6, 1329, a proclamation was made

[75] *Ibid.*, p. 21, see also p. 23.   [76] *Ibid.*, pp. 24–6.
[77] *Ibid.*, pp. 28–30. The quote is on p. 29.
[78] *CCR, 1318–23*, p. 287; *Foedera*, vol. 2 pt. 1, p. 442.

against forestalling.[79] Then the next day six men, three knights and three serjeants, that the sheriff of Northamptonshire chose, were charged to assess the maximum prices for poultry, wine, and ale "in such wise that the sellers may make a fair profit and the buyers pay no more than a fair price."[80] When the six returned with their price assessments, on November 8, the justices ordered the sheriff to proclaim them as the maximum prices.[81]

It is clear that the price setting at the eyre, like the York ordinances of 1301 and the other regulatory measures associated with meetings of parliament, were designed to benefit major consumers of food stuffs and renters of lodgings such as the justices, other government officials, those summoned to parliament, and those with business in the law courts. In this regard, it is striking that at the opening of the eyre of Northamptonshire in 1329 the justices proclaimed that no one was to demand payment for lodgings from the justices or anyone else officially associated with the eyre and that townsmen should not raise the price of lodgings for common people who had come to town for the eyre.[82] Despite all this, the likely benefits to the crown do not provide the full explanation for these regulatory measures. Any limitations imposed on prices, which would otherwise rise rapidly in anticipation of a parliament or a meeting of the eyre, would also prevent profiteering and benefit consumers generally. Moreover regulations, such as the assizes of ale, bread, wine, and weights and measures and the statute of forestallers that underpinned the ordinances of York and other geographically limited measures, had long left the confines of the household. During the second half of the thirteenth century, they had become laws recognized and enforced nationwide, usually by local courts and officials.[83]

In origin, the regulations represented a major expansion of royal authority, which appears to indicate a willingness on the part of the crown to take responsibility for the regulation of the market in the interest of consumers generally. Nonetheless, there are some indications that, by the reign of Edward I, the crown was becoming conscious of the needs of poorer consumers, although not all scholars are totally convinced of that.

Seaborne has argued that the aim of the assizes of bread, ale, and wine was "to prevent abusive pricing in particular fields." In the example of bread and ale, regulation was required because these were "staple goods required by the whole population."[84] She also sees a similar aim

---

[79] Sutherland (ed.), *The Eyre of Northamptonshire*, p. 9.   [80] *Ibid.*, pp. 14, 24.
[81] *Ibid.*, pp. 29.   [82] *Ibid.*, pp. 32–4.   [83] Davis, *Market Morality*, pp. 137–273.
[84] Seaborne, *Royal Regulation*, p.123.

to prevent or reverse excessive price rises on behalf of all consumers lying behind regulations such as the York ordinances of 1301 and the statute of forestallers.[85] At the same time, Seaborne tends to dismiss any official desire to aid the poor by pointing to the scarcity of any expressions of such sentiment, in particular the infrequency of contemporary condemnation of forestallers as oppressors of the poor.[86] Finally, she finds that the traditional regulations appear to be little influenced by the teachings of canon lawyers and theologians in favor of a just price and in condemnation of sharp practices like forestalling as sinful and immoral.[87]

In fact, one does not have to look far to find contemporary moral condemnation of the sharp practices of dealers. The works of Owst provide a rich catalog of examples of forestalling, false weights, and other corrupt practices condemned as sinful oppression of the poor drawn from the sermons of the fourteenth-century Dominican John Bromyard and others.[88] An additional source that includes many examples of corrupt market practices and their punishment is the medieval London letter books.[89] Moreover, the price setting actions of the itinerant justices during the eyres of 1313–14, 1321, and 1329–30 and regulations like the York ordinances and the statute of forestallers, if not directly influenced by scholastic ideas, were consistent with the current teaching of theologians on the just price. The just price was the current market price, that was set either by the operation of an open, free, and public market or by duly constituted authorities that regulated the market and prices. To operate effectively, markets needed to be free of "private monopolistic practices such as forestalling, engrossing, and regrating."[90] In setting prices for food, the itinerant justices aimed for a just price by sending out groups of substantial men to canvas the markets for the prevailing prices and by issuing proclamations against fraudulent practices such as forestalling. Similarly royal enforcement of the forestalling statute had as its main aim the punishment of activities that drove up food prices

---

[85] *Ibid.*, pp. 117–24, 150–7.
[86] There are a number of instances of such dismissals in Seaborne, *Royal Regulation*, pp. 117–24, 150–7. The reference to the infrequency of contemporary condemnations is on p. 152.
[87] Seaborne, *Royal Regulation*, pp. 128, 152.
[88] Owst, *Literature and Pulpit*, pp. 352–9 and *Preaching*, p. 124 nt. 1. For a more recent discussion of medieval moralists' views of sharp practices see Davis, *Market Morality*, pp. 34–136.
[89] *CLB*. See also Riley (ed.), *Memorials*.
[90] Baldwin, "Medieval Theories," 1–92. The quotation comes from p. 76. See also De Roover, "Just Price," 418–34; Gilchrist, *The Church and Economic Activity*, pp. 58–62, 116–8; Little, *Religious Poverty*, p. 177; Wood, *Medieval Economic Thought*, pp. 132–58; Davis, *Market Morality*, pp. 55–64.

above what would have been the just price, if there had been no corrupt attempts at market manipulation.

In contrast to Seaborne, Britnell describes the early version of the statute of forestallers, produced by the king's marshalsea around 1275, "as a landmark for the principles of the Moral Economy" in its condemnation of the activities of forestallers, who are described as oppressors of the poor and deceivers of the rich, interested only in "evil profit."[91] Britnell also argues for a direct influence of scholastic theory on the language and ideas behind the statute.[92]

More recently, Davis has examined in great detail the nature and limits of medieval market morality. For example, he situates the assize of bread in the context of ideas about the just price as well as the social and economic developments of the thirteenth and early fourteenth centuries, particularly population growth and the increase in the marketing of foodstuffs, especially bread grains. The development of such marketing reflected a demand for food from a growing segment of the population that did not produce its own. Davis shows that the assize of bread was a measure designed to maintain social peace and order that aimed not only to meet the needs of consumers in general but also to guarantee to the most vulnerable among them the availability of bread "at a constant price whatever the price of grain."[93] While the poorer consumers would continue to pay a farthing for a smaller loaf and might be compelled to decrease their bread intake, they also had the option of buying larger "brown loaves" of lesser quality.[94]

Davis also places the assize of bread in the larger context of "medieval ideas of social structure, justice, and morality."[95] Those engaged in trade, especially in foodstuffs, were often suspected of fraudulent dealings that destroyed social cohesion. Thus bakers, among all tradesmen, should be "honest, hard working, and conspicuously aware of their responsibilities to the community."[96] Underlying the assize of bread then were contemporary ideas of both social justice, including the needs of the poor, and the just price rooted in the teachings of such scholastics as Albertus Magnus and Thomas Aquinas. The role of the crown in enforcing regulations like the assize of bread was to insure that foodstuffs should be sold at reasonable prices, which produced moderate rather than excessive profits for the seller.[97] In the end, Davis confirms

---

[91] Britnell, "Forestalling," 94; *SR,* vol. 1, pp. 203–4.

[92] Britnell, "Forestalling," 94–5. See also Davis, *Market Morality,* p. 259, which offers a similar assessment of the statute.

[93] Davis, "Baking for the Common Good," 467–9; the quotation comes from 469.

[94] *Ibid.,* 469–70.   [95] *Ibid.,* 480.   [96] *Ibid.,* 482.   [97] *Ibid.,* 483–5.

E. P. Thompson's point about the popular demand for the enforcement of the assize of bread in the eighteenth century, that it was regarded as among "the visible paraphernalia of paternalism."[98]

In his new book on medieval market morality, Davis examines the whole range of market regulations, including the statute of forestallers, the assizes of bread, ale, and weights and measures and many others as well. He argues that the aim of such regulations was the common good. In particular, those regulations that were focused on foodstuffs, especially grain, were designed to provide reasonably priced victuals to consumers, including the poor, and to prevent protests that might destabilize the social order. Fear of rising grain prices brought on by harvest failure or market manipulation lay behind such regulatory measures.[99]

While Davis does recognize the influence of the ideas of moralists on the market regulations, he notes that such influence was tempered by the practical necessity of allowing markets to operate efficiently enough to provide for the common good. For example, the fines regularly imposed on brewers for violating the assize of ale were small but regular enough to be considered a license fee rather than punishment. A similar situation existed in the case of forestallers and regrators, most of whom were small dealers, hawkers, and hucksters, who bought and sold in small quantities, which met the needs of poorer consumers. Moderation in enforcement appears to have been motivated by a realization that heavy fines or corporal punishment might drive bakers, brewers, and hucksters out of business and disrupt the market. Only the most egregious offences were punished with large fines or the pillory. Such offences were often connected with dealing in grain, a primary product whose fluctuations in price and availability could have a major impact on the price of bread and ale as well as social stability.[100]

While Davis focuses mainly on enforcement of regulatory measures at the local level, it is clear from his work and Britnell's that in the course of the thirteenth century, certainly before the end of the reign of Edward I, the crown had taken on the obligation of enforcing regulations of food marketing in the interests of consumers in general but with an added focus on the needs of the poor and more vulnerable among them. A small but striking example of that concern is to be found in the records of the Michaelmas parliament of 1302 in which Edward I pardoned a

---

[98] *Ibid.*, 491; Thompson, "The Moral Economy," 106. In her article "Assize Matters" published in 2007, four years after her book, Seaborne appears to have a perspective on the assize of bread much closer to Davis's, see especially p. 36.
[99] Davis, *Market Morality*, pp. 29, 139, 141, 237, 253, 259, 271.
[100] *Ibid.*, pp. 274–409.

woman, Alice de la Chapele of Guernsey, who had stolen thirty-five sheaves of the king's share of a grain crop in order to feed her child. She had been indicted for theft, fled to sanctuary, and then was compelled to abjure the island.[101]

The evidence from Edward II's reign indicates that, at least in the enforcement of market regulations, he continued his father's policies. His commitment to enforcing the traditional regulations meant that, when faced with famine and a longer period of difficult times between 1315 and 1322, the king took action to try to ameliorate the situation of his subjects. There can be little doubt that the king's actions in response to the famine were motivated by a religiously grounded moral sense that it was his duty to try to aid his subjects, including the poorest, in a time of hunger and suffering. While Edward II was not notably successful, he set certain precedents for the royal response to dearth that his successors would follow.

[101] *Parl. Rolls*, "Original Documents Edward I Parliaments: Petition 2," item 1.

2 The response of Edward II and his government to the great famine

The most devastating famine that England (and northern Europe) experienced in the middle ages was that of 1315–17, at a time when the vast majority of the population depended for about 75 percent of their calories on a grain based diet of bread, pottage, and ale. The failure of the harvests of 1315 and 1316 in England drove the price of grain to unprecedented heights. Munro's price series shows that during the first fifteen years of the fourteenth century the average annual price of a quarter of wheat ranged from a low of 3.95s in 1305–6 to a high of 8.36s in 1314–15. In the harvest year 1315–16 it rose to 14.9s and even further in 1316–17 to 15.99s. Chronicles report even higher wheat prices, ranging from 20s–40s the quarter at the height of the famine.[1] The harvest of 1317 was better with wheat at 8.29s the quarter, and there was a run of good harvests from 1318–20, which reduced prices to prefamine levels. Harvest failure returned in 1321–2 driving up the average price of a quarter of wheat to 11.66s.[2]

On top of the failure of the wheat harvests in 1315 and 1316, the harvests of the other two significant grain crops, oats and barley, failed as well, thereby intensifying the distress of the population.[3] One other measure of the gravity of the famine is the decline in grain yields. Yields for all grains were 39 percent below long term average in the harvest of 1315, 43 percent below in 1316, 10 percent below in 1317 and 33 percent below in 1321.[4] As grain prices rose, the real wages of laborers plummeted.[5]

To add to the misery, at Easter 1319 a cattle plague arrived in England and spread throughout the kingdom in subsequent months killing an estimated 62 percent of the bovine animal population. Not only did this

---

[1] Munro, "Revisions of the Commodity Price Series." Chronicle reports of grain prices are summarized in Kershaw, "The Great Famine," 8.

[2] Munro, "Revisions of the Commodity Price Series."

[3] Campbell and Ó Gráda, "Harvest Shortfalls," 869.

[4] Campbell, "Nature as Historical Protagonist," 288–9; Campbell, "Three Centuries of English Crop Yields."

[5] Clark, "The Long March of History," 110.

affect dairy production but it also reduced manure output and the number of oxen available for haulage and ploughing, which made agricultural recovery following the famine all the more difficult.[6] Another sign of the subsistence struggles of the populace is the increase in crime. Hanawalt shows that the number of crimes recorded in gaol delivery rolls rose markedly as the price of wheat increased and fell when it declined. In Essex, Norfolk, and Yorkshire during the years 1315–19 there was an increase in recorded crime of over 200 percent beyond the average for 1300–14. Much of that crime involved robbery and theft of foodstuffs, clothes, and other readily disposable objects, an indicator of destitution and distress.[7] The period 1315–22 was thus one of recurrent dearth and deprivation during which, it has been estimated, 10 to 15 percent of the population died from hunger and disease.[8]

Over the past few years, scholars have increased our understanding of the famine. Campbell has demonstrated that the long periods of heavy rain in 1315–17, which ruined the crops, were part of a longer climatic cycle between 1300 and 1353.[9] During those years, recurrent wet weather periodically reduced grain yields and produced scarcity and sometimes famine. He and others have also argued persuasively that the famine was particularly disastrous because it hit a society with a large population of vulnerable small holders, subtenants, and laborers, many of whom were indebted to wealthier neighbors and did not have sufficient land to produce their own food, even in the best of times.[10] In his study of the manor of Hinderclay in Suffolk during the early fourteenth century, Schofield provides a graphic example of the vulnerabilities of smallholders and laborers. From at least 1294 until the famine, substantial tenants became increasingly involved in the market, buying and selling small parcels of land and lending money. As a consequence of that market orientation the better-off, when they looked at the survival struggles of their poorer neighbors, saw not objects of compassion but opportunities to buy land. In effect, the social cohesion of the community was destroyed not by the famine but by the intrusion of market values before it occurred.[11]

---

[6] Campbell, "Nature as Historical Protagonist," 289; Slavin, "The Great Bovine Pestilence,"1239–66; Newfield, "A Cattle Panzootic," 155–90.

[7] Hanawalt, *Crime and Conflict*, pp. 238–60.

[8] Kershaw, "The Great Famine," 11; Jordan, *The Great Famine*, 116–20.

[9] Campbell, "Nature as Historical Protagonist," 284–98; Campbell, "Four Famines," pp. 32–3.

[10] Campbell, "The Agrarian Problem," 3–70. See also Campbell, "Land Markets and the Morcellation of Holdings," pp. 197–209.

[11] Schofield, "The Social Economy," 38–63. For a similar study of a community in the West Midlands, see Razi, *Life, Marriage and Death*, pp. 32–50, 76–98.

Schofield's work raises an issue that has attracted little scholarly attention but is the focus of this chapter. If neighbors were unable or unwilling
to help one another during the famine, were any attempts made to
provide relief? What, in particular, was the crown's response? While we
have evidence of the crown's involvement in enforcing regulation of food
marketing during the second half of the thirteenth century, there appears
to be scant evidence of sustained governmental responses to dearths or
famines before that of 1315–17. For example, the previous severe famine
of 1257–8, the result of two harvest failures in a row in 1256 and 1257, is
quite well documented in chronicles but it has left virtually no trace in
the records of the crown.[12] The chronicle of Matthew Paris paints a grim
picture of widespread starvation and death in the face of rapidly rising
grain prices and crops ruined by torrential rain.[13] Paris emphasizes the
high death toll, with the unburied dead including many of the poor lying
where they died and gravediggers overwhelmed by the numbers of the
dead. In the end, they were often buried in common graves.[14] According
to the chronicler, the famine only ended when the church organized
fasts, prayers, and barefoot processions around the time of St. Oswald's
day (August 5) 1258 that resulted in divine intervention to improve
weather conditions, which undoubtedly brightened prospects for the
forthcoming harvest.[15]

Paris also describes attempts to alleviate the effects of the famine. In
London, a proclamation was issued that certain noblemen would distribute bread to the poor.[16] Real relief came in the week before Easter 1258
(March 17–24) when fifty ships from Germany arrived in London
with cargoes of wheat, barley, rye, and bread. They were sent by the
King of the Romans, that is, Germany (Henry III's brother, Richard, earl
of Cornwall), possibly at the request of Henry but Paris is silent on that
point. According to Paris, after the grain arrived a royal proclamation was
issued that no citizen of London should be allowed to buy any of the
imported grain with the intention of storing it and selling it later at a
higher price. The chronicler notes that this was a normal practice among
Londoners during scarcities.[17] While there is no official record of the

---

[12] Aside from a letter that Henry III sent to the sheriffs of Essex, Lincolnshire, Norfolk, on
April 16, 1258 regarding the burial of the bodies of the poor, *CCR, 1256–59*, p. 212 there
are no other references to dearth or famine in *CPR, 1216–1314* and *CCR, 1227–1314*.
For a recent more detailed treatment of the famine see Keene, "Crisis Management,"
pp. 49–57.

[13] *Chronica Majora*, vol. 5, pp. 628, 630, 660–1, 710–11, 728–9.

[14] *Ibid.*, pp. 690, 701–2, 728–9.   [15] *Ibid.*, pp. 711–12.   [16] *Ibid.*, pp. 693–4.

[17] *Ibid.*, pp. 673–4. See also Riley (ed.), *Chronicles of the Mayors and Sheriffs*, pp. 31–42,
which mentions relief provided to the populace by the arrival of grain ships from
Germany.

arrival of the grain, there is other evidence that England was importing grain from Germany and the Baltic from at least 1257 onward.[18]

In contrast to the lack of official evidence for any crown response to the famine of 1257–8, the response of Edward II's government to the Great Famine is well documented. When necessity drove Edward II to attempt remedial measures, it is not surprising, given the crown's involvement in the regulation of food marketing in the thirteenth century, that he urged the enforcement of traditional regulations like the assizes of ale and weights and measures. In addition, the king turned to a number of other remedies such as encouraging the import of grain and, most significantly, imposing prohibitions on the export of grain that were explicitly justified by domestic scarcity and high prices. Keene claims that English kings "since at least as early as the twelfth century" had imposed prohibitions on the export of grain in times of scarcity but he offers no supporting evidence.[19]

Clearly, the crown's responses to the famine were woefully inadequate to the task; it is hard to imagine that any fourteenth-century government would have had the means or the measures to respond effectively to a catastrophe like that of 1315–17. Nonetheless, Edward II's successors regularly implemented similar measures when faced with scarcity or famine, and sometimes food riots, on a number of occasions between 1347 and 1440.[20] While attempting to implement remedial measures, Edward II was compelled to continue the war against the Scots through the famine period. After the victory at Bannockburn on June 23–24, 1314, the initiative was with the Scots king. That meant, until 1322, regular Scots raids ever deeper into northern England. The raids involved burning of farmsteads, destruction of crops, seizure of cattle, and extortion of protection money, all of which intensified the suffering of the local population, especially during the famine.[21] At the same time, Edward II's demands for military provisioning and taxes in order to defend the kingdom probably intensified the distress of those of his subjects who lived beyond the reach of the Scots raiders.

Edward II's ordinance of early 1315, that fixed the prices of cattle, pigs, sheep, poultry, and eggs though not of grain, has often been regarded as a harbinger of the coming famine.[22] The magnates in a parliament at

---

[18] Hybel, "The Foreign Grain Trade," pp. 215–17; Hammel-Kiesow, "Lubeck and the Baltic Trade," pp. 70–4.
[19] Keene, "Crisis Management," p. 47. None of the sources listed in nt. 8 refers to such prohibitions.
[20] See Chapters 3–5.   [21] McNamee, *The Wars of the Bruces*, pp. 72–122.
[22] Lucas, "The Great European Famine," p. 51; Kershaw, "The Great Famine," 6–7; Jordan, *The Great Famine*, p. 171.

Westminster pressed the king to agree to the ordinance because prices were beginning to spiral upwards.[23] On March 14, the sheriffs nation-wide were ordered to proclaim the ordinance with two sets of prices one for London and another, lower on some items, for the rest of the country.[24] In less than a year, on February 20, 1316, the king withdrew the ordinance, again at the insistence of the magnates in another parliament at Lincoln.[25]

Some historians have attempted to connect the price ordinance to the famine but that connection is not clear. For one thing, the ordinance predates the failure of the 1315 harvest by 6–7 months. While it has been asserted occasionally that the 1314 harvest failed as a result of wet weather, there is no substantiation for this in the surviving evidence. Campbell's crop-yield data shows that the harvest was within the long-term average.[26] This is confirmed by the price data with a quarter of wheat at 8.36s, 56 percent of the price it would be in the harvest year 1315–16. The prices of other grains in the 1314–15 harvest year were also much lower than in 1315–16.[27] Moreover, the chronicle accounts of a wet summer appear to refer to 1315 not 1314.[28] Even if heavy rains in the autumn of 1314 led people to anticipate a poor harvest in 1315, it is hard to imagine that enough of them turned to meat and poultry as an alternative and thus caused the price rise that led to the ordinance. Virtually everyone who would suffer from the projected dearth of grain could not have afforded to trade up to meat and the like. Finally, it is odd that, since the failure of the grain crop was the cause of the famine, the ordinance did not attempt to regulate grain or bread prices.

The ordinance needs to be situated in the context of rising prices that Edward I and Edward II had faced for a number of years before

---

[23] Childs (ed.), *Vita Edwardi Secundi*, pp. 102–3; *Parl. Rolls*, "Edward II: January Parliament 1315," items 35–7.

[24] *CCR, 1313–18*, p. 160; *Foedera*, vol. 2 pt. 1, p. 263; *CLB*, vol. E, pp. 43–4; Kershaw, "The Great Famine," 6.

[25] *Parl. Rolls*, "Edward II: January Parliament 1316: SC 9/20," item 2; *CCR, 1313–18*, p. 325; *Foedera*, vol. 2 pt. 1, p. 286.

[26] Campbell, "Crop Yields."   [27] Munro, "Revisions of the Commodity Price Series."

[28] Lucas, "The Great European Famine," p. 51 and Kershaw, "The Great Famine," 6 assert that the summer of 1314 was wet and adversely affected the harvest. They give as their source *Vita Edwardi Secundi*. The relevant passage on p. 111 is undated and could as easily refer to the summer of 1315. Elsewhere on 6 nt. 17 Kershaw states that other chronicle references to heavy rain in 1314 actually refer to 1315. He concludes that "A number of chronicles are very wayward in their chronology of the famine." Jordan, *The Great Famine*, pp. 18, 171, follows Lucas. In the introduction to *Parl. Rolls*, "Edward II: January Parliament 1315," item 3, the editors assert that the ordinance was the result of high prices produced "by the bad weather of 1314–15 and consequent crop failures." For another example of the unreliability of chronicle accounts of the famine see Marvin, "Cannibalism," pp. 73–86.

the famine. In Edward I's case the government's focus had been on the inflationary effects of the so-called pollards and crockards, coins minted in Flanders that resembled English pennies but contained less silver. They circulated widely in England during the 1290s and, as in the case with debased coins generally, over time they drove up prices.[29] In response to the price rise, the Easter parliament of 1299 passed a statute that prohibited the bringing of counterfeit money into England from abroad and authorized the appointment of two wardens in every port to confiscate the coins and arrest those who imported them. The statute also imposed a limit on the use of already circulating pollards and crockards. Only "good and lawful sterlings" were to be used to buy wool, woolfells, leather, lead, or tin.[30]

Then, in late December of 1299, Edward I issued a proclamation that two pollards or crockards should have the same value as one English silver penny and that no one should refuse to accept them in payment, a clear admission of their continued circulation.[31] A month later, the king instructed the mayor and sheriffs of London to enforce the proclamation and to ensure that the prices of goods did not rise any further.[32] In the following weeks, officials in London conducted a vigorous judicial campaign against scores of cordwainers, tanners, curriers, butchers, fishmongers, and the like, who either raised their prices or refused to accept pollards or crockards, in defiance of the king's policy. Many were found not guilty at trial, but some were bound over to appear before the king at the next parliament.[33]

That parliament, in Lent 1300, passed an ordinance stating that pollards and crockards should no longer circulate as currency and on March 30, 1300 the sheriffs were instructed to enforce it.[34] While it appears that most of the pollards and crockards were soon withdrawn from circulation and their silver turned into new minted sterling pennies, some must have continued to circulate. The York ordinances of August 29, 1301 blamed the continued circulation of pollards and crockards as one cause of the price rise in the city.[35]

---

[29] Pollards and Crockards do not appear to be so debased compared to sterling pennies as Edward I's decision in late 1299 to value one of them as equal to one half-penny would lead one to believe. See Mate, "Monetary Policies," 66 and Mayhew and Walker, "Crockards and Pollards," pp. 125–46.

[30] *SR*, vol. 1 pp. 131–5; *Parl. Rolls*, "Edward I: Easter 1299, Introduction," item 1.

[31] Prestwich, "Edward I's Monetary Policies," 412; Mate, "Monetary Policies," 66; Riley (ed.), *Chronicles of the Mayors and Sheriffs*, pp. 208–28, 237–48.

[32] *CLB*, vol. C, pp. 56, 61.

[33] *Ibid.*, pp. 57–8; Thomas (ed.), *Calendar of Early Mayor's Court Rolls*, pp. 59–66.

[34] *Parl. Rolls*, "Edward I: Lent 1300," legislation item 3; *CCR, 1296–1302*, pp. 385–6, 390–1.

[35] Mate, "Monetary Policies," 66–70; Prestwich (ed.), *York Civic Ordinances*, pp. 5, 14–15.

Rising prices and monetary problems continued into the early years of Edward II's reign. On August 24, 1307 the king ordered the sheriffs to proclaim that the currency would continue to have the same value that it had in his father's reign.[36] A few months later, on December 24, he reiterated the point when he issued commissions of the peace conveying the power to arrest and indict forestallers, accompanied with instructions to announce that the currency would remain at the same value and weight and prices at the same level as in the reign of Edward I.[37] The commissions were renewed with some revisions on March 17, 1308 and, over the next few years, the statute of forestallers was vigorously enforced, no doubt as a result of a belief that forestalling was behind the rise in food prices.[38] Nonetheless, in the face of rumors of a forthcoming debasement of the coinage, the king was forced, on August 5, 1309, to resort to another proclamation indicating that he did not intend to make any alteration in the currency because that would raise the price of foodstuffs and other essentials.[39] Two years later, Edward II reissued the proclamation, noting that since his earlier proclamation "the dearness of victuals and other goods is not reduced but increased."[40]

Mate has argued that the explanation for the upward pressure on prices in the last years of Edward I, and the early years of Edward II, was an influx of foreign silver, which led to an increase in the money supply and consequently prices.[41] Recently, Allen has shown that 90 percent of the total silver received at English mints in the period 1302–30 was of foreign origin.[42] The ordinance of 1315 should be seen as another response to the resultant price rise, which largely affected the consumers of beef, mutton, pork, and fowl, that is the well-off including the magnates sitting in parliament, not the ordinary consumers whose diet was largely grain based. Nonetheless, the author of *Vita Edwardi Secundi* describes the action of the earls and barons in supporting this ordinance as supporting the *rei publice*, which is a version of the original justification of the ordinance contained in the royal proclamation that announced it to the king's subjects, *pro communi utilitate populi*.[43]

[36] *CCR, 1307–13*, p. 41.   [37] *CPR, 1307–13*, p. 29–31.
[38] *Ibid.*, pp. 53–5; *CCR, 1307–13*, pp. 21–3, 39, 73, 92; Cam, "Some Early Inquests," pp. 168–72; Britnell, "Forestalling," 100.
[39] *CCR, 1307–13*, pp. 224–5.   [40] *Ibid.*, p. 343.
[41] Mate, "High Prices," 1–16; Prestwich, "Edward I's Monetary Policies," 406–16; Childs (ed.), *Vita Edwardi Secundi*, p. 103 nt. 200.
[42] Allen, "Silver Production," 127. See also Allen, *Mints and Money*, pp. 259–61.
[43] Childs (ed.), *Vita Edwardi Secundi*, pp. 102–3. The editor's translation of "*rei publice*" is "welfare of the state"; I prefer "public good" or "commonwealth."

The withdrawal of the Ordinance of 1315 was the direct result of a problem that the official attempt to control prices encountered. When dealers in the regulated commodities concluded that they could not make a living selling at the fixed prices, they withdrew from dealing altogether, at least in the regulated markets, and took their business elsewhere if they could. This problem arose almost immediately after the proclamation of the ordinance on March 14, 1315. On April 10, the king wrote to the sheriffs nationwide ordering a proclamation that prohibited forestalling, which was regularly blamed for scarcity and high prices.[44] The surviving full text is directed to the sheriff of Middlesex and relates specifically to London. After an opening, which recapitulates the terms of the price fixing ordinance, the king's letter indicates that "divers forestallers" were reputed to be meeting merchants and others bringing victuals to the city and compelling them, sometimes with violence, to sell the victuals before they reached market.[45] In response to the king, the mayor and sheriffs of London ordered an inquest by sworn juries drawn from the city wards to identify forestallers and others who violated the ordinance.[46]

The author of *Vita Edwardi Secundi* was certainly of the opinion that the main result of the attempt to fix food prices was the withdrawal of suppliers from the market: "as a result of that statute little or nothing was exposed for sale in the markets, whereas formerly the market had been full of goods, even though they seemed dear."[47] This reality no doubt lay behind the withdrawal of the ordinance in early 1316 at the behest of the magnates, who had come to realize that the only effect of price fixing was to make prized foodstuffs scarcer.

The problems that enforcement of the price ordinance of 1315 encountered were hardly unique and had little to do with the famine. A similar situation arose during the 1321 London Eyre. On January 19, the justices set the prices of victuals in London for the duration of the Eyre, as was their custom. Five days later, they had to raise the prices for poultry because the poulterers complained that they could not afford to sell at the original fixed price. The next day, Edward II wrote to the justices ordering them, in effect, to withdraw their proclamation of fixed prices and let dealers in foodstuffs trade at reasonable prices, without being

---

[44] *CCR, 1313–18*, p. 227.   [45] *Foedera*, vol. 2 pt. 1, p. 266.

[46] *CLB*, vol. E, pp. 43–4. See also the commissions of oyer and terminer to inquire into forestalling in Norfolk and Suffolk, May 28, 1315 and in Yorkshire, March 6, August 20, and October 1, 1316, *CPR, 1313–17*, pp. 326, 494, 587, 594.

[47] Childs (ed.), *Vita Edwardi Secundi*, p. 121.

charged with forestalling, otherwise many of them would refuse to supply London markets and thereby produce scarcity.[48]

One unique response of the crown to the actual famine of 1315–17 is a letter that Edward II sent, presumably, to all the bishops of England on April 24, 1316. Two copies of it survive: one in the register of Richard de Kellawe, Bishop of Durham, the other in the register of Roger Martival, Bishop of Salisbury.[49] Two scholars have discussed the letter but only briefly.[50] It opens with a statement that the kingdom had been long accustomed to having wheat, along with other grains and victuals, in greater abundance than other regions. As a consequence of rainstorms, which resulted from the sins of the people in disobeying God's laws, they are suffering from scarcity and dearth of grain.

Then the letter gets to the heart of the matter. The king asserts there is in fact grain in the country that could be used to feed the populace, but some who have it keep it in their granges and refuse to put it up for sale, in order to sell it at a higher price later. As a result the poor and beggars die of starvation. The king then laments that the bishops and others in the kingdom, like the king himself, feel pain and sorrow in the depth of their hearts. The letter then compares past with present: "Who of pious mind carefully considering the situation does not sigh in sorrow at the wealth and fertility of the past and does not feel compassion for his neighbor in the present time of such scarcity and dearth when people are dying of famine and starvation."[51]

Finally, the king's letter provides a solution, which would offer salvation to his people. The bishops are urged, with whatever ways and means, to warn those in their dioceses, both laity and clergy, who have grain in their granaries, to make it available for sale while keeping back only enough to feed themselves and their families until after the next harvest. Otherwise, those who have grain and refuse to sell it will be responsible for suffering and death among the population. The letter concludes with one final, but vague, warning that if the men who have grain refuse to sell it, and this comes to the king's attention, then he will, on account of urgent necessity and the need to do his utmost for the sustenance of the people, seek an appropriate remedy in consultation with his council.

---

[48] Cam, (ed.), *The Eyre of London*, pp. 28–30; CCR, *1318–23*, p. 287; *Foedera*, vol. 2 pt. 1, p. 442.

[49] Hardy (ed.), *Register of Richard de Kellawe*, vol. 2, pp. 1118–20; Reynolds (ed.), *Registers of Roger Martival*, vol. 3, pp. 13–14. The printed Durham register contains the full text of the letter while the printed Salisbury register has only an English summary.

[50] Jordan, *The Great Famine*, p. 172; Braid, "Economic Behavior, Markets and Crises," p. 349.

[51] Hardy (ed.), *Register of Richard de Kellawe*, vol. 2, p. 1119.

The only known result of this letter is that the Bishop of Salisbury ordered the clergy of his diocese to carry out the king's wishes "concerning the public welfare."[52]

No doubt the king's extraordinary letter had little practical effect, but it appears to be the earliest surviving example of a written statement by an English monarch that he regarded meeting the food needs of his subjects in time of scarcity to be a moral obligation.[53] Such exhortations to lay and ecclesiastical officials, phrased in the language of moral obligation and full of religiously colored rhetoric, were to become a part of royal policy in future times of dearth. Moreover, while it is highly unlikely the king's proposal that those who had grain beyond the needs of their families should put it up for sale was ever implemented at the time, such a remedy eventually became a major governmental response to dearth.

Another response of Edward II's government to the famine was to impose a prohibition on the use of wheat in brewing and urge the enforcement nationwide of traditional regulations like the assizes of ale and weights and measures. At the parliament of January 1316, after the failure of the 1315 harvest, the king accepted a petition from the burgesses of Winchester requesting the issue of a proclamation that "no brewers or ale-wives in the same town are henceforth to make malt from wheat, because the wheat in that country is ruined." The proclamation, sent to the sheriffs nationwide, opened with the following: "On the account of the dearth of corn."[54]

The setting of the price of ale was a standard practice under the assize and not necessarily connected to famine.[55] For example, in 1305 Edward I set the price of a gallon of ale in London at 1d for the better and .75d for the lesser. Soon after the failure of the 1316 harvest, the government of London set the prices of ale considerably higher at 1.5d a gallon for the better and 1d for the lesser, no doubt in response to the rise in grain prices. Following on this action, the crown, on January 24, 1317, instructed the sheriffs to proclaim the same prices in all cities and boroughs and 1d a gallon for the better in the countryside. All lords with franchises, which included the assize of ale, were ordered to enforce the new prices. The price setting was a result of complaints from the people, including a petition presented to the king's council, that brewers were

---

[52] Reynolds (ed.), *Registers of Roger Martival*, vol. 3, p. 14. These volumes contain only English summaries of the original documents to which I have not had access. This makes it impossible for me to determine the Latin phrase translated as "public welfare."

[53] I found none in *CCR, 1227–1327* and *CPR, 1216–1327*.

[54] *Parl. Rolls*, "Edward II: January 1316: SC9/19," item 35.

[55] Bennett, *Ale, Beer and Brewsters*, pp. 21–2; Seaborne, *Royal Regulation*, pp. 84–5; Davis, *Market Morality*, pp. 241–8.

brewing and selling ale "too dearly at their pleasure." In addition, the proclamation noted that wheat and barley, which could have been saved for making bread during the past two years of scarcity, were being converted to malt for brewing in such quantities that "unless a remedy be provided a great part of the lower and poor people will shortly suffer from famine."[56] A few months later, on April 14, another proclamation repeated the terms of the first, but added that the sheriffs should summon juries of inquest to discover the names of the brewers and lords of liberties who had not observed the assize as ordered in the earlier proclamation and send their names to the king.[57] The proclamation also indicated that the king planned to send out commissioners to enquire into these matters in each county, although there appears to be no evidence that such commissions were ever established. Nonetheless, the London authorities took matters into their own hands and on August 24, 1317 prohibited the use of barley in the brewing of ale.[58]

On February 20, 1317, a royal proclamation directed the sheriffs to enforce the assize of weights and measures. Merchants, under pain of forfeiture, were to use only one measure, the London quarter, when buying and selling grain. The proclamation was grounded on *Magna Carta*, clause 35, which specified a single national standard measure for grain. Complaints, frequently made in parliament, had reached the king that merchants were using "great measures to buy with and small to sell by to the great deception and manifest injury of the people of this realm."[59] It is obvious that the problem of false or nonstandard measures would be of particular concern in years of scarcity. As promised in the proclamation, commissioners were soon appointed on March 1 to go round the country in circuits to enquire into these practices and punish the offenders.[60] In April and May the king ordered the mayor and sheriffs of London to deliver bushel measures for grain of the London standard to the commissioners appointed for a number of different counties.[61]

While there does not appear to be any evidence of further actions that the weights and measures commissioners might have undertaken, the issue remained a live one, testimony to the lasting effects of the famine. In the face of further complaints in the Michaelmas Parliament of

---

[56] *CCR, 1313–18*, p. 449; *CLB*, vol. E, pp. 71–3.   [57] *CCR, 1313–18*, p. 463.

[58] *CLB*, vol. E, p. 77; Braid, "Economic Behavior, Markets and Crises," p. 346.

[59] *Foedera*, vol. 2 pt. 1, p. 316; *CCR, 1313–18*, p. 455; Holt, *Magna Carta*, pp. 460–1.

[60] *CPR, 1313–17*, pp. 688–9; *Parliamentary Writs*, vol. 2 pt. 2, appendix, pp. 111–12. A year later, on March 6, 1318, a new commission was issued for the counties of Essex and Cambridge, *CPR, 1317–21*, p. 173.

[61] Two surviving copies of the king's orders are *CLB*, vol. E, pp. 74, 76. The counties involved were Norfolk, Suffolk, Kent, Surrey, and Sussex.

1320 that some merchants continued to use fraudulent measures for grain, Edward II wrote to the treasurer and barons of the exchequer, on November 25, 1320, ordering the London bushel of grain to be assayed and proved and identical measures made and sent to the principal town of each county "so that other measures in the said counties may be made by such proved measures, which are to be used in the buying and selling of corn."[62] Following this, on March 2, 1321, the king ordered the mayor, aldermen, and sheriffs of London to permit his clerk of the market to assay the measures known as the "standards of London" in order that "there shall be one measure of wine, one of ale, and one of corn throughout the realm."[63]

Again, as is the case with the commissions of 1317, it is unclear what the effects of the weights and measures activity in 1320–1 might have been. Nonetheless, concern about the matter continued throughout much of the rest of Edward II's reign. According to Ormrod, further action on weights and measures was considered in a legislative agenda produced for the king's council in 1322.[64] Nothing appears to have come of this until November 3, 1324 when, in response to complaints in parliament, new commissioners were appointed to enforce the assize.[65] There is other evidence, from early 1326, of the commission's continued existence, when Edward II wrote to the Norfolk commissioners on the enforcement of the assize in the city of Norwich.[66]

Anxiety about the availability of bread grains and their price could also directly affect the king. On December 22, 1321, during the scarcity that followed the poor harvest of that year, Edward II, who was at Cirencester with some of his magnates, complained of the high price and scarcity of grain. He blamed unnamed people in Gloucestershire, Worcestershire, and Wiltshire of withholding it from the market in order to sell at higher prices. The king directed the sheriffs of the three counties to aid two of his servants to look for grain that they could buy at reasonable prices to be delivered to bakers and brewers, who would then sell the finished products to the magnates.[67]

Even after harvests improved and grain prices fell, concerns about shortage and high prices continued. On April 20, 1325, Edward II wrote to the magistrates of London that he was coming to the city with magnates and others, probably for a parliament, and they needed to act in order to ensure that merchants, who had forestalled and hoarded large amounts of grain recently imported from Flanders, would not sell it at an

---

[62] *CCR, 1318–23*, p. 280.   [63] *Ibid.*, p. 362; *Foedera*, vol. 2 pt. 1, p. 443.
[64] Ormrod, "Agenda for Legislation, 1322–c. 1340," 6–7, 22–3, 26, 29, 31.
[65] *CFR, 1319–27*, pp. 314–16.   [66] *CCR, 1323–7*, p. 532.   [67] *CPR, 1321–4*, p. 43.

excessive price to the great detriment of the people. In response, the mayor, aldermen, and sheriffs summoned a number of local representatives from the different neighborhoods and charged them to prevent anyone from carrying grain out of the city for sale elsewhere. They were also instructed to ensure that grain would only be sold openly in the markets and that no sales took place before the hour of prime.[68]

The most significant response of Edward II's government to the famine of 1315–17 and the harvest failure of 1321 was to issue proclamations prohibiting the export of grain that were justified mainly by rising prices and scarcity brought on by bad weather. His predecessors had routinely regulated the export of grain and other victuals for military or diplomatic reasons. For example, during the French wars of King John, export of grain to the king's enemies was forbidden.[69] In 1233, Henry III imposed a ban on the export of grain from Ireland to Wales to prevent it reaching Llewellyn the Great.[70] In July of that year, Henry III also instructed the sheriff of Devon to prohibit the shipment of victuals and other goods to Wales. Later, in November 1245, the justiciar of Chester was ordered to impose a similar ban on trade with the king's enemies in Wales.[71] Finally, Edward I imposed prohibitions on the shipping of grain, other victuals, and weapons to his enemies in Scotland and Wales while encouraging English merchants to bring grain to the king and his army.[72] Conversely, when in an alliance with the count of Flanders against the French king in 1297, Edward I encouraged the export of grain and other wares to Flanders to help the count to sustain the war against France.[73]

Like his father and his successors into the early modern period, Edward II ordered proclamations prohibiting the export of grain and other victuals to his enemies. Four of his seven prohibitions had as their sole justification the war with the Scots, although there was considerable variation in their details.[74] More significantly, the other three refer to scarcity and high prices as a major justification.[75] The first dates

---

[68] *CCR, 1323–7*, p. 286; *CLB*, vol. E, pp. 196–7; *Foedera*, vol. 2 pt. 1, p. 597.

[69] Cam, "Studies in the Hundred Rolls," p. 20; Miller and Hatcher, *Medieval England: Towns*, pp. 190–1.

[70] Britnell, *Britain and Ireland, 1050–1530*, p. 132.   [71] *Foedera*, vol. 1 pt. 2, pp. 88, 264.

[72] *CCR, 1272–9*, pp. 366–7, 410, 426; *CCR, 1288–96*, p. 435; *CCR, 1296–1302*, pp. 190, 192, 400, 489; *CCR, 1302–7*, pp. 471–2, 488, 522.

[73] *CCR, 1296–1302*, p. 15.

[74] *CCR, 1307–13*, pp. 225, 337, 338, 588; *CCR, 1318–23*, p. 134; *CLB*, vol. D, pp. 240–2.

[75] Edward II was probably not the first English monarch to issue such proclamations in response to scarcity. There is evidence that Edward I issued one in 1284 prohibiting the export of grain because recent shipments by alien merchants had caused scarcity in England. See Lloyd, *Alien Merchants*, p. 109; *CPR, 1281–92*, p. 117. Braid, "Economic Behavior, Markets and Crises," p. 349 is mistaken when he states that Edward II did not prohibit the export of grain during the famine.

from September 1, 1315, after the failure of the harvest. That failure is blamed directly on intemperate weather that produced heavy rains in the summer and devastated the grain crop. The prohibition is described as for *commodo populi nobis*. To enforce the proclamation, the crown instructed the sheriffs nationwide and the warden of the Cinque Ports to appoint two searchers in every port to survey ships that might have cargoes of grain or other victuals to ensure that nothing would be carried out of their areas without their knowledge. Merchants intending to ship such foodstuffs were required to find sureties that they would only take them to other parts of England or to Berwick in support of the king's war effort. On returning home, such merchants had to bring back letters from the officials of the port where they unloaded their cargoes testifying to that fact and to the amount unloaded. If they returned without such letters, then the sheriff was to arrest and imprison them until further orders.[76]

Edward II's next proclamation that mentions scarcity dates from February 14, 1317, at the height of the famine. It banned export from England of grain, meat, fish, and other victuals. While this action was justified by the king's need for a large supply of foodstuffs to maintain his subjects defending the marches of Scotland and the land of Ireland, it was admitted that there was less grain in England than usual because of bad weather over the previous two years.[77] The third and final proclamation in this series dates from December 28, 1322, towards the end of a year of grain scarcity and high prices that came after the famine years. It prohibited export of grain from England, because prices were high and might be higher in future, if export continued. It also stated that it was necessary to have an abundant supply of grain available for the support of the planned military campaign in Scotland during the coming summer.[78]

No prohibition on export was absolute. All of them, whether justified by scarcity or by diplomatic and military necessity, included the proviso that exceptions could be granted by the king's special license. In fact, the prohibition of September 1, 1315, at the beginning of the famine, included one major exception for diplomatic reasons. Merchants in the allegiance of the king of France were allowed to export grain from England "to parts beyond the seas" except Scotland, if they produced letters patent from their king.[79] Despite this exception and the king's

---

[76] *CCR, 1313–18*, pp. 308–9; *Foedera*, vol.2 pt. 1, p. 276. See also the many commissions issued in 1315–17 to inquire into illegal shipments of grain and other goods to the Scots, *CPR, 1313–17*, pp. 259, 316, 418–20, 423, 429, 431, 503, 598, 679, 686, 693–4; *CCR, 1313–18*, pp. 395, 517–18, 686.
[77] *CCR, 1313–18*, p. 455.   [78] *Ibid.*, p. 691.
[79] *CCR, 1313–18*, pp. 308–9; *Foedera*, vol. 2 pt. 1, p. 276.

right to issue licenses, there is little evidence that much, if any, grain was shipped out of England during the famine except that destined to victual the king's supporters in Berwick and other towns in Scotland. At the same time, there is no way to measure the domestic effects of export prohibitions. Nonetheless, from the famine of 1315–17 onward through the seventeenth century such prohibitions allied with bonds for good behavior to control licensed shipments remained one important dimension of the crown's response to dearth.[80]

In addition to banning export of grain, the crown also encouraged its import. On December 18, 1315 Edward II wrote to both the king of France and the duke of Brittany requesting that merchants of Newcastle on Tyne be allowed to buy grain in their lands and ship it home. At the same time, the English king ordered the seneschal of Ponthieu, one of his French possessions, to permit the same merchants to buy grain there.[81] Later, on March 16, 1316, Edward II extended his protection and safe conduct first for a year, then immediately increased to two years, to all foreign merchants, except those of Scotland and Flanders, to encourage them to bring grain to England.[82] Finally, to encourage the trade in grain and other foodstuffs, the king, on September 13, 1317, ordered that such commodities should be imported free of customs duties.[83]

The export prohibition of February 14, 1317 contains a reference to the import of grain that reveals the difficult food supply situation in England. The sheriffs, to whom the prohibition was directed, were instructed to exclude from a general order to arrest the goods of foreign merchants not only grain and other victuals but also any foreign ships importing such goods into England. According to the instructions, fewer foreign merchants than in the past were shipping foodstuffs to England as a consequence of frequent arrests.[84] In fact, the major reason for this decline may well have been famine conditions in northern Europe rather than fear of arrest. Later, in the spring of 1322, the mayor and aldermen of London requested, apparently to no avail, that the king should issue a similar order to encourage foreign merchants to bring victuals to London and "an end be put to the sudden scarcity that has arisen in the land."[85] Then on April 11, a number of Londoners were elected to guard the various market places where grain was sold to prevent it from being either shipped out of the city or withdrawn from the market.[86]

---

[80] See Chapters 3–8.   [81] *CCR, 1313–18*, pp. 318–19; *Foedera*, vol. 2 pt.1, p. 282.
[82] *CPR, 1313–17*, pp. 440, 450.
[83] *CCR, 1313–18*. p. 498; Keene, "Crisis Management," p. 59.
[84] *CCR, 1313–18*, p. 455. See also p. 392.   [85] *CLB*, vol. E, p. 166.   [86] *Ibid.*, p. 167.

In addition to general encouragements to import, there are enrolled on the patent rolls for 1315–17 thirteen safe conducts and letters of protection for individuals who planned to go to foreign parts and return with grain and other foodstuffs either for sale or for use in their own households.[87] Sometimes the foreign destination is named, most commonly France or Gascony, once Spain. In the same period, sixty-seven safe conducts and letters of protection were issued for the movement of grain from one part of the king's dominions to another. Most are for merchants or ship masters who intended to buy grain elsewhere in England to supply areas that were suffering either from the famine or the depredations of the Scots. Some are for landowners who wanted to transport grain from one manor to another for their own consumption; others are for individuals who sought to buy grain for their own households. A few safe conducts were issued for the purpose of shipping grain from Ireland to deficient areas of Wales and northwest England. Merchants of Southampton also obtained safe conducts to visit the Channel Islands in search of grain.[88] In addition, when Edward II wrote to the Seneschal of Ponthieu on December 18, 1315 ordering him to allow the burgesses of Newcastle to buy grain there, he also sent letters in similar terms on the behalf of the sheriffs of fourteen English counties and issued safe conducts for the burgesses.[89] It appears that under Edward II government policy was to encourage the movement and marketing of grain as much as possible in hope that it would enable whatever surplus grain might exist to get to areas with shortages. This certainly was standard operating procedure for future royal governments facing dearth. At the same time, one must admit that an overriding concern of Edward II's government remained the Scottish war.

The movement of grain for military purposes continued to be a major consideration during the famine in order to sustain the king's attempts to respond to repeated Scots raids on northern England. If the crown managed to have some success in encouraging the import of grain from foreign sources, provisioning for campaigns in the north was, understandably, a priority. When the galley, *St. John* of Genoa, arrived at Sandwich in May 1316 with 2,100 quarters of wheat the king authorized Peter Bard, bailiff of Sandwich and Nicholas, clerk of Antonio Pessagno a Genoese merchant and major creditor of the crown, to buy part of her

---

[87] *CPR, 1313–17*, pp. 370, 373, 383, 386–7, 401, 450, 467, 478, 520, 613, 624.

[88] *Ibid.*, pp. 378, 380, 382–4, 387, 389–90, 394–401, 439, 447, 450, 459, 470, 540–3, 553, 560, 568, 614, 622, 624–5, 627, 657; *CPR, 1317–21*, p. 38.

[89] *CCR, 1313–18*, pp. 318–19.

cargo for the supply of Berwick.[90] What happened next was not entirely clear at first to the king. An apparently early report led the king to believe that "certain malefactors" were attempting to carry off the *St. John* and its cargo.[91] This has led some modern historians to believe that the ship "was seized by a mob at Sandwich."[92] On closer inquiry, it turned out that on May 20 when the *St. John* anchored at the dunes off Sandwich, a fleet under the command of Berenger Blance, a French admiral, captured the ship and took her to Calais.[93]

Apparently Edward II never received any satisfaction from the French despite a number of requests for either restitution of the ship and her cargo or monetary compensation, estimated at £5,716 1s.[94] At one point the English king heard from Berenger, who justified the seizure of the *St. John* on the basis of his belief that the ship was bound for Flanders to victual the enemies of the French king.[95] For good measure, he added another justification that the *St. John* had once traded with the Saracens. This was not the only time Berenger Blanc struck at English interests. Later in 1316, he seized another English ship, the *Petite Bayard*, bound for Antwerp with a cargo of wool and took her also to Calais, claiming that she was actually a Flemish ship. In November 1318, the French crown agreed to pay 2,000 marks in compensation for this action, but only half that amount was actually paid and that in 1324.[96]

Two months after the French seizure of the *St. John*, Pessagno had apparently managed to buy replacement wheat in Southampton, which was then shipped to Sandwich before being moved on to Berwick.[97] Pessagno had acted in the past as a supplier of foodstuffs for the royal household and army, providing three quarters of the wheat and oats shipped to Berwick in support of the English army that the Scots defeated at Bannockburn in 1314.[98] Later, on December 16, 1316, Pessagno made an agreement with Edward II to supply 17,000 quarters of wheat and 2,600 tuns of wine for the war against Scotland, half to be delivered

---

[90] Fryde, "Antonio Pessagno of Genoa," pp. 159–78. *CPR, 1313–17*, pp. 466, 571–2.
[91] *CPR, 1313–17*, p. 466.
[92] Prestwich, *The Three Edwards*, p. 248. See also Lucas, "The Great European Famine," p. 69 and Jordan, *The Great Famine*, p. 174.
[93] *CCR, 1313–18*, pp. 291, 425, 475–6; *CPR, 1313–17*, pp. 501–2, 571–2; *Foedera*, vol. 2 pt. 1, p. 502.
[94] *CCR, 1313–18*, pp. 345–6, 425, 475–6; *CCR, 1318–23*, pp. 496, 692.
[95] *CCR, 1313–18*, pp. 341, 475–6.
[96] *Ibid.*, pp. 444, 552–4: *CCR, 1318–23*, pp. 9, 13–14, 52, 259, 710–11; Lloyd, *Alien Merchants*, pp. 68–70.
[97] *CFR, 1307–19*, p. 287.
[98] Fryde, "Antonio Pessagno of Genoa," p. 170; McNamee, *The Wars of the Bruces*, pp. 125–6.

to Berwick, one quarter to Newcastle, and the other to Skinburness, on the Solway near Carlisle. In addition, Pessagno agreed to provide 5 fully equipped Genoese galleys each manned by a crew of 200 to carry grain for the king's use from Ireland to Skinburness.[99] Following this agreement, on January 31, 1317, Edward II requested the authorities at Genoa to permit Leonardo Pessagno, Antonio's brother, to outfit five galleys for his service.[100] These arrangements were made in anticipation of a major royal campaign in Scotland in 1317 that in the end did not happen. Instead, it was replaced with a considerably smaller enterprise that the Earl of Arundel led. Moreover, the plan to hire Genoese galleys to operate in the Irish Sea appears to have foundered because of lack of funds.[101]

While it has been suggested that Pessagno successfully acquired the 17,000 bushels of wheat in England during the worst period of the famine, there is no clear evidence to support that conclusion.[102] It appears that he aimed to buy at least some of the grain overseas. For instance, Edward II wrote to the rulers of Spain, on January 31, 1317, requesting that Pessagno be allowed to buy 1,000 razed bushels of wheat in that realm.[103] It is also not certain how much of the promised 17,000 quarters of wheat he actually delivered. In early November 1317 it appears that the king expected the arrival momentarily at Sandwich of 5,000 quarters of wheat and 630 pipes of wine. Orders were issued to distribute the supplies mainly to Newcastle, Berwick and three castles in the north of England, Barnard in Durham and Alnwick and Wark in Northumberland.[104] A month later, in early December, the king was still waiting for the grain and wine to arrive. Two months later, on February 1, 1318, the cargo had still not come.[105] Finally, the total amount of wheat received from Pessagno at Berwick and Newcastle in the year July 8, 1317–July 7, 1318 was around 2,000 quarters instead of the planned 12,750, while in the same period Carlisle appears to have received nothing of its allotted 4,250 quarters.[106] Pessagno may have been unable to supply the full amount of wheat because famine in northern Europe forced him to go south to Gascony and Spain, where

---

[99] *CPR, 1313–17*, p. 603.   [100] *CCR, 1313–18*, p. 452.

[101] McNamee, *The Wars of the Bruces*, pp. 125, 128, 151, 181.

[102] *Ibid.*, p. 151. The supporting reference is to Fryde, "Antonio Pessagno of Genoa," p. 173, which only discusses the earlier case of the 2,100 quarters of wheat on the *St. John* not the 17,000 quarters that Pessagno later contracted to deliver.

[103] *CCR, 1313–18*, p. 452.   [104] *Ibid.*, pp. 506–7.

[105] *CPR, 1317–21*, pp. 44–5, 58–9; *CCR, 1313–18*, pp. 506–7, 522.

[106] McNamee, *The Wars of the Bruces*, pp. 126–7. McNamee's chart on p. 126 also shows that in 1314–15 and 1315–16, Pessagno supplied no wheat to Berwick and Newcastle.

he would have run into stiff competition from merchants, including other Italians, who were seeking grain for Flanders and northern France. Italy did not seem to be a possibility. Jordan claims that during the famine no grain was shipped from there to England.[107]

A related question is how frequent and extensive was royal purveyance of grain during the famine? Maddicott has documented the oppressive nature of purveyance, a burden that fell largely on the peasantry. Purveyance was the prerogative right of the king "to purchase compulsorily the victuals and means of transport which his household needed" that was extended to supply royal armies. Complaints about purveyance included "private profiteering, the seizure of goods without payment or consent, and payments made inadequately or after long delays."[108] During the reign of Edward I, as the king became more deeply involved in war especially in Scotland, his armies became larger and purveyance more frequent and oppressive. McNamee's charts on wheat and oats received at Carlisle, Berwick, and Newcastle, the three main northern supply bases, indicate the scale of the king's demands on the peasantry, when he was preparing for campaigns in Scotland. For example, in 1299–1300 a total of 5,300 quarters of wheat (1,500 from Ireland) and 4,975 quarters of oats (1,600 from Ireland) were received. In 1302–3 the totals were wheat 5,400 quarters (500 from Ireland) and oats 4,125 (500 from Ireland). For Edward I's planned final campaign in 1306, the totals were 8,000 quarters of wheat (1,200 from Ireland) and 7,750 quarters of oats (700 from Ireland).[109]

The only early campaign of Edward II that came close to his father's in the amount of wheat and oats purveyed was that which led to Bannockburn. In 1313–14, 7,000 quarters of wheat and 3,750 of oats were received, all at Newcastle and Berwick. For many other years of Edward II's reign the amounts received were much more modest. In fact, during the first year of the famine, 1315–16 nothing was received at Carlisle, Newcastle, and Berwick, while in the second year, 1316–17, 1,650 quarters of wheat and 1,425 of oats (300 from Ireland) were received. Finally, in 1317–18, the totals received were 2,900 quarters of wheat and 900 of oats. The period 1316–18 was one of planned campaigns that never materialized.[110] One reason may well be that the king's

---

[107] Jordan, *The Great Famine*, pp. 158–62, 167–9, 173–4.
[108] Maddicott, "The English Peasantry," p. 299.
[109] The figures for the reigns of the first two Edwards are approximations extrapolated from the charts in McNamee, *The Wars of the Bruces*, pp. 126–7. The years are regnal, Nov. 20–Nov. 19 for Edward I and July 8–July 7 for Edward II. In 1316 Berwick ceased being used as a supply base, *ibid.*, p. 125.
[110] *Ibid.*, p. 125.

purveyors were unable to squeeze enough grain out of the famine struck population. Although these amounts are less than those associated with earlier military activities of either Edward II or his father, in a time of famine they must have been hard targets to meet and the amounts purveyed could easily have disrupted local grain markets.

Later in his reign, in 1319 and 1322, Edward II was able to mount and support two sizeable campaigns against the Scots. In 1319–20, 4,300 quarters of wheat and 1,675 of oats were received at Newcastle and Carlisle. The totals for 1321–3 were 4,550 quarters of wheat (350 from Ireland) and 3,425 of oats (300 from Ireland).[111] While the totals to support the 1322 campaign are quite substantial, particularly since this was a scarcity year, they are much less than the amounts the king demanded: 6,200 quarters of wheat and 8,500 of oats from his English subjects and 6,000 quarters of wheat and 4,000 of oats from his Irish.[112] One must conclude that the demands of the king far exceeded the capacity of his subjects to supply them in an age of famine, destitution, and death.

Finally, one other demand of the king for resources to support his military efforts needs to be examined for its possible effects on the population during the famine, is taxation. During the period 1290–1322 the crown imposed fourteen lay subsidies on the moveable wealth of its subjects in order to finance war, an unprecedented level of taxation that produced £636,700. The single heaviest tax was that of 1290 which yielded £114,400, 97 percent of the assessed amount. Beyond the amount demanded of the taxpayers by any individual subsidy, the real and cumulative burden was the frequency of taxation, on average a new subsidy every 2.33 years. Nonetheless, the most striking aspect of this taxation, noted by Ormrod, was that the net yield of the taxes only fell below 90 percent of the assessment once, in 1295 when it was 87 percent, not surprising because this was the third year in a row in which a new subsidy was levied. In other years the yields ranged from a low of 91.7 percent in 1294 to a high of 98.7 percent in the famine year 1316.[113]

Maddicott provides numerous examples of the ways in which lay subsidies in the period 1294–1341 burdened the peasantry. First, taxes levied on movables hit tenants harder than landlords. Second, there is considerable evidence that some taxpayers paid more than the official assessment as subtaxors, men drawn from the local community who

---

[111] *Ibid.*, pp. 126–7.   [112] *CPR, 1321–4*, pp. 93–5.
[113] Omrod, "The Crown and the English Economy," pp. 151–6; Maddicott, "The English Peasantry," pp. 290–1.

actually assessed and collected the taxes, skimmed a portion off the top
for themselves. Finally, despite the fact that poor peasants who owned
moveable goods worth 10s or less were exempt from paying taxes, subtaxors on their own initiative sometimes taxed "the nontaxables."[114]
Maddicott's general assessment of some subtaxors is that they "may have
regarded temporary office holding as a means to self advancement."
In drawing this conclusion he expresses skepticism about the idea of
"the common interests of the village community."[115]

The two lay subsidies levied during the famine years 1315 and 1316
must have imposed a heavy burden on the poorer peasants who faced a
number of different obligations but probably lacked the means to meet
them all. These included feeding their families and saving enough seed
for the following year's crop, while having to sell grain to pay rent and
taxes. Not surprising, there was some resistance to taxes during those
years but it appears scattered and localized. In June 1315 there was
opposition in Staffordshire and Shropshire. Then on January 1, 1316 a
commission was appointed to enquire into resistance in Yorkshire by
manorial bailiffs of the king and other lords. They were accused of
preventing tenants from coming before the taxors to be assessed. Then,
when the taxors distrained upon the non payers by seizing and impound-
ing (unidentified) animals, the bailiffs broke the pounds and freed them,
no doubt with the intension of returning them to their owners. Similar
opposition appeared later in 1316 in three royal manors in Buckinghamshire, in the estates of the earls of Lancaster and Pembroke in Derbyshire
and Nottinghamshire and again in Yorkshire. Finally, on February 20,
1317, the king instructed the taxors and collectors in each county to send
him the names of all those who resisted paying the subsidy or aided their
tenants to resist.[116]

The resistance of the bailiffs to taxation appears to have been the
consequence of local knowledge of the dire social situation on the
manors that they managed. They were no doubt aware of the demands
with which the tenants were struggling, especially the difficulty they faced
in paying taxes and rents. If their animals were distrained upon for the tax
debt they owed to the king, this was another blow to their livelihood,

---

[114] Maddicott, "The English Peasantry," pp. 291–9. See also Kershaw, "The Great
Famine," 47.
[115] Maddicott, "The English Peasantry," p. 294. Maddicott's conclusion is similar to that
on the relationship between the better-off peasants and their poorer neighbors in
Schofield, "The Social Economy," pp. 59–61.
[116] CPR, 1313–17, pp. 324–5, 424; CCR 1313–18, pp. 363, 365, 453; Willard,
Parliamentary Taxes on Personal Property, pp. 170–2; Maddicott, "The English
Peasantry," p. 298.

especially if the animals were plough horses or oxen. This would make it all the more difficult to plant another crop, recover from the famine, and pay their rents. While we do not know what sort of animals were distrained, Maddicott believes that, in some instances, they were plough beasts, despite the fact that the legislation *Articuli super Cartas* of 1300 prohibited their distraint for debt owed to the king.[117]

Edward II was not the only European ruler who attempted to respond to the famine. The French king, Louis X, also imposed prohibitions on grain export and encouraged import, but he took a bolder stroke on September 25, 1315 when he issued an ordinance condemning merchants who hoarded victuals and salt. This was followed by government officials searching for, and confiscating, stores of salt in a number of towns including Paris and Rouen.[118] On July 30, 1316, Haakon V, king of Norway issued an edict allowing the export of butter and stockfish only by merchants "who imported grain and grain products in return."[119] Some European cities had more effective responses to famine. In 1317 the town council of Bruges, for example, bought 6,875 quarters of imported grain and sold it to the populace at cost.[120]

The English crown's commitment to the regulation of the market for bread grains in the interest of all consumers, with an express commitment to the particular needs of the poor, predated the reign of Edward II. Nonetheless, when the famine began, after the 1315 harvest failed, and dragged on to 1322, the king made an effort to enforce the traditional measures that were to hand, including the assizes of ale and weights and measures. Beyond those, the crown also imposed prohibitions on the export of grain and encouraged its import. Finally, in his letter to the bishops in 1316 Edward II indicated his moral commitment to aiding the poor and the hungry. At the same time he faced a difficult military situation after 1314 in a war inherited from his father. Repeated Scots raids and depredations on the north of England meant that he had to call on his famine struck people for provisions and money that they could ill afford to part with.

During future scarcities and famines, later medieval English kings followed policies similar to those of Edward II. They imposed prohibitions on export, encouraged the import of foreign grain, pushed for vigorous enforcement of the statute of forestallers and the assize of

---

[117] Maddicott, "The English Peasantry," pp. 295–6; *SR*, vol. 1, p. 139, 28 Edw. I c. 12.
[118] Braid, "Economic Behavior, Markets and Crises," p. 349; Jordan, *The Great Famine*, pp. 168–9.
[119] Jordan, *The Great Famine*, p. 182.
[120] *Ibid.*, pp. 158–9; Nicholas, *Medieval Flanders*, p. 207.

weights and measures, and encouraged the domestic movement of grain to places in need, especially London.[121] New policies were also tried such as the purchase of grain overseas by the government of London.[122] Also, the crown appointed commissions with power to search for fore-stallers and hoarders of grain, who would be punished according to the forestalling statute of 1351 renewed in 1378, which meant forfeiture of their grain to the king and its likely sale in the market.[123]

Finally, there appears to have been no food riots or other protests during the Great Famine. It may be that there were some but they remain buried in legal records. On the other hand, those people who were suffering the most from hunger and, ultimately, starvation may have lacked the strength to protest. Nonetheless, one is tempted to speculate that the crown's regulatory actions in the reigns of Edward II and his son created an expectation among those who brought grain in the market place for their own domestic consumption that it was a duty or obligation of the crown to protect the subsistence rights of consumers. Thus, when the crown appeared to be lax in fulfilling its obligations, in 1347 and beyond, riot followed either as a means of popular direct enforcement or as a shaming tactic designed to compel the king and his officials to do their duty.

---

[121] See Chapters 3–5.
[122] Martin (ed.), *Knighton's Chronicle 1337–1396*, pp. 538–9; Taylor, Childs, and Watkiss (eds.), *St. Albans Chronicle*, vol.1, p. 915; *CLB*, vol. H, pp. 92–4, 100; Lloyd, *England and the German Hanse*, pp. 222–3.
[123] TNA, C54/232 m. 16; TNA, C66/332 m. 15d; 441 m. 35d; 443 m. 27d, 25d, 23d; *CCR, 1389–92*, p. 250; *CPR, 1389–92*, p. 441; *CPR 1436–41*, pp. 145, 266, 369.

3 The food riots of 1347

It is not until the late spring and early summer of 1347 that we find the first clear evidence of food riots in medieval England, when there were outbreaks in five different locations: Bristol; Lynn and Thetford in Norfolk; Boston in Lincolnshire; and unidentified ports in Kent. The first encounter with the best documented of them, the riots at Lynn and Boston, produces an immediate shock of recognition. The crowd actions – stopping transport of grain, seizing shipments, and selling grain at less than the prevailing price – fit well with the behavior of eighteenth-century crowds described by Thompson and, more generally, with the behavior of English food rioters at any time from the sixteenth century onward. An even more striking similarity between the food riots of 1347 and early modern riots is the participants' appeal to crown policy and established law as a means of legitimating their actions. In 1347 the crowds appear to have claimed to be acting in the king's name when they ordered the unloading of ships that had taken on cargoes for export overseas, in effect implementing prohibitions on export, one of the crown's main responses to scarcity and rising grain prices.[1]

One conclusion that can be drawn from the behavior of the crowds in 1347 is that these protests were fully formed, mature examples of the genre. As Walker has noted in his discussion of an anti-tax riot by women of Bristol in 1401 and a food riot at Lynn in 1405: "Where the records allow a sufficiently detailed view of the tactics of popular protest, it seems that the vocabulary of ritual gesture and defiance, familiar from the better-documented early modern period, was already in place."[2]

Given the apparent maturity of the 1347 riots, one question comes immediately to mind, namely were there earlier riots that preceded them?

---

[1] Sharp, "The Food Riots of 1347," pp. 33–54. For the early modern situation see Thompson, "The Moral Economy," 76–136; Walter and Wrightson, "Dearth and the Social Order," 22–42; Walter, "Grain Riots and Popular Attitudes to the Law," pp. 85–129; Sharp, *In Contempt of All Authority*, pp. 10–81; Sharp, "Popular Protest," pp. 271–308; Bohstedt, *The Politics of Provisions*.

[2] Walker, "Rumour, Sedition and Popular Protest," 56–7. The quotation is on 56.

The answer might well be yes but the evidence, if it exists, has not yet been discovered. There is some evidence for disorders over food before 1347, especially in the first two decades of the fourteenth century, but that evidence is not sufficient or clear enough to allow us to describe them as food riots.[3] Nonetheless, the awareness of the law demonstrated by the 1347 crowds provides another indication that a popular sense of the rightness of a regulated market in food had emerged from the mid-thirteenth century onward. As R. H. Britnell has concluded: "the formal market was regulated in the interests of customers to monitor weights and measures and to suppress forestalling, areas in which thirteenth-century monarchy extended its concern."[4]

The riots and the rioters

Our knowledge of the 1347 riots comes from related sources, the special commissions of oyer and terminer that the crown issued to try the rioters plus the record of the trials before the special commissioners in the Lynn case and the proceedings in king's bench in the Boston case, when it was transferred there after indictments before the special commissioners. Usually, a special commission consisted of a group of prominent individuals, a mixture of judges and local notables, assigned to hear a specific complaint. For the food riots of 1347 a different commission was issued in response to each outbreak, except that the commission to try the protesters at Lynn also included authority to try those responsible for the disorders at Thetford.

Such commissions "were initiated at the suit of the injured party, and were obtainable from Chancery, like writs de cursu, on the Chancellor's own authority."[5] To begin the process it was necessary for the injured party to submit a petition or complaint, addressed to the king, his council, or the chancellor stating his case then the commission was issued on payment of the appropriate fee. Beyond assigning justices to hear the matter at issue, the commission, at least in the fourteenth and fifteenth centuries, contained a statement of the complainant's case.[6] In addition to the evidence of the surviving commissions, the records

---

[3] See for example the disorder over grain in Gloucester marketplace on June 11, 1304 in TNA, JUST 1/286 m. 1. It is discussed, although misdated to 1302, in Hilton, *A Medieval Society*, p. 181. See also an attack on a cart carrying salt fish through Tottenham in 1310 in Pam, *The Hungry Years*, p. 18.

[4] Britnell, "The Proliferation of Markets," 212. See also Dyer, *Standards of Living*, p. 272.

[5] Powell, "Special Oyer and Terminer Proceedings," p. 2.

[6] *Ibid.*, 2; Kaeuper, "Law and Order in Fourteenth Century England," 747–58; Musson and Ormrod, *The Evolution of English Justice*, pp. 48–50, 119–22.

of the trials of the Lynn and Boston rioters provide invaluable information about the events that occurred, the names and sometimes, occupational status of the accused rioters plus the punishments imposed.

The first of the 1347 riots took place at Bristol, in May or early June, certainly before June 6. During the 1340s, William Casse or Caas, a Bordeaux wine merchant, shipped cargoes of grain from England to Bordeaux with some regularity. In December 1343, Casse was licensed to export wheat and peas from London. He also received one royal license in November 1346 to ship 900 quarters of wheat from Sandwich and a second in February 1347 for another 200 quarters of wheat from the same port. Later, in the spring, Casse obtained a further license to ship 700 quarters of wheat from Bristol. On April 28, 1347, the king ordered the mayor and bailiffs of Bristol to let Casse have suitable ships to carry the grain to his lieges in Bordeaux and commanded all admirals and local officials to let the grain pass to its destination without hindrance.[7] On the day of the riot, according to the first commission of oyer and terminer issued on June 18, 1347, a crowd assumed the royal power, elected a captain, issued proclamations, boarded the loaded ship in Bristol harbor "in a warlike manner" and carried the grain away.[8] It is clear from the wording of a letter dated June 6, 1347 from the king to the sheriff of Gloucestershire, to allow Casse to leave the port of Bristol with a replacement cargo of grain, that Casse was the source of the information about the events described in the first commission of oyer and terminer.[9]

In a revised commission, issued on July 12, 1347, the rioters were described as boarding the ships "with armed force" as well as "in a warlike manner."[10] In yet another revised commission, of February 8, 1348, the rioters were accused of assaulting and beating the merchants and sailors and taking away grain and unspecified foodstuffs plus other goods worth a total of £2,000.[11] This final revised version also expanded on another charge made in the first two commissions. In the original commission, the rioters were accused of committing other unspecified

---

[7] Thomas (ed.), *Calendar of Plea and Memoranda Rolls*, vol. 1, p. 207; *CPR, 1345–8*, pp. 198, 251, 280; *CCR, 1346–9*, pp. 116, 224, 458–9, 464.

[8] TNA, C66/221 m. 28v, "*more guerrino.*" A full text of the commission is in *Foedera*, vol. 3 pt. 1, p. 126. See also *CPR, 1345–8*, p. 376.

[9] TNA, C54/181 m. 6. See also *CCR, 1346–9*, p. 224.

[10] TNA, C66/221 m.11v, "*armata potentia.*" See also *CPR, 1345–8*, p. 392.

[11] TNA, C66/221 m. 19v. See also *CPR, 1348–50*, p. 72. Cohn, *Popular Protest*, pp. 141–3 misreads this commission as evidence for a second riot at Bristol, when it is in fact a revised commission for the trial of the suspects who participated in the original riot of mid-1347.

misdeeds in neighboring places to the terror and disturbance of the king's subjects. In the first revised version, neighboring places had become the counties of Gloucester and Somerset, while the final version stated that the rioters gathered to themselves a great multitude of malefactors, wandered in the fairs and markets of Gloucestershire, and seized goods "with force and arms" from men whom they beat and wounded.[12] Unfortunately, beyond the commissions, no other records of the events at Bristol seem to have survived.

The next two outbreaks of riot, at Lynn and Boston, began on the same day, Saturday June 16, 1347. On the following Monday and Tuesday, June 18 and 19, there were further disorders at Lynn while at Boston the actions with which the rioters were charged all took place on June 16. At Lynn popular ire was aimed at export of grain to Gascony, which the crown had licensed. One exporter was William Merton who, on June 2, 1347, obtained a license to ship 300 quarters of grain from Lynn to Bordeaux on the *James* of Lynn.[13] The other was John Wesenham, the king's butler in the period 1347–51, a sometime customs farmer and prominent citizen of Lynn, who was heavily involved in the wool, wine, and grain trades. In the period 1347–61, he supplied Calais with 6,600 quarters of grain purveyed in England and in 1363 he was mayor of the town.[14] During the years 1333–60, he was regularly the recipient of licenses to export grain from England to a variety of foreign locations including Norway, Flanders, Holland, and Zealand as well as Gascony. In 1358, and again in 1360, in one of his other capacities as the king's farmer of the temporalities of the bishopric of Ely, Wesenham was licensed to ship one cargo of 500 quarters of wheat and 120 tuns of ale and another of 500 quarters of wheat from Lynn to the Low Countries.[15]

In the weeks before the Lynn riots of June 16–19, Wesenham received three licenses to ship grain from Lynn to Bordeaux and to return with

---

[12] TNA, C66/221 m. 19v, "*vi et armis.*" [13] *CPR, 1345–8*, p. 282.

[14] Gras, *The Evolution of the English Corn Market*, p. 173; Fryde, "The English Farmers of the Customs," 1–17; Burley, "The Victualling of Calais," 53. See also Owen (ed.), *The Making of King's Lynn*, pp. 449–53; *CPR, 1350–4*, p. 314, license for Wesenham to ship 400 quarters of rye (originally purveyed in England for the supply of Calais) to Gascony for his profit because he could not sell it in Calais for as much as he paid for it in England, February 5, 1350; *CPR, 1354–8*, p. 511, commission authorizing Wesenham to arrest sufficient ships in Lynn and other Norfolk ports to transport grain and other victuals purveyed to supply Calais, February 27, 1357.

[15] Licenses for Wesenham to export grain are to be found in *CPR, 1330–4*, p. 415; *CPR, 1334–8*, pp. 80, 539; *CCR, 1348–50*, p. 469; *CPR, 1350–4*, pp. 196, 318; *CPR, 1354–8*, pp. 545, 637; *CPR, 1358–61*, pp. 20, 432. See also *CIM*, vol. 2, p. 386; *CFR, 1356–69*, pp. 28, 172, 287.

wine for the king, one on May 8, for 1,000 quarters of wheat and two on June 2 for a total of 600 quarters of various kinds of grain on two ships, the *Nicholas* of Lynn and the cog *Seinte Marie* of Bayonne.[16] A commission of June 18 that instructed a king's serjeant-at-arms, Walter del Haye, to arrest four suspected rioters confirms that Wesenham was a victim of the riots and the probable source of the complaint laid out in the commission of oyer and terminer.[17]

At Lynn on June 16, 1347, a crowd acting "with force and arms and in breach of the king's peace," compelled John of Cokesford, the mayor of the town, to issue proclamations ordering the owners of two loads of wheat, one of forty quarters, the other of twenty quarters, to sell the grain to members of the crowd at 6s per quarter instead of the prevailing price of 6s 8d, which they did but only against their will.[18] The crowd, accompanied by three bailiffs of the town, who also went along against their will, also boarded the *James* owned by William Merton and forced the unloading of its cargo of 200 quarters of wheat, 60 quarters of rye and 60 quarters of beans. The crowd then caused the grain to be returned to the granaries of the owners, four named men who were probably local merchants or dealers in grain.[19]

On Monday June 18, the crowd returned to its work and forced the unloading of 60 quarters of wheat from a ship of Bayonne and the return of the grain to the owner's granary in Lynn. The ship was unnamed, but probably the cog *Seinte Marie* of Bayonne. The crowd also made proclamation that no one could ship grain out of the port until after the Feast of St. Peter ad Vincula (August 1) unless it was intended for the king at Calais. Finally, at the guildhall, the crowd compelled the mayor, aldermen, and other ministers of the king and prominent citizens of the town such as Thomas Melchebourn, another merchant active in the

[16] *CPR, 1345–8*, pp. 282–3.
[17] TNA, C66/221 m. 28v; *Foedera*, vol. 3 pt. 1, 126. This document also confirms that Wesenham was to bring back wine for the king. See also *CPR, 1345–8*, p. 376.
[18] TNA, JUST1/612/5 m. 1, indictments before the justices of oyer and terminer sitting at Lynn, July 30, 1347. The language "*vi et armis et contra pacem Regis*" comes from the indictment. The actual commission issued to the judges uses stronger language much like that of the second commission regarding the Bristol riots, such as describing the Lynn rioters as assuming to themselves the power of the crown and exercising the power of arms in a warlike manner. In addition the "proclamations" of the indictment had been "quasi royal proclamations" in the commission, TNA, C66/221/m. 16v and JUST, 1/612/5, m. 1. See also *CPR, 1345–8*, p. 388.
[19] TNA, JUST1/612/5, m. 1, indictment before the justices of oyer and terminer sitting at Lynn, July 30, 1347. The owners of the 200 quarters of wheat were John Crewe and Thomas Blome and, of the 60 quarters of rye and 60 quarters of beans, Thomas Feltewelle and John Newelond.

grain trade and in royal service during the years 1327–55, to swear to uphold all of their actions and complaints.[20]

Towards the end of the roll containing a record of the indictments and other judicial process relating to the Lynn riots there is a brief, somewhat cryptic and incomplete entry, which appears to relate to the grain riots. At some point in the proceedings of the commission, four men were indicted for activities that took place on Tuesday June 19. They were accused of placing a baker of Wiggenhall, a village on the Ouse four miles south of Lynn, in the thewe (a form of pillory usually reserved for women) located in the Lynn market place, without legal process.[21] This action no doubt lies behind the accusation, contained in the commission of oyer and terminer, that the rioters by their own authority and without legal process condemned people to the pillory.

On July 28, 1347 there was one final echo of the June 16–19 events at Lynn. The commission of oyer and terminer began its first session on Monday July 30. The first item of that session, recorded on the roll, is the indictment of ten men for an assault on Robert son of John the miller. According to that indictment, Robert had come to the market of Lynn on Saturday July 28 to sell half a quarter of peas. He was approached by Thomas Crede, who offered to buy the peas for 2s. When Robert refused to sell at that price, he was assaulted and beaten by Thomas and a number of other men. While the commission was expressly charged with hearing the June riot cases, no doubt it and the sheriff took advantage of a timely arrival to deal with the similar case that arose out of the events of July 28.[22]

While the records of the commission of oyer and terminer, before which the Boston rioters were indicted, have apparently not survived, after the case was moved to the court *coram rege* in Michaelmas term

---

[20] TNA, JUST1/612/5 m. 1, indictment before the justices of oyer and terminer sitting at Lynn, July 30, 1347. In 1327 and 1335 Melchbourn shipped victuals to Newcastle and Berwick in support of military operations against the Scots and in 1337 he was licensed to ship 400 quarters of wheat to Holland and Zealand to accompany an English diplomatic mission which included the Bishop of Lincoln, the Earl of Salisbury and the Earl of Huntingdon, *CPR, 1327–30*, p. 104, *CCR, 1334–8*, pp. 98, 456–67; Melchbourn regularly received licenses to export grain from Lynn in the period 1332–55, see *CPR, 1330–4*, pp. 302–3, 424; *CPR, 1334–8*, pp. 57, 74, 339, 542; *CCR, 1341–3*, pp. 694–5; *CPR, 1348–50*, p. 287; *CPR, 1350–4*, p. 477; *CPR, 1354–8*, pp. 148, 285, 307. See also *CFR, 1337–47*, pp. 41–2, 233 and *CIM*, vol. 2, pp. 368–9.

[21] TNA, JUST1/612/5 m. 2. See *CLB*, vol. G, pp. 175, 216 for two cases from 1364 and 1367 of women "condemned to the pillory for women called 'la thewe'" for market frauds. See also a case from 1375 of a woman sentenced as a scold to the thewe "for women ordained" in Riley, *Memorials*, pp. 385–6.

[22] TNA, JUST1/612/5 m. 1, indictment before the justices of oyer and terminer at Lynn, July 30, 1347.

1347 the king's bench plea rolls contain references to the substance of the indictments and record subsequent proceedings. These records plus the commission of oyer and terminer itself provide enough evidence to permit at least a partial reconstruction of events.[23] There appear to have been two riotous incidents at Boston on June 16. In the first, a crowd led by their elected captain and mayor, Thomas of Okeham cordwainer, assumed the royal power, rose up in a warlike manner, feloniously boarded two ships loaded with grain, and carried away 120 quarters of wheat valued at £36 or 6s per quarter. Other charges in the indictment included the ringing of a bell, no doubt the market bell, as a means to assemble the crowd and coordinate their actions, which included forcing other men, who would not support them willingly, to swear to uphold their activities and more generally committing other unspecified evil acts with swords, bows and arrows, and other arms.[24] The ringing of the common bell seems to have been a standard means of summoning a crowd in the period.[25] In the second action, a crowd led once again by Thomas of Okeham assumed the royal power, feloniously boarded the two grain ships once again, and carried away eighty-five quarters of wheat from one and fifty-three quarters from the other. The crowd then sold the wheat at 4s per quarter and, with force and arms, compelled five men to hold the money.[26]

Although the actual commission of oyer and terminer claims that the Boston rioters issued quasi-royal proclamations, including one that those inhabitants who had left the town because of the disorders had to return by a given deadline or their houses would be destroyed, there is no clear evidence in the surviving king's bench records of this charge being included in the indictments. It might be included in the charge

---

[23] TNA, C66/221/m. 22v. See also *CPR, 1345–8*, p. 381. An English translation of the commission of oyer and terminer can be found in Musson with Powell (eds.), *Crime, Law and Society*, pp. 48–9.

[24] TNA, KB27/350 (Mich. 21 Ed. III) m. 101.

[25] See for example, *CPR, 1313–17*, p. 314 and *Parliamentary Writs*, vol. 2 pt. 2, appendix, p. 89, use of the common bell at Nottingham to summon the community, April 7, 1315; *CPR, 1317–21*, p. 277 and *Parliamentary Writs*, vol. 2 pt. 2, appendix, pp. 125–6, ringing of common bell (so described in full text) to summon a crowd in Norwich, August 6, 1318; *CPR, 1317–21*, p. 469, ringing of town bells to summon a crowd in Bury St. Edmunds, October 25, 1319.

[26] TNA, KB27/350 (Mich. 21 Ed. III) m. 101. What I have described as the first action is consistently dated in KB27 as the Saturday before the festival of St. Botolfus, June 16, 1347, while the second action is consistently dated as the Saturday before the translation of St. Edward, June 16, 1347, if the saint's day refers to the second translation of Edward the Martyr. It is the two different ways of dating the same day that lead me to believe there were two separate actions and consequently two separate indictments.

against the participants in both riots that they assumed the royal power.[27] As in the Bristol and Lynn cases, the Boston grain shippers, four London merchants, appear to have obtained the king's license to export the grain but the destination is not clear, although it was likely Gascony or Calais.[28]

According to the commission of oyer and terminer issued to try the rioters at Lynn, the events there inspired the inhabitants of Thetford, and other unnamed towns in Norfolk, to similar actions.[29] Unfortunately, the actual actions are undocumented. There is no mention of Thetford or events there in the surviving roll of the commission of oyer and terminer. The disorders in Kent are also poorly documented. A commission of oyer and terminer was issued to hear charges that, sometime before September 1, 1347, disturbers of the peace prevented victuals, which were intended to supply Edward III and his army in France, from being loaded on ships in unnamed ports in the county, but little else can be discovered.[30]

It is only for the Lynn and Boston riots that we have evidence about the numbers of people indicted for participation, their occupational status, and the punishments imposed. A total of 103 men were indicted for their part in the Lynn riots of June 16 and 18. Two were found not guilty, 63 were found guilty and made fines, and 38 did not appear to answer the charges and were ultimately outlawed. The fines ranged from 2s to one mark (13s 4d) except in the case of two men who were noted as very poor and fined 1s each. The occupations of 38 of the 103 indicted rioters are known and not unexpectedly they range over a number of mainly artisanal and laboring occupations, the kind of people who no doubt depended on the market for most, if not all, of their food: 7 tailors; 5 glovers; 4 porters; 3 smiths; 3 weavers; 2 cordwainers; 2 barkers (tanners) and one each of the following: poulterer, currier, brewster, cooper, souter, coucher, upholsterer, shearman, cutler, cook, boatman, and *famulus*. If, in this period, surnames are still a reliable guide to occupations then 2 curriers, 2 weavers, 1 chandler, 1 smith, 1 cardmaker, 1 woolwinder, and 1 cook (a total of nine) can be added to the list of the 38 indicted Lynn rioters with known occupations.[31]

---

[27] TNA, C66/221 m. 22v.

[28] There is no license enrolled on the patent rolls; the only reference to a license is in the commission of oyer and terminer, TNA, C66/221 m. 22v. The four London merchants were Walter Mortoun, John Lonekyn, Adam de la Pole, and Richard Sprot, TNA, KB 27/350 m. 101.

[29] TNA, C66/221 m. 16v.   [30] TNA, C66/221 m. 3v. See also *CPR, 1345–8*, pp. 398–9.

[31] TNA, JUST1/612/5, mm. 1–2.

One woman, Juetta wife of John Claymond, and 110 men were indicted for their involvement in the Boston riots of June 18.[32] They were indicted before the commission of oyer and terminer on August 8, 1347, after which the proceedings were moved to the court *coram rege*. There is no indication in the king's bench records of a subsequent trial. In fact, few of the rioters ever appeared to enter pleas. At most only 21 were ever in custody and 18 of them entered pleas of not guilty.[33] A number of accused rioters only appeared in court in order to plead royal pardons for their offences after April 10, 1348 when the crown began to issue them. At least 46 pardons were granted including one to Juetta Claymond and one to Thomas of Okeham cordwainer, the captain and mayor of the crowd.[34] The occupational status of 45 of the 111 indicted Boston suspects is known and the information follows much the same pattern as that found among the Lynn suspects. There were 10 tailors, 6 butchers, 4 porters, 3 fishers, 2 cutlers, 2 mariners, 2 skinners, 2 farriers, 2 servants, and one each of the following; cordwainer, sadler, shearman, spicer, glover, lawner (linen weaver), weaver, knifesmith, shipman, woolwinder, sociller, and farrier. If surnames are included then five more can be added: a taverner, a flesher, a draper, a weaver, and a tailor.[35]

One significant point about the judicial proceedings against the rioters of 1347 needs to be emphasized, the distance between the language used to characterize the offences and the actual punishments imposed. The king's bench records in the Boston case describe the rioters as assuming the royal power and acting in a warlike manner.[36] Similar language was also used in the commissions of oyer and terminer to describe the actions not only of the Boston rioters but also those of the Lynn and Bristol rioters. In the Boston and Lynn cases the commissions also accuse the participants in the riots of issuing quasi-royal proclamations

---

[32] TNA, KB27/350 Rex (Mich. 21 Edward III) m. 49. The names of six men appear twice in this list of the indicted: John Besage, Robert Davy, Henry or Reginald Pakkere, Richard Pakkere, John Claymond, and William Sutton. In three instances this duplication was cleared up when pleading a pardon: Robert Davy was one and the same as Robert Davy, glover; Reginald Pakkere was one and the same as Henry, son of Petronille atte Pratte; John Besage, tailor, was one and the same as John Besage, glover. See TNA, KB27/352 (Eas. 22 Ed. III) m. 49 and 353 Rex (Trinity 22 Ed. III) m. 28v.

[33] TNA, KB27/350 (Mich. 21 Ed. III) m. 101.

[34] The forty-six recipients of pardons are named in *CPR, 1348–50*, pp. 52–3, 59 and *CPR, 1350–4*, p. 181. At least twenty of the indicted men appeared in King's Bench and successfully pleaded pardons. See TNA, KB27/352 Rex (Eas. 22 Ed. III) mm. 3v, 49; 353 Rex (Trin. Ed. III) m. 28v; 354 Rex (Mich. 22 Ed. III) m. 1.

[35] TNA, KB27/350 (Mich. 21 Ed. III) m. 49.

[36] TNA, KB27/350 (Mich. 21 Ed. III) m. 101.

(*proclamationes quasi regias*).[37] The king's bench records refer to the Boston rioters as acting feloniously while both the records and the commission refer to them as felons and wrongdoers and their actions as felonies, seditions, and crimes.[38] Finally, the Bristol oyer and terminer commission of June 18 and the Lynn commission of July 12 mention that the king was concerned that if the participants remained unpunished it would encourage others to commit similar misdeeds bringing intolerable harm to the realm, especially in his absence, undoubtedly pursuing military glory in France.[39]

Most of the language in the records would thus lead the reader to believe that the rioters had committed felonies, perhaps approaching rebellion, sedition, or even treason.[40] Yet the offences were treated as criminal trespasses or misdemeanors, a category of crime less than felony that evolved rapidly from the mid thirteenth century onward.[41] The repeated use of the phrase with "force and arms" (*vi et armis*) in the actual commissions of oyer and terminer and in the surviving judicial records to describe the actions of the rioters in Bristol, Lynn, Boston, and Kent, with the addition in the indictments for the June 16 and 18 Lynn riots of the words "against the king's peace" (*contra pacem Regis*) provides an important indicator of how the law actually regarded the actions. The phrase, *vi et armis et contra pacem regis* was already becoming a term of art necessary to the definition of forceful criminal acts not encompassed by felony. It was to have a long future history as an essential component of the legal description of riot.[42] Another indicator of the actual state of affairs was the law's leniency, fines for the Lynn rioters and pardons for the Boston rioters.[43]

There is one final and fascinating question about the Lynn and Boston riots that cannot, at present, be answered on the basis of available evidence.

---

[37] TNA, C66/221 mm. 16v, 22. The Bristol rioters were accused of issuing proclamations, m. 28d.

[38] TNA, KB27/350 (Mich. 21 Ed. III) m. 101 and Rex m. 49; C66/221 m. 22v.

[39] TNA, C66/221 mm. 16v, 28v.

[40] See the discussion of accroaching or assuming the king's power, including a brief discussion of the Bristol, Lynn, and Boston riots, in Bellamy, *The Law of Treason*, pp. 65–8.

[41] Harding (ed.), *The Roll of the Shropshire Eyre*, pp. xlii–lviii; Musson and Ormrod, *The Evolution of English Justice*, pp. 119–27.

[42] Baker, *An Introduction to English Legal History*, pp. 71–5. For the development of the crime of riot see Bellamy, *Criminal Law and Society*, pp. 54–89.

[43] It is clear from the indictments for the June 16 and 18 riots at Lynn that the crimes were treated as criminal trespasses "*vi et armis et contra pacem Regis.*" Since the actual indictments for the Boston riots have not survived it remains a possibility that the rioters were charged with felony. In either case the argument about leniency still stands, given the granting of pardons.

Was it only a coincidence that the riots in both places broke out on the same day or was there some measure of coordination between the people of the two towns? Lynn and Boston are both on the Wash, about thirty-three miles apart by road, so that communication between them must have been relatively easy even in the fourteenth century. Both towns drew grain from extensive hinterlands and were engaged in shipping considerable quantities either overseas or coastwise to other parts of England. Moreover, where we have evidence, the occupational status of the accused rioters in both towns is similar. Such similarities could argue for some sort of prior communication before the riots or it might be that both towns experienced simultaneously the same social strains under the same circumstances. Thus the June 16 opening day for riots in both could have been purely coincidental.

Harvest deficiency and grain export

To explain the causes of the food riots of 1347, they need to be put in the context of a combination of elements, which include a below average harvest in 1346, a rapid increase in grain exports shipped to sustain Edward III's supporters in Gascony, and purveyance for military purposes, particularly to support the English siege of Calais. The period of the riots was not one of severe dearth of grain. The harvest of 1346 was deficient, with grain yields 20 percent below the long term average, but the deficiency did not come anywhere near the severity of the famine of 1315–17. In 1346–7 the average price of a quarter of wheat was 6.85s, 46 percent of the average price in 1315–16 and 44 percent of the price in 1316–17.[44] Moreover, the poor harvest of 1346 occurred during a run of good to bountiful harvests. "In 18 out of the 26 harvests between 1322 and 1348 net grain yields were at least 10 percent above their long-term average."[45] There were only four harvests in the same period, including that of 1346, in which net yields were lower than the long term mean but by no more than 20 percent. Finally, during the period 1322–48 there were no catastrophic consecutive harvest failures such as occurred during the Great Famine. Campbell attributes this run of good harvests to improvement in the weather.[46] Edward III must have been prescient, when he observed in a letter to the mayor and other officials of London on July 31, 1331 that urged them to enforce the assizes of bread and

---

[44] Campbell, "Population Pressure," pp. 115–16; Campbell, "Grain Yields;" Campbell, "Nature as Historical Protagonist," 297; Munro, "Revisions of Commodity Price Series."

[45] Campbell, "Nature as Historical Protagonist," 299.   [46] *Ibid.*, pp. 299–300.

ale and to ensure the prices of victuals were kept at reasonable levels,
"now that a time of plenty has succeeded to a time of scarcity."[47]

Despite the largely good harvests in the years 1322–48, the plight of
smallholders and laborers revealed during the Great Famine appears to
have been little altered. Campbell argues that, despite the high death rate
caused by the famine, the countryside in grain growing regions, such as
Norfolk, continued to be overcrowded with impoverished smallholders.
It may well be that it was the good harvests, which allowed them to
survive. In Norfolk the peasant survival strategy of selling land to buy
food became increasingly common in the course of the first half of the
fourteenth century.[48] One possible implication of Campbell's argument
is that the catastrophic years 1315–22 did not put a permanent break on
population increase. Instead population resumed its upward course in
the better years of the 1330s and 1340s, thereby accelerating the margin-
alization and impoverishment of a larger proportion of the rural population and making more people vulnerable to the negative effects of a single
deficient harvest of 1346, especially in an overcrowded, productive agricultural county like Norfolk. If Campbell is right in his argument that
"the progressive build-up of population may have pressed hard upon
resources" until the eve of the Black Death, then one wonders if it is
only a coincidence that the first recorded English food riots occurred
in 1347.[49]

Whatever the impact of the scarcity of 1346–7 on peasant producers,
its effects on consumers were magnified by the export of grain, mainly to
Gascony. There are no grain export licenses recorded on the patent rolls
for the year 1346 until October, that is after the harvest. Beginning in
October 1346 and running through June 1347, licenses were issued for
the export of 24,380 quarters of grain, 21,540 for Gascony, 2,840 for
Spain, and 400 for Calais. Of the total of 24,380 quarters, 16,210 were
shipped from Hull, London, and Lynn. In 1347, Gascony was the only
overseas destination for licensed grain shipments, with all licenses issued
during the first six months of the year. During that period licenses were
issued to ship a total of 17,870 quarters of grain, with export of 14,370
through Hull, London, and Lynn alone. Even more remarkable is the
concentration of licenses between April 28 and June 14, when exports
totaling 14,250 quarters were authorized, 12,350 from Hull, London,

---

[47] *CLB*, vol. E, p. 219.

[48] Campbell, "Population Pressure," pp. 115–20; Campbell, "The Agrarian Problem,"
60–70; Campbell, "Land Markets and the Morcellation of Holdings," pp. 197–209.

[49] Campbell, "Population Pressure," p. 120; Campbell, "Nature as Historical Protagonist,"
296–7.

and Lynn[50] Such large shipments within a short period of time must have either driven up prices or created the expectation of high prices in the areas from which the grain was obtained and in the ports through which it was shipped, especially towards the end of a poor harvest year when grain stocks would have declined.[51]

Lynn was one of the leading grain exporting centers in England from the early fourteenth century through at least the early eighteenth. The town's rise to importance as a grain port began in the late thirteenth-early fourteenth centuries when it became the main outfall of the system of East Anglian rivers which fed the Great Ouse. This was a result of natural changes in the courses of those rivers aided by the cutting of artificial channels.[52] Towards Lynn, the river system directed grain from a highly productive and extensive agricultural hinterland, although it is also the case that the town was well served with a road system, which moved grain on wagons and pack horses from that hinterland as well.[53] From Lynn, the grain was either shipped coastwise, north as far as Newcastle and south as far as London or Portsmouth, or exported to various European destinations depending, in part, upon royal political and diplomatic considerations.

For thirteenth and early fourteenth century East Anglian grain producers with a surplus to sell on the market, all roads and rivers led to Lynn. For example, Huntingdonshire river traffic from Yaxley on the Nene and St. Ives on the Ouse "had direct and unobstructed access" to Lynn. As a result, both market centers acted as collection points for grain later shipped down river to Lynn.[54] Customary tenants of the abbey and bishopric of Ely, which had estates in a number of East Anglian shires, were required to do carrying service to move grain – sometimes on their backs, but usually by pack horse or cart – to riverine market centers like St. Ives or Thetford in Norfolk where it was collected and then moved by

---

[50] *CPR, 1345–8*, pp. 198, 201–2, 204, 206–7, 209–10, 212–13, 215–16, 219, 225, 246, 251, 280–3, 287, 291, 350; *CCR, 1346–9*, pp. 116–17, 219, 224, 226, 228, 308. I have reworked the figures since I first published them in Sharp, "The Food Riots of 1347," p. 37.

[51] Martin (ed.), *Knighton's Chronicle*, pp. 88–9 records that a great dearth of grain occurred in August 1347 but abated once the new harvest was gathered.

[52] Darby, *The Medieval Fenland*, pp. 93–100; Williams, *The Maritime Trade*, pp. 54–5. See Campbell, "The Sources of Tradable Surpluses," pp. 15–16, 21–3 and "Ecology versus Economics," p. 81.

[53] Campbell, "Population Pressure," pp. 89–92; Williams, *Maritime Trade*, pp. 54–5; Parker, *The Making of King's Lynn*, pp. 3–18.

[54] Masschaele, *Peasants, Merchants, and Markets*, pp. 190–5. The quotation is from p. 190. On pp. 189–212 Masschaele discusses the complex "transport infrastructure" of thirteenth and fourteenth-century Huntingdonshire. See also Owen, (ed.), *The Making of King's Lynn*, pp. 48–51.

boat to Lynn. The abbey and bishopric of Ely were also entitled to other tenant services that included transporting grain and other victuals by water to various locations on the river system or to the final destination at Lynn. Other great ecclesiastical landlords, like Ramsey abbey, which also had extensive estates across East Anglia, shipped large quantities of grain to Lynn.[55]

Reflection on the weight of a cargo of grain and transportation costs reveals the importance of movement by river. A bushel of grain weighs 56 lbs while eight bushels, one quarter, weigh 448 lbs or four hundred weight. It has been estimated that a led packhorse in the medieval and early modern periods could carry a maximum of 200 weight or 4 bushels. Thus two packhorses were required to carry one quarter of grain.[56] In contrast "a fully loaded cart could carry 10 or 11 times as much" as one packhorse.[57] While horse drawn carts were a more efficient and cheaper way of transporting grain than packhorses their costs were much higher than carriage by river or sea.[58]

Evidence is lacking that would allow a calculation of the full extent of grain movements from Lynn or any other medieval port. In addition, it is impossible to estimate the amount smuggled out of the country. Neville Williams, in his study of the ports of East Anglia in the second half of the sixteenth century, has argued that illegal exports of grain from Norfolk ports, including Lynn, could have run as high as 20,000 quarters a year, which probably equalled the amount of legal exports that were duly licensed and paid customs duties in some years.[59] There is no reason to believe that customs officials were any more willing or able to control smuggling in the fourteenth century than in the sixteenth.

The fullest evidence we have for legal grain exports from Lynn and other ports in the period prior to the 1347 riots comes from licenses to export enrolled on the patent rolls, supplemented by royal mandates sent to local officials ordering them to permit specific licensed shipments to sail. Such licenses were required as exceptions whenever the crown had

---

[55] Farmer, "Marketing the Produce of the Countryside," pp. 347–9, 354; Miller, *The Abbey and Bishopric of Ely*, pp. 84–5; Gras, *The Evolution of the English Corn Market*, pp. 62–3, 174–6; Masschaele, *Peasants, Merchants, and Markets*, pp. 204–7, 217–19.

[56] Zupko, *A Dictionary of English Weights and Measures*, p. 25; Masschaele, *Peasants, Merchants, and Markets*, p. 202; Willan, *The Inland Trade*, pp. 11–12.

[57] Masschaele, *Peasants, Merchants, and Markets*, p. 202. See also *A Medieval Capital*, p. 58.

[58] Modern scholars are all in agreement that transport by water was much cheaper than overland transport but they differ quite widely on the cost ratios. See Masschaele, *Peasants, Merchants, and Markets*, pp. 207–10; Masschaele, "Transport Costs in Medieval England," 266–79; *A Medieval Capital*, pp. 60–3 and 193–8; Dyer, "The Consumer and the Market," p. 309; Childs, "Moving Around," p. 265.

[59] Williams, *Maritime Trade*, pp. 25–33, 35–49, 72.

imposed a prohibition or restriction on export of grain. Even this evidence does not provide a complete account of exports. It is clear, for example, from the evidence of royal mandates that not all licenses were enrolled on the patent rolls.[60] Thus any figures for exports of grain based on recorded licenses must be regarded as incomplete.

For the year 1347, all the licenses enrolled on the patent rolls that authorize export from Lynn are concentrated in one month, May 1 – June 2, when 4,600 quarters of grain were licensed for shipment to Gascony.[61] This month was matched in known exports from Lynn by only one other period in the 1340s, December 17, 1342 – January 16, 1343, when 4,900 quarters of grain, plus five other shiploads and a further unspecified amount, were licensed for shipment to Flanders.[62] In addition to Lynn, Hull and London were major shippers of grain to Gascony in the spring of 1347. During May and June 1347 2,600 quarters of grain were licensed for shipment from Hull and 5,150 quarters plus another shipload from London.[63]

The explanation of Gascony's need is simple. It was a classic monoculture region that could not feed its population, but depended on the import of grain and other foodstuffs in return for the wine it produced and sold overseas, particularly in England. In 1346–7 warfare between the French and English crowns was being conducted on at least two fronts, Gascony and northern France. Gascony, which was under English lordship, was invaded by a French army in 1345 and was the location of intermittent fighting until the summer of 1347.[64] The provisioning needs of Anglo-Gascon forces undoubtedly made it necessary to send even more grain than usual to the duchy. A number of the export licenses make it clear that the grain cargoes were intended to meet military requirements. For example, at least two shipments to Bordeaux, one from Sandwich the other from London, licensed in January 1347 and totaling 900 quarters of wheat and 200 of oats, and two others both from London, licensed on May 7, 1347 and totaling 1,000 quarters of wheat,

---

[60] In *CCR, 1341–3*, pp. 627–8, 694–5, and *CCR, 1343–6*, pp. 81–2, 116, 205, 274–5, 384, 390–9. For the period December 1342–June 1344 there are twenty-four royal orders to local officials in various ports to allow the shipment of particular cargoes with sureties as to specific foreign destination (twenty-two of them were in fact bound for Flanders.) Only one of the twenty-four cargoes is recorded on the patent rolls as licensed, *CPR, 1340–3*, p. 579. Licenses were also enrolled on the Gascon and the French Rolls, which I have not searched.
[61] *CPR, 1345–8*, pp. 281–3.   [62] *CCR, 1341–3*, pp. 627–8, 694–5.
[63] *CPR, 1345–8*, pp. 281–3, 291; *CCR, 1346–9*, pp. 219, 224, 226, 228. For Hull as a supplier of grain to Gascony in the period 1325–50, see Kermode, *Medieval Merchants*, pp. 177, 180.
[64] McKisack, *The Fourteenth Century*, pp. 132–7.

were destined for the maintenance of Bernard Ezii, Lord d'Albert and his men in the king's service in Gascony. Another, of 400 quarters of wheat licensed on May 8, 1347, was to supply John Warryn, constable of Bordeaux and the king's lieges. Finally, on June 17, 1347 two serjeants of the Earl of Lancaster were allowed to send grain in two ships from London to Bordeaux to supply the earl and his men serving the king in Gascony, while on July 4 a ship of Lübeck and her master received royal protection and safe conduct for a year to purvey victuals in England and foreign parts also for the Earl of Lancaster.[65] Most licenses or related documents, however, simply indicate that the grain was intended for the king's lieges in Gascony.

The other main overseas demand for grain in 1346–7 was a result of the English military campaign in northern France that Edward III led personally. The victory at Crecy on August 26, 1346 was soon followed by the eleven month siege of Calais, which ultimately fell on August 4, 1347. To sustain the king's campaign, foodstuffs were purveyed in England and shipped from Lynn, Hull, Boston, London, and Maldon in Essex to Portsmouth for movement to France. In 1346 at least 843 quarters of wheat (which produced 731 quarters of flour) 455 quarters of oats, and 60 quarters of peas and beans, plus other victuals, purveyed in the counties of Cambridge, Huntingdon, and Northampton were shipped through Lynn.[66] The work of James Masschaele has examined the specific case of the movement of purveyed foodstuffs from Huntingdonshire to Lynn in support of various military campaigns in the first half of the fourteenth century. He emphasizes the important point that the sheriff in collecting, storing, and shipping grain and other victuals to Lynn took advantage of the existing and well established commercial trading network of roads, collection and storage points, and waterborne transport that moved grain and other bulky goods.[67] No doubt the Huntingdon situation held good for elsewhere in the country where purveyance occurred.

With the context of overseas shipment of grain in mind let us return to the actions of the Lynn protesters in 1347. While the export of grain from Lynn, particularly the 4,600 quarters in May and early June 1347,

---

[65] *CPR, 1345–8*, pp. 216, 225, 282, 350; *CCR, 1346–9*, pp. 219, 226, 228. Earlier, on October 25, 1343, the Lord d'Albert, because of the king's affection, received a license to buy 1,400 quarters of grain in England to supply his castles in Brittany, *CPR, 1343–5*, p. 131. See also Hewitt, *Organization of War*, pp. 62–3.

[66] Hewitt, *Organization of War*, p. 55.

[67] Masschaele, *Peasants, Merchants, and Markets*, pp. 219–24. See also Owen (ed.), *The Making of King's Lynn*, pp. 258–9, sheriff's accounts for cost and carriage of grain for the king from Cambridge and St. Ives to Lynn, 1302.

could easily have driven up local prices, an even more important trigger for protest must have been the sight of such large quantities of grain being sent to foreign parts over a relatively short period. Visible export clearly created fears or expectations of rising prices among the towns-people. Confirmation of this point is provided in the crowd's actions on June 16 and 18, 1347 when they forced the unloading of the grain cargoes from two ships and then made a proclamation prohibiting the export of grain.[68]

Other actions of the crowd provide further indicators of possible rising prices and fear of dearth at Lynn. One, on June 16, 1347, was the seizure and sale of two loads of wheat at less than the prevailing price. The grain was being brought into the town to be marketed, presumably having been transported by road or river from the agricultural hinterland. The other, on June 19, was the condemnation of a baker to the thewe without legal process.[69] This act may indicate that the crowd considered the baker to have been guilty of selling underweight bread contrary to the assize. The crowd may also have believed that those people bringing grain to market in Lynn, who were compelled to sell it at popularly set prices, were forestallers and had bought the grain from the original producers before it reached market in order to sell it themselves on a rising market.[70]

The tactics of seizing grain, compelling its sale at a popularly set price, and proclaiming a prohibition on exports were obviously designed to prevent future shortages and price rises as a result of continued export. It is also worth recalling that the Lynn protests triggered similar actions at Thetford, a community on the Little Ouse, where grain was collected for transport to Lynn. Here again, frequent outward grain shipments, this time down river, must have raised the possibility of local scarcity and thereby provoked remedial action by the populace.

Unfortunately, we cannot put much contextual flesh on the bare bones of the Boston riot. There are no licenses for export of grain from the port in 1347 recorded on the patent rolls, another indication that enroll-ment was not always regular or systematic; the commission of oyer and terminer for trial of the Boston rioters states that the merchants whose ships were forcibly unloaded had been licensed to export the grain.[71] There is also other evidence of grain exports from Boston in 1346. In November, a license was issued to a Spanish merchant allowing the export of 1,000 quarters of wheat from Boston to Spain at the request

---

[68] TNA, JUST1/612/5, m. 1v.
[69] TNA, JUST1/612/5, mm. 1, 2; PRO, C66/221, m. 22v; *CPR, 1345–8*, p. 381.
[70] Britnell, "Forestalling," 94, 96, 102.
[71] TNA, C66/221, m. 22v; *CPR, 1345–8*, p. 381.

of the king's daughter Joan.[72] For the campaign in northern France in 1346, at least 652 quarters of wheat yielding 552 quarters of flour, 300 quarters of oats, and 100 quarters of peas and beans, plus other victuals, which had been purveyed in Lincolnshire, were shipped from Boston and Hull to Portsmouth. An additional 975 quarters of wheat yielding 890 quarters of flour, 304 quarters of oats, 168 quarters of peas and beans plus other victuals purveyed in Derbyshire, Nottinghamshire, and Yorkshire were shipped through Hull alone.[73] While it is surprising that records of grain export from Boston in 1347 are scarce, the actions of the crowd, in forcing the unloading of grain cargoes from ships and compelling the sale of some of the grain at popularly set prices, were much like those of the Lynn crowd and reveal a fear of local scarcity and high prices if export continued.[74]

The effects of purveyance appear to provide much of the context for the riots in Kentish ports. While there is evidence for the purveyance of grain and other victuals in Kent during 1346 and 1347, there are no available figures on actual amounts. Nonetheless, during the siege of Calais (September 7, 1346–August 4, 1347) Sandwich became a major collecting and shipping point to supply English forces with grain and other victuals purveyed in a number of counties, including Kent itself.[75] The importance of Kent in this regard is further indicated by a royal proclamation of October 25, 1346 that prohibited the export of wheat from Sandwich and the other Cinque ports except to Calais.[76] This proclamation was superseded by another, five days later, that imposed a nationwide prohibition on the export of wheat, except licensed shipments to Calais, Gascony, and Flanders.[77] Between November 1346 and February 1347 at least four licensed cargoes of wheat totaling 2,500 quarters were sent from Sandwich to Gascony, while in December 1346, two unspecified cargoes of victuals and, in May 1347, 800 quarters of wheat were shipped to the same destination from Winchelsea.[78] It also should be noted that once Calais fell the provisioning of the English besiegers, now occupiers, continued. In September 1347 and again in January 1348, royal mandates instructed a number of English sheriffs to provide wheat, malt, and other victuals for the supply of Calais. In the

---

[72] *CPR, 1345–8*, p. 201.   [73] Hewitt, *Organization of War*, p. 55.

[74] TNA, KB27/350 (Mich. 21 Ed. III), m. 101.   [75] Hewitt, *Organization of War*, p. 57.

[76] *Foedera*, vol. 3 pt. 1, p. 92. This proclamation was enrolled on the French Rolls not the Close Rolls.

[77] *CLB*, vol. F, p. 155. A full text of the proclamation preserved in Letter-Book F is in Delpit (ed.), *Collection Generale Des Documents Francais*, pp. 72–3. This proclamation does not appear to have been enrolled on the Close Rolls.

[78] *CPR, 1345–8*, pp. 198, 215–16, 246, 251, 283.

case of the September mandate, the provisions totaled 1,240 quarters of wheat and 1,100 quarters of malt.[79]

It is clear from the language of the commission of oyer and terminer issued to deal with the food riots in Kent that the rioters were trying to stop the flow of supplies to the English army besieging Calais, which was led by the king in person. The protesters "impeded with force and arms" some of the king's servants and others assigned to send victuals to the king and his lieges campaigning in France, "so that they were unable to place any kinds of victuals on those ships." The commission also contains an interesting admission regarding the situation in Kent. The commissioners were assigned to try not only the protesters but also officials who, by virtue of their offices, extorted victuals and took fines at will from the king's lieges. The document's association of food riots in Kentish ports and the activities of purveyors can hardly be coincidental.[80] By March 11, 1348, a royal letter to the sheriff of Kent admitted that grain and other victuals were scarce in the county because of shipments to Calais.[81]

In the late middle ages and the early modern period, Bristol was the major outlet for the agricultural produce and manufactures of the west midlands, shipped down the river Severn. The town depended on the river not only for its own food supply but also for the grain cargoes it sent coastwise and overseas. Grain came down river by boat from Shrewsbury, Worcester, Tewkesbury, and Gloucester.[82] Illegal export in a poor harvest year appears to provide the most plausible explanation for the real or threatened scarcity that produced the Bristol riot of 1347.

There certainly was purveyance in the counties of the Severn valley during 1346–7 but we do not know a great deal about its effects. On May 3, 1346 a commission was issued to Richard Talbot, steward of the king's household, to investigate the oppressive behavior of sheriffs and other officials in the counties of Gloucester, Hereford, and Worcester, among others, who extorted money from the wealthy in return for exemptions from purveyance, while they took grain and other victuals for the king from "poor and simple men" who could not afford to part with them.[83]

By the spring of 1347, there were signs of grain scarcity in Gloucestershire caused, or at least aggravated, by transportation out of the area.

---

[79] *Foedera*, vol. 3 pt. 1, pp. 135–6, 149.

[80] TNA, C66/221, m. 3v; *CPR, 1345–8*, pp. 398–9.   [81] *CCR, 1346–9*, p. 502.

[82] Hilton, *A Medieval Society*, pp. 194–9, 207–17; Carus-Wilson, "The Overseas Trade of Bristol," pp. 185–9.

[83] *CPR, 1345–8*, p. 113.

On May 30, around the time of the Bristol riot, royal letters sent to the sheriff of Gloucestershire and to the mayor and bailiffs of Gloucester indicate scarcity in the town. According to the letters the "men of Gloucester town" had petitioned the king that merchants, both with and without royal warrant, had bought up so much grain in Gloucestershire that dearth had resulted, thereby impoverishing the populace who, "unless a remedy is speedily supplied ... will succumb." As a remedial measure, the letters ordered a proclamation in both the town and the county of Gloucester placing a prohibition on the export of grain, except for properly licensed shipments to "the king's lieges" in Gascony.[84] One properly licensed grain shipment was the 700 quarters that William Casse intended to export to Bordeaux, the only 1347 grain cargo outward bound from Bristol for which evidence of a license survives.[85]

After the Bristol crowd seized Casse's grain cargo, three royal letters on his behalf were issued on June 6, 1347. The sheriff of Gloucestershire and the bailiffs of Gloucester were instructed to allow a replacement cargo of grain to move down the Severn to Bristol and then on to Bordeaux, notwithstanding the earlier order to prohibit the export of grain. Local magistrates in Gloucester had taken the opportunity offered by the order of May 30 to arrest and stop the movement down river of Casse's new cargo. At the same time, the king ordered the mayor and bailiffs of Bristol to allow Casse to ship the replacement 700 quarters of grain from Bristol to Bordeaux.[86]

Soon, however, the crown became concerned about illegal export from the Severn. On February 16, 1348, a commission was appointed to inquire into such export and arrest those responsible. According to the commission, merchants daily shipped grain down river in boats from Tewkesbury and other places, claiming that the cargoes were for sale at Bristol. Instead, the grain was transferred to ships anchored down river from Bristol harbor and then shipped overseas illegally to the king's enemies. In addition, the commissioners were to survey all boats loaded with grain going past Gloucester and take sureties from the shippers that the cargoes were bound only for Bristol. The shippers were also required to bring back to the commissioners letters from the mayor and bailiffs of Bristol testifying to the arrival and discharge of the grain there. The commissioners were also authorized to arrest all shippers of grain, along with their cargoes, if they refused to find sureties. They were to be held secure until further notice, and their names and the amount of grain arrested certified to the chancery from time to time.[87]

[84] *CCR, 1346–9*, p. 281.   [85] *CPR, 1345–8*, p. 280.   [86] *CCR, 1346–9*, p. 224.
[87] *CPR, 1348–50*, pp. 67–8.

Six months later, on July 10, 1348, a commission of oyer and terminer was issued, headed by William Shareshull, to try the many "evildoers" who took victuals from Gloucestershire to La Rochelle and elsewhere in the power of the French king at a time when there was open war between the English king and his enemies.[88] It appears from the work of Evan Jones that Bristol merchants continued smuggling into the early modern period. In the 1530s and 1540s, a number of them obtained licenses to ship given quantities of grain and then actually shipped much larger amounts. To facilitate their activities they either bribed customs officials or loaded their ships in the channel outside Bristol harbor, presumably from smaller boats that brought the grain from further up the Severn, much like their medieval predecessors.[89]

By late summer 1347, the crown was persuaded, no doubt in part by the riots, that the scarcity was the product of excessive export. Sometime in August, a royal mandate ordered that two shiploads of grain licensed for shipment from London to Bordeaux should be stayed, unloaded, and sold because of growing dearth in the capital.[90] On August 20, the king ordered the sheriffs of London to issue regulations on the activities of purveyors who had been taking victuals from people bringing them to London for sale without "paying the reasonable price." As a result sellers had stopped coming into the city to sell foodstuffs, thereby creating scarcity. The king ordered the sheriffs to arrest and keep in prison until further notice any purveyor who did not pay for victuals taken.[91] Finally, on October 16, a prohibition was imposed on the export of grain from England, except to Calais, unless licensed by the king and his council.[92] The express justification for the prohibition was that the export of great quantities of grain had produced scarcity in the kingdom.

One further indication of the clampdown on the grain trade is that from late July 1347 to the end of the year no licenses permitting export of grain from England are recorded on the patent rolls. Another indicator of growing official concern about grain scarcity was the crown's appointment of a commission on March 25, 1348 to inquire into mills, weirs, and other obstructions on the rivers Thames, Severn, Ouse, and Trent in response to a commons petition in parliament. One of the main justifications for the inquiry was that obstructions on the rivers were impeding the movement of victuals and causing prices to rise.[93] Nonetheless, it had

---

[88] *Ibid.*, p. 165.
[89] Jones, "Illicit Business," 17–38; Jones, *Inside the Illicit Economy*, pp. 96–111.
[90] *CPR, 1345–8*, p. 372.   [91] *CCR, 1346–9*, p. 375; *CLB*, vol. F, p. 167.
[92] *CCR, 1346–9*, p. 403. The full text is in *Foedera*, vol. 3 pt. 1, p. 139.
[93] *Parl. Rolls*, "Edward III: January 1348," item 34; *CPR, 1348–50*, p. 76.

taken some time given other pressing needs for the crown to respond to the grain shortage. On a number of occasions, from mid-June through July 1347, royal orders were issued, in the face of known scarcity, to permit already licensed shipments of grain to leave London for Gascony, largely for political and military purposes.[94]

The crown and the crowd

The crown's prohibition on grain export in 1347 and its attempt in 1348 to regulate the movement of grain on the Severn in order to prevent illegal export from the Bristol area indicate that Edward III continued the regulatory policy of his father. To begin consideration of that regulatory policy and its relationship to popular expectations, it is worthwhile considering some of the larger implications of the riots of 1347. The actions of the rioters reflected the role that the law and royal government had come to play in the regulation of grain marketing. In the case of the Lynn riots, the accusation that the crowd condemned to the pillory people who brought grain into the town to sell reflected popular knowledge of existing law on the crime of forestalling and its punishment. That knowledge no doubt came from direct observation, since pillories, thewes, and other restraining devices used to punish offenders against market regulations were physically located in market places.[95]

An even more significant reflection of the crown's role in regulating the grain market is to be found in other accusations against the 1347 rioters. The Bristol rioters were accused of assuming the royal power and issuing proclamations.[96] In the commission of oyer and terminer, the Boston rioters were accused of assuming the royal power and issuing quasi-royal proclamations; the indictments of the rioters included the charge of assuming the royal power but there was no direct mention of issuing proclamations.[97] The Lynn rioters were also accused in the commission of oyer and terminer of assuming the royal power and issuing quasi-royal proclamations. The indictments do not refer to assuming the royal power but the rioters were indicted for forcing the mayor of Lynn to issue a

---

[94] *CCR, 1346–9*, pp. 226, 228, 308.
[95] TNA, JUST1/612/5, m. 2; C66/221, m. 16d; Britnell, "Forestalling," 89–102; Masschaele, "The Public Space of the Marketplace," 400–6. For general discussions of the widespread dissemination of knowledge of the law among the English populace, see Neville, "Common Knowledge," 461–78; Musson, *Medieval Law in Context*, pp. 84–134, 241–64; Musson with Powell (eds.), *Crime, Law and Society*, pp. 39–66.
[96] TNA, C66/221, m. 11v; *CPR, 1345–8*, p. 392.
[97] TNA, C66/221, m. 22v; *CPR, 1345–8*, p. 381; TNA, KB27/350 (Mich. 21 Ed. III) m. 101.

proclamation on June 16, 1347 compelling the owners to sell two loads of wheat at less than the market price and for issuing their own proclamation on June 18, 1347 prohibiting the export of grain from Lynn until after August 1.[98]

These charges of assuming the king's power and issuing proclamations were closely connected, if not identical. It was in making proclamations in the king's name or compelling local officials to issue them that the rioters assumed or, as the law would have it, accroached the royal power.[99] The assumption of royal power probably involved uttering, in the king's name, prohibitions to stop the export of grain, orders to seize and unload cargo, and instructions to sell grain at less than the market price. What lies behind such behavior is knowledge that the king's government took some hand in the regulation of the grain trade; in turn that knowledge sanctioned or legitimized popular direct action. In effect, the crowd could claim that it acted in support of royal authority and established law.

This point about legitimation is confirmed by two other significant acts, one by the Lynn crowd and the other by the Boston. The proclamation that the Lynn crowd issued on June 18 prohibiting export of grain excluded grain headed for the supply of the king at Calais.[100] This can be read as a carefully crafted attempt to represent the crowd as loyal supporters of the king and his legitimate needs, while asserting the larger need to implement a ban on grain export in the face of rising prices and possible scarcity. It is also an indication of the crowd's awareness of larger political events that affected them and the rest of the kingdom. When the Boston rioters on June 16 compelled the sale of grain forcibly removed from two ships, they put the money in the hands of five men for safe keeping, probably with the intention of giving it to the owners of the grain.[101] Clearly the crowd wanted to signal that they were not common criminals profiting from the sale of the goods of others but acting in defence of what they regarded as established and legitimate market regulations. Similar actions were also to be found later in some early modern food riots.[102]

The actions of the rioters of 1347 in defence of established market regulations not only indicate an understanding of existing law and government but they match well with the actions of the participants in

---

[98] TNA, C66/221, m. 16v; *CPR, 1345–8*, p. 388; TNA, JUST1/612/5, m. 1.
[99] Bellamy, *Law of Treason*, pp. 66–8, 218.   [100] TNA, JUST1/612/5, m. 1.
[101] TNA, KB27/350 (Mich. 21 Edward III) m. 101.
[102] Sharp, "Popular Protest," pp. 271–2, 281–2.

the Great Revolt of 1381 and with those of thirteenth and fourteenth-century peasants who appealed to Domesday book to defend their rights against encroachment by landlords. Modern scholarship on the revolt has unearthed a great deal of circumstantial detail about the actions and beliefs of rebels in a variety of locations outside of London, including a number of instances of popular appropriation of royal authority. In the aftermath of the revolt, John Greyston of Bottisham in Cambridgeshire was indicted for claiming that he had a "commission from the King to seek out traitors, and used this to raise bands of insurgents." John Stanford, saddler, of London and Geoffrey Cobbe of Cambridgeshire were also indicted for similar offenses.[103] Then there is the case of Geoffrey Lyster, the leader of the rebels in Norfolk, who was called "King of the Commons."[104] He "assumed judicial powers and appointed local members of the gentry to serve him in a mock royal court."[105] In June 1381, proclamations were issued in Lister's name to rouse the Norfolk population.[106] According to Eiden "The whole of Lyster's action indicates that he was prepared to take over lordship (in terms of governing and dispensing justice)."[107] Brooks notes that in the period June 6–9, 1381 there was a "crescendo of public proclamations" in Essex, which aimed to persuade villagers to join the rising.[108] In Suffolk during June 1381, insurgents took "charge of their localities" with a series of acts that implied an intention "to create an alternative government." An effort was made "to force the constable of Hoxne hundred to levy ten archers from the hundred for the rebel forces, at a wage of 6d per day each." The rebels at Brandon were accused of "assuming to themselves the royal power."[109] Finally, four accused rebels in Derbyshire, who were indicted for seizing Horston royal castle on June 18, 1381 and raising a Saint George banner, were also accused of "taking upon themselves the royal jurisdiction in prejudice to the Crown of the lord king and to the terror of the whole country."[110]

One notable feature of the 1381 revolt at the local level is that in counties such as Norfolk, Suffolk, and Essex, the leadership came from the middling and upper peasantry who often shared a common

---

[103] Prescott, "Writing about Rebellion," 12 and 25 nt. 108.
[104] Ormrod, "The Peasants' Revolt," 15; Dobson (ed.), *The Peasants' Revolt of 1381*, pp. 257–8.
[105] Prescott, "Writing about Rebellion," 17.   [106] Eiden, "Joint Action," 16.
[107] *Ibid.*, 20.
[108] Brooks, "The Organization and Achievements of the Peasants," p. 255. See also Eiden, "Joint Action," 13.
[109] Dyer, "The Rising of 1381 in Suffolk," 275.
[110] Crook, "Derbyshire and the English Rising of 1381," 9–10.

experience in holding local manorial or hundredal offices.[111] Such experience undoubtedly underlay the organization and coherence of the local revolts, especially in the choice of targets to be attacked, which reached beyond individual lords to encompass the persons and properties of those involved in local and national government. The common target was "unjust and bad exercise of lordship on the manorial, communal, and governmental level."[112]Although the majority of the rebels were undoubtedly engaged in agriculture either as landholding tenants or laborers, a substantial minority were artisans. In both Essex and Norfolk, there were sizeable numbers of individuals in the textile trades among the rebels, a reflection of the development of rural industry in the two counties. There were also rebels who earned their livings in the wide range of other trades and occupations found in both town and country-side. In this respect, the occupational profile of the 1381 rebels closely resembles that of the food rioters of 1347.[113]

The market place figures prominently in any discussion of medieval or early modern protests over the price or availability of food. It was the place where prices were not only set but seen to rise. It is also the place to which grain was returned after the crowd unloaded ships and where the crowd established new, lower prices. Finally, the market place was the location of the pillory or the thewe where offenders against market regulations received public punishment. Recent work by Masschaele has highlighted the 1381 rebels' use of the marketplace as a site for asserting their authority and punishing their enemies. At St. Albans, the claim of access to a rabbit warren and local woods was accompanied by the tethering of a live rabbit to the pillory in the marketplace. The same space was used to burn the abbot of St. Albans' charters of liberties that the king had granted. Also at St. Alban's, after holding mock trials of

---

[111] Eiden, "Joint Action," 26–8; Dyer, "The Social and Economic Background," pp. 17–19; Dyer, "The Rising of 1381 in Suffolk," 276, 282–5; Ormrod, "The Peasants' Revolt," 15–17.

[112] Eiden, "Joint Action," 29. See also Dyer, "Social and Economic Background," pp. 41–2, Brooks, "The Organization and Achievements of the Peasants," pp. 260–70, Müller, "Conflict and Revolt," 1–19 and Musson with Powell (eds.), *Crime Law and Society*, pp. 39–43.

[113] Eiden, "Joint Action," 26–8. Eiden's figures are as follows: Essex, 22 tailors, 11 weavers, 9 cordwainers, 5 skinners, 5 tanners, 3 fullers, 1 dyer, 1 glover, 7 butchers, 6 smiths, 6 brewers/taverners, 4 carpenters, 4 wrights, 4 carters, 3 masons, 3 cutlers, 3 fishermen, 2 millers, 2 bowmakers, 2 parkers (barkers?), 1 dauber, 1 cooper, 1 sawyer, and 1 thatcher; Norfolk, 11 tailors, 9 weavers, 6 cordwainers, 2 dyers, 2 tanners, 2 glovers, 1 fuller, 1 skinner, 10 carpenters, 7 smiths, 4 brewers/taverners, 3 coopers, 3 cutlers, 3 daubers, 3 gelders, 2 wrights, 1 goldsmith, 1 mason, 1 thatcher, 1 bowmaker, 1 cook, 1 carter, 1 miller, and 1 thresher.

prisoners released from jail, the rebels beheaded one and placed his head on the pillory. When the rebels in Suffolk found chief justice John Cavendish in the village of Lakenheath, they beheaded him and carried his head fifteen miles to Bury St. Edmunds and put it on the pillory in the marketplace.[114]

Modern scholars have also explored, in considerable detail, a number of examples of peasant resistance to the demands of lords for increased services or dues before the Revolt of 1381.[115] That resistance, which fell short of open revolt, often took the form of attempted legal appeals to Domesday Book in order to defend customary rights against encroachment. Recent work on peasant resistance in 1348 on the manor of Bradbury in Wiltshire shows how peasants attempted, unsuccessfully in the end, to establish through such an appeal that the manor was originally ancient demesne of the crown. Success in establishing that claim would have limited labor services and rents and provided means of legal recourse to bring cases to court if a lord oppressed his tenants with extra labor services or increased rents.[116] Almost thirty years later, in 1377, tenants of Bradbury along with those in about forty villages in Devon, Hampshire, Surrey, Sussex, and Wiltshire attempted to obtain exemplifications (copies) of relevant sections of Domesday Book to prove that they were tenants on ancient demesne.[117]

Such appeals to Domesday Book and the idea of ancient demesne of the crown might be regarded as one further example of the traditionalist mentality of the peasantry, which involved an invocation of an idealized past where the king as landlord guaranteed fair and just treatment of his tenants. Yet their frequency, financial cost, and the fact that the leading participants appear to have been individuals of some substance with considerable local administrative and legal experience, much like that of the local leaders of the rising of 1381, lead to other conclusions. Like the leaders of the 1381 rebels, those who appealed to Domesday Book demonstrated considerable legal and political sophistication. While the appeals may have idealized Domesday Book and revered it as the Book of Judgment from which there was no appeal, they also frightened landlords with the possibility of the loss of control over the lives and labor of their tenants. Dyer has argued that the real threat the appeals posed to

---

[114] Masschaele, "The Public Space of the Marketplace," 416–18. See also Davis "The Cross and the Pillory," pp. 251–9.

[115] Hilton, "Peasant Movements," pp. 73–90; Razi, "The Struggles between the Abbots of Halesowen and their Tenants," pp. 151–67.

[116] Müller, "The Aims and Organization of a Peasant Revolt," 1–20.

[117] Faith, "The Great Rumour," pp. 43–73.

landlords was the abolition of serfdom altogether and, from the point of view of the peasantry, the restoration of freedom that had been lost.[118]

Like the insurgents of 1381 and the peasants who appealed to Domesday Book, the food rioters of 1347 were knowledgeable about legal and governmental matters and knew how to use or appeal to them for their own purposes. In particular, the crowd actions of 1347 would be meaningless without an already established and popularly known tradition of active monarchical regulation of the grain trade through proclamations. Indeed throughout his reign Edward III continued his predecessor's practice of regularly issuing proclamations to prohibit or regulate the export of grain. During the first twenty years of his reign (1327–47) there were at least nine such proclamations issued. The first, on October 27, 1330, prohibited the export of grain without the king's license because it was believed that shipment overseas was driving up prices in England.[119] For the months before the prohibition was issued, there is considerable evidence of shipments overseas of sizeable quantities of grain and other victuals, virtually all of it purveyed and shipped to support the earl of Cornwall and other English magnates campaigning in Gascony.[120]

Soon after the prohibition of October 27, 1330 was in place, Edward III began to license shipments of grain from Somerset and Gloucestershire to Ireland and Wales, both of which were suffering from grain scarcity.[121] One royal mandate, of February 5, 1331, that ordered the sheriff of Gloucestershire to allow a licensed shipment of 600 quarters grain to Ireland, indicates the king's compassion for the state of his people of Ireland who were enduring a great scarcity of grain (*compacientes tamen statui populi nostri de partibus Hibern', ubi magna bladorum caristia habetur*).[122] Similar language, regarding the king's people of Wales, can be found in a mandate of February 15, 1331 that instructed the sheriff of Somerset to allow 500 quarters of grain to be sent to Wales.[123]

The next five proclamations are grouped in two years, 1333 and 1336, and were closely connected to the crown's military needs. On February 3, 1333 a prohibition was imposed on the export of grain without the king's special license.[124] While this proclamation offered no explanation for the prohibition, the king's aims were made clear in the subsequent one of

---

[118] Dyer, "Attitudes towards Serfdom," pp. 277–95, esp. 291–5. See also Müller, "The Aims and Organization of a Peasant Revolt," 15.

[119] *CCR, 1330–3*, p. 159.   [120] *CCR, 1330–3*, pp. 15–16, 17, 18–19 28–9.

[121] *CCR, 1330–3*, pp. 168, 275, 284, 294, 298; *CPR, 1330–4*, pp. 20, 75, 80, 232.

[122] *CCR, 1330–3*, p. 275. The full text is in *Foedera*, vol. 2 pt. 2, p. 807. See also *CCR 1330–3*, p. 168.

[123] *CCR, 1330–3*, p. 284.

[124] *CCR, 1333–7*, p. 82. The full text is in *Foedera*, vol. 2 pt. 2, p. 850.

March 20, 1333, which urged all merchants with grain or other victuals for sale to bring them to Northumberland to supply the king's planned expedition against the Scots. At the same time, the prohibition on export was reiterated.[125] Again on May 8, 1336, a prohibition on grain export without royal license was announced, this time to prevent it getting to the king's enemies, presumably the Scots and the French.[126] A month later, on June 6, an explanatory proclamation was issued clarifying that it was not the king's intention to prevent merchants from shipping grain overseas for their own benefit as long as they were licensed and provided sureties that they would not ship to his enemies.[127] Finally, on December 15, 1336, a new proclamation was issued prohibiting the export of victuals and other merchandise, even if licensed, in order to prevent them from being seized by enemy warships. Merchants were urged instead to bring victuals and other goods to Berwick, Stirling, or Perth to support another royal campaign in Scotland.[128]

A few years later parliament began to become involved in the regulation of the export of grain. In the October parliament of 1339, it was agreed that the king should issue a proclamation that no one was to export grain from England until such time "that the king should ordain otherwise."[129] The following year, the March parliament of 1340 ordained that no victuals should be shipped out of England to the king's enemies in Scotland.[130] This parliamentary interest may reflect a growing concern among the commons about the price and availability of bread grains, an interest that became more obvious later in the century.

The next three proclamations of Edward III that regulated the export of grain come from the years preceding the riots of 1347. These three are the first examples in the reign of responses to possible scarcity, whatever the cause. Although the first proclamation, on December 24, 1342, prohibited the export of grain without the king's special license but provided no explicit justification, a few days earlier the king had written to the bailiffs and customs collectors of Boston ordering them to prohibit unlicensed export because so many victuals were being taken to the king's enemies in France that it was causing scarcity in England.[131] In a second proclamation of December 23, 1343, the prohibition was renewed, naming the locations to which licensed export

---

[125] *CCR, 1333–7*, p. 98. The full text is in *Foedera*, vol. 2 pt. 2, p. 855.
[126] *CCR, 1333–7*, p. 675.   [127] *Ibid.*, p. 683.
[128] *Ibid.*, p. 731. The full text is in *Foedera*, vol. 2 pt. 2, pp. 954–5. There appears to have been an earlier version of this proclamation ordered on October 2, 1336, see *CLB*, vol. E, p. 302.
[129] *Parl. Rolls*, "Edward III: October 1339," item 20.
[130] *Parl. Rolls*, "Edward III: March 1340," item 52.   [131] *CCR, 1341–3*, pp. 666, 691.

was permitted – Gascony, Ireland, Flanders, Brittany, Brabant, Spain, Holland, Zealand, and Germany (which was suffering a scarcity of grain) – all places either in the English king's friendship or under his lordship.[132] This proclamation states that a great deal of grain had been shipped out of the country, which might cause harm and peril to the kingdom if it continued, thereby alluding to the possibility of scarcity although there is no confirming evidence from either prices or grain yields.[133] The third, of October 28, 1346, prohibited the export of wheat except to Flanders, Gascony, and for the king's army besieging Calais.[134]

During the period 1342–7, Edward III's government made a sustained effort to enforce the prohibitions or limitations on grain export. Royal mandates were sometimes sent to bailiffs or sheriffs commanding them to seize unlicensed grain shipments and arrest the ships and their masters.[135] Local magistrates and customs officials were regularly reminded to allow grain cargoes to sail only if the shippers were licensed and had found sureties as to their destination.[136] Early in 1344, the crown concluded that the terms of the prohibition on export were being "daily disregarded." Consequently, on January 16, 1344, Saier Lorimer was appointed to arrest ships carrying unlicensed grain for export or other goods upon which customs had not been paid, and to certify the arrests to the Chancery. Lorimer's commission was renewed regularly thereafter up through 1349.[137]

Although such a commissioner may have had an occasional success, as in January 1344 when Lorimer arrested two ships loaded with unlicensed grain, it is doubtful that he could stem the tide of illegal exports.[138] But the effectiveness of regulations is not the issue. What mattered were the public and known intentions of the crown. Since proclamations were proclaimed in the county court and market places in each shire, the

[132] *CCR, 1343–6*, pp. 267–8; *CLB*, vol. F, pp. 93, 207. A full text of the copy in the Letter Books is in Delpit (ed.), *Collection Generale De Documents Francais*, pp. 69–70.

[133] Campbell, "Nature as a Historical Protagonist," 298–9; Campbell, "Grain yields"; Munro, "Revisions of Commodity Prices."

[134] *CLB*, vol. F, p. 154. The full text of the copy in the Letter Books is in Delpit, (ed.), *Collection Generale Des Documents Francais*, pp. 72–3. This proclamation does not appear to be enrolled on the Close Rolls.

[135] *CCR, 1343–6*, pp. 99, 207, 261, 410–11.

[136] *CCR, 1341–3*, pp. 628, 695; *CCR, 1343–6*, pp. 81–2, 205, 207; *CCR, 1346–9*, pp. 219, 226.

[137] *CPR, 1343–6*, pp. 186–7; *CPR, 1345–8*, pp. 30, 304; *CPR, 1348–50*, p. 311. It is noted in *CPR, 1345–8*, pp. 97–8 that John Marreys was appointed for the same purpose on February 10, 1346. It is not clear if Marreys was a one-year replacement for Lorimer or appointed in addition to him.

[138] *CCR, 1343–6*, p. 261.

populace knew those intentions.[139] Moreover, the continued attempt over the five years 1342–7 to implement a regulatory policy grounded on royal proclamations, despite the exceptions contained within them, may have created a general impression that a more stringent prohibition was in force than actually was the case. Or perhaps that was the intentional misreading of the situation on the part of both the crowds that boarded ships to prevent the export of grain in the summer of 1347 and the local magistrates who occasionally stopped licensed shipments of grain with the claim that an export prohibition was in force.

Any shipment stayed by local officials was only allowed to proceed on receipt of a royal mandate that ordered its release because the cargo was properly licensed for shipment and the shipper had found sureties guaranteeing the cargo's final destination.[140] One such cargo of 900 quarters of grain, stayed at Sandwich and then released by royal order to proceed to its destination at Bordeaux on October 3, 1346, was part owned by William Casse, another of whose cargoes was seized by the Bristol rioters in 1347.[141]

With this background of royal attempts to impose controls on grain export in the 1340s, one can understand why the protesters of 1347 apparently made proclamations in the king's name to prohibit export, unload ships, and sell grain at less than the market price. Their actions were sanctioned by a history of regulation of the grain trade through proclamations that reached back at least to the second decade of the fourteenth century. The 1347 protesters could have plausibly argued that, in the face of dearth and rising prices, they were acting either in support of a royal proclamation or in place of a tougher one, which ought to have been in force. Eventually, in October 1347, the crown found itself in agreement with the protesters and issued a more stringent prohibition on grain export, except to Calais, without the king's special license, on the advice of the council.[142]

The 1347 food riots and their larger context indicate that the moral economy of the crowd was firmly in place no later than the mid fourteenth century. The actions of the crowd in stopping outward bound shipments of grain and in compelling sale of grain at less than the market price and the legitimation of their actions by appeals to already

---

[139] Doig, "Political Propaganda," 253–60; Masschaele, "The Public Space of the Marketplace," 390–9. See also Owst, *Preaching in Medieval England*, p. 196.
[140] *CCR, 1341–3*, p. 694; *CCR, 1346–9*, pp. 116–17, 308.
[141] *CCR, 1346–9*, p. 116. While this mandate refers to 90 quarters of wheat, the license in *CPR 1345–8*, p. 198 has 900 quarters.
[142] *CCR 1346–9*, p. 403.

established law and regulation are all characteristic of later food riots in the sixteenth through eighteenth centuries. The fact that the riots occurred in a year following a deficient harvest, after a long period of good harvests, is not particularly surprising. The occurrence of food riot should not be taken by itself as an indicator of severe food shortage. One reason why there were apparently no food riots in 1315–22 may well be the direct result of the severity of the famine, which weakened people so that they had no strength for protest. In a famine people either managed to buy, scrounge, beg, or steal food, or sickened and died.[143]

On other occasions, such as 1347, when scarcity or fear of scarcity arose, the politically savvy acted while they could to prevent the worst before real shortage and hunger set in. This meant the rioters drew on their past experience, their knowledge of the law, which included awareness of the royal commitment to a regulated market, and finally an understanding of the state of the local market. That state was one of rising prices and potential scarcity that resulted from a deficient harvest combined with royal military provisioning needs in Gascony and around Calais.

In the years 1342–9, the crown did demonstrate a commitment to one of the major components of market regulation through proclamations that prohibited the export of grain without licenses, which could be issued by the king usually for a price.

Grants of licenses were based on a number of different considerations. There was the diplomatic necessity to support foreign allies in an age when England was engaged in major military operations in Scotland and France. Then those military operations needed to be victualed, in part, by directing licensed shipments of grain to the campaign's location.[144] The English king's own subjects in Gascony and Calais required provisioning. During the late fourteenth century both places were often exempted from export prohibitions.[145]

Finally, powerful commercial interests, sources of loans, and royal agents, represented by John Wesenham and the other equally wealthy Lynn merchant Thomas Melchebourn, were regularly rewarded with export licenses. While licensed shipments contributed to the likelihood of local scarcity, so too did the crown's overseas shipment of

---

[143] See Appleby, *Famine in Tudor and Stuart England*, for a powerful account of hunger and starvation in the northwest of England in 1597 and 1623.

[144] For examples of royal proclamations in 1347 urging merchants to bring victuals and other supplies to Calais, see *CLB*, vol. F, pp. 165–6 and Delpit (ed.), *Collection Generale Des Documents Francais*, pp. 73–5.

[145] Hewitt, *Organization of War*, pp. 60–3; Burley, "Victualling of Calais," 49–57.

purveyed grain and other victuals in support of military campaigns. Tensions and difficult to resolve conflicts between competing aims and interests such as the desire to prevent movement of grain to satisfy local needs and the necessity to keep grain moving to serve larger ambitions and policies remained characteristic of the crown's market regulation well into the future.

4   Royal paternalism and the response to dearth 1349–1376

The first twenty-two years of Edward III reign (1327–49) had experienced largely good or abundant harvests and low grain prices. There were only four years with deficient harvests, 1328, 1331, 1339, and 1346 and no disastrous famines like that of 1315–17, when two harvests in a row failed.[1] In contrast, during most of the next twenty-seven years of the reign (1349–76) there were consistently high grain prices and low grain yields. Moreover, three harvests in a row in the years 1349–51 failed, at a time when England had been struck by the first outbreak of bubonic plague, which killed an estimated 40 percent of the population.[2] Over the period 1349–76, the crown continued what had become by now its standard policy of issuing prohibitions on the export of grain in response to scarcity and high prices. There was also a particular governmental focus on forestallers and other offenders against market regulations, who were blamed for driving up grain prices. This meant a new parliamentary statute of forestallers in 1351, which resulted in the establishment of commissions authorized to seize the grain of forestallers and sell it in the open market in 1370. In addition, the crown made considerable efforts to enforce the assize of weights and measures.

Another recurring major issue for the government throughout the period 1349–76 was the need to ensure that the grain needs of the London populace were met, usually by encouraging the movement of grain to the capital, which included seeking supplies from distant parts of the kingdom beyond the city's normal supply zone. Aside from London, Bristol also encountered problems with food supply in the period 1363–76 that required crown intervention.

Despite an active royal response to dearth that can be described as paternalistic, there is little doubt that other crown policies played a role in creating some strain in the grain marketing system in the years 1349–76.

[1] Campbell, "Nature as Historical Protagonist," 298–300.
[2] *Ibid.*, 301–5; Campbell, "Physical Shocks, Biological Hazards, and Human Impacts," p. 29.

While the demands of purveyance for military purposes clearly moderated over the period, the crown, on at least two occasions, urged or
ordered dealers to bring grain and other victuals to sell in market towns
in areas where troops were being assembled for embarkation to the
continent. It is likely that these actions produced at least temporary
scarcity or disruption in local markets in the south and east of the
kingdom.

Poor harvests

For a considerable time historians struggled to understand why, for
roughly twenty-seven years after the outbreak of the Black Death in
1348–9, the price of grain in England was above pre-plague levels. The
mean of the average price of a quarter of wheat for the years 1331–49
was 4.92s per quarter. In the years 1350–76 the mean was 7s. In the case
of barley the mean for 1331–49 was 3.73s while that for 1350–76 was
4.92s.[3] Finally for oats, the mean for 1331–49 was 1.99s and for 1350–76
it was 2.67s.[4] It was not until the harvest year 1376–7 that grain prices
began a sustained, long-term decline, although there would still be some
years of scarcity and high prices in the future.[5] It would be reasonable to
assume that the death in 1348–9 of an estimated 40 percent or more of
the population, having greatly reduced the number of mouths to feed,
would have led to a marked drop in food prices, especially since later
outbreaks of plague in 1361–2, 1369, and 1375 probably further reduced
population numbers. Some years ago Dyer called the phenomenon of
"prices of grain, which held up when they should have fallen" one of the
unsolved mysteries of the post-plague period.[6]

Recently, Campbell has offered a multifaceted argument that provides a solution to the mystery. First, he addresses the situation during
the plague and its immediate aftermath, when the yields of wheat,
barley, and oats in the harvests of 1349–51 were respectively 33 percent,
28 percent, and 46 percent below average.[7] Although major environmental changes that produced colder, wet weather adversely affected
harvests, another important contributor to the poor yields, frequently

[3] Munro, "Revisions of the Commodity Price Series;" Hatcher, *Plague, Population and the English Economy*, pp. 50–1.
[4] Clark, "The Price History of English Agriculture," pp. 63–4.
[5] Munro, "Revisions of the Commodity Price Series."
[6] Dyer, "Trade, Urban Hinterlands and Market Integration," p. 108. See also Dyer, "Changes in Diet in the Late Middle Ages," p. 96.
[7] Campbell, "Nature as Historical Protagonist," 300–5; Campbell, "Four Famines and a Pestilence," pp. 34–5; Campbell, "Grain Yields," pp. 121–74.

mentioned in chronicle accounts, was the high death rate that meant there were insufficient numbers of laborers to bring in the harvest on lords' demesnes. Moreover, peasant production must also have been disrupted sufficiently to result in a further reduction in the amount of grain brought to market.[8] Substantiating evidence of the disruption caused by the plague is to be found in the records of the parliament that met in February 1351, when the commons resisted the king's recent demand for purveyance of 24,260 quarters of grain plus other victuals to support military enterprises in Calais, Gascony and Brittany.[9] The commons complained that, as a result of the plague, local communities were depopulated, "land lies fallow and uncultivated" and there was a "great lack and scarcity of grain." As a consequence, they petitioned the king to withdraw the purveyance commissions altogether. In his response, the king indicated that Calais's needs were too great to end the commissions but to "assist the king's commonalty" he agreed to cut the demand for grain in half.[10]

According to Campbell, there is a paradox in the records of the agrarian situation of 1349–52 that needs explanation. Grain yields dropped much more precipitously than grain prices rose. One would expect that under normal circumstances the decline in yields in 1349–52 would produce grain prices like those during the great famine of 1315–17 but they did not. For example, in the harvest year 1349–50 the average price of a quarter of wheat was 5.49s, a price that would be well within the norm for an average to good harvest. In the harvest years 1350–1 and 1351–2 respectively, the average price of a quarter of wheat was 8.78s and 10.21s. These are high average prices but not as high as they were after the harvest failures of 1315–16 and 1316–17, when they were 14.9s and 15.99s[11] Campbell's solution to the paradox is that the plague killed so many people, it resulted in a drastically reduced demand for grain. As a consequence, prices did not rise as dramatically as they would have otherwise. Without the outbreak of plague, the decline in yields in 1349–52 alone would have been catastrophic for the population.[12]

---

[8] For accounts of the disruption of agricultural activities that stemmed from the outbreak of plague, see Martin (ed.), *Knighton's Chronicle*, pp. 100–5, Horrox, (ed.), *The Black Death*, pp. 62–82, Campbell, "Agriculture in Kent in the High Middle Ages," pp. 45–6, and Stone, "The Black Death and its Immediate Aftermath," pp. 213–45.

[9] *CFR, 1347–55*, pp. 273–7.   [10] *Parl. Rolls*, "Edward III: February 1351," item 11.

[11] Munro, "Revisions of the Commodity Price Series."

[12] Campbell, "Nature as Historical Protagonist," 301–5: Campbell, "Physical Shocks, Biological Hazards, and Human Impacts," pp. 28–9; Campbell and Ó Gráda, "Harvest Shortfalls," 869–72.

After the crisis of 1349–52 had passed, grain yields remained low and, according to Campbell, "it took twenty-five years for yields of all three principal grains [wheat, barley, and oats] to regain their pre-plague level on a majority of demesnes."[13] This meant high grain prices over most of the period 1353–76, despite the continued population decline following subsequent outbreaks of plague. That population decline meant, of course, upward pressure on wages as labor became scarce. Despite the crown's attempts, in the interest of landowners, to hold down wages through the ordinance of laborers of 1349 and the statute of laborers of 1351, there is no question that real as well as nominal wages rose.[14] While landowners responded to the declining demand for grain by converting marginal land to pasture and diversifying into stock rearing, their resort to heavier stocking densities of animals such as cattle and sheep as well as changes in crop rotations should have increased yields. At the same time, however, to reduce costs they appear to have sown seed thinner than before and cut back on labor-intensive activities like spreading manure and weeding, which reduced yields. It is also likely that further outbreaks of plague in 1361–2, 1369 and 1375 disrupted work on the harvest in those years. Above all, the continuation of poor weather conditions stood in the way of any efforts to increase yields.[15]

Export prohibitions 1350–1376

Over the period 1350–76, the crown was clearly aware that grain prices were high and that it was necessary to respond. One response was prohibitions on export. During those years, eighteen proclamations imposing prohibitions on the export of grain and, sometimes, other victuals without a license were issued, many with the usual exclusions of Calais and Gascony.[16] Seven prohibitions were explicitly justified by domestic scarcity caused by poor harvest, excessive export, or a combination of both. Six contained no explicit justification. Six others appear to have originated from a range of military concerns, such as preventing

---

[13] Campbell, "Grain Yields," p. 148.
[14] Campbell, "Nature as Historical Protagonist," 285; Hatcher, "England in the Aftermath of the Black Death," 3–35; Hatcher, *Plague, Population and the English Economy*, pp. 48–9.
[15] Campbell, "Grain Yields," pp. 123–4, 142–9.
[16] For the eighteen proclamations, see *CCR, 1349–54*, pp. 199–200, 223, 274, 402–3, 593: *CCR, 1355–60*, pp. 190, 208, 401–2; *CCR, 1360–4*, pp. 138, 240 436, 542–3; *CCR, 1364–9*, pp. 288, 370–1; *CCR, 1369–74*, pp. 114–16; *CCR, 1374–7*, pp. 103, 208–9; *Foedera*, vol. 3 pt. 1, pp. 199, 207, 250–1, 298, 553; *Foedera*, vol. 3 pt. 2, pp. 603, 683, 710, 797, 823, 1016, 1026. See also *CLB*, vol. F, pp. 225, 241–2; *CLB*, vol. G, pp. 39, 82–3, 123–4, 208, 215, 256, 329.

food and weapons reaching the king's enemies, encouraging the export of grain only to possessions of the English crown including Berwick, Calais, and Gascony, and directing domestic supplies of grain and other victuals towards the provisioning of the navy and army, in anticipation of either overseas campaigns or actions in defense of the English coast during the hundred years war. There is other evidence that at least two of the proclamations that did not mention scarcity as a justification were, at least partially, the result of scarcity. One of the six proclamations with a military focus, that of February 28, 1357, was followed up the same day with letters from the king to the mayor and bailiffs of Hull and the sheriffs of Lincolnshire and Yorkshire ordering them to take action against excessive export of grain that was causing scarcity in their counties.[17] In addition, one of the six proclamations that contained no explanation for their issue, which dates from October 8, 1363, was the result of a petition from the commons in Parliament complaining of high prices caused by excessive export of grain and malt.[18]

Five export prohibitions date from the plague years and their immediate aftermath. The first from January 28, 1350 blames scarcity on excessive export while the second of June 23 contains no specific justification.[19] The next prohibition, of October 27, 1350, refers to export as one cause for the scarcity of grain (*caristia bladorum*) and to a poor harvest as another, which is mentioned in a statement about the scarcity of grain that had befallen that year (*sterilitatem bladorum quae contigit hoc anno*).[20] The prohibition of December 4, 1351 also makes it clear that it was issued because of scarcity caused by export and a poor harvest, while the last in the series, dating from a month later, was designed to strengthen the prohibition by ordering the forfeiture to the king of both unlicensed export shipments of grain and the ships carrying them but it contains no specific justification.[21]

No export prohibition was issued in harvest year 1375–6 despite a commons petition in the parliament of April 1376 complaining of high prices and requesting that no grain should be exported in the future without approval of an ordinance in parliament, "except to Calais and other lands of our lord the king." The negative reply to this petition indicates that the crown was particularly concerned with protecting the royal prerogative: "The king's lieges should be free to export it where it seems best to them for their profit, except in time of prohibition, which will be made by the continual council."[22] Nonetheless, prohibitions seem

---

[17] *CCR, 1355–60*, p. 403.   [18] *Parl. Rolls*, "Edward III: October 1363," item 16.
[19] *CCR 1349–54*, pp. 199–200, 223.   [20] *Ibid.*, p. 274; *Foedera*, vol. 3 pt. 1, p. 207.
[21] *Ibid.*, pp. 402–3.   [22] *Parl. Rolls*, "Edward III: April 1376," item 156.

to have been in force throughout the whole period 1350–76, with licenses required to export grain, except in some instances when it was destined for Calais or Gascony.

While it is obvious that the crown and its officials were aware of the problems that were associated with grain scarcity and high prices in the period 1350–76, it is not always clear that their prevailing belief in export of grain as a major cause was correct. Perhaps it all comes down to terminology. Grain exports could either be licensed and lawful or unlicensed and illegal contrary to royal proclamations. If the export licenses enrolled on the patent rolls, supplemented by the close rolls, can be trusted to provide a reasonably accurate sense of the magnitude of licensed exports during the period 1349–76, then that evidence does not appear to support fully the claims of excessive export contained in royal proclamations and other pronouncements.

The first of two export prohibitions issued during the harvest year 1349–50 blamed excessive export for scarcity of grain, while the second contains no explicit justification.[23] The enrolled licenses do show that 4,850 quarters of grain were exported in that harvest year, but it is difficult to imagine that such an amount would have been as significant a cause of scarcity as the disruption to the grain harvest that resulted from the plague.[24] It is also difficult to reconcile the content of export prohibitions in 1350–2 with the evidence of licensed exports. The prohibitions of October 27, 1350 and December 4, 1351 blamed excessive export of grain as the cause of scarcity but there is little indication of that in the export licenses, 1,220 quarters for the harvest year 1350–1 and 710 quarters for 1351–2.[25]

The harvest year 1360–1 was another where a great scarcity of grain (*magna caristia bladorum*) was blamed on export and a poor harvest in two prohibitions, using similar language, issued on November 14, 1360 and February 17, 1361.[26] The first also stated that it was for the benefit and tranquility of the populace. The second was probably the consequence of a statute that the parliament of January 1361 passed imposing a prohibition on the export of grain, except for licensed shipments to Calais and Gascony.[27] Nonetheless, there is little evidence for licensed exports, which totaled only 1,200 quarters for the harvest year 1360–1.[28] It may

---

[23] *CCR 1349–54*, pp. 199–200, 233; *Foedera*, vol. 3 pt. 1, p. 199.
[24] *CPR 1348–50*, pp. 469, 485, 501–2, 510, 513, 550, 555; *CCR 1349–54*, 184, 194, 248.
[25] *CCR, 1349–54*, pp. 274, 402–3; *Foedera*, vol. 3 pt. 1, p. 207; *CPR 1350–4*, pp. 44, 54, 126, 130, 196, 318–19; *CCR 1349–54*, p. 331.
[26] *CCR 1360–4*, pp. 138, 244; *Foedera*, vol. 3 pt. 1, 553 and pt. 2, p. 603.
[27] *SR*, vol. 1, p. 368, 34 Edw. III c. 20.   [28] *CPR 1358–61*, pp. 472, 479, 562, 574.

well be the case that the relatively heavy licensed exports (8,245 quarters) of the previous year, 1359–60, had an influence on prices or perceptions in 1360–1.[29] In October 1363, parliament again successfully petitioned the king for an export prohibition on the grounds of excessive export and no export licenses are recorded on the patent rolls for the harvest year 1363–4.[30]

In the harvest year 1356–7, there appears to have been a clearer connection between actual grain export and fear of scarcity, despite the fact that the proclamation of February 28, 1357 was apparently a fairly standard wartime one that imposed a prohibition on the export of grain, other victuals, horses and weapons except to Bordeaux, Calais, and Berwick and to Brittany and Normandy in order to supply the king's subjects and supporters there.[31] Nonetheless, on the day of the issue of the prohibition, the king sent additional instructions to the mayor and bailiffs of Hull and the sheriffs of Lincolnshire and Yorkshire emphasizing that no one should be allowed to ship grain, ale, and other victuals overseas except to Calais and Bordeaux with the king's license because merchants were exporting so much that they were creating a grain scarcity in those counties "to the damage of the people."[32] In fact during the harvest year 1356–7 a considerable amount of grain, 6,724.5 quarters, was licensed for export.[33] Moreover it was the second of three years of substantial grain export in a row that may have contributed to keeping grain prices high. In 1355–6, 6,840 quarters were exported and for 1357–8 the total was 7,310.[34]

During the harvest year 1364–5, when the average price of a quarter of wheat was high at 7.4s, a possible indication of a deficient harvest, no new export prohibition was issued although licensing did continue in force.[35] In fact enrolled licenses for shipments of grain overseas for that year totaled 6,770 quarters yet there is no mention in official documents regarding the effects of export either on domestic grain supply or prices.[36] With the average price of a quarter of wheat at 6.03s the harvest year 1365–6 appears not to have experienced scarcity, although the export prohibition of July 22, 1366 mentions as its justification a rise in

---

[29] *CPR 1358–61*, pp. 187, 312, 335, 338–9, 343, 432, 438, 440; *CCR 1360–4*, pp. 27, 94–5.
[30] *Parl. Rolls*, "Edward III: October 1363," items 7, 16; *CCR, 1360–4*, 542–3.
[31] *CCR, 1355–60*, pp. 401–3.   [32] *Ibid.*, p. 403.
[33] *CPR 1354–8*, pp. 457, 467–8, 471–2, 477, 483, 518, 545, 589; *CCR 1354–60*, p. 337.
[34] *CPR 1354–8*, pp. 285, 287–8, 299–300, 307–8, 311, 314, 324–5, 346, 406, 607–8, 621, 625, 636–7, 642, 645, 648–9; *CPR 1358–61*, pp. 5–6, 11–13, 15, 20, 22, 25, 27, 29, 31; *CCR 1354–60*, p. 438.
[35] Munro, "Revisions of the Commodity Price Series."
[36] *CPR 1364–7*, pp. 29, 32, 35–6, 49–50, 56, 59, 61, 86–7, 101, 127–8, 130.

the price of grain caused by bad weather.[37] If the price of grain was rising in late July, roughly a month before the new harvest, because supplies were short perhaps the real, but unmentioned, culprit was the licensed export of an unprecedented amount of grain in any harvest year of the period, 18,140 quarters between October 3, 1365 and July 3, 1366.[38]

If we cannot rely on licensed exports to provide consistent support for the contemporary claim that in some years export caused scarcity, should we look instead at illegal, unlicensed export to provide an answer? Certainly contemporaries regarded this as a major problem. A good example of that view is contained in the export prohibition of February 17, 1361. Particular emphasis was placed on the complaints to the king from the commons in the current parliament that, even after the issue of the earlier prohibition of November 14, 1360, merchants and others had exported large quantities of grain and malt in contempt of the king and to the grave injury of the people of the kingdom.[39] In addition, the export prohibition of October 8, 1363 was issued as a result of similar parliamentary pressure.[40]

Since at least the reign of Edward II, export prohibitions often contained language ordering sheriffs and other officials to arrest all ships and their masters with cargoes of grain intended for export without a license and to certify their actions to the Chancery from time to time. Such ships and cargoes were subject to forfeiture to the king. As a further means to enforce prohibitions, the crown periodically appointed commissions, with varying powers, to inquire through juries into the names of those who were involved in various illegal commercial activities, including export of uncustomed goods and unlicensed grain. Sometimes they were instructed to seize only ships and cargoes; on other occasions they were given power to seek indictments of the merchants or masters of ships and then imprison them until further orders from the king. Occasionally, commissions included the power to try the indicted suspects. Between 1350 and 1376, Edward III's government issued or renewed many such commissions, which usually covered one to four counties.[41]

---

[37] *CCR, 1364–9*, p. 288; *Foedera*, vol. 3 pt. 2, p. 797; Munro, "Revisions of the Commodity Price Series."

[38] *CPR 1364–7*, pp. 162, 176, 181, 187, 189, 192–5, 211, 218, 224, 235, 248, 255, 258–9, 291–3.

[39] *CCR, 1360–4*, p. 240; *Foedera*, vol. 3 pt. 1, p. 603.

[40] *Parl. Rolls*, "Edward III: October 1363," items 7, 16: *CCR, 1360–4*, pp. 542–3; *Foedera*, vol. 3 pt. 2, p. 710.

[41] *CPR, 1348–50*, p. 4 (Cornwall); *CPR, 1350–4*, p. 275 (Yorkshire, Water of Thames), p. 289 (Kent, Essex, Surrey, Sussex), p. 334 (Kent etc.), p. 395 (Yorkshire), p. 448 (Water of Thames and Kent etc.), p. 512 (Kent etc.); *CPR, 1354–8*, p. 66 (Kent etc.), p. 125 (Kent etc.), pp. 163, 497, 613–14 (Norfolk and Suffolk), pp. 614, 617 (Essex),

Sometimes single individuals were commissioned to focus on unlicensed grain export in specific areas. For example, on December 28, 1352, John Pecche, sheriff of London, was appointed to arrest all ships loaded with unlicensed grain for export in ports between London and the Isle of Sheppey, at the mouth of the Thames. His appointment was a result of many complaints reaching the king's ears that grain was being shipped overseas without license, contrary to the prohibition, presumably that of January 12, 1352.[42] On March 18, 1358, Thomas Dautry, king's serjeant at arms, was given a similar appointment to inquire into unlicensed grain export from Hampshire.[43]

On other occasions, judicial commissions were appointed to discover and punish those responsible for unlicensed grain exports. On December 8, 1362, a commission of oyer and terminer was issued to try those who illegally exported grain from Boston. The bailiffs of Boston were accused of failing to proclaim a prohibition on the export of grain and other victual without the king's license. Moreover, the bailiffs were accused not only of exporting unlicensed cargoes of grain in their own ships but also allowing other merchants to do the same.[44] Faced with scarcity in 1374–5, the crown, on February 24, 1375, issued instructions to the justices of the peace in thirteen counties, plus the mayor and sheriff of Bristol, to inquire into the export of grain contrary to the proclamation of the previous November. Such illegal export was blamed for causing increasing scarcity in the kingdom.[45]

Although surviving evidence provides us with a sense of how seriously contemporaries regarded the problem of unlicensed exports, there is no way of measuring the success of attempts to stop it or even how big a problem it actually was. Scattered throughout official records for the years 1349–76 are occasional references either to the seizure of individual shipments or to pardons issued to those who engaged in illegal export,

---

p. 653 (Lincolnshire); *CFR, 1356–68*, p. 32 (Water of Thames); *CPR 1358–61*, p. 159 (Essex), p. 223 (Yorkshire); *CPR, 1361–4*, pp. 62–3 (Essex, Norfolk and Suffolk, Gloucester, Somerset, Dorset, Devon); *CPR, 1364–7*, p. 438 (East Riding of Yorkshire); *CPR, 1367–70*, p. 60 (Yorkshire and Northumberland), p. 264 (Yorkshire, Northumberland, Cumberland, Westmoreland); *CPR, 1374–7*, p. 332 (Hampshire, Essex, Devon, Cornwall, Suffolk, Norfolk, Dorset, Sussex, Yorkshire, Lincolnshire, Cinque Ports, Bristol).

[42] *CFR, 1347–55*, p. 351.   [43] *CPR, 1358–61*, p. 73.

[44] *CPR, 1361–4*, p. 294; see also p. 359, a second commission appointed for Boston, February 22, 1363.

[45] *CPR 1374–7*, p. 146. The counties named were Hampshire, Sussex, Kent, Norfolk, Essex, Lincoln, Dorset, Somerset, Devon, Gloucester, Northumberland, the three Ridings of Yorkshire, Lindsey and Holland in Lincolnshire, and Huntingdon. The justices of the peace are called justices of oyer and terminer in the commissions.

but there are only a handful for any single year.[46] In addition, there are a few surviving records of the results of judicial inquiries. Two surviving cases resulted from the instructions to the justices of the peace in February 24, 1375 to inquire into illegal export of grain in violation of the prohibition of November 24, 1374. One, of June 30, 1375, comes from Holland in Lincolnshire and names one suspect who shipped 300 quarters of grain illegally to Scotland. The other, of April 9, 1375, from Dorchester names two men who shipped grain from Dorset ports to Bordeaux, Southampton, Plymouth and Dartmouth but there is no indication if these shipments were properly licensed or in violation of the prohibition.[47] This is a recurring problem in other surviving records of inquiries into illegal export, where juries often responded by listing grain shipments but frequently indicated ignorance about whether they were licensed or not.[48] Two other records related to Yorkshire survive from the work of the commission of July 23, 1376, appointed to examine illegal export of grain and other goods from ten counties plus the Cinque Ports and Bristol. One from Whitby found no evidence of illegal export. In the second, from Cleveland, two merchants were accused of shipping 60 quarters of peas and beans to parts of Scotland against the king's prohibition.[49] At present, it is impossible to begin to measure the amount of grain exported illegally without a license at any point during the period, although further research might uncover more extensive evidence.

Market regulation and grain supply

During the years 1349–76, a significant response of Edward III's government to scarcity and high prices was to encourage the enforcement of traditional market regulations such as the assize of weights and measures and the statute of forestallers, particularly the new statute of 1351. In addition, close attention was paid to the supply of grain in urban areas, especially London and Bristol, which included an attempt to regulate prices in the ordnance of laborers of 1349 and efforts to encourage the movement of grain especially to London from distant parts of the realm and from Ireland.

An effort to enforce the assize of weights and measures began in 1340 and continued with fits and starts until 1361, when jurisdiction

---

[46] *CCR, 1349–54*, pp. 10, 15; *CPR, 1350–4*, pp. 55, 464, 467, 479; *CFR, 1356–68*, pp. 4–5, 88, 149–50, 228, 291; *CPR, 1354–8*, pp. 444, 553; *CCR, 1354–60*, 571, 578–9, 580; *CCR, 1360–4*, p. 347; *CPR, 1361–4*, p. 294; *CPR, 1364–7*, pp. 40–1, 43, 50, 72, 443; *CFR, 1368–77*, pp. 5–6; *CPR, 1367–70*, pp. 235, 270; *CCR, 1369–74*, pp. 152, 369.
[47] *CIM*, vol. 3, pp. 371–2.   [48] *Ibid.*, pp. 147–8, 206, 247–8.
[49] *Ibid.*, pp. 401–2; *CPR, 1374–7*, p. 332.

was turned over to the recently created justices of the peace in each county. Despite organizational difficulties and the corrupt practices of the commissioners, Edward III's government, regularly prodded by the commons in parliament, stuck with the policy throughout the 1350s probably because it was regarded as necessary to deal with the problem of high grain prices.

In a parliament of 1340, in response to a petition of the commons, Edward III approved a statute that confirmed the traditional assize of weights and measures grounded in Magna Carta and authorized the creation of commissions to go round the country enforcing the use of standardized weights and measures that would be made under the supervision of the Treasurer and sent to every county.[50] Over the next few years, the king issued or renewed a series of commissions covering virtually every English county.[51] At the same time, the commons in the parliament of April 1343 petitioned the king "that the commissions should be issued to good people ... so that remedy is made for the profit of the king and his people."[52] The commons also requested that "those who use false measures ... should be punished individually according to the seriousness of his trespass."[53] This last request was intended to prevent the practice of imposing a common fine on whole communities where false weights and measures were used rather than on guilty individuals. Such a practice was a money raising device that the clerk of the market and commissioners appointed to enforce the statute frequently employed.

While we have no details of the specific complaints against fraudulent measures that led to the statute of 1340 and the establishment of the commissions, examples of fraud from the period are relatively easy to discover. The printed fourteenth-century London records contain numerous examples of trade and market offences, including false measures. Two cases involved "thickening the bottom of a quart measure with pitch" so that it would hold up to one-third less volume. In both instances the accused women were sentenced to the thewe.[54] Other cases involved false measures for fish, grain, or ale.[55] In one instance a turner

---

[50] *SR*, vol. 1, p. 285, 14 Edw. III Stat. 1 c. 12. The surviving parliament rolls for this year do not contain any reference to a commons petition on weights and measures. For somewhat different treatments of weights and measures in this period see Ormrod, *The Reign of Edward III*, p. 79 and Musson and Ormrod, *The Evolution of English Justice*, p. 92.

[51] *CPR, 1340–3*, pp. 310, 318, 363, 441, 446, 580–1, 587; *CPR, 1343–5*, pp. 72, 282–3.

[52] *Parl. Rolls*, "Edward III: April 1343," item 40.

[53] *Ibid.*, item 39.

[54] *CLB*, vol. G, p. 175 (1364), p. 216 (1367); Riley, *Memorials*, p. 328.

[55] *CLB*, vol. C, pp. 157–8 (1307); vol. E, p. 42 (1315), p. 46 (1315); vol. G, p. 269 (1370); Riley, *Memorials*, p. 78 (1310), pp. 116–17 (1315); Thomas (ed.), *Calendar of Plea and Memoranda Rolls*, vo. 2, p. 186 (1375), pp. 188–9 (1375).

who made false measures for ale, called chopyns, was sentenced to jail but released when he agreed not to make them in future.[56]

There is one other kind of fraud that may also have lain behind the commons pressure for the regulation of weights and measures. A good example of it is to be found in pardons that Edward III issued on May 26, 1347, at the request of Henry, earl of Lancaster, to Sir Thomas Bekeryng and his wife Isabel in return for a heavy fine. Bekeryng had been sheriff of Nottingham and Derby and was convicted of using false measures to defraud the commonalty of Nottingham and enrich himself, when authorized to buy victuals for the king. His wife was also convicted for aiding Bekeryng in his use of false measures and for other activities, including "thrusting her hand into the said false bushel while wheat, peas, oats, and other corn were falling into it to be measured."[57] This tale of the corrupt sheriff and his lady reminds us of the long-standing accusations of fraudulent practices against royal purveyors.[58]

In the end, it was another form of official corruption that alienated the commons and forced the king to abandon the first set of commissions on weights and measures. One early indication of that corruption comes from 1342 when, on September 16, Edward III ordered the arrest Thomas Shirburn, one of the commissioners for Lincolnshire. Shirburn was accused of planning to leave the country with money that came from the fines levied on offenders against the statute and thereby defrauding the king.[59] While the king continued to order Shirburn's arrest, by February 1343 he had succeeded in fleeing the country with the money.[60] The crucial corruption problem that plagued the weights and measures commissions, however, was not commissioners absconding with the proceeds of the fines levied on the guilty but commissioners extorting large sums of monies for their own use from guilty and innocent alike. On April 26, 1343, Edward III appointed three men to investigate the activities of the commissioners in Suffolk who were accused of extortion "touching fines and ransoms as well as gifts received and moneys collected" in the course of their official duties.[61] Despite this enquiry it is not at all clear the king was aware of the extent of the corruption, for the commissions were renewed between February and May 1344.[62]

It was only in June 1344 during a meeting of parliament that the widespread discontent with the behavior of the commissions became public. The commons, which in the parliaments of 1340 and 1343 had

---

[56] Thomas (ed.), *Calendar of Plea and Memoranda Rolls*, vol. 2, p. 124 (1370).
[57] *CPR, 1345–8*, pp. 535–6.   [58] Madicott, "The English Peasantry," pp. 307–18.
[59] *CPR, 1340–3*, p. 553.   [60] *CPR, 1343–5*, p. 70.   [61] *Ibid.*, p. 84.
[62] *Ibid.*, pp. 282–3.

been strongly in favor of the commissions as a means of enforcing the statute on weights and measures, now petitioned against their extortionate practices and urged their abolition. The king bowed to the commons' grievances and agreed to put an end to the commissions. Soon thereafter, Edward III ordered the sheriffs to proclaim that the commissions would cease to operate and that anyone with a complaint against the commissioners should bring it before the treasurer and barons of the Exchequer. At the same time, the king wrote to the treasurer and barons of the Exchequer ordering them to hear the cases of those with complaints and compel the commissioners to account for the money they had collected.[63]

The abolition of the commissions in 1344, at the commons' request, did not diminish their support for enforcement of the weights and measure statute. In the parliament of February 1351 the commons petitioned the king to order the making of the standard measures for distribution to each county, to which the king gave his assent.[64] Almost a year later, in the parliament of January 1352, the commons again petitioned the king for the enforcement of the statute. He responded with approval of a renewal of the statute and a statement that "whenever it is necessary" he would appoint justices to enforce the statute locally.[65] In the parliament of September 1353, the commons returned to the matter of enforcement, petitioning the king "that the justices of labourers and keepers of the peace shall be appointed from the most worthy men dwelling in the counties" and be given jurisdiction over weights and measures and other market offences such as regrating. The king's response was general and evasive, namely "that good and suitable justices shall be elected to do justice."[66] Clearly the commons wanted regular enforcement of the weights and measures statute through locally established, fixed, and ongoing institutions. The king on the other hand, after the failure of the first round of commissions, appears to have settled for ad hoc arrangements. This is indicated in the fact that in the three years 1352–5 the only enforcement actions he took on weights and measures was to issue a four commissions of oyer and terminer, three for Suffolk and one for Suffolk and Norfolk.[67]

---

[63] *Parl. Rolls*, "Edward III: June 1344," items 12, 13, 47, 48; *SR*, vol. 1, p. 301, 18 Edw. III Stat. 2, c. 4; *CCR, 1343–6*, pp. 391, 422; *CLB*, vol. F, p. 107. In their discussion of the withdrawal of the commissions in 1344, Ormrod in *The Reign of Edward III*, p. 79 and Musson and Ormrod in *The Evolution of English Justice*, p. 92 appear to have overlooked the significance of the commons' discontent in June of that year.

[64] *Parl. Rolls*, "Edward III: February 1351," item 38.

[65] *Parl. Rolls*, "Edward III: January 1352," item 26; *SR*, vol. 1, pp. 321–2, 25 Edw. III Stat. 5 c. 10.

[66] *Parl. Rolls*, "Edward III: September 1353," item 36.

[67] *CPR, 1350–4*, pp. 510, 541; *CPR, 1354–8*, pp. 121, 236.

The commons, however, were not about to give up their quest for more rigorous and regular enforcement. In the parliament of April 1354, they petitioned the king, insisting that the statute was not being enforced and requesting that standard measures should be made for each county and distributed to the sheriffs who would keep custody of them "to serve the king and the people." The king replied that those who wanted standard measures should come to the treasury and pay for copies of those stored there.[68] Some months later, in November, when the statute was again proclaimed, it was made clear that "all who use measures in buying and selling shall bring them to Winchester castle and have them made to agree with the measures there placed."[69] Within less than a year, this particular approach was abandoned. Instead, the king had new measures to the London standard made and sent to the sheriffs, on October 1, 1355, with instructions to proclaim that all those in their counties, including royal purveyors, who used measures to buy or sell grain or other victuals, should bring them to the relevant sheriff to be converted to the London standard and that no one should use any other measures.[70]

In the parliament of November 1355, the commons returned once more to the question of the enforcement of the statute of weights and measures. They again petitioned the king that the justices of laborers should be given the power to enforce it. Once more the king was evasive in his answer that the statute would be enforced by "suitable and wise judges ... assigned whenever necessary."[71] The consequence was that, at least for the short term, the king continued with ad hoc measures of enforcement and issued, over the period April–November 1356, a number of commissions of oyer and terminer that covered at least eleven counties.[72] In the end, however, the king gave in to the commons and in 1357 appointed new commissions of justices to enforce the statutes of laborers and weights and measures.[73] Finally, a statute was passed in the parliament of January 1361 that defined the jurisdiction and powers of the new justices of the peace who replaced the keepers of the peace in the counties. Included among their powers was enforcement of the weights and measures statute.[74]

---

[68] *Parl. Rolls*, "Edward III: April 1354," item 37.   [69] *CCR, 1354–60*, pp. 101–2.

[70] *Ibid.*, pp. 162–3, 183, 226. See also *CCR, 1354–60*, pp. 376, 383.

[71] *Parl. Rolls*, "Edward III: November 1355," item 19.

[72] *CPR, 1354–8*, pp. 396–7; *CCR, 1354–60*, p. 365. It may well be that not every commission was recorded because *CCR, 1354–60*, p. 365 contains the only reference to a commission for Somerset.

[73] *CPR, 1354–8*, pp. 549–51. The commissions were renewed in 1358, see *CPR, 1358–61*, pp. 67–8.

[74] *SR*, vol. 1, p. 365, 34 Edw. III cc. 5, 6.

The crown's focus on the food supply of London and other urban areas began in the immediate aftermath of the plague and continued through to 1376. The particular concern with London's food supply in the years 1349–54 provides another indication of the depth of the disruption caused by the plague and the poor harvests of those years. Already, in one of the sections of the ordinance of laborers of 1349, the king had ordained that all sellers of victuals should sell them at reasonable prices established by the prevailing prices in nearby markets so they would "have moderate gains and not excessive, reasonably to be required according to the place from whence the said victuals be carried." The mayors and bailiffs of all towns were authorized to inquire into such matters and fine those guilty of charging excessive prices.[75]

Two years later, in the parliament of February 1351, a statute was passed confirming an earlier one of 1335 that all merchants, whether "aliens or denizens" should be able to trade freely in all goods including victuals and bring such goods to London or any other town with a market or a fair without hindrance or interference from any official or anyone else.[76] On March 22, 1351 the king wrote to the mayor and sheriffs of London informing them that he had found out that victuallers, engrossers, and regrators in London "seeking their own gain" were interfering with trade contrary to the statute by setting the price of victuals brought to the city and not permitting them to be sold for less. As a result, foodstuffs had become more expensive than before the statute, when it was the king's intention that they should be less expensive after its passage. The letter concluded by instructing the mayor and sheriffs to investigate this situation, punish the offenders, and end the practice so that victuals "may be freely sold at a reasonable price" (*rationabile precium*).[77]

In a related matter, on January 22, 1351, Edward III instructed the mayor and sheriffs of London to issue a proclamation that purveyors and others were not to forestall grain and other victuals bound for the city, in order to prevent scarcity that would affect a forthcoming parliament. A similar proclamation of November 28, 1351 encouraged dealers to come to Westminster to sell victuals to help supply another parliament. The king promised that no one, including his purveyors, would force them to sell at less than an agreed upon price.[78] A more significant step

[75] *SR*, vol. 1, p. 308, 23 Edw. III c. 6.
[76] *SR*, vol. 1, pp. 314–15, 25 Ed. III stat. 3 c. 2; *Parl. Rolls*, "Edward III: February 1351," item 43. The statute confirms 9 Edw. III stat. 1 c. 1.
[77] *CCR, 1349–54*, pp. 360–1; *Foedera*, vol. 3 pt. 1, p. 217; *A Medieval Capital*, pp. 104–7.
[78] *CLB*, vol. F, pp. 227, 240.

had already been taken in the parliament of February 1351 when it passed a statute of forestallers, whose enforcement was regularly urged by Edward III's government. The statute established that a convicted forestaller would be liable to forfeit the goods he purchased or their value either to the king, if indicted at the king's suit, or half to the king and half to a private party who brought the suit.[79]

On October 20, 1351, the crown's continuing concern with London's food supply resulted in the proclamation of a royal ordinance restating the traditional London grain marketing regulations that had developed from the early thirteenth century onwards and continued to be reissued by London officials for much of the fourteenth century.[80] The opening of the ordinance observes that it was made for the "common wealth" (*commune profit*) of the people of London. The ordinance then states that no foreigners ought to sell grain by sample but should bring it into the city by land or water and sell it openly at the four traditional grain markets, Billingsgate, Queenhithe, Newgate, and Gracechurch. No grain was to be put up for sale at Queenhithe, Newgate, and Gracechurch before prime (sunrise) and at Billingsgate before demi prime. All market transactions were confined to three days: Monday, Wednesday, and Saturday. No one was to go out to meet any victuals being brought by land or water to the city in order to buy them before they reached market. No cornmonger or any other dealer was to buy grain from a stranger and leave it in his hands to sell it at a higher price later. All grain being moved to the city for sale ought to come to the markets to be sold to the people for their sustenance, and to bakers and brewers "to serve the common people" (*pur servir le commune poeple*). No cornmonger or regrator was to buy grain in the market to sell again at a profit. Those who wished to deal in grain should buy it in other counties and sell it for a profit in the city's markets. Similar regulations governing the sale of poultry, fish, cattle and pigs were also included in the ordinance.[81]

The aims of such regulations are clearly stated by Bruce Campbell. They "were to ensure that the market in grain in the city was an open one and not subverted by dealing in secret places; that the market should be accessible to the common people of the city, who should be able to meet their needs for sustenance by buying in small quantities and not be excluded by wholesale dealers; that prices be not enhanced by successive

---

[79] *SR*, vol. 1, p. 315, 25 Edw. III c. 3; *Parl. Rolls*, "Edward III: February 1351," item 44.
[80] An earlier version of the regulations that the Mayor and Aldermen of London issued in 1316 is in *CLB, vol.* E, pp. 56–7. For later versions, see *CLB*, vol. F, pp. 100–2 and vol. G, p. 103. See also *A Medieval Capital*, pp. 104–7.
[81] *CCR, 1349–54*, pp. 391–2; *Foedera*, vol. 3 pt. 1, pp. 233–4.

sales of the same grain."[82] In fact, a 1344 version of the regulations that the mayor and aldermen issued is described as "articles for avoiding dearness of corn."[83]

There is other evidence from the early 1350s that reveals the crown's interest in maintaining London's grain supply, along with its continuing concern about the price of food in the capital and nationwide. This includes the proclamation of December 4, 1351 that prohibited export of grain, to which a clause was added that "the king does not wish the taking of corn to London by water to be impeded by reason of this order."[84] A few months later, on April 10, 1352, while a nationwide export prohibition was still in effect, the king ordered a prohibition on export of grain from London, except by Ralph, Earl of Stafford, Bernard Ezii, Lord of Lebret, and John Charnels, Constable of Bordeaux who were permitted to supply Gascony.[85] In the parliament of September 1353, a commons petition urged that the justices of laborers and the keepers of the peace in every county should be given the power to punish "regrators of victuals" and "innkeepers for their outrageous prices."[86] The result was a statute, which stipulated that "justices learned in the law" should be appointed to inquire into the activities of hostlers and regrators and punish them "for the great and outrageous dearth of victuals." This "would do right to the king and his people."[87] Finally, there were further complaints by the commons in the parliament of April 1354 that poor governance in the city of London, including failure to enforce regulatory measures, had resulted in a "great scarcity of victuals" so that "they are sold for three times more than the cost at which they were bought." The king replied that the activities of the responsible officials would be examined by inquests of people drawn from the counties around London and those who were found guilty would be heavily amerced.[88]

In the early 1360s, the issue of the high price of food arose again, first in London, and then in other towns. An early indication of the crown's concern is revealed in the wording of three appointments of searchers for the illegal export of uncustomed goods and unlicensed grain made on April 16 and May 30, 1361. The first appointment covered Essex, the second Norfolk, and the third Gloucestershire, Somerset, Dorset, and Devon. If the searchers found merchants who planned to export grain,

---

[82] *A Medieval Capital*, p. 104.   [83] *CLB*, vol. F, pp. 100–2. The quotation is on p. 100.
[84] CCR, 1349–54, pp. 402–3.   [85] *CLB*, vol. F, p. 244.
[86] *Parl. Rolls*, "Edward III: September 1353," item 36.
[87] *SR*, vol.1, p. 330, 27 Edw. III Stat.1 c. 3.
[88] *Parl. Rolls*, "Edward III: April 1354," item 26.

they were to take sureties that they would ship it instead to London to sell "for their own profit." If the grain merchants did not provide sureties then the searchers themselves were to arrange to ship the grain to London.[89]

On October 30, 1361, the king wrote to the mayor and sheriffs of London that the price of bread, wine, beer, and other victuals in London and the suburbs was very high because of the regrating that sellers practiced and the city authorities allowed. According to the royal letter, every new mayor had taken an oath to oversee the sale of victuals, enforce the assize of weights and measures, and punish abuses but none had acted accordingly. The king ordered the mayor and sheriffs to assemble the aldermen and other important men to enforce the assize of weights and measures and to establish a price for victuals in the city based on the original purchase price so that the sellers would get "a reasonable but not excessive profit." The letter ends by ordering that these reforms should be publicly proclaimed in London and the suburbs.[90] In response to this letter, the mayor and other officials of London issued an order to search for and punish "forestallers and regrators of victuals" so "that no one shall have cause to complain of the price of victuals being enhanced."[91]

Soon parliament picked up on the issue. In October 1362, the commons complained of the high prices of victuals and wine in London, York, Bristol, Hull, Boston, and other towns, which were "fixed at so great a price for individual profit, to the great damage and misfortune of the people." As a remedy, they requested the king to order the enforcement of the relevant statutes and ordinances, no doubt those dealing with market offences such as forestalling and the like. The king, in turn, promised to enforce those laws.[92] The commons in the parliament of October 1363 returned to the problem of high prices. They were emphatic that "merchants, innkeepers, regrators, forestallers, and other such people" engrossed all kinds of victuals and drove up prices so much so that what they bought for 1s they sold for 3s or more and petitioned for a statute setting the price of poultry. In reply, the king not only stated that the relevant laws would be fully enforced but accepted the need for the statute as well.[93] It was also in this parliament that the commons succeeded in getting the king to impose a prohibition on the export of

---

[89] *CPR, 1361–4*, pp. 62–3.   [90] TNA, C54/199 m. 16v; *CCR, 1360–4*, p. 284.
[91] *CLB*, vol. G, p. 122. The king's letter provides the most obvious context for this undated order. See also p. 138 for an ordinance against forestalling grain and other foodstuffs probably from 1361–2.
[92] *Parl. Rolls*, "Edward III: October 1362," item 19.
[93] *Parl. Rolls*, "Edward III: October 1363," items 15, 21; *SR*, vol. 1, pp. 378–9, 37 Edw. III c. 3.

grain and malt because the merchants of London and elsewhere were shipping so much out of the country that prices were being driven up.[94]

In the face of scarcity seven years later, the government of London and the crown returned once again to market offences as the cause. In January 1370, the bailiff of Southwark was authorized to seize all malt that strangers brought to London and Southwark with the intention of shipping it overseas. Two months later, in March, the mayor and sheriffs of London ordered a prohibition on the export of grain and malt from the city.[95] The king became involved in October 8, 1370 when he urged enforcement of the 1351 statute of forestallers. This involved a much more aggressive policy of search and seizure of forestalled grain than that implemented by Edward III's predecessors.

In urging the enforcement of the statute, the king instructed the sheriffs of London and Middlesex plus the sheriffs of eight other counties and the bailiffs of the town of Beverley to issue a proclamation blaming forestallers, regrators, and embracers for the increasingly high cost of grain and the "clear impoverishment" (*depauperatum manifestam*) of the people.[96] It is difficult to know what embracers meant in this context, since embracery was the crime of corrupting a jury through bribery or threats of force. It may simply mean indulging in corrupt practice. According to the proclamation, the forestalling of grain in large quantities before it came to market, including the purchase of it while still in stacks or granges and the withholding of that grain from the market (in anticipation of rising prices), were the cause of the scarcity. Forestallers and others who bought grain in order to withhold it from the market and those who sold it to them were to be imprisoned and the grain forfeited and put up for sale in the open market. Two days later, commissions were established for the relevant counties and authorized to summon juries to discover the names of those involved in these corrupt practices and arrest them.[97]

---

[94] *Parl. Rolls*, "Edward III: October 1363," items 7, 16.

[95] Thomas (ed.), *Calendar of Plea and Memoranda Rolls*, vol. 2, p. 114; *CLB*, vol. G, p. 260.

[96] TNA, C54/208 m. 8v; *CCR, 1369–74*, pp. 193–4. The other counties were Kent, Hertford, Essex, Bedford, Buckingham, Cambridge, Huntingdon, and Lincoln.

[97] TNA, C66/282, m.4v; *CPR 1367–70*, pp. 474–5; *CLB*, vol. G, pp. 266. Throughout the reign Edward III's government regularly authorized commissions to investigate forestalling in particular communities. See *CPR, 1334–8*, p. 445 (Exeter); *CPR, 1338–40*, p. 64 (Exeter); *CPR, 1343–5*, p. 398 (Yorkshire), p. 426 (Holderness); *CPR, 1345–8*, p. 320 (Exeter), pp. 387–8 (Nottinghamshire); *CPR, 1348–50*, p. 453 (Exeter), p. 527 (Yorkshire); *CPR, 1350–4*, p. 94 (Yorkshire), p. 157 (Lincolnshire), p. 275 (Yorkshire), pp. 334 and 512 (Kent, Essex, Surrey, and Sussex), p. 509 (Colchester); *CPR, 1354–8*, p. 65 (Lincolnshire), p. 125 (Kent, Essex, Surrey and Sussex), p. 129 (Yarmouth), p. 162 (Kent) pp. 165, 399, 458 (Scarborough), p. 236 (Norfolk and Suffolk); *CPR, 1358–61*, p. 76 (Cumberland), pp. 220–1 and p. 223 (Yorkshire); *CPR, 1361–4*, p. 281 (Gloucestershire); *CPR, 1370–4*, p. 391, (Gateshead and Newcastle). See also *CPR, 1364–7*, pp. 40–1, 43, 50–1 and *CPR, 1377–81*, p. 79, pardons for forestalling.

It is particularly significant that the royal condemnations of fore-stalling, regrating, and engrossing in the period 1351–70 imply that these three market offences were so similar that they could be punished as violations of the 1351 statute against forestalling, which, in fact, does not specifically mention engrossing and regrating.[98] It may be that those offences were considered crimes at common law and thus did not require statutory authority to be prosecuted. This latter point is probably con-firmed by the fact that there are numerous examples from the fourteenth and fifteenth centuries of town ordinances that condemned forestalling, engrossing, and regrating.[99] It was not until the reign of Edward VI that an actual statute was passed against engrossing and regrating along with forestalling.[100]

Later, on October 28, 1370, the king ordered the sheriffs to issue another proclamation to modify that of October 8, which made it clear that it was not the king's intention to interfere with the activities of nobles, lords, bishops and other churchmen, who sold their grain in large or small amounts directly from their houses or granges rather than in the market. They could continue to do so lawfully. Imprisonment and forfeiture of the grain were to be reserved for common forestallers, regrators, and embracers.[101] It is probable that in authorizing such a proclamation the king was attempting to make a distinction between forestallers who bought and hoarded grain in order to sell it later at a profit and those who produced large quantities of grain that they kept in their own granaries until it was sold. Nonetheless, it is also possible that whatever the nature of the great men's out of market sales, it was too sensitive a matter for the king to touch; it was much easier to go after the offenders whose lower social standing and reputations for unscrupulous profiteering made them easier targets. Finally, in what now had become standard practice, Edward III ordered the mayor and sheriffs of London to issue a proclamation in February 1371 "against enhancing the price of victuals" when a forthcoming parliament met.[102]

Another city with food supply problems was Bristol, which depended on grain from a number of counties shipped overland or down the river Severn. Some of the difficulties along the Severn had been clear earlier, around the time of the 1347 Bristol food riot. The immediate object of the food rioters on that occasion was to stop the export of grain to Gascony, whether licensed or not, but there was also a growing official worry about illegal export from Bristol of grain that had come

---

[98] *SR*, vol. 1, p. 315, 25 Edw. III c. 3.   [99] Davis, *Market Morality*, pp. 253–63.
[100] *SR*, vol. 4, pp. 148–50, 5 and 6 Edw. VI c. 14.
[101] *CCR 1369–74*, p. 195; *Foedera*, vol. 3 pt. 2, p. 901.
[102] *CLB*, vol. G, p. 278; Riley, *Memorials*, pp. 347–8.

down river.[103] During the harvest year 1363–4 the food supply difficulties of Bristol again came to the attention of the crown through a petition from the city's inhabitants. The petition stated that Bristol had always depended on grain shipped from Gloucestershire, Worcestershire, and Herefordshire, since the grain grown in its immediate neighborhood was insufficient for its needs but now sheriffs and other royal officials were blocking grain from these counties reaching the city, probably in fear of either unlicensed export overseas or creating scarcity in their own bailiwicks.

In response, on November 5, 1363, the king ordered that, since three citizens of Bristol had put up sureties that grain brought to the city would not be shipped overseas, those individuals in the three neighboring counties with grain and other victuals to sell should be allowed to transport them to Bristol freely by land or water.[104] Nonetheless, the crown continued to be concerned with illegal export from Bristol. On November 26, 1369, an order to proclaim a prohibition on the export of grain, gold, silver, weapons, and armor was issued; this was followed up on January 18, 1370 with a letter from the king to the mayor and bailiffs of Bristol ordering them to publish and enforce the proclamation, particularly against unlicensed export of grain.[105]

The continuing difficulty that Bristol encountered with its grain supply in scarcity years is revealed in a royal mandate of May 20, 1375 addressed to a number of sheriffs and other local officials instructing them to allow merchants and others to take their grain and other victuals to Bristol to sell without being hindered. Once again, the townsmen had petitioned the king that locally grown grain was insufficient for their needs, while sheriffs and other officials in neighboring counties had imposed restrictions on the activities of those who normally supplied the city with grain. Finally, like the previous mandate, this one noted that three citizens of Bristol had put up sureties that all grain and victuals brought to the city would not be shipped elsewhere.[106]

The crown's concern with the grain supply of Bristol was part of a continuing worry about scarcity and high prices in the larger region. On January 16, 1376, the king directed the sheriffs of Warwickshire, Worcestershire, and Gloucestershire to issue a proclamation against embracery. It had come to his attention, through frequent complaints,

---

[103] TNA, C. 66/221 m.1v; *Foedera*, vol. 3 pt. 1, p. 126; *CPR, 1345–8*, p. 224; *CPR, 1348–50*, pp. 67–8, 165; *CCR, 1346–9*, p. 281.

[104] *CPR, 1361–4*, pp. 409–10. See also a commission of oyer and terminer issued on June 10, 1363 to deal with forestalling and regrating in Gloucestershire, *CPR, 1361–4*, p. 281.

[105] *CCR, 1369–74*, pp. 114–16.   [106] *CPR, 1374–7*, pp. 101–2.

that merchants who embraced large quantities of grain and shipped it out of these counties were driving up local prices to the "great peril" (*periculum maximum*) of the people. As a consequence, no merchant was to buy, or ship from those counties any grain beyond that necessary to support his own household.[107]

Within a month, unforeseen complications had arisen. On February 20 the king ordered the sheriff of Gloucestershire to issue a proclamation that merchants and others could buy grain in that county and sell it without hindrance in Bristol for the sustenance of its population.[108] It seems that the proclamation of January 16 against embracery provided the justification for people in Gloucestershire to prevent grain from leaving their county for Bristol. The result was that the inhabitants of Bristol had once again petitioned the crown complaining of scarcity and pointing out this time that there was not enough grain growing within ten leagues of the city to feed its population. The king's letter claimed that the people of Gloucestershire who prevented the movement of corn to Bristol misunderstood the January 16 proclamation, but did not elaborate upon the nature of that misunderstanding. No doubt the king did not intend to cut off Bristol from its grain supply, but the proclamation had certainly provided legitimation or legal cover for the unnamed people of Gloucestershire to keep grain from moving out of their localities in a time of scarcity.

Despite the complications that surrounded Bristol's grain supply, the king remained committed to the substance of the proclamation of January 16, 1376. On April 8 of that year, the crown concluded that despite the proclamation the scarcity was unabated in the three counties because of continued embracery. As a result, a commission was set up to identify those who continued to ship grain out of Warwickshire, Worcestershire, and Gloucestershire and return their names to the Chancery.[109] Meanwhile one other possible way of meeting Bristol's needs was tried in 1377, encouraging the shipment of grain from Ireland to the city.[110]

One other response of Edward III's government to the grain supply problem of 1349–76, especially in London, was to encourage the shipment of grain from distant parts of the kingdom and Ireland. Galloway, in his discussion of London's grain supply, has noted a "disruption of one of the city's core supply routes, the middle Thames, in the 1350s and 1360s." Although the exact nature of that "disruption" is never made clear, Galloway does mention poor harvests as a possibility. To find

---

[107] *CCR, 1374–7*, p. 285; *Foedera*, vol. 3 pt. 2, p. 1047.
[108] TNA, C54/214 m. 23v; *CCR, 1374–7*, pp. 324–5.
[109] TNA, C66/294, m. 26v; *CPR, 1374–7*, pp. 319–20.   [110] *CCR 1374–7*, p. 491.

grain, London buyers were forced to seek supplies in areas "beyond the city's normal wheat supply radius." These areas included East Anglia, Lincolnshire, and north of the Humber.[111]

Galloway briefly discusses letters of protection and licenses for merchants shipping grain by sea to London from distant parts of England, as evidence for disruption of the city's normal grain supply zone in the 1350s and 60s.[112] Export prohibitions were normally extended to coastal shipments as a means to prevent fraudulent export overseas; licenses with sureties were required to ensure that such cargoes reached their domestic destinations. Such letters of protection and licenses provide useful indications of the places to which merchants turned to obtain grain in times of scarcity. On March 21, 1352, a protection was issued to ship an unspecified amount of grain and other victuals from north of the Humber to London.[113] Between October 20 and November 8, 1352, licenses or protections were issued to ship to London 3,000 quarters of wheat from Lincolnshire and Yorkshire, 1,000 quarters of grain from north of the Humber, and another 1,000 quarters from Newcastle.[114] Towards the end of the same year, on December 13, a further protection was issued to ship unspecified amounts of grain and victuals from north of the Humber also to supply London.[115]

Galloway also notes a few licenses that might indicate the shipping of foreign grain to England in the early 1350s, but he does not refer to a major source of the grain imported into England in this period, namely Ireland.[116] Between August 2, 1351 and May 17, 1353, the crown issued licenses to permit the export of 7,160 quarters of wheat and 3,400 quarters of other grains from Ireland mainly to England alone, but occasionally with an additional destination, usually Gascony. Also a license was issued in 1352 to ship 600 quarters of wheat and 200 of other grain from Ireland directly to Gascony for the use of the Earl of Warwick.[117]

The importance of Ireland as a source of grain for England in the early 1350s is revealed in a letter of March 18, 1354 that Edward III sent to the justiciar and other government officials in Ireland. The king instructed them not to interfere with the merchants of Ireland who had shipped grain to England and Gascony during the recent period of scarcity

---

[111] Galloway, "One Market or Many?" pp. 32–4. The quotes come from p. 33. See also *A Medieval Capital*, pp. 69–71.
[112] Galloway, "One Market or Many?" p. 33.   [113] *CPR, 1350–4*, p. 244.
[114] *CPR, 1350–4*, pp. 347, 353, 363.   [115] *CPR, 1350–4*, p. 375.
[116] Galloway, "One Market or Many," p. 33.
[117] *CPR, 1350–4*, pp. 126, 192, 196, 235, 242, 253–4, 305, 312, 320–1, 346, 356, 365, 415, 439.

contrary to his own proclamations that prohibited export from Ireland. The king had already pardoned these violations in consideration of the benefit that they had produced for his lands. It was, in his opinion, unreasonable to impose punishments in such a situation. The letter ended with the king granting his Irish subjects freedom to export grain and other victuals to England until he issued a future prohibition.[118] At least one pardon for an Irish merchant is enrolled on the patent rolls. John Bek of Dublin was pardoned on August 22, 1352 for shipping grain from Ireland to England and to Bordeaux and Bayonne on different occasions contrary to royal prohibitions. He was pardoned because his actions helped alleviate the scarcity in England and "succoured" its people. Nonetheless, Bek did have to pay 20s for his pardon.[119] In effect, during the early 1350s, Ireland was used as an emergency granary for England and Gascony in a time of poor harvests.

After the early 1350s the size of coastwise licensed shipments of grain to London from outside its usual range of supply varied widely. In some years nothing or a shipment of one or two cargoes of only a few hundred quarters of grain is recorded on the patent rolls, while in other years substantial amounts were licensed. Sometime before December 10, 1354, two merchants agreed to ship 1,000 quarters of grain from Holland Fen to London.[120] In early 1356, cargos totalling 2,400 quarters of grain were licensed for shipment from the Humber to London and, in early 1358, 1,000 quarters again from the Humber, 200 quarters from Northumberland and Yorkshire, and 400 quarters from Nottingham-shire. Also, on June 25, 1355 a merchant, William Kirketon, received a protection for one year to go around England buying grain for the supply of London, while in December 1356 two London cornmongers were licensed to buy unspecified amounts of grain in Leicestershire, Lincolnshire, and Yorkshire for supply of the city[121]

For three later years, some large licensed coastwise shipments of grain to London from outside its normal supply zone are recorded. In 1369–70, a year in which the average price of a quarter of wheat reached 11.85s, licenses were issued for the shipment by sea to London of

---

[118] *CPR, 1354–8*, p. 25.

[119] *CPR, 1350–4*, p. 313. There are no export licenses in Bek's favor enrolled on the patent rolls, further confirmation that the enrollment of licenses was inconsistent.

[120] *CPR, 1354–8*, p. 148.

[121] *CPR, 1354–8*, pp. 252, 338, 359; *CPR, 1358–61*, pp. 15, 23, 43. References to individual shipments of grain to London from Yarmouth, Norfolk, and Lincolnshire in 1350, the Humber and Newcastle in 1352, Boston, Lowestoft, and Lynn in 1356, and Yarmouth in 1358 can be found in Sharpe (ed.), *Calendar of the Letters from the Mayor*, pp. 9–10, 12–13, 29, 42, 75, 78, 95. See also Kermode, *Medieval Merchants*, p. 187.

560 quarters of grain from Sussex and 5,150 quarters of grain from an area stretching from Orwell on the Essex-Suffolk boundary north to Newcastle.[122] The following year, 1370–1, 1,500 quarters of grain were licensed for shipment to London from Yarmouth, Blakeney, and Yorkshire.[123] In addition, grain was imported from Prussia and Brittany.[124] Finally, in 1374–5, licenses were issued for the transport to London of 3,730 quarters of grain, virtually all from Suffolk and Norfolk except for one shipment that was to be bought between Maldon in Essex and Newcastle.[125] Later, on March 20, 1375, the king wrote to the mayor and bailiffs of Southampton ordering that the 900 quarters of wheat carried on a ship headed from Flanders to Valencia, which was forced to unload its cargo in Southampton because of damage incurred off the Isle of Wight, should be sold in England to help sustain the king's subjects in a time of high prices.[126]

The recorded licenses for shipments of grain to London from elsewhere in England during the harvest year 1374–5 were concentrated in the period February 4–May 16, 1375. It is certain that the recorded license during that harvest year do not tell the full story of the movement of grain to the city. On July 8, 1375 a commission of oyer and terminer was issued to hear the complaint of Walter Sibile, citizen and merchant of London, against twenty-three named suspects who had assaulted him at Yarmouth, took away 160 quarters of his wheat worth £100 (12.5s the quarter), chased him with drawn swords, and so threatened his servants that he was unable to continue his business.[127] While no further evidence about this incident has yet been discovered, it seems likely that Sibile was a regular shipper of grain from Yarmouth to London, although only one license for him, to ship 500 quarters of wheat from Yarmouth to London and dated March 14, 1375, is recorded on the patent rolls.[128] Much like the disturbance at Boston and Lynn in 1347 the events at Yarmouth were probably driven by fear of scarcity and high prices that would result from continued outward shipment of grain, on this occasion to London. The 12.5s a quarter valuation of Sibile's wheat indicates that prices at Yarmouth were already reaching dearth levels.

[122] *CPR, 1367–70*, pp. 339, 341–2, 362–4, 369, 391, 416.
[123] *CPR, 1370–4*, pp. 22, 48, 54. See also Kermode, *Medieval Merchants*, p. 185.
[124] *CPR, 1367–70*, pp. 337, 441.
[125] *CPR, 1374–7*, pp. 70, 81, 83–4, 90, 101; *CCR, 1374–7*, pp. 119, 126–7.
[126] *CCR, 1374–7*, pp. 125–6.
[127] TNA, C66/292, m. 2v; *CPR, 1374–7*, p. 160. Presumably this was the same Walter Sibile who was indicted for his role in aiding the rebels to enter London during the Great Revolt of 1381, but later acquitted. See Dobson (ed.), *The Peasants' Revolt*, pp. 212–13, 215–18, 223–35.
[128] *CPR, 1374–7*, p. 81.

After the early 1350s, Ireland's role as a supplier of grain to England appears to have been much reduced. There is only surviving evidence of the occasional cargo such as one shipment of 300 quarters of grain licensed on February 26, 1355 and another of 600 quarters on November 26, 1356.[129] For the 1370s there are records of five licenses for grain exports from Ireland; the biggest by far was issued on February 4, 1375 for 1,200 quarters of grain to supply the Prince of Wales' castles.[130]

Part of the reason for the limited movement of grain from Ireland to England in the later years of Edward III's reign may have been scarcity in Ireland. In March 1361, the king ordered the justiciar and chancellor of Ireland to proclaim a prohibition on the export of grain and other victuals without the king's special license. The stated reason was that Ireland was deprived of victuals (*victualibus destituator*), the result of attacks by the king's Irish enemies that laid waste to estates.[131] Later, in November 1368, a similar prohibition was imposed on the export of grain, other victuals, and horses from Ireland.[132] Although in 1376 there was strong royal encouragement for the export of grain from Ireland to England, the first time that had happened since the early 1350s, it was not until April 16, 1377, much too late in the day as a response to scarcity in England, that the king addressed the problem of the Irish export prohibition.[133] On that date Edward III wrote to his officials in Ireland instructing them not to trouble a number of English masters who had sailed their ships to Ireland to buy wheat and other grain to supply Bristol. According to the king's letter, when he ordered the prohibition on November 1, 1368, it was not his intention to prevent the shipment of grain from Ireland to England, which English merchants should be able to do at will.[134]

Military provisioning

During the years 1349–76 purveyance for military purposes continued, especially to supply Calais, Gascony, and, on at least one occasion, England's ally, Brittany. Aside for the large amount of grain demanded in 1351, purveyance in this period involved modest amounts compared to those raised during the wars of Edward I and Edward II and, in the main, probably had little impact on English grain markets.

---

[129] *CPR, 1354–8*, pp. 186, 476.
[130] *CPR, 1374–7*, pp. 70, 342, 393. See also *CPR, 1367–70*, p. 362, and *CPR, 1370–4*, p. 8.
[131] *CCR, 1360–4*, pp. 255–6; *Foedera*, vol. 3 pt. 2, pp. 610–11.
[132] *CCR, 1364–9*, p. 453.   [133] *CCR, 1374–7*, pp. 318, 383.   [134] *Ibid.*, p. 491.

Nonetheless, closely connected to purveyance was the crown's practice of either encouraging merchants to ship grain to its overseas possessions or directing them to bring grain to locations in England where the king was assembling military forces for embarkation overseas. On at least two different occasions, in 1359 and 1370, such practices probably disrupted, at least temporarily, normal grain marketing.

The biggest single purveyance demanded in the period 1349–76 was that of January 2, 1351 when commissions were issued to the sheriffs and other officials in 24 counties to purvey 8,200 quarters of wheat and 16,060 quarters of other grain to support forthcoming royal military campaigns against France in Calais, Gascony, and Brittany. The king eventually reduced the amount of grain and other victuals demanded because of a commons petition in the parliament of February 1351 that pointed out the disruption to the harvest caused by the plague.[135] Edward III issued new commissions covering 22 counties on February 23, 1351 for a revised total of 4,190 quarters of wheat and 7,610 quarters of other grain, still sizeable amounts in a year where the harvest was adversely affected by plague and low yields.[136] Beginning on March 20 and running through June 26, letters were directed to the relevant sheriffs ordering them to have the purveyed corn ground and then shipped overseas along with other victuals.[137]

The crown itself recognized the distorting effects that purveyance could have on grain marketing. Already on January 24, 1351, the king had ordered the mayor and sheriffs of London to proclaim that no one appointed to purvey corn and other victuals for royal use should take it from those who were bringing it to the city for sale. According to the proclamation, fear of the activities of purveyors had resulted in fewer sellers of victuals coming into London, thereby reducing available supplies.[138] This situation was of particular concern to the king because of an upcoming parliament at the palace of Westminster, the kind of occasion with its influx of attendees, officials, and the retinues of magnates

---

[135] CFR, 1347–55, pp. 273–7. In addition to grain, the commissions were ordered to purvey a total of 5,420 beef carcasses and 11,060 bacon pigs. See also Parl. Rolls, "Edward III: February 1351," item 11. The purveyance ordered on January 2, 1351 is roughly of the same order of magnitude as that authorized on March 22, 1333 for a forthcoming campaign in Scotland: 11,200 quarters of wheat; 21,100 quarters of other grain; 1,000 quarters of hay; 900 quarters of salt; 2,000 bacon pigs; 30 lasts of herring; and 6,000 stockfish. See CCR, 1333–7, pp. 25–6.

[136] CFR, 1347–55, pp. 288–91. The beef and bacon amounts were reduced to 2,580 and 4,060 respectively. For reasons that are unclear Kent and Warwickshire were left off the revised commissions.

[137] CPR, 1350–4, pp. 61; CCR, 1349–54, pp. 290–4, 299, 304.

[138] CCR, 1349–54, p. 278.

that sharply increased the need for food and fodder. Two months later, on March 8, when the grain supply of London remained a royal concern, the king ordered that 160 quarters of wheat and malt that John Took, mariner, had bought in Norfolk for the supply of London should be freed from arrest and allowed to come to the city without interference from purveyors. The order notes that the king had taken Took and his cargo into his special protection.[139]

After the English capture of Calais in 1347, the defence of the town and its environs against French attack was one of the crown's major military commitments. This meant the provision of grain and other victuals for a garrison of 1,100-1,200 men.[140] The accounts of the keeper of the victuals at Calais show that over the period 1347–61 the garrison received a total of 14,188 quarters of wheat and 14,650 quarters of other grains. Of that total, 13,138 quarters of wheat and 12,901 quarters of other grains came from purveyance in England.[141] The rest must have come from individual merchants who shipped grain and other victuals from England to Calais to sell, a practice that the crown encouraged.[142] On average per year during 1347–61, Calais was obtaining 1,013 quarters of wheat and 1,044 quarters of other grains, small enough totals that would have little effect on English domestic grain supplies. Later, there is further evidence of purveyance for Calais that might have driven up local prices. On February 2, 1371, the sheriffs and other prominent men from seven counties were commissioned to buy 3,500 quarters of wheat and 3,000 of malt to supply the town and the surrounding garrisons.[143] Among the seven counties, there were four that had been mentioned in the October 1370 proclamations as suffering high prices as a consequence of the activities of forestallers and regrators: Kent, Essex, Cambridgeshire, and Huntingdonshire.[144]

On a number of occasions export prohibitions were issued in order to ensure that grain would be directed to Calais or Gascony. One was proclaimed on April 14, 1355 prohibiting the export of grain without the king's license except to Calais with a second on January 28, 1356.[145] Neither proclamation provides a reason for its issue but there is other

---

[139] *CPR, 1350–4*, p. 55.   [140] Burley, "The Victualling of Calais," 50–1.
[141] *Ibid.*, 53. The garrison also received 3,168 beef carcases and bacon pigs, 2,814 of which were obtained through purveyance.
[142] *Foedera*, vol. 3, pt. 1, pp. 135, 149; *CCR, 1354–60*, p. 223.
[143] *CPR, 1370–4*, pp. 98–9.
[144] TNA, C54/208/m. 8v; *CCR, 1369–74*, pp. 193–4. The other counties where grain was purchased were Sussex, Norfolk, and Suffolk.
[145] *CCR, 1354–60*, pp. 190, 298. The calendar entry on the prohibition of April 14, 1355 on p. 190 notes that it was on the export of wheat but the full text in *Foedera*, vol. 3 pt. 1, p. 298 has the prohibition on *blada* (grain).

evidence that the crown was particularly concerned to sustain Calais and Gascony and support other military endeavors. On February 16, 1355 the king ordered one of his serjeants at arms to seize three ships in the port of Southampton to take victuals to supply the king's castles in Gascony, while two weeks later, on March 1, the sheriff of Hampshire was instructed to supervise the threshing of the wheat purveyed for supply of those castles and to arrange for its carriage to nearby ports for shipment.[146] Finally, on July 22, 1355, the king ordered the sheriffs of all counties and the mayor and bailiffs of twenty-seven ports, ranging along the east and south coasts from Newcastle in the north to Southampton in the south, to issue a proclamation urging merchants, who had grain, especially oats, to sell to take it to Calais where there was a great dearth.[147] During the same period Edward III was planning a naval enterprise to defend the south coast against French attack. In support of that endeavor, the sheriffs of Essex, Kent, Surrey, Sussex, Dorset, Devon, Somerset, and Gloucester were commanded, on July 12, 1355, to issue proclamations that everyone in their bailiwicks who had grain and other foodstuffs for sale should bring them to places on the coast where the king intended to make landfall in order to buy victuals "for the refreshment of himself and of the lieges in his company."[148]

The next export prohibition, that of February 28, 1357, was also clearly connected to military needs; it was a typical wartime proclamation that prohibited the export of grain, wine, ale, horses and weapons except to Bordeaux, Calais, and Berwick-on-Tweed on condition the merchants would find sureties that the mayor and bailiffs of the towns with which they traded would return letters within a month to certify that the goods had arrived there.[149] At the same time, supplementary instructions were sent to the mayors and bailiffs, or other officials, of twenty-two ports on the south and southwest coasts, ranging from Dover in the southeast to Bristol in the southwest and to the sheriffs of the six counties in which the ports were located. These instructions indicated that the king was sending soldiers to Normandy and Brittany on his service and wanted to ensure that the men departing for those destinations would be exempt from the prohibition on taking grain, horses, and weapons out of the country. Moreover, it was the king's will that merchants should be allowed to ship grain to Normandy and Brittany on the same terms as contained in the prohibition that allowed shipment to Calais, Bordeaux, and Berwick.[150]

---

[146] *CPR, 1354–8*, p. 178; *CCR, 1354–60*, p. 118.
[147] *CCR, 1354–60*, p. 223; *CLB*, vol. G, p. 42.   [148] *Ibid.*, p. 214.
[149] *Ibid.*, pp. 401–2.   [150] *Ibid.*, pp. 402–3.

Over two years later, on September 18, 1359, the king ordered the sheriff of Kent to issue a proclamation regulating food markets in that county so that the needs of a new military expedition would be met. The only fairs or markets selling victuals to be allowed in the county were at Sandwich where an army was assembling, it turns out for transport to Calais, and at Canterbury and Dover where many of the soldiers had gone searching for victuals. The king also ordered that all inn keepers along the road from London to Sandwich should have sufficient victuals on hand to sell at reasonable prices to the magnates and other of his lieges passing by.[151] About a month later, on October 14, the king ordered the sheriffs to issue a proclamation that merchants should bring victuals to Sandwich to supply his army.[152] These royal orders certainly had the potential to disrupt the normal operations of food markets in Kent.

Grain was only part of a larger list of goods whose export was prohibited in a proclamation of November 1369–70. It included gold, silver, bows, arrows, and other arms and armor and was in fact another example of the kind of wartime proclamation that the crown periodically issued in advance of a military campaign.[153] Over the course of March and April 1370 it appears that the crown's own subsequent military preparations seriously disrupted the marketing of grain in the south east of England. On March 22, 1370 the king ordered the sheriffs of Essex, Norfolk, Suffolk, Cambridgeshire, Huntingdonshire, and Hertfordshire, to issue a proclamation that had apparently unanticipated consequences. The king's order indicated that he planned to assemble his army and navy at the port of Orwell, a haven at the confluence of the Stour and Orwell rivers next to Harwich, and sail against the French by May 1.

To provision this enterprise, the king instructed the six sheriffs to proclaim that everyone within their counties, who had victuals for sale, should bring them to market towns within twelve leagues of Orwell, beginning no later than April 21. After that date, no one was to be allowed to sell victuals anywhere in the six counties except in the market towns close to Orwell. Anyone who violated this command was to be arrested and held until further orders from the king. The dealers in victuals were to remain in those market towns and continue to sell their provisions as long as the king was at Orwell.[154] One day after the March 22, 1370 proclamation, the king ordered the sheriff of Kent to issue a proclamation urging all of those in that county, who had grain or other victuals to sell, to obtain licenses from the Chancery to ship them

---

[151] *Ibid.*, p. 647; *Foedera*, vol. 3 pt. 1, p. 448.   [152] *CLB*, vol. G, pp. 111–12.
[153] *CCR, 1369–74*, pp. 114–16.   [154] *Ibid.*, p. 177; *Foedera*, vol. 3 pt. 2, p. 889.

to Calais.[155] It was later modified in one respect; the licenses were to be issued, on security, by the mayors or bailiffs of the main Kentish ports.[156]

Soon, however, problems arose with the royal plan. On April 23, 1370 the king was compelled to order the sheriff of Cambridgeshire to issue a new proclamation that it was lawful for those within the county, who had victuals, to sell them within the town of Cambridge. This order was issued in response to complaints from scholars at Cambridge University that the proclamation of March 22, which directed grain and other foodstuffs towards Orwell to support the king's military forces, had resulted in a scarcity of victuals in Cambridge and its environs. As a consequence, without remedial action, the scholars would have to leave the university and their studies.[157] By April 27 the king had completely abandoned his Orwell provisioning plan altogether. On that day he issued an order to the sheriffs of the six counties plus the sheriff of Kent that anyone in those counties who had victuals could lawfully bring them to London or any other market town to sell, notwithstanding the proclamation of March 22.[158] While the proclamation of April 27 does not offer any explanation for the crown backing away from its provisioning plan beyond the vague "particular causes laid before the king and council," there can be little doubt that it was driven by concerns over the disruption of food marketing in general, but with special concern for the supply of London.

The period 1349–76 was one of consistently high grain prices and low grain yields caused largely by bad weather but also intensified by plague, especially in the years 1349–52, which drastically reduced population and disrupted harvests. Recurrent outbreaks of plague in 1361–2, 1369, and 1375 meant further reduction in population numbers. Declining population had a number of different consequences for agriculture. It meant a decline in the demand for grain and the withdrawal of marginal land from grain production and an increase in stock raising. One result of the decline in demand was that prices in 1349–51, times of catastrophic harvest failures, rose much less than they would have if they had occurred in the pre-plague years when the population was much larger. At the same time, high mortality meant that labor was scarce and increasingly expensive, hence the attempts by landlords to reduce their labor costs, which meant sowing seed thinner and reducing labor intensive work such as manure spreading and weeding. The consequence was declining grain yields per acre and high prices.

---

[155] *CCR, 1369–74*, p. 177.   [156] *Ibid.*, p. 188.   [157] *Ibid.*, pp. 179–80.
[158] *Ibid.*, pp. 180–1.

The government of Edward III responded actively to the problems associated with this long period of high grain prices. It relied to a considerable extent on traditional measures such as prohibitions on export of grain, enforcement of the assize of weights and measures and of laws against forestallers and other offenders against market regulations. Although, it should be pointed out that when the king enforced the new 1351 statute of forestallers in 1370 he ordered the seizure of grain that forestallers had bought from stacks and granges before it went to market with the aim of driving up market prices. Such grain was to be seized and sold in public markets. In addition, the crown attempted, on a number of occasions, to respond to high prices and made considerable efforts to help meet the grain needs of urban areas like London and Bristol.

While the crown did continue to purvey grain for military purposes throughout the period, it appears that the only purveyance substantial enough to have any effect on local grain markets was that demanded in 1351. It is also important to remember that in response to parliamentary opposition to that purveyance, the king cut his demands in half. The crown's other military supply strategy of directing merchant to bring grain and other victuals to areas where he was mustering an army to embark overseas probably had negative effects on local food markets, nonetheless it is again worth remembering that when the provisioning scheme to direct grain and other victuals to Orwell in 1370 had unanticipated effects on normal marketing, it was dropped.

Overall the government of Edward III was active and engaged with issues of grain prices, supplies, and marketing throughout the period 1349–76. The crown took its responsibilities seriously and attempted to fulfill its obligation to meet the basic subsistence needs of its subjects. Finally those responsibilities were expressed in a language of obligation for the common good that, if not new, became increasingly frequent in Edward III's reign and those of his successors.

5   Scarcity and food riots 1377–1439

From 1376 through 1399, grain yields rose and prices fell, largely the result of improved weather.[1] The only notable exception was the deficient harvest of 1390–1 when the average price of a quarter of wheat was 8.75s, while a quarter of barley was 6.17s[2] As a result of the return of a cycle of wetter and colder weather, deficient harvests returned in 1400–3, 1408–10, and 1416–17. These deficient years culminated in the poor harvest of 1428–9 and finally in the famine of 1437–9, the result of two poor harvests in a row, "the worst of the fifteenth century" and "the most disastrous since 1349–51."[3] One consequence of the poor harvests and the resultant high prices and scarcity of bread grains during the first four decades of the fifteenth century was riot and other disorders.

   The main crown responses to scarcity remained the traditional ones of export prohibitions, accompanied in especially hard years with the encouragement of imports from foreign countries, plus attempts to invigorate the enforcement of such measures as the statute against forestallers and the assize of weights and measures. The governments of Richard II and Henry VI, following the precedent of Edward III in 1370, created commissions with powers to inquire into the activities of forestallers, regrators, and engrossers, seize their surplus stocks of grain, and sell them in the market to drive down prices. Moreover, official documents that the crown issued in response to scarcity during the reigns of Richard II through Henry VI continued to refer to the *commune profit* or *rei publice* as justifying its responses to scarcity. There was, however, one change in the language in some official documents of Henry VI's. They had a moral tone far more intense than that of his predecessors, especially in the areas of the crown's obligations to the hungry and the wickedness of those who hoarded or forestalled grain. There was one other innovation that began in 1390–1 and reappeared in the reign of

---

[1] Campbell, "Grain Yields," pp. 149–50.
[2] Munro, "Revisions of the Commodity Price Series."
[3] Campbell, "Four Famines and a Pestilence," p. 30; Campbell, "Grain Yields" pp. 152–5.

Henry VI, namely the government of the city of London began to buy grain on the European continent to sell in the city's markets in order to moderate prices. It is also worth noting that while the crown continued the policies of Edward III to ensure provisioning of Calais and Gascony, along with other military requirements, there appears to be no evidence that the crown's needs were so great that they had negative effect on local markets.

Grain supply and market regulation in the reign of Richard II

It is no doubt true, as documented by Dyer and other scholars, that over the long haul after 1376 peasants, artisans, and even laborers became less dependent on bread and pottage for their caloric intake and had a more varied diet, which included meat, fish, cheese, and other dairy products. Given the drastic decline in population, more land became available for raising cattle and sheep as the demand for grain decreased. At the same time, the growth in industries such as cloth making provided new opportunities for labor. Shortage of labor for agriculture and for various trades and industries, a consequence of the population decline following the repeated recurrence of plague after 1349, meant rising real wages for laborers of all kinds, despite government attempts to set fixed wage rates through parliamentary legislation.[4] Nonetheless, the continued significance of bread grains in the diet of a substantial proportion of the population is reflected not only in the behavior of some of the participants the Great Revolt of 1381, but also in the actions and pronouncements of government and in the recurrence of food riots up though the famine of 1437–9.

At Saint Albans Abbey, a few days after the opening of the Great Revolt on Corpus Christi day (June 13) 1381, a crowd of peasants entered the abbey's parlor and removed the millstone paving from the courtyard floor, broke up the stones, and passed out pieces to those present.[5] This act was the culmination of a long struggle, since at least 1274, between the abbey's tenants and the abbots over grain milling and other matters. At an earlier point in the struggle, Richard of Wallingford, abbot in the years 1328–36, had successfully compelled the tenants to give up their hand mills, which he used to pave the abbey's parlor, and

---

[4] Dyer, "English Diet," pp. 191–216; Dyer, "Changes in Diet," pp. 77–99; Campbell, "The Land," pp. 215–22; Kowaleski, "A Consumer Economy," pp. 238–59.
[5] Taylor, Childs and Watkiss (eds.), *The St. Albans Chronicle*, vol. 1, pp. 456–9.

forced them to bring their grain to the abbey's mill, which meant they would have to pay multure (a percentage of the grain) for using that mill.[6]

A number of scholars have commented on the symbolic significance of the tenants' actions.[7] The breaking of the stones and the sharing of the pieces among the actors was a re-enactment of the ceremony of the holy loaf, bread that the priest blessed and then distributed in pieces every Sunday to the congregation.[8] Although not the same as the consecrated host that the laity received once a year at the end of mass, the holy loaf ceremony clearly had Eucharistic resonance. Certainly, an event such as that at St. Albans a few days after Corpus Christi day, which celebrated the Eucharist, makes such resonance even more likely. Moreover, the actions of the tenants in sharing the pieces of stone can be regarded not only as an expression of their communal solidarity against injustice but also as a judgment against a landlord who was depriving them of some of their hard earned daily bread. Finally, Margaret Aston has documented the large number of medieval allegorical or metaphorical connections "of Christ with grain, milling, grinding, flour and bread, related specially to Corpus Christi." Much of that linkage was spiritual, that is "Christ as spiritual food, ground and milled for the salvation of mankind."[9] Yet the choice of metaphors surely reflects the vital importance of bread for the sustenance of life in medieval England.

There are two other indicators from the reign of Richard II of the continued significance of bread. One is the repeated official efforts to produce farthings and half pennies so that the poor could pay for their food. The other is a continuing concern with weights and measures. In the parliament of April 1379, the commons petitioned the king that the poorer commons did not have small coins to pay for bread and ale and requested that he "order half pennies and farthings to pay for the small measures and other small items of merchandise, for God and by way of charity." The king replied that as soon as he had bullion, he would do it "for the general benefit of the kingdom" (*pur commune profit*).[10]

The commons submitted a similar petition in the parliament of November 1380 to which the king answered that he would see that half pennies and farthings were issued.[11] Meanwhile in London, sometime in

---

[6] Faith, "The Class Struggle in Fourteenth Century England," pp. 53–9; Faith, "The 'Great Rumour' of 1377," pp. 63–8.

[7] Duffy, "Religious Belief," pp. 333–5: Justice, *Writing and Rebellion*, pp. 156–60; Justice, "Religious Dissent, Social Revolt and 'Ideology'," pp. 210–13.

[8] Rosser, "Going to the Fraternity Feast," 433–4.

[9] Aston, "Corpus Christi and Corpus Regni," 26–32. The quotes come from 28 and 29.

[10] *Parl. Rolls*, "Richard II: April 1379," item 44.

[11] *Parl. Rolls*, "Richard II: November 1380," item 32.

1382, the mayor and aldermen issued an ordinance that bakers should produce farthing loaves and brewers should sell ale by the farthing measure in order to help the poor. In addition, the mayor and aldermen authorized the making of farthing measures for the brewers and arranged for £80 sterling to be made into half pennies and farthings at the Tower to distribute to the brewers and bakers so they would not "fail to give change for a half penny."[12] Finally, at the January parliament of 1394, the commons submitted yet another petition claiming that farthings and half pennies were once again scarce. In response, the king agreed to order the making of more. This commons petition pointed out the importance of small coins for the poor. "When a poor man buys his victuals and other goods necessary to him and has nothing but a penny, which he wishes to change for a half penny, he often loses his penny through lack of a half penny. And also, although many worthy people of the community in their devotions wish to give alms to poor mendicants, they abstain from giving alms because of the scarcity of half pennies and farthings, to the great reduction in the sustenance of poor mendicants."[13]

Another continuing concern of Richard II's parliaments was weights and measures. In fact, the first weights and measure raised in Richard's reign, in the parliament of January 1390, had already been raised in Edward III's parliament of April 1376 when two petitions were submitted to the king, one by the commons the other by the citizens of Rochester, with similar complaints against the clerk of the market.[14] According to the commons' petition, the clerk's role in the past had been to ensure that proper weights and measures were used within the verge of the royal household and to fine those who used false measures, but now he was imposing fines for false measures, not just on guilty individuals but on whole communities both inside and outside the verge. The commons remedy, which the king accepted, was that the weights and measure statute of 1361 should be strictly enforced and the clerk of the market should confine his activities to the verge and only impose fines on guilty individuals, not on whole communities.

In the parliament of January 1390, the commons once again petitioned the king with complaints about the clerk of the market inflicting communal fines for false weights and measures "with no remedy provided to help the common people." Instead of such fines, the commons requested that the false weights and measures should be destroyed and the guilty "such as inn-keepers, taverners, bakers, brewers, tapsters, and others

---

[12] *CLB*, vol. H, p. 183.   [13] *Parl. Rolls*, "Richard II: January 1394," item 38.
[14] *Parl. Rolls*, "Edward III: April 1376," items 87 and 152; Given-Wilson, *The Royal Household*, p. 50.

who sell by measure or weight be corporally punished," twelve days in prison for the first offence, twenty four days in prison for the second, and one hour a day in the pillory in the market place for three market days, followed by prison at the king's will for the third. Finally, the commons proposed that if the clerk of the market or his deputies contravened the proposed legislation then they should be subject to a fine of £20 and loss of their offices.[15] The king's answer, enshrined in the statute, agreed that the false measures should be burned and that the clerk of the market should not inflict communal fines but it said nothing about the punishment of those guilty of using false measures. The king also agreed to fines for offences by the clerk but on a sliding scale of £5 for the first, £10 for the second, and £20 for the third.[16]

The commons returned to the issue of the clerk of the market and weights and measures in the parliament of January 1393, when they petitioned that, while past statutes insisted there should be one standard of weights throughout the realm established by the Exchequer, in fact there were two standards. One was the Exchequer pound and the other was the Marshalsea pound of the king's household, "which weighs two shillings six pence more." The clerk of the market used the Marshalsea pound when he assayed the weights across England. When the clerk discovered weights that did not agree with the Marshalsea pound they were destroyed or seized and those who used them were fined "to the great deceit and destruction of the common people."[17] The king agreed with the commons that the Exchequer standard of weight and measures should be the only one used in the kingdom. In the actual statute it was also specified that all the weights and measures used by the clerk of the market, when assaying weights and measures anywhere in the kingdom, should be marked with the sign of the Exchequer.[18]

The other weight and measure of concern to Richard II's parliaments was the size of a quarter of grain. The commons in the parliament of November 1390 petitioned the king that "it had been ordained and established by statute" the standard quarter of grain in England was "eight bushels levelled and not heaped." Nonetheless, brewers in many towns bought malt in nine bushel quarters "to the very great wrong and injury" of the whole community of the realm. The commons requested that the king issue a proclamation upholding the statutes on weights and measure, a request that the king accepted.[19] In the following parliament,

---

[15] *Parl. Rolls*, "Richard II: January 1390," item 35.
[16] *SR*, vol. 2, p. 62, 13 Ric. II, stat. 1, c. 4.
[17] *Parl. Rolls*, "Richard II: January 1393," item 25.   [18] *SR*, vol. 2, p. 83, 16 Ric. II, c. 3.
[19] *Parl. Rolls*, "Richard II: November 1390," item 28.

of November 1391, the commons requested, "for the common profit of the king and kingdom" (*pur commune profit de roi et de roialme*) that penalties be imposed on those who used false measures, otherwise they would continue that practice "to the great injury and oppression of all the common people."[20] As a consequence, the king agreed to a statute that those who bought grain in nine bushel quarters would be liable to forfeit it to him.[21]

Later, in the parliament of January 1394, the commons faced an unanticipated problem raised by the prohibition of the nine bushel quarter. According to their petition, "since time immemorial" those who brought malt to London sold it by the nine bushel quarter "because when malt is transported, nine bushels scarcely make eight bushels washed and clean in pure malt." Now sellers from Huntingdonshire, Cambridgeshire, Hertfordshire, Northamptonshire, and Bedfordshire "for their singular profit" (*pur lour singuler profit*) only sell malt by the eight bushel quarter unwashed and uncleaned, which means buyers get "a mere seven bushels or less of pure clean malt per quarter, to the very great wrong and injury of all." The commons requested "for the common profit, and as right and reason demand" (*pur commune profit et come droit et reson demandent*) that malt should be sold either in nine bushel quarters uncleaned or eight bushels quarters cleaned.[22] In the end, the statute that the king approved stated that malt should be sold in eight bushel quarters "well and sufficiently sifted, cleansed, and purified." The statute also gave to the magistrates of towns "where such malt shall be sold" authority, on the complaint of any buyer, to "see the said malt and if default be found thereof to make due redress."[23]

During his reign, Richard II, like his predecessors, issued a number of proclamations regulating the grain trade. Twice, in 1378 and again in 1394, the king proclaimed that his subjects were free to export grain without license to any place not in his enmity. The king's action in 1394 took the form of a statute in response to a parliamentary petition, although in his answer to the petition he reserved the right to impose restrictions on the trade when necessary.[24] One regular restriction of long standing was prohibitions on export of grain and other goods to the king's enemies in Scotland issued in 1383, 1385, and 1386 (twice).[25]

---

[20] *Parl. Rolls*, "Richard II: November 1391," item 31.
[21] *SR*, vol. 2, p. 79, 15 Ric. II c. 4.   [22] *Parl. Rolls*, "Richard II: January 1394," item 53.
[23] *SR*, vol. 2, p. 88, 17 Ric. II c. 4. See also *CCR, 1392–6*, p. 282 and *CLB*, vol. H, p. 411.
[24] *CCR, 1377–81*, p. 207; *Parl. Rolls*, "Richard II: January 1394," item 39; *SR*, vol. 2, pp. 88–9, 17 Ric. II c. 7.
[25] *CCR, 1381–5*, p. 601; *CCR, 1385–9*, pp. 136, 289, 619; *Parl. Rolls*, "Richard II: October 1383," item 60 and "Richard II: October 1386," item 27; *SR*, vol. 2, p. 35, 7 Ric. II c. 16.

The crown still had possessions in France and campaigns to fight, which called for supplies of grain and other victual. Consequently, royal policy on the grain trade included directing merchants to supply overseas possessions and armies. In the parliament of October 1382, the commons petitioned the king for a prohibition on export, except properly licensed shipments to Calais, Bordeaux, and Berwick, because so much grain was being exported that there was a threat of scarcity and dearth. The king agreed to the petition except that Bordeaux was replaced with Gascony along with Cherbourg and Brest also held by the English, which were added to the list of places exempted from the prohibition.[26] On October 2, 1389, the crown issued another proclamation, this time a general prohibition on grain export without the king's license. The stated reason was that heavy rains during the summer had reduced the grain crop and rising prices were feared unless export was prohibited.[27] This proclamation was followed ten days later with a mandate to John de Beaumond, lord of Barton upon Humber, that repeated the dire prediction about rising prices of grain following the wet summer and ordered him not to allow any of his tenants or other people of the town to sell grain or other victuals to "aliens or strangers" nor to allow the export of any grain from the town without the king's license. The king threatened that anyone who disobeyed his command would be punished in such a way that it would be "an example and a terror to others who rebel against his commands."[28]

Over the next two months, despite such threats and dire predictions, the king directed officials in sixteen major ports and the sheriffs nationwide to allow merchants to export grain and other victuals to Calais, Bordeaux, Bayonne, Brest, and Cherbourg after they had given sureties that they would only ship to the permitted destinations, "any proclamations or commands to the contrary not withstanding."[29] When the king was in Calais in 1396 he ordered the mayor and sheriffs of London, the sheriff of Kent, and the mayor and bailiffs of eleven south and south eastern ports to proclaim that victuallers should come to Calais with wheat, oats, hay, bread, ale, and other victuals for the supply of the king's household and his other lieges. Such suppliers would be exempt from paying customs but required to give sureties that they would ship only to Calais.[30]

Finally, there were proclamations directing grain to specific destinations in England and Ireland for military or other purposes. On July 16,

---

[26] *Parl. Rolls*, "Richard II: October 1382," item 54; *CCR, 1381–5*, p. 236.
[27] *CCR, 1389–92*, p. 80.   [28] *Ibid.*, p. 24.   [29] *Ibid.*, pp. 30, 99.
[30] *CCR, 1396–9*, p. 59.

1385 the king, on his way north with an army to invade Scotland, ordered the bishop of Durham and the sheriffs of Yorkshire, Northumberland, Cumberland, and Westmorland to issue a proclamation for all victuallers to "follow the king and his army with all victuals needful for maintenance of man and horse and to sell them to the army at a reasonable price for ready payment." The proclamation also instructed the inhabitants of the towns through which the army would march to "bake and brew" and sell victuals to the army. Finally, the holding of markets other than in those towns was forbidden for the duration of the campaign.[31] On September 26, 1394, and again on February 20, 1395, while Richard II was campaigning in Ireland, he instructed the sheriffs of a number of counties in the west and southwest of England to proclaim that all who had grain, wine, and other victuals to sell should bring them to Ireland to sustain the king and his army. "Prompt payment" was guaranteed.[32]

On April 30, 1392, just before a meeting of the king's council at Stamford to discuss a possible peace treaty with France, Richard II ordered the sheriffs of Lincolnshire and Northamptonshire to proclaim that all who had grain, wine, and other victuals to sell should bring them to Stamford to sell "for the sustenance of the king and of a great number of lords, princes, great men and gentlemen" who had been summoned to the council meeting.[33] Later on August 27, 1397, in anticipation of a parliament and the arrival of many "lords, great men and others daily," Richard II issued a similar order to the sheriffs of London and fifteen counties close to London to proclaim that victuallers and others should bring foodstuffs of all kinds to sell in the city's markets and that purveyors buying victuals for households of the great should "should make ready payment" for everything they buy. All purveyors who violated "this ordinance made for the commonweal" (*pro commodo rei publice*) would be imprisoned and fined "at the king's will." If a seller believed himself to be wronged by the activities of any purveyor buying for the king's household, "he shall sue with the king and council and have his remedy."[34] Finally, on March 14, 1398, while the king was at Bristol, he directed a similar order to the sheriff of Bristol and the sheriffs and bailiffs of three counties and five towns in the vicinity to proclaim that all with grain and victuals should come to the city to sell for

---

[31] *CCR, 1385–9*, p. 5. See also *CPR, 1381–5*, p. 573.
[32] *CCR, 1392–6*, pp. 364, 405–6. The sheriffs of the same six counties were to issue both proclamations. Lancashire, Cheshire, Somerset, Cornwall, Devon, Dorset, and Bristol were added to the second.
[33] *CCR, 1389–92*, pp. 562–3.
[34] *CCR, 1396–9*, p. 211. The Latin comes from the full text printed in *Rotuli Parliamentorum*, vol. 3, p. 410. See also *CLB*, vol. H, p. 438.

the consumption of the king, his household, and others arriving there. "Ready payment" was again promised but potential forestallers were warned not to buy any grain or victuals before they arrived at the Bristol market.[35]

The prohibitions on export of grain issued in October 1382 and 1389, in response to fear of scarcity and rising prices, were the only ones issued for that explicit reason in the reign of Richard II but the feared scarcities did not appear to materialize. It may be that the readiness of Richard II's government to relax the export prohibition of October 1389 over the following two months, in order to encourage the supply of the crown's French possessions, reflected a growing belief that the threat of scarcity had either disappeared completely or was much diminished. The only real scarcity during Richard II's reign was in the harvest year 1390–1.

Although the scarcity of 1390–1 did not produce a new export prohibition it appears that the prohibition of October 1389, with its emphasis on the need for grain exports and domestic coastal shipments to be properly licensed, continued in effect. Few shipments overseas were actually licensed. The only recorded licensed exports on the patent and close rolls for the harvest year 1390–1 are 1,000 tuns of wheat for Genoa and Pisa, 120 quarters of grain and other victuals to supply Oye castle in Picardy, 120 quarters of grain and other victuals for Calais and Guyenne castle in Gascony, and another shipment of unspecified victuals for Guyenne.[36] In contrast, during that scarcity year licenses were issued for coastal shipments of 7,400 quarters of grain of all kinds to London. Of that total 5,100 quarters were to be bought in Lincolnshire and Yorkshire, 100 quarters in Hampshire, and the rest in unspecified locations.[37] In addition, licenses for shipment of 2,000 quarters of grain from Ireland to London were issued.[38] Such grain shipments to London clearly reflected the city's food needs, which became more obvious as the scarcity year unfolded.

The first recorded indication of scarcity is a mandate dated January 31, 1391 from the king to the sheriffs of London ordering a proclamation that all merchants, whether native or alien, could bring grain and other victuals to the city for sale without paying "any custom or subsidy," because of the great scarcity and rising prices of foodstuffs. This action was for "the commonweal and relief of the people" (*pro republice et relevatio populi*).[39] That same day royal mandates, with substantially the

[35] *CCR, 1396–9*, p. 290.   [36] *CCR, 1389–92*, pp. 226, 234, 252, 322.
[37] *Ibid.*, pp. 239, 306, 308, 311, 374–5, 385–6, 406.
[38] *Ibid.*, pp. 398, 476; *CCR, 1392–6*, p. 17.
[39] TNA, C54/232, m. 10v; *CCR, 1389–92*, p. 348.

same terms, were sent to the customers and subsidy collectors in the ports of London, Southampton, Newcastle upon Tyne, Boston, Lynn, and Great Yarmouth.[40] Between February and May 1391 similar mandates were sent to officials in Bristol, Exeter, Hull, and Colchester as well as the sheriff of Devon.[41] In addition to suspending custom duties on food imports, Richard II on February 4, 1391 ordered the suspension of the collection of duties on grain and other victuals being carried on the road between Oxford and Woodstock until Michaelmas, in effect after the next harvest. The king had granted the right to collect such duties for five years on November 6, 1390 in order to pay for the repair of the road but it was now withdrawn in order to make provision *pro republice et relevatio populi*.[42]

While the king was removing custom duties on the import of foodstuffs, the mayor and aldermen of London took the unprecedented step of buying grain for the supply of the city, a step that would recur during later scarcities up through the late sixteenth century. On February 8, 1391, Richard Odyham, city chamberlain, with the agreement of the alderman, gave £400 from the orphans' fund to mayor Adam Bamme, goldsmith, to buy grain from overseas.[43] A few days later Bamme entered into a recognizance that he would repay the fund by the following Michaelmas, no doubt out of the proceeds from the sale of the grain in the city.[44] Knighton's chronicle reports that, in addition to Bamme's efforts, twenty-four aldermen of London "each contributed £20 to make similar purchases for fear of a famine in the city." The purchased grain was stored in various places and made available to the poor "at a fixed price enough to sustain their families." Those who did not have the money to buy the grain "could pledge to pay within the following year, and thus they were relieved, and no one perished of hunger."[45] One unintended consequence of this London purchase of grain was that Hanse merchants, who were encouraged by the king's proclamation and bought grain in Prussia to sell duty free in London, had no sale for

---

[40] *CCR, 1389–92*, p. 237.   [41] *Ibid.*, pp. 239, 255, 265.
[42] TNA, C54/232, m. 16v; *CCR, 1389–92*, pp. 332–3; see also p. 239, another mandate, dated February 4, 1391, that encouraged native and alien merchants to bring grain and other victuals to Oxford customs free because prices were increasing daily.
[43] Thomas (ed.), *Calendar of Select Pleas and Memoranda*, vol. 3, pp. 174–5. Although this source and the one in note 44 below do not mention where Bamme intended to buy the grain, Taylor, Childs, and Watkiss (eds.), *The St. Albans Chronicle*, vol. 1, p. 915 mentions that it was overseas as does the later Stow, *Survey of London*, vol. 1, p. 108 and vol. 2, p. 169.
[44] *CLB*, vol. H, pp. 360–1.
[45] Martin(ed.), *Knighton's Chronicle*, pp. 538–9. See also Hector and Harvey (eds.), *The Westminster Chronicle*, p. 475.

their cargoes because the mayor of the city proclaimed that the stored grain had preference in the market. As a result, two Hanse merchants were allowed to take their cargo of 300 quarters of wheat to Bordeaux or Bayonne in Gascony to sell and two others their cargo of 300 quarters of rye to Dordrecht in Holland. One other cargo of barley brought to great Yarmouth by three Hanse merchants, who did pay customs, rotted before it could be sold.[46]

Another significant response of Richard II's government to the scarcity of 1390–1 was the enforcement of the statute of forestallers, which was first passed by Edward III's parliament of February 1351 and then renewed by Richard II's parliament of October 1378. The copy of the renewal contained in the *Statutes of the Realm* indicates that it was intended "for the common profit of the realm." (*pur commune profit roialme*).[47] On February 3, 1391, at the point when the crown had become aware of the existence of scarcity, Richard II directed a mandate to the mayor and bailiffs of the city of Winchester ordering them to conduct a search for grain and malt in the houses of all suspected forestallers and regrators and to distribute what they had found to the inhabitants for reasonable prices payable to the owners.[48] Then, on April 20 of that year, a commission was established to enquire by a jury of good and lawful men into forestalling and regrating in Tamworth in Staffordshire and Warwickshire, which had resulted in high prices for grain and other victuals. The commissioners were to search "houses and granaries" for such grain and victuals, put them up for sale in the principal markets in the town and "punish offenders according to the statutes."[49] While the mandate of February 3, did not mention the forfeit of the forestalled grain and seemed to imply that the proceeds of the sale would go to the forestallers, the implication of the commission of April 2 is that the forestallers would forfeit the grain in accord with statute. Although these actions were modest in their geographical range, they did represent a revival of Edward III's effort against forestallers in 1370. Also, like Edward III's actions in 1370 Richard II's appear to have conflated forestalling and regrating.

Grain scarcity and disorder 1400–1439

Some of the grain related disorders and market disruptions of 1400–1 are reminiscent of similar problems along the Severn during the reign of

---

[46] *CCR, 1389–92*, pp. 388, 390–1, 403; see also Lloyd, *England and the Hanse*, pp. 81–2.
[47] *SR*, vol. 2, p. 8, 2 Ric. II, stat. I, c. 2. See also *Parl. Rolls*, "Richard II: October 1378," item 75.
[48] TNA, C54/232, m. 16; *CCR, 1389–92*, pp. 250.
[49] TNA, C66/332, m. 15v; *CPR, 1388–92*, p. 441.

Edward III. On March 18, 1400, Henry IV sent a mandate to the bailiffs of Gloucester to cease arresting, "with a strong hand," boats carrying grain down river and to allow them to pass freely to supply ships at Bristol that had been requisitioned for the king's navy. The king complained that the "mayor and commonalty" of Gloucester had put the seized grain up for sale, doubtless because of rising prices in the local market.[50]

A year later, a commission of oyer and terminer was issued to Thomas Berkeley and others to inquire into complaints from Shropshire, Staffordshire, and Herefordshire that the bailiffs of the towns Gloucester and Worcester had been levying illegal tolls on grain and other victuals moving down the Severn. At the same time, according to the commission, the inhabitants of the forest of Dean had compelled those who carried grain and other victuals down river to sell them "against their will." Another charge was that some inhabitants of Worcester and Tewkesbury had regrated grain and prevented it coming to market in Gloucester.[51]

On August 22, 1401, a further commission of oyer and terminer was issued to Sir Hugh Burnell and others to inquire into disruptions of the trade in grain and other victuals along the roads in the west midlands between Birmingham, Alcester, and Stratford and between Birmingham and the markets of Coleshill, Walsall, and Dudley. According to the commission, the disruption was caused by men who lay in ambush along the roads "with gladmeres and other instruments," assaulted corn mongers and cut grain sacks carried by horses, causing the animals to bolt and throw off their riders, including women and children, some of whom were injured, sometimes fatally. To hide their identities the attackers wore masks and clothing like torturers.[52]

In further confirmation of scarcity, on March 31, 1402, the mayor of London wrote to the aldermen urging them to persuade the people of their wards "to lay in a store of corn" in anticipation of coming shortage.[53] Although no royal proclamations imposing prohibitions on the export of grain seem to have been issued in 1400–2, there is little evidence of actual export taking place.[54] One other piece of evidence that may provide further confirmation of the severity of the scarcity is the

---

[50] TNA, C54/246, m. 16; *CCR, 1399–1402*, pp. 146–7.

[51] TNA, C66/364, m. 31v; *CPR, 1399–1401*, p. 516; see also *CCR, 1399–1402*, p. 374. The tolls on the Severn were also a matter of complaint from the commons in the parliaments of January 1401 and November 1411, see *Parl. Rolls*, "Henry IV: January 1401," item 100 and "Henry IV: November 1411," item, 41.

[52] TNA, C66/365, m. 14v; *CPR, 1399–1401*, p. 552.   [53] *CLB*, vol. I, p. 17.

[54] No export licenses for these years are recorded on the Patent Rolls. Smit (ed.), *Bronnen tot de Geschiedenis*, vol. 1, p. 555 records of two shipments of oats totaling 400 quarters from Lynn to Holland and Zeeland.

return of the issue of the lack of half pennies and farthings previously raised in three parliaments of Richard II's reign. In the parliament of September 1402, the commons petitioned the king that the scarcity of small coins was a "great hardship among the poor people," who had to resort to small foreign coins, "such as Scottish half pennies" to meet their needs. The king's answer was that a third of all silver coins brought in for recoining would be made into half pennies and farthings.[55]

The next outbreak of grain related protest took place at Lynn in Norfolk in October, 1405, when the town bell was rung to draw a crowd together, which then marched through the town, accompanied by banner and trumpet, and insisted that a ship loaded with grain for Bordeaux should be unloaded and the cargo sold to the crowd for 5d the bushel (3s 4d the quarter). The mayor of the town offered the grain to the crowd at 6d the bushel (4s the quarter), the likely asking price at Bordeaux. The protestors refused, demanded the right to choose a new town government, and announced that anyone bringing orders from the king that the ship should be allowed to sail on its way would be assaulted.[56] To deal with the disorder, the crown appointed a commission to inquire into "insurrections, felonies and trespasses" in Lynn, which included as a member John Cockayn, a recently appointed justice of the common bench.[57] When the commission met, nine men were identified as participants in the disorder, three goldsmiths and one each of the following trades, skinner, smith, carpenter, tailor, fuller, and patternmaker. Although orders were issued for their attachment, in the end they were all pardoned.[58]

This crowd action at Lynn in 1405 reminds us of the earlier food riot there in 1347 although the context is quite different. In 1347 grain prices were much higher, large quantities were being shipped to Gascony and scarcity was a real possibility. In 1405 grain prices were low, shipments to Gascony were much fewer, and scarcity did not threaten. The demand for the right to choose a new government for Lynn probably connects the protest with the long, complex four cornered power struggle in the town between the Bishop of Norwich who was its lord,

---

[55] *Parl. Rolls*, "Henry IV: September 1402," item 46; *SR*, vo. 2, p. 136, 4 Hen. IV c. 10. The problem of lack of half pennies and farthings that would enable the poor to buy victuals and other goods in small quantities they could afford was addressed in another commons' petition in the parliament of 1445, *Parl. Rolls*, Henry VI: February 1445," item 36 and Bolton, *Money in the Medieval English Economy*, pp. 239–40.

[56] TNA, KB27/580 Rex Eas. 7 Hen. IV, m. 5; Walker, "Rumour, Sedition and Popular Protest," 56–7.

[57] *CPR, 1405–8*, p. 152. Cockayn's appointment is on p. 11.

[58] TNA, KB27/580 Rex Eas. 7 Hen. IV, m. 5; KB 27/582 Rex Mich. 8 Hen. IV, m. 10.

the *potentiores* who held power in the town and the *mediocres* and *inferiores* who aspired for a share of that power.[59]

The final scarcity period in the reign of Henry IV occurred in the harvest years, 1408–9 and 1409–10. The first indication of difficulty dates from late 1408 when, on November 26, the king ordered the mayor of Lynn and the customers of the port "for particular causes which concern the common weal of the realm" that no one should be allowed to ship grain of any kind overseas without the king's special license.[60] This mandate was followed a month later, on December 17, with the issue of a license to William Sevenoke, a merchant of London to buy 1,000 quarters of wheat in Yorkshire and elsewhere in the kingdom to supply London, where the prices of wheat and other grain were particularly high.[61] Originally, Sevenoke's license was to run to Easter when he had to bring to Chancery written evidence from the customers of London that he had discharged his cargo in the city's port, but by March 24, since he had only managed to buy and ship to London 480 quarters of wheat, his license was extended to Whitsuntide.[62] In February 1409, a further license was issued to a merchant of Burham, Norfolk for the shipment of 40 quarters of wheat, 200 of barley and 100 of oats from Lynn to London. A month later yet another license was issued to two London fishmongers to buy 500 quarters of wheat in Yorkshire and Lincolnshire to ship to London where grain prices were still high.[63]

As the scarcity persisted the king, on January 3, 1409, ordered the mayors or bailiffs, in thirteen major east and south coast ports, stretching from Newcastle to Southampton, to issue a proclamation, again "for particular causes which concern the common weal of the realm" that shipments of any kind of grain overseas should be prohibited without the king's license, except to Calais.[64] This was followed in February of that year with a further royal order to the sheriffs of eleven counties and the town of Bristol plus the chancellor of the county palatine of Lancaster to proclaim that no grain should be exported overseas from creeks without the king's license. This order was renewed in August 1409. On November 23, 1410, the same order was sent again but only to the sheriff of Yorkshire and the mayor of Hull.[65] The emphasis on stopping export from creeks probably reflected a concern to stop unlicensed export. Creeks were places with access to the sea, which

---

[59] The fullest account of this struggle is Alsford "The Men Behind the Masque," chap. 7. See also Rigby, *English Society in the Later Middle* Ages, pp. 172–3.
[60] *CCR, 1405–9*, p. 480.   [61] *CPR, 1408–13*, p. 41.   [62] *CCR, 1405–9*, p. 434.
[63] *Ibid.*, p. 429; *CPR, 1408–13*, p. 55.   [64] *CCR, 1405–9*, p. 482.
[65] *Ibid.*, pp. 485, 527; *CCR, 1409–13*, p. 187.

were outside established towns but under the jurisdiction of customs officials in the nearest port. As they tended to be remote that probably made creeks places where it was easier to avoid the gaze of customs officers and ideal for smuggling.

Like many of his predecessors, Henry IV occasionally issued proclamations before the meeting of a parliament in order to ensure that plentiful supplies of food at reasonable prices were available for the members and their entourages. On September 14, 1404, the king ordered the sheriff of Warwickshire to ensure that there was no forestalling of grain, other victuals, and wine when the parliament met at Coventry on October 6. The king also insisted that the asking price for such goods should be no higher than they were on August 22. Rumors had reached him that forestallers had begun to buy large quantities of foodstuffs in Coventry and nearby towns to hold them off the market until parliament met, when they would sell the victuals at higher prices.[66]

On November 1409, the king issued an order for a similar proclamation before the meeting of a parliament at Bristol but the context was quite different. Not only was the proclamation issued in a deficient harvest year but, instead of a mandate to the sheriff either of Bristol or Gloucestershire to make the proclamation, a commission of three men was appointed to proclaim the king's will in the forest of Dean and elsewhere in Gloucestershire. The king's will was that the inhabitants of the county should allow all persons to bring grain and other victuals to Bristol without hindrance.[67] Clearly the events of 1400–1, when the inhabitants of the forest intercepted grain supplies bound down the Severn for Bristol, were still fresh in the official mind.

One other response of the Crown to the scarcity of 1408–10 was to issue a commission on April 24, 1410 to investigate the regrating of grain in Suffolk and Norfolk, which produced "great dearness of corn and consequent impoverishment and commotion."[68] While the nature of the commotion to which the commission referred is unclear, in November of the following year another commission was issued to investigate a report that some inhabitants of Suffolk were preventing merchants from buying and selling grain and other victuals in a number of places within the county.[69]

Perhaps the most fascinating occurrence of the scarcity period is that contained in a commission of oyer and terminer issued on March 18, 1411. The commission was issued in response to information that groups of "certain evildoers" had met in different parts of Norfolk and sent

---

[66] *CCR, 1402–5*, p. 386.   [67] *CPR, 1408–13*, p. 175.   [68] *Ibid,*, p. 222.
[69] *Ibid.*, p. 374.

anonymous letters to abbots, priors, and others threatening arson or murder unless money was left in particular locations.[70] While there is no direct link between the sending of such letters and the grain scarcity of 1408–10, it is certainly a possibility especially since, as Thompson has demonstrated for the late eighteenth early nineteenth centuries, the sending of such anonymous threats increased considerably in times of social distress.[71] Even more to the point, this occurrence provides further support for Walker's observation that where there is sufficient evidence to document popular protests in the early fifteenth century "the vocabulary of ritual defiance, familiar from the better-documented early modern period, was already in place."[72]

Beyond responses to grain scarcity and disruptions of the domestic grain trade, a major concern of Henry IV's government was military matters that included preventing grain from getting to the king's enemies and provisioning the king's forces and his dependencies in France. In 1401–2 attempts were made to prevent grain, other victuals, and weapons being shipped through Shrewsbury, Bristol, and Herefordshire to the Welsh rebels led by Owain Glyn Dŵr.[73] Also, in the period 1402–4, regular efforts were made to ensure that victuals of all kinds were bought and shipped from shires close to Wales to towns on the Welsh marches in order to supply either the king's field army or his garrisons in Wales.[74] The other areas of royal concern were Calais and Gascony whose needs for food supplies were regularly met throughout the reign.[75]

There are few signs of poor harvests or disruptions of grain supplies in Henry V's reign except for the harvest year 1416–17. On March 2, 1417, the king wrote to the Master of the Teutonic Order requesting that he "encourage the exportation of corn from Prussia into England" because heavy rains had produced scarcity.[76] Sometime before July 8, 1417, William Baker of Southampton, who had been authorized by the king to buy 100 quarters of wheat in Dorset for the supply of that town, informed the king that some people of Dorset "hindered him from bringing it to the town." The king then ordered that Baker and the grain should pass without hindrance, if he paid a price for the wheat that he

---

[70] *Ibid.*, p. 316.   [71] E. P. Thompson, "The Crime of Anonymity," pp. 255–308.

[72] Walker, "Rumor, Sedition and Popular Protest," 56.

[73] *CCR, 1399–1402*, pp. 478–9; *CPR, 1401–5*, p. 135.

[74] *CPR, 1401–5*, pp. 137, 296–7, 310; *CCR, 1402–5*, pp. 109, 401–2.

[75] *CCR, 1402–5*, pp. 13, 191, 325, 220, 240, 243, 263, 327, 336, 339, 397, and 461; *CCR, 1405–9*, p. 42; *CCR, 1409–13*, p. 176; *CPR, 1405–8*, p. 89; *CPR, 1408–13*, pp. 168 and 176.

[76] *CLB*, vol. I, p. 174.

and the seller agreed upon.[77] Aside from these few scraps there appears to be no other evidence of grain scarcity in the reign of Henry V. In fact, virtually all the crown's dealing with grain supply for the entire reign related to military campaigns in France between 1415 and 1422, including orders on provisioning armies before departure, purchases of grain and other victuals for shipment to wherever the king was in France, and regular proclamations that urged merchants to bring victuals of all kinds to Harfleur, Rouen, Caen, or Calais to support the crown's forces.[78] In addition, prohibitions were placed on grain exports except to Calais and Harfleur in 1415 and 1419 in order to give priority to the king's military campaign in France.[79] As an added incentive for merchants to ship grain and other victuals to the king in Normandy, sheriffs in London, Bristol, and Newcastle and eleven counties were instructed to proclaim that such shipments would be customs free.[80]

In the reign of Henry VI there were two significant periods of scarcity, 1428–9 and 1437–9. Both periods experienced food riots, export prohibitions, and major efforts to supply the city of London. In addition, the years 1437–9 were marked by a vigorous crown campaign to punish forestallers and hoarders of grain. Aside from these two scarcity periods, the trajectory of grain prices for much of the reign of Henry VI and his immediate successor was largely flat.[81] As a consequence, there was mounting pressure from the commons in parliament to free up the export of grain and to establish base domestic market prices below which grain could be freely exported.

In October 1423, the crown had issued an order to the keepers of the passage in fifteen major ports to ensure that no one exported grain without the king's license.[82] This was not in response to any scarcity but rather a statement of the king's government that it would continue to maintain the long-standing system of licensing that stretched back to the time of Edward II. On August 20, 1428, probably in anticipation of a deficient harvest, the king ordered the sheriffs of the city of York, Yorkshire, and Lincolnshire as well as the keepers of the passage at Hull and adjoining ports to enforce the export prohibition of 1423.[83] Fear that grain was being exported in violation of this prohibition led the crown, on May 31, 1429, to appoint a commission, which included the customs

[77] CPR, 1416–22, pp. 109–10.
[78] CCR, 1414–19, pp. 214, 237, 278, 301, 438–9; CPR, 1413–16, pp. 354, 361, 364, 409, 412–14; CPR, 1416–22, pp. 7–8, 11, 46, 60, 71, 253, 271, 274–5, 319, 326, 327, 387–8, 421; CLB, vol. I, pp. 161–2, 172, 174, 188, 197–8, 200.
[79] CCR, 1414–19, pp. 236, 498.   [80] CCR, 1419–22, p. 58.
[81] Munro, "Revisions of the Commodity Price Series."   [82] CCR, 1422–9, pp. 85–6.
[83] Ibid., pp. 408–9.

collectors of Hull and Boston, to inquire by sworn inquest into the quantities of grain and other victuals shipped to foreign parts from ports in Yorkshire and Lincolnshire since Easter 1428, plus the dates, the names of those responsible, and the circumstances of the shipments.[84] This commission was followed by another to arrest all grain brought to any port in Lincolnshire for export.[85]

By the spring of 1429, scarcity had affected both the town of Lynn in Norfolk and the city of London. At Lynn, sometime in April, the mayor and council on their own authority imposed a prohibition on the export of grain until Michaelmas, in effect after the next harvest.[86] In London, the situation was serious enough that, on April 22, the common council decided to send an agent, William Rider fishmonger, to buy grain in Normandy "at the City's risk of any loss by sea or otherwise."[87] Rider was also provided with a letter addressed to the Duke of Bedford, Henry VI's uncle who governed Normandy on behalf of the young king. This excessively obsequious letter never actually states its purpose directly, but beseeches the Duke, "our good and gracieux lord" for help "at this time in tharticle of our grete necessite" that Rider himself would explain. It concluded, "after our soveraign lord ther nys no person in erthe that us ought or semeth so tristily to seke unto for grace and socour in tyme of need as unto you in your gracieux lordship, which God of his endlesse mercy kepe and preserve in all honure and joye to his plesanche and our singler confort."[88] The letter appears to have done the job, because the next time we find mention of William Rider, on September 6, 1429, the mayor and aldermen had relieved him of service on juries as a reward for obtaining grain from Normandy.[89] In addition to Rider's actions, seven domestic cargoes of wheat, totaling 1,210 quarters, were licensed for shipment to London between February and June 1429, five from Sandwich in Kent, one from Ipswich in Suffolk and one from any port in East Anglia.[90]

The disorders of this scarcity period took place along the Severn. Some time before May 13, 1428, three merchants of Bristol bought wheat and barley worth 100 marks in Worcestershire and Gloucestershire and loaded the grain on trows to be moved down river to supply Bristol. According to the account of the merchants, the trows were seized at Minsterworth, about six miles down the river from the town of Gloucester, by "certain malefactors and disturbers of our [the king's]

---

[84] *CPR, 1422–9*, p. 553.   [85] *Ibid.*, p. 555.

[86] Jenks, "The English Grain Trade 1377–1461," p. 522.   [87] *CLB*, vol. K, p. 92.

[88] *Ibid.*, p. 94. This appears to be a full transcript of the letter.   [89] *Ibid.*, p. 100.

[90] *CPR, 1422–9*, p. 532; *CCR, 1422–9*, pp. 424, 426, 431–2, 434.

peace of the said county of Gloucester, armed and arrayed in a warlike manner," who assaulted the crews and took away the grain. Minsterworth is roughly three miles from the boundary of the Forest of Dean. Since, in 1401, the inhabitants of Dean had already compelled shippers of grain to sell grain to them against their will and in November 1409 Henry IV had ordered a proclamation to be publicly announced in the forest that those shipping grain down the Severn to Bristol should be allowed to pass without interference, it is highly likely that the people of Dean were behind this attack as well. In response to the petition of the three plundered Bristol merchants, the crown appointed a commission to inquire into the events by sworn inquest and to arrest those responsible and imprison them in Gloucester castle.[91]

In the parliament of September 1429, the commons submitted a petition on behalf of the inhabitants of the town of Tewkesbury, another Severn town upriver from Gloucester. This petition claimed that the people of Tewkesbury regularly carried all sorts of goods down river to Bristol. Over time and up until recently, although no dates are given, grain of all kinds and other goods worth £500 were loaded on trows to be shipped to Bristol. When the trows reached the Forest of Dean, they were attacked and all the goods taken by "a grete multitude of peple, and rowte of the communes of the same forest and of the hundredes of Bledislowe [Bledisloe] and Wesebury [Westbury], with greete ryot and strengthe in maner of werre, as enemys of a straunge lande."

According to the commons petition, after the king and his council were informed of these attacks, the king sent letters to a number of people in the forest to proclaim that no one should attempt to stop any shipments of grain and other merchandise on the river "upon the payne of treson." In contempt of the proclamation, "the saide trespassours come to the saide rever, with grettur rowtes and riotes thenne ever they dede by fore." Then, at different times, they plundered eight trows carrying grain and other goods, threw their crews overboard, and severed the hawsers of the boats, no doubt letting them drift off with the current. The plunderers then warned the owners of the goods and the crews of the trows that, in future, they should not ship any victuals on the river in either direction "for lorde ne lady." If they did, then their trows would be destroyed. As a result, no one in Tewkesbury or its neighborhood was willing to carry goods on the river. Moreover, the victims of the attacks could obtain no legal redress because the inhabitants of the forest were disorderly and showed no respect for the law, while officers of the law did not dare enter the forest to execute any process against the inhabitants.

---

[91] TNA, C66/424 m. 9v; *CPR, 1422–9*, p. 551.

Having described the problem in great detail, the commons then offered a solution. In every such case, when a complaint was brought to the sheriff of Gloucestershire or the bailiffs of the town of Gloucester, one of them should proclaim at Gloucester that the plunderers must return the stolen goods or their monetary equivalent plus compensation for damages within fifteen days after the issue of the proclamation. If this did not happen or if the plunderers were not arrested and imprisoned in Gloucester castle pending trial, then the statute of Winchester should come into operation. This allowed the victim of a robbery to sue the inhabitants of the hundred where the crime took place for return of the goods or the equivalent monetary value plus damages.[92]

While Henry VI approved this petition, thereby making it law, it is hard to imagine it making any difference.[93] It did not, and in this period could not, address the problem of lack of enforcement. Even if accused plunderers or the inhabitants of the hundreds where they lived were identified and sued, who was going to be able to execute process to bring them into court or arrest them if they failed to appear since the petition had already indicated that officials were afraid to enter the forest to enforce any legal judgment. In the late sixteenth century, William Camden expressed the long standing opinion of the forest and its inhabitants held by many: "This formerly was so thick with Trees, so very dank and terrible in its shades, and various crossways, that it rendred the Inhabitants barbarous, and emboldened them to commit many outrages."[94]

In that same parliament of 1429, the issue of anonymous threats arose again. A commons petition was submitted on behalf of the town of Cambridge as well as Cambridgeshire and Essex that written threats had been made recently to people in those areas, who were ordered to leave money in certain places at specific times, otherwise their houses and goods would be set on fire. In some instances, the petition avers, when the money was not paid arson followed.[95] The petitioners requested and obtained a statute that such acts of arson, back to September 1, 1422, be deemed treason.[96] While there is no direct evidence to link this activity to scarcity, this was the second outbreak anonymous threats in a scarcity year, the other being in Norfolk in 1411.[97]

From the harvest of 1430 until that of 1437 the prices of grain largely moderated and levelled off, although there was a threat of scarcity in 1432–3 at both Lynn and London. In June 1432 a merchant, who had a

---

[92] *Parl. Rolls*, "Henry VI: September 1429," item 30.
[93] *SR*, vol. 2, pp. 258–61, 8 Hen. VI c. 27.   [94] Camden, *Britannia*, column 232.
[95] *Parl. Rolls*, "Henry VI: September 1429," item 37.
[96] *SR*, vol. 2, pp. 242–3, 8 Hen. c. 6.
[97] There was another recurrence in Lincolnshire in 1452, *CPR, 1446–52*, p. 579.

license to export 400 quarters of wheat to Bordeaux from Lynn was persuaded, after some haggling, to sell 100 quarters to the mayor and council for 5.52s, less than the prevailing market price, no doubt so the wheat could be used to moderate prices in Lynn market. The following year, two merchants, who had a royal license to export grain from Lynn, were arrested on order of the mayor and council when they attempted to load their ship. The town authorities seized the grain and held it for seven days when it eventually rotted. Also, at different times during 1433, the mayor and the constables of the town were authorized to buy grain to supply the town's needs.[98] On October 11, 1432 a petition was presented to the mayor and aldermen of London asking them to request the king and his council to restrict the export of grain because of the possibility of scarcity.[99] This request must have been quickly communicated to the crown because two days later a royal mandate was sent to the keepers of the passage in fifteen major ports, including London, that no grain of any kind should be exported to foreign parts unless licensed by the king.[100] While there is no evidence of nationwide scarcity, the prohibition was renewed on August 12, 1433.[101]

In the years 1430–7, one other royal intervention in the grain market consisted of two proclamations related to the victualing of an army led by the king's uncle, the Duke of Gloucester, that embarked from Sandwich in late July 1436 to relieve Calais, which was besieged by a Burgundian army allied with the French. This army, of 7,675 men, was one of the largest that England had sent to France since the reign of Henry V.[102] On July 5, 1436, the king directed the mayor and sheriffs of London to issue a proclamation that no one, either in the city or its suburbs, should raise the price of armor, wine or any victuals in anticipation of the arrival in London of men mustered to serve under the Duke of Gloucester passing through on the way to Sandwich.[103] That same day, another order was directed to the sheriffs of London, Kent, Surrey, Sussex, Norfolk, Suffolk, and Essex to proclaim that all merchants with any grain and other victuals plus bows and arrows should take them to Calais to supply Gloucester's army "for ready payment."[104]

Grain scarcity returned in the years 1437–9, the worst dearth period since the famine of 1315–17. In the harvest year 1437–8 the average price

---

[98] Jenks, "The English Grain Trade, 1377–1461," pp. 522–3.   [99] *CLB*, vol. K, p. 146.
[100] *CCR, 1429–35*, p. 199.   [101] *Ibid.*, pp. 219–20.
[102] Griffiths, *The Reign of King Henry VI*, pp. 202–5.
[103] *CCR, 1435–41*, p. 65; *CLB*, vol. K, p. 206.
[104] *Ibid.*, pp. 65–6. The copy of the proclamation in *CCR* only names the sheriff of London as addressee. The other sheriffs can be found in the printed full text in Rymer (ed.), *Foedera*, vol. 5 pt. 1, p. 32. See also *CLB*, vol. K, p. 205.

of a quarter of wheat was 9.31s, while the price of a quarter of barley was 4.57s. In the following year, 1438–9, the average price of wheat rose to 14.63s and the price of barley to 7.05s.[105] Despite its severity, this dearth has attracted little scholarly attention compared with the famine of 1315–17, beyond discussion of high mortality rates, especially in the north east of England.[106] Throughout the crisis one government response was the repeated resort to prohibitions on export of grain without the king's license. The first prohibition was directed to the customers and keepers of the passage of London and fourteen other major ports on May 15, 1437, probably in anticipation of a poor harvest.[107] It was renewed on September 1, 1437 "for urgent causes which affect the common good" (*commune bonum*).[108] That same day, the order was also sent to the sheriffs of eleven counties to proclaim a prohibition on the export of wheat.[109]

On receiving reports of great quantities of unlicensed wheat being exported from the Thames, despite the prohibition, the king, on September 17, 1437, issued a commission to the mayor of London to search ships between the mouth of the river and the port of London, seize all unlicensed cargos of wheat, and return them to the city to feed the population, which was suffering from high prices and scarcity. A similar commission was issued a week later to the mayor and customers of Southampton.[110] The following year, on September 18, 1438, a further order prohibiting the export of wheat and other grain without the king's license, Calais excepted, was sent to the customers and keepers of the passage in Ipswich, Great Yarmouth, Lynn, and Sandwich. The express justification was the high price of grain throughout the kingdom.[111]

While it is always difficult to assess the effectiveness of such an export prohibition, if a commons petition in the parliament of November 1439 is to be believed it was, at least from one perspective, too effective. While accepting that the rising price of grain justified the prohibition on the export of grain, the commons argued that the prohibition also prevented the movement of any grain by ship from one part of England to another without the king's license as if such shipments were intended

---

[105] Munro, "Revisions of the Commodity Price Series;" Hatcher, "The Great Slump of the Mid-Fifteenth Century," p. 246.
[106] Fryde, *Peasants and Landlords*, pp. 147–9; Fryde, "Economic Depression in England," p. 216; Goldberg, "Mortality and Economic Change," 44–6, 49; Pollard, "The North-Eastern Economy," 88–105, esp. 93–5, 98–105.
[107] TNA, C54/287 m. 8; *CCR, 1435–41*, p. 89.
[108] TNA, C54/288 m. 20; *CCR, 1435–41*, p. 138.
[109] TNA, C54/288 m. 20v; *CCR, 1435–41*, p. 157.
[110] TNA, C66/441 m. 35v; *CPR, 1436–41*, p. 144.
[111] TNA, C54/289 m. 33; *CCR, 1435–41*, p. 194.

for export overseas, "whiche in this derthe of corne is right grete hurt unto the kyng's pouere poeple." The solution, according to the petition, was to allow the customs official in every port to permit domestic shipments of grain by sea if the owner entered surety of double the value of the grain that he would not send it overseas. If the owner or shipper of the grain did not return within five months with written evidence that the shipment had been delivered to a domestic port then the surety would be forfeited to the king.[112] The king's answer was that he would give this more consideration but since the scarcity began to moderate after the harvest of 1439 any further response was probably regarded as unnecessary.

As in other earlier periods of scarcity, there was considerable effort undertaken to meet London's grain needs. Between December 22, 1438 and May 6, 1439, Stephen Broun, grocer and mayor of London, received three royal commissions to buy a total of 6,000 quarters of grain in Lincolnshire, Northamptonshire, Norfolk, Suffolk, Kent and Sussex for the supply of London. On November 11, 1439, he was also a recipient of two licenses to buy a further 1,000 quarters for London in Yorkshire, Lincolnshire, Norfolk, and Suffolk.[113] In addition, between November 1437 and January 1440, eleven other licenses were issued to a various London merchants to buy a total of 1,500 quarters of mixed grains plus 1,400 of wheat, 660 of barley, 720 of malt, and 100 of beans to supply the city. Virtually all of it was to be bought in Suffolk and Norfolk.[114] In another action to aid in the supply of London the king, on December 22, 1438, wrote to a number of officials commissioned to purvey grain for the king's needs in Norfolk and Suffolk ordering them not to interfere with the activities of merchants of London, who had gone to those counties to buy grain for the city. This was the king's response to a petition from the mayor "praying for the king's consideration for the present dearness and scarcity of corn and the multitude of inhabitants of the said city."[115]

To meet the food needs of London and elsewhere, the crown and the city government also turned to foreign suppliers. In December 1437, Henry VI and the mayor of London wrote to the Master of Prussia requesting ten to twenty shiploads of grain. On May 21, 1438, the Prussian authorities permitted the export of wheat to England and on June 2, 1438 the export of rye and other grains. When the harvest of 1438 failed,

---

[112] *Parl. Rolls*, "Henry VI: November 1439," item 57.
[113] *CPR, 1436–41*, pp. 232, 253, 345.
[114] *Ibid.*, pp. 99, 137–8, 154, 163 225, 236, 344, 349, 358, 366.
[115] TNA, C54/289 m. 26; *CCR, 1435–41*, pp. 199–200; *CPR, 1436–41*, pp. 226–7.

the king wrote to the Master requesting that the export of grain to England be again allowed, which was approved. On February 28, 1439, Henry VI wrote again to the Master thanking him for his help and asking for more because grain prices in England were still high.[116] Earlier in the month the king had also written to Eric, king of Denmark, to allow Robert Chapman, citizen of York, to buy grain in his kingdom for that city because intemperate weather had produced floods in England and created a scarcity of wheat and rye.[117] According to John Stow, sometime in 1438 or 1439, the mayor of London was successful in requesting rye from Prussia at a time when wheat was at an extremely high price of 3s the bushel (24s the quarter). The arrival of the rye caused the price of wheat to drop by half.[118] One important result of the scarcity in London was the erection of a public granary at Leadenhall, which appears to have been finished around 1446. The construction was financed by both public funds and individual donations. In 1443, a well-off merchant, John Rainwell, left a bequest of money to buy wheat for the granary.[119]

A significant indicator of the severity of the dearth of 1437–9 is the frequency, and at times outrage, of the crown's responses to various market offences, particularly forestalling, engrossing, and regrating, which appear to be treated once again as virtually identical offences. On October 7, 1437, three men were commissioned to make a proclamation in Alton, Hampshire, where some people taking advantage of the scarcity were "forestalling or regrating of wheat and other corn." The purpose of the proclamation was to forbid these practices "under pain of imprisonment and the forfeiture of such wheat and corn."[120] The next day the king ordered the sheriff of Hampshire to make a proclamation throughout the county on similar terms and to imprison anyone who continued to forestall or regrate any grain after the proclamation was announced.[121]

Between December 4, 1437 and May 5, 1438 five separate royal commissions were issued to inquire into the export of uncustomed goods and other offences in Lincolnshire, Yorkshire, Sussex, Kent, and Essex (twice).[122] The record of the inquest held at Canterbury on March 15, 1438 before the commissioners appointed for Kent and Essex

---

[116] Lloyd, *England and the Hanse*, pp. 222–3; Brie (ed.), *The Brut*, pt. 2, p. 507; Von Runstedt (ed.), *Hansisches Urkundenbuch*, vol. 7 pt. 1, pp. 124, 156–7, and 204. See also *CCR, 1435–41*, p. 195.

[117] Rymer (ed.), *Foedera*, vol. 5 pt. 1, p. 58.

[118] Stow provides two separate but similar accounts of Broun's actions, one dated 1438 and the other 1439 in his *Survey of London*, vol. 1, p. 173 and vol. 2, pp. 109–10.

[119] Thomas, "Notes on the History of the Leadenhall, A. D. 1195–1488," 17–19; *A Medieval Capital*, pp. 103–4; Keene, "Crisis Management," pp. 60–1.

[120] TNA, C66/441 m. 35v; *CPR, 1436–41*, p. 145.

[121] TNA, C54/288 m. 20v; *CCR, 1435–41*, p. 157.   [122] *CPR, 1436–41*, p. 147.

on February 12 of that year survives. It records the activities of one "common regrator" and four "common forestallers." In the week after Michaelmas 1437 John Qwynchaunt, husbandman, of Milstead bought 40 quarters of grain, which did not come to the markets of Milton Regis or Faversham for a year. Four men, all mariners of Milton Regis, were found to have bought various amounts of grain and held it off the market for a year. No doubt the aim in all cases was to increase the asking price as the scarcity intensified. These actions were reported as being "to the great damage of the common people."[123]

On December 12, 1438, a further commission was appointed for Kent and another for Buckinghamshire to inquire through juries or any other means into those who had recently bought large quantities of wheat and other grain far beyond their household needs in order to advance their "individual interest" (*singulari commodo*) without "bowels of pity" (*visceribus pietatis*) in a time of scarcity. Such offences drove the price of grain even higher and undermined "the politic governance of the common wealth" (*gubernationus politice rei publice*). The offenders were to be punished for violations of the statute of forestallers, which meant forfeiture of the grain to the king.[124] A few days later, commissions were appointed for Essex, Middlesex, and Surrey to inquire into the activities of millers who had conspired in this time of scarcity to raise the customary fixed price for grinding grain to the great harm of the king's subjects.[125] The pursuit of engrossers, forestallers, and regrators expanded on January 23, 1439 when the king issued commissions for Warwickshire, Leicestershire, Staffordshire, Cambridgeshire, and Huntingdonshire, similar to those for Kent and Buckinghamshire, in which the offenders were described again as acting against "politic governance and the common wealth" (*gubernatione politicam et bonum publice*).[126] Finally, on October 14, 1439, another commission was issued to deal with engrossers and the like in Kent was issued with language similar to that of December 12, 1438.[127]

Only a single record of one of these inquests appears to have survived, that for the Kent commission of December 12, 1438 and it makes for interesting reading.[128] The commission met at Canterbury on at least two occasions, during the second week of Lent and on the Monday after Palm Sunday, 1439 and three different juries made presentments that

[123] *CIM*, vol. 8, p. 57.   [124] TNA, C66/443 m. 27v; *CPR, 1436–41*, p. 266.
[125] TNA, C66/443 m. 25v; *CPR, 1436–41*, p. 267.
[126] TNA, C66/443 m. 23v; *CPR, 1436–41*, p. 268.
[127] TNA, C66/445 m. 25v; *CPR, 1436–41*, p. 369.
[128] TNA, C145/308/6; *CIM*, vol. 8, pp. 67–9.

covered the period from late 1438 to early 1439, with most of the activities under scrutiny having occurred in October and November 1438. In one case Constance, wife of John Lynde and "hosewyff" of Canterbury, was accused of buying eight quarters of wheat at 10s the quarter on October 20, 1438 and selling it for 13s 4d the quarter "making an excessive gain of 3s 4d contrary to the statute." Depending on the circumstances under which the wheat was bought and sold this was the crime of either forestalling or regrating. This was the only clear case of such crimes identified by the commission.

All the other offences that the commission discovered were clearly violations of the statute of weights and measures, although that statute is not mentioned in any of the commissions that Henry VI's government issued in response to the scarcity of 1437–9. Constance Lynde was also guilty of violating that statute by buying and the selling grain by the quarter measured at eight bushels plus a heap. The man who bought the grain from her, William Stephene of Whitstable husbandman, also acted contrary to the statute in buying the oversized quarters. Five other transaction presented by the juries involved the purchase of grain in heaped measures, while a sixth involved two malt makers and six brewers, including John Lynde, Constance's husband, all of Canterbury using a false, oversize bushel measure of nine instead of the standard eight gallons, when buying their malt. After the presentments, the accused were examined under oath. Nine men admitted that they had sold grain in heaped measures, some more than once, and one man admitted that he had bought grain with such measures. John Lynde, brewer, admitted to buying barley at various times at 6s 8d and 8s the quarter, and over the year accumulating another 1,000 quarters of barley at 5s the quarter but there was no mention of any offence committed against the statute of weights and measures although he may have been considered an engrosser. Under oath, however, Edmund Wykes esquire did state that he sold 120 quarters of barley to Lynde using the brewer's oversized nine gallon bushel measure while Henry Wright in his examination admitted that he sold 20 heaped quarters of barley to Lynde.

The effort to standardize weights and measures involved a long campaign that began with Henry III, when he sent out commissions in 1255–6 to enforce the assize of weights and measures and other regulatory measures nationwide. The campaign continued on through the reigns of his successors, especially Edward III and Richard II. Richard II's parliaments of November 1390 and November 1391 had advocated the standard eight bushel quarter as a measure for grain, a position supported by the king who also agreed that those who used the nine bushel quarter would be liable to forfeit the grain to the king.[129] Nonetheless, the practice of using the nine bushel quarter continued in London, and probably elsewhere among buyers of grain. In response, the May 1413 parliament of Henry V renewed the statute of weights and measures with its standard of an eight gallon bushel and a level eight bushels to the quarter. The use of any other measure could then result in a year's imprisonment and a fine of £5 to the king with a possible further £5 in damages to the wronged person, who would have the right to sue the culprit.[130] Despite this statute, purchasers of grain in London and other towns continued to use the nine bushel quarter. In London, it was long standing practice to use the "stand," a vessel that held nine bushels, in measuring out a quarter. In Henry VI's parliament of July 1433 complaints by the commons about the continued use of false measures led to another statute of weights and measures, which in substance was a renewal of Henry V's statute of 1413.[131]

Despite this legislation oversized measures did not disappear. It was to take a very long time, until the early nineteenth century, before traditional practices and uses were eradicated and standardized measures became the norm.[132] Their persistence and popularity in the fifteenth century is nicely illustrated in the case of John Bredon, friar and professor of theology. On Friday, in the first week of Lent in 1440, Bredon was indicted before the keepers of the peace of Warwickshire for causing a disturbance at Coventry. He had come to the town and claimed that the king and his council, at a parliament held at Reading, had given him authority to proclaim that the inhabitants should use a nine gallon bushel in measuring grain instead of the eight gallon bushel specified in the statute. When he uttered his proclamation Bredon "caused riotous gatherings against the mayor and bailiffs and other officers of the town to the danger of the people and the subversion of the laws (*subversionem legum*)." In the end, however, he received a royal pardon.[133]

During the dearth of 1437–9 there were at least two food riots in Suffolk, one at Ipswich and the other at Southwold Haven, sometime before May 24, 1438 when two separate commissions of oyer and terminer were issued to the same body of commissioners, headed by the earl

---

[129] *Parl. Rolls*, "Richard II: November 1390," item 28; "Richard II: November 1391," item 31; *SR*, vol. 2, p. 79, 15 Ric. II c. 4.

[130] *Parl. Rolls*, "Henry V: May 1413," item 42; *SR*, vol. 2, p. 174, 1 Hen. V c. 10.

[131] *Parl. Rolls*, "Henry VI: July 1433," item 54; *SR*, vol. 2, p. 11 Hen. VI c. 8; *CCR, 1429–35*, p. 315. See also *CLB*, vol. K, pp. 184–6, 192.

[132] Sheldon, Randall, Charlesworth, and Walsh, "Popular Protest and the Persistence of Customary Corn Measures," pp. 25–45.

[133] *CPR, 1436–41*, p. 545.

of Suffolk, to conduct trials of the rioters.[134] According to the complaint of four London merchants in the first case, a crowd in Ipswich, estimated at 300 in number and led by John Blankpayne and William Talyfer, assaulted their servants and seized and carried away 52 quarters of wheat, worth 104 marks, that they had bought in the town. If these figures are accurate this means that the price of a quarter of wheat in Suffolk had reached the extraordinarily high level of 26s 8d greater even than the 24s reported by some London chronicles.[135] No wonder then that the crowd seized the wheat. It was probably going to be shipped to London for its supply and, since most of the licensed grain shipments to London during this scarcity came from Suffolk and Norfolk, the grain purchases by city merchants must have drawn the ire of the local populace as the cause of rising local prices.

The events at Southwold, as reported in the commission of oyer and terminer, were considerably more violent than those at Ipswich. Clays Yandisson, a merchant of Haarlem in Holland, had recently sold a shipload of linen cloth, "osemund" (Swedish iron), and other merchandise in Southwold. With the money he received, he bought 90 quarters of barley and four lasts of "sperlyng" (smelt), which he loaded on his ship, no doubt to return to Holland. Instead, a crowd of about eighty men led by Henry Sterlyng, yeoman, and Henry Joye, shipman, boarded the ship, assaulted, and drove off Yandisson and his crew and seized a chest containing eight marks that they discovered on the ship. Then the rioters went below and, using an axe, cut a hole three foot long and one foot wide in the hull. As a result, the ship sank along with its cargo of barley and smelt. After that the crowd left. No doubt the sinking of Yandisson's ship with its cargo reflected the long standing and wide spread popular hostility to the export of grain during periods of scarcity.

In both commissions, the actions of the crowds were described in terms very much like those used to describe the food rioters of 1347. They were "armed and arrayed in a warlike manner" (*armatis et modo guerrino arriatis*) and acted "with force and arms" (*vi et armis*), "against the king's peace" (*contra pacem nostram*). The events at Ipswich might qualify as merely a riot, except the carrying away of the grain would have made the rioters vulnerable to a charge of theft. Similarly the events at Southwold might also be construed as a riot except for the taking of the eight marks, which again would have left the possibility open to a charge of theft. We will probably never know what happened to the rioters

[134] TNA, C66/442 m. 30v; *CPR, 1436–41*, p. 199.
[135] Thomas and Thornley (eds.), *The Great Chronicle of London*, p. 174; Nicolas (ed.), *A Chronicle of London*, p. 124.

because no indictments or trial records appear to have survived for either riot, although we do know a little more about the Southwold rioters because a few records of the proceedings of the commission of oyer and terminer survive.[136] In addition to the two Henries who led the crowd, there were six other known suspects a husbandman, four ship-men, and a laborer. Seven of the eight suspects never appeared before the commission, despite numerous summonses and orders to the sheriff to arrest them during the period July 14, 1438–February 20, 1439. In the end they were outlawed. The only person who did appear, Henry Joye, was bailed on November 19, 1438. What happened to him after that is not known.[137]

Perhaps the most intriguing popular response to the scarcity of 1437–9 is contained in what R. L. Storey calls "The molecatcher's tale," a fantastic tale of magic and treason told on January 12, 1440 by Robert Goodgroom of Ospringe Kent, moletaker, alias Robert Green late of London, currier.[138] Goodgroom had been indicted at Canterbury on May 29, 1439 for three thefts for which he could be hung if convicted. He confessed his crimes but then turned approver, which meant that, if he charged named individuals with felony or treason and they were convicted, then he would go free. If the accused were found innocent or the charges were in some way insufficient then the approver would be executed. In Goodgroom's case, since he levied charges of treason at a number of people but failed to prove any of them, he died a traitor's death on May 4 1440.

The approver's tale survives in the records of king's bench, in English. At the heart of it is a conspiracy of a number of gentlemen in Kent and elsewhere, hatched between late 1438 and early 1439, to kill Henry VI, the Duke of Gloucester, and the Duke of Norfolk with a magical potion created from ground up herbs and human flesh, which was to be put in an earthenware container capped with wax for forty days and nights. Then the potion was to be distilled; three drops would be enough to kill a man. Despite all this fantasy and more, the striking aspect of this imagined conspiracy is Goodgroom's explanation of the cause that lay behind it. The king and the two dukes were to be killed because of their role in creating grain scarcity. According to Goodgroom, when one of the conspirators, John Sinclair, explained the motives behind the plot he said

---

[136] TNA JUST1/862/8.   [137] *Ibid.*

[138] There are two printed versions of the tale. One, which I have quoted here, is a modernized English version in an appendix to Story, *The End of the House of Lancaster*, pp. 199–209. The other, in the original Middle English with an interesting introduction, is Margaret Aston, "A Kent Approver of 1440," 82–90.

"Lo, Robert, thou knowest well the great wars of France is hindering to this realm, and also the dear years of corn, and also the taking of corn by the king and other certain lords, the which is to the said realm and commons great destruction."[139] Such a point of view is an entirely plausible one for an ordinary person, whether mole catcher or currier to hold in 1438–9 and it resonates with the seditious words uttered by ordinary folk during later harvest failures.[140]

One of Goodgroom's accusations, that against John Dandelion, a gentleman of the Isle of Thanet in Kent, is closely related to Sinclair's opinion on the dearth of grain. Dandelion was accused of traitorously shipping sixty quarters of wheat and eighty of barley to the king's enemies in Flanders on the night of April 28, 1438.[141] This is such a specific and plausible accusation, lacking any of the colorful and fantastic attributes of much of the rest of the tale that it makes one wonder how much Goodgroom knew of Dandelion's business. There is no doubt that Dandelion was engaged in the grain trade. On October 16, 1429 he received a license to ship 400 quarters of grain from Kent to London.[142] Even more to the point, Dandelion's grain dealing came to the attention of the commission appointed on December 12, 1438 to inquire into engrossing, regrating, and forestalling of grain in Kent. At the session held at Canterbury, on Tuesday in the second week of Lent in 1439, it was found that a year earlier Dandelion had bought twenty-one quarters of wheat at 8s the quarter and twenty-one of barley at 3s 4d from William Haghe, also of the Isle of Thanet, but the grain had not yet been paid for.[143] There is no indication in the record of any law being broken but one surmises that the commission found this to be an odd situation worth recording. At the very least, Goodgroom's accusation against Dandelion had some air of plausibility.

At the same time, one must admit that not everyone accused of trade offences was guilty. Take the case of William Bodevyle brewer who was accused of engrossing 8,000 quarters of malt and other grain that he bought in Cambridge and neighboring townships. After investigating the charge, the chancellor of the university found that it was baseless. The chancellor then issued letters testimonial to that effect that Bodevyle then submitted to the mayor and aldermen of London on February 1, 1439, no doubt to show that he was a respectable man of business.[144]

---

[139] Storey, *End of the House of Lancaster*, p. 204.
[140] Sharp, *In Contempt of All Authority*, pp. 36–7.
[141] Storey, *End of the House of Lancaster*, p. 207.   [142] *CPR, 1429–36*, p. 4.
[143] TNA C145/308/6; *CIM*, vol. 8, p. 68.
[144] Jones (ed.), *Calendar of Plea and Memoranda Rolls of the City of London, 1437–1457*, pp. 8–9.

While there is no denying the recurrence of grain scarcity in the period 1377–1440, scarcities were considerably less frequent than they had been in the reign of Edward III (1327–77). Moreover, there were signs in the period that the balance between food supply and population was beginning to swing more favorably towards surplus and away from dearth, although that took some time to achieve. Two early signs of that improvement are to be found in the reign of Richard II with the king's proclamation of 1378 allowing export of grain without a license to all foreign places in the king's friendship and the similar statute passed by the parliament of January 1394.[145] It was no doubt wise of the king to make it clear that he retained the right to restrict export of grain when necessary, as it was later in his reign. Nonetheless, the commons petition that originated the statute made the case that the domestic price of grain was so low that without the right to export freely the commons "cannot pay their rent." After the restoration of licensing later in Richard II's reign and its continuation into the reign of Henry VI, the commons in the parliament of February 1426 petitioned the king on behalf of the commons of Kent that the requirement to obtain a license to export grain resulted in "great harm and impoverishment of your said commons." The king, in response, agreed to uphold and enforce Richard II's statute of 1394 allowing export of gain without a license, with the same proviso that he retained the authority to enforce export prohibitions when necessary.[146]

Since the king once again issued prohibitions on export of grain without his license in 1432–3, the matter returned again in the January parliament of 1437 some months before the deficient harvest of that year. In that parliament, the commons petitioned the king once again requesting the lifting of the prohibition because domestic prices were low so that English farmers needed to be able to export grain to make a living. This time, however, the commons proposed an additional remedy. That was to set a base price for grain, below which it could be freely exported without license except to the king's enemies, 6s 8d for a quarter of wheat and 3s for a quarter of barley. The king approved this measure but only until the next parliament.[147] By the time the next parliament met in November 1439, the bad harvests of 1437 and 1438 had already occurred, licensing had been reintroduced and prices had risen well above the base line set in the statute of 1437 so there was no chance of the statute's renewal. The commons in the parliament of

---

[145] *CCR, 1377–81*, p. 207; *Parl. Rolls*, "Richard II: January 1394," item 33; *SR*, vol. 2, p. 88, 17 Ric. II c. 7.
[146] *Parl. Rolls*, "Henry VI: February 1416," item 37; *SR*, vol. 2, pp. 230–1, 4 Hen. VI c. 5.
[147] *Parl. Rolls*, "Henry VI: January 1437," item 21; *SR*, vol. 2, pp. 295–6, 15 Hen. VI c. 2.

November 1439 accepted the need for licensing given the rise in the price of grain, but they did request a loosening of the regulations on the domestic shipping of grain coastwise, which the king dodged by saying he would consider it further.[148] In the parliament of January 1442 the statute of 1437 setting the base price below which grain could be freely exported was approved until the next parliament or ten years passed, whichever came first. The next parliament, of February 1445, renewed the statute permanently.[149] No doubt the temporary renewal of the statute in 1442 reflected official fear that scarcity would recur but it did not. England had entered into a long scarcity free period with low grain prices except for a few years 1481–4 and 1502–5. This also meant an absence of disorder and protest that resulted from high prices and scarcity. In 1463 Edward IV's parliament passed a statute that correlated with the export statute. No foreign grain was to be imported into England if grain prices were below the base of 6s 8d for a quarter of wheat, 4s for a quarter of rye, and 3s for a quarter of barley in order to protect English agriculture from cheap foreign imports.

While it is clear that scarcity and famine years became less frequent and devastating from 1377 through 1440 compared with those experienced in the period 1315–76, nonetheless when scarcity and famine did occur the crown acted with alacrity in response to apply traditional remedies such as prohibitions on export of grain, encouraging import of grain, and enforcing laws against forestalling, regrating, and false measures. In addition, the governments of Richard II and Henry VI, like that of Edward III, issued commissions to search for forestallers, imprison them, seize their grain, and sell it in the market. One important innovation with a long future began in 1391 and continued on into later scarcities, when the government of London raised money to buy grain overseas to supply the needs of the city's population.

From 1440 until the reign of Henry VIII dearth measures were rarely implemented, because of the decline in grain prices and the infrequency of harvest failures.[150] When scarcities did occur, the long term rise in real wages and continued population decline or stagnation meant that they did not have the negative consequences, such as increased mortality, they had in the past when population numbers were much higher and wages much lower. This appears to have been the case when two poor harvests

---

[148] *Parl. Rolls*, "Henry VI: November 1439," item 57.
[149] *Parl. Rolls*, "Henry VI: January 1442," item 23; "Henry VI: February 1445," item 33; *SR*, pp. 319–20, 20 Hen. VI c. 6; pp. 331–2, 23 Hen. VI c. 5.
[150] Hatcher, "The Great Slump," pp. 248, 271.

in a row occurred in 1481–2 and 1482–3.[151] The deficient harvest of 1481 drove up the average price of a quarter of wheat to 8.56s and barley to 6.18s in 1482. The poor harvest of 1482 resulted in even higher average prices of 10.33s for wheat and 7.16s for barley.[152]

The years 1481–3 are the only ones between 1440 and 1527 for which record survives of a crown response to scarcity. On February 11, 1482 Edward IV ordered the sheriffs of Norfolk and Suffolk to proclaim a prohibition on the export of grain except to Calais because of a fear that more grain was being exported than had been properly licensed, as a result of the negligence of customers and other port officials. Then, on May 10 and July 11 of that year, the sheriffs nationwide were instructed to prohibit the export of grain and other victuals without a license.[153] The supply of grain to London was of particular concern to Edward IV. On November 21, 1482 he wrote to a number of sheriffs ordering them that, as a result of great scarcity in London, grain should be shipped freely to the city without being intercepted by the king's purveyors. Those who shipped the grain by sea were instructed to use named ports and to give sureties to the customers of the port that they would ship only to London.[154] A few days later the king instructed Thomas Roggers, clerk of the king's ships, to seize vessels for the king's use except for ships that brought victuals to London.[155] When major scarcity and popular disorders returned in the reign of Henry VIII the crown revived and reinvigorated the policies of its predecessors while adding new initiatives.

---

[151] Campbell, "Four Famines and a Pestilence," pp. 39–40, 46.

[152] Munro, "Revisions of Price Series."

[153] *CPR, 1476–85*, pp. 264, 320. Full texts of the proclamations can be found in Steele (ed.), *A Bibliography of the Royal Proclamations*, pp. clxxvii–viii. The only other prohibition on export of the period is one by Henry VII on September 19, 1492 that refers to scarcity of grains caused by excessive export, *CPR, 1494–1509*, p. 391.

[154] A full text of the letter is in Gras, *The Evolution of the English Corn Market*, pp. 447–8. See also *CLB*, vol. L, p. 199. The counties were Sussex, Surrey, Cornwall, Devonshire, Somerset, Dorset, Oxfordshire, Berkshire, Hampshire, Hertfordshire, Buckinghamshire, Kent, Essex, Norfolk, Suffolk, Lincolnshire, and Cambridgeshire. The letter does not appear to have been enrolled on either the Patent Rolls or the Close Rolls.

[155] Hughes and Larkin (eds.), *Tudor Proclamations*, vol. 1, p. 27; *CPR 1476–85*, p. 329.

6 Harvest failure and scarcity in the reign of Henry VIII

The years 1440–1519 experienced consistently low wheat price. According to Munro's price series, the average annual price of a quarter of wheat in virtually every harvest year of the period ranged from a low of 4s to a high of 6.5s. In one year, 1509–10, it was particularly low at 3s per quarter. The exceptions were the harvest years 1460–2 (7.02s and 7.45s), 1481–4 (8.56s, 10.33s, and 7.27s), 1501–3 (8.44s and 8.06s), 1512–13 (9.1s), and 1516 (6.81s).[1] Hatcher has argued persuasively that the key to understanding this phenomenon is the continued decline in population, which meant that "food became cheaper in a period when the acreage under cultivation shrank and *per capita* consumption probably increased substantially." As a consequence, from the 1440s to the end of the century "annual fluctuations in price caused by variations in the quality of the harvest were among the narrowest in recorded history."[2]

Any attempt to evaluate the quality of the harvests in Henry VIII's reign is made difficult because of the lack of an equivalent to Campbell's "Three Centuries of English crop yields 1211–1491." As a consequence, we must depend on the evidence of price series supplemented by other contemporary evidence, including official sources that comment on the state of the harvest. In contrast to the period 1440–1519, the reign of Henry VIII from the harvest year 1519–20 through 1545–6 experienced a number of multiple harvest runs when the average annual prices of a quarter of wheat were high and ranged between 7.17s at the low end to 15.56 s at the top. The first of these runs was 1519–22 (7.17s, 9.37s, and 7.88s). Second was 1527–33 (12.92s, 8.85s, 8.83s, 8.41s, 8.21s, and 8s). Third was 1535–7 (10.29s and 10.6s). Finally there was 1541–6 (9.02s, 7.93s, 9.27s, 9.02s, and 15.56s).[3] Some of these high price years

---

[1] Munro, "Revisions of the Commodity Price Series." See also Clark "The Price History of English Agriculture," pp. 66–7. While Clark's prices differ slightly from Munro's, the larger trends are similar.

[2] Hatcher, *Plague, Population and the English Economy*, p. 52.

[3] Munro, "Revisions of the Commodity Price Series;" Clark, "The Price History of English Agriculture," pp. 67–8; Hoskins, "Harvest Fluctuations," 44–5. Gwyn, *The King's Cardinal*,

undoubtedly had more negative effects on the population than others. For example, harvest years 1527–8 and 1545–6 were times of severe scarcity and very high prices. In 1528 real wages declined just over 25 percent.[4] Nonetheless, the most striking point about these figures is the multi year runs of high prices, which meant continued distress for many wage earners and small holders who did not produce enough food for themselves and needed to enter the market to obtain it. A further complication, especially in 1528, was disruption of the cloth industry, which imposed even more economic stress on wage earners.

Whatever the cause or causes, whether climatic cycles or the long contraction in land under the plough that left the country with a grain deficiency in the face of a rapid rise in population between the mid-1520s and 1541, with somewhat slower growth thereafter, crises produced by harvest deficiencies were regular occurrences in the reign of Henry VIII.[5] In respect to the official response, the years 1527–9 were crucial. Under the direction of Cardinal Wolsey, the lord chancellor, medieval precedents were revived, such as prohibitions on export of grain and proclamations that urged the enforcement of laws against market offences like forestalling, regrating, and engrossing. Most significantly, searches for stores of grain, attempted in the reigns of Edward III, Richard II and Henry VI, were also revived, expanded in scope and energized. Later in the reign, during the period when Thomas Cromwell had risen to power and influence, he continued Wolsey's policies and supplemented them with a campaign against unlawful export of grain. Moreover, beginning with the scarcity of 1519–22, town governments conducted surveys of grain stocks and raised money to buy grain and sell it at reduced prices to those in need, on their own initiative.

The urban response to the scarcity of 1519–1522

Virtually all the surviving evidence that documents the effects of the high grain prices of 1519–22 is found in town records. There is little in the records of Henry VIII's government. Coventry was particularly hard hit.

---

p. 456 in a comparison of the pre-scarcity average price of a quarter of wheat in 1526–7 with that of the scarcity year 1527–8 misread the sources. He lists the prices as £6.53 and £13.37 instead of 6.53s and 13.37s. Among his sources was Hoskins, "Harvest Fluctuations," 28–46. Hoskins makes it clear at the beginning of his price table on 44 that his prices are in shillings.
[4] Campbell, "Four Famines and a Pestilence," pp. 38–40. On p. 38, 1538 should be 1528.
[5] Wrigley and Schofield, *The Population History of England*, pp. 208, 566–9 estimate population at 2.259 million in the mid-1520s, 2.774 million in 1541, and 2.854 million in 1546.

Here the high prices ran from the harvest year 1518–19 through 1520–1. After the 1518 harvest, the price of a quarter of wheat in the city was 10s. The next harvest in Warwickshire was probably worse as a result of near constant rain from early May until Christmas, which resulted in a further rise in the price of a quarter of wheat in Coventry to 14s. After the 1520 harvest, wheat prices peaked at 18s per quarter, a famine price.[6] In response, the city authorities did what they could. On October 11, after the poor harvest of 1519, they issued new market regulations to benefit the city population. On market day no one, whether inhabitant of Coventry or stranger, was permitted to buy grain outside of the market so that it could be brought to the market place to be sold. Only townsmen could buy grain between 9 am, when the market opened, and noon. After noon, countrymen could buy. Those who violated the ordinance were to be fined 6s 8d. Anyone who forestalled grain in the city or brought forestalled grain to the market was to be subject to the same penalty. Finally, a prohibition was imposed on selling malt out of town when it cost above 5s the quarter. Violators were also to be fined 6s 8d.[7]

One year later, on October 10, 1520, as grain prices began a further rise after another deficient harvest, the mayor and other magistrates of Coventry undertook a census of the population and the existing grain supply in the city. They discovered 47 quarters of wheat, 100 quarters and 1 strike of rye and maslin, 2,405 quarters of malt, 39 quarters and 2 strikes of oats, and 18 quarters and 2 strikes of peas. The census also noted that the Coventry brewers used 86 quarters and 1 bushel of malt every week, while the bakers used 120 quarters of wheat and 12 of rye and peas.[8] What are we to make of these figures? Phythian-Adams made a perfectly reasonable attempt to understand them and drew the conclusion that they indicated the dire straits of the population. He divided the 2,405 quarters of malt by the weekly amount used and concluded that the beer supply would run out sometime in February, 1521. Then he divided the total of all the other grains by the weekly amount used by the bakers and concluded they had less than a two weeks supply.[9]

[6] Phythian-Adams, *Desolation of a City*, pp. 55–7.

[7] Harris (ed.), *The Coventry Leet Book*, pt. 3, p. 666; Phythian-Adams, *Desolation of a City*, 56. On September 16, 1521 the mayor and magistrates of Leicester passed a similar ordinance that no one should buy grain on market day before it came to the market place to be sold, Bateson (ed.), *Records of the Borough of Leicester*, pp. 18–19.

[8] Harris (ed.), *The Coventry Leet Book*, pt. 3, pp. 674–5; Tawney and Power (eds.), *Tudor Economic Documents*, vol. 3, pp. 141–3. The strike is a customary and variable measure ranging from ½ to 4 bushels. See Zupko, *A Dictionary of English Weights and Measures*, p. 165.

[9] Phythian-Adams, *Desolation of a City*, p. 59.

Nonetheless, there is an insurmountable difficulty with Phythian-Adams conclusion, one that is also encountered in any attempt to assess the later grain surveys of 1527–8.

The Coventry census is a single static record of a moment in time. It tells us nothing about how much grain would be coming into Coventry market from the surrounding countryside in subsequent days, weeks, and months. Moreover, the census shows that the wards that had little bread grain per capita on hand were those that contained many poorer households of textile workers. It is likely that such households did not normally have grain on hand since they probably did not bake their own bread but depended on bakers.[10] Moreover, the city did not rely solely on the bread baked by its own resident bakers. Bakers from Warwick and the countryside also came to Coventry every Wednesday and Friday to sell bread. Later, in 1533, the city government passed an ordinance that any bread brought in from outside not sold on those days should be left at three named tippling houses to be sold later to the common people.[11] Also, at the end of the census it is noted that just before Christmas 1520 the mayor and his friends bought 97 quarters and 6 strikes of various grains "to helpe to susteyne the Cyte."[12] What we do not know is if there were subsequent purchases of grain by city officials. It is clear, nonetheless, that we cannot use the census alone to draw definitive conclusions about the severity of the scarcity in Coventry.

One other response of the mayor and alderman of Coventry to the scarcity of 1520–1 was to issue an order on May 22, 1521 that the tenants of the town's common pasture should convert between half and all of their holdings to arable.[13] The reason for the conversion is made clear in a later order of April 1534, which observes that then there was a "great darthe and scarsenes of corne." Now "Corne is comon to good plentie and to easie and reasonable price" and pasture should be restored throughout the common.[14]

While we have no direct evidence from grain prices, it is reasonably certain from the town's ordinances that Leicester also experienced scarcity in 1520–1. In November 1520, the town council passed an ordinance regulating bakers and brewers. Country bakers were instructed to bring good and wholesome bread into the town on Wednesday and Friday market days and sell it at the High Cross for one or two pennies.

---

[10] Lee, "Grain Shortages in Late Medieval Towns," pp. 66–8.
[11] Harris (ed.), *The Coventry Leet Book*, pt. 3, p. 717.   [12] *Ibid.*, p. 675.
[13] Phythian-Adams, *Desolation of a City*, p. 58; Harris (ed.), *The Coventry Leet Book*, pt. 3, pp. 679–80.
[14] Harris (ed.), *The Coventry Leet Book*, pt. 3, pp. 719–20.

Such bakers, on pain of forfeiture of their wares, were not to carry bread directly to their customers. Those townsmen who baked bread for the poor were to make it good and wholesome from rye and bran. Brewers were instructed to make good and wholesome ale for the poor at a half-penny the gallon so that they "maye the better be relieved."[15] A year later, another ordinance was passed to prevent forestalling of grain. On market days, when grain was brought into the town, no one was to receive it in his house until it was set down in the market place and sold. Also, no one was to receive grain in his house after the market closed, with the intention of selling it on the next market day. Those who violated the ordinance were to be fined 6s 8d.[16]

Norwich and Bristol certainly suffered from high prices and scarcity in 1520–2. In 1521 the aldermen of Norwich paid for a stock of wheat to meet the needs of the city population. A year later, in March 1522, the aldermen agreed that each of them would provide money to buy 20 combs (10 quarters) of wheat "to serve the people dwellyng within the said citie or elles to have redy xx combz to thentent aforesaid." At least eighteen of the twenty-two aldermen supplied the requisite amount of wheat.[17] At Bristol in 1519–20, the town government imposed new rules on the activities of bakers, including prohibitions on buying grain in the countryside close by and on shipping wheat bread or wheat out of Bristol to Wales or anywhere else without license from the mayor. In addition, the bakers were urged to "have sufficyent stuffe of bred as well whyte as wheten bothe in their houses and in their hucksters houses to serve the comons of this towne at all houres."[18] In 1522 rising grain prices compelled the mayor of Bristol, "inclynyng his charitie towardes the comen wele and profite of this Towne," to authorize a Mr. Ware and others to travel to Worcestershire to purchase grain. Ware was successful in this mission and brought back a great deal of grain that reduced the prices in Bristol market and relieved the people of the town.[19]

London was the main urban center whose government bought grain during the scarcity years 1519–22. Earlier, in 1514, the city authorities ordered the building of a granary at the Bridgehouse.[20] In 1520 a former

---

[15] Bateson (ed.), *Records of the Borough of Leicester*, pp. 15–16.   [16] *Ibid.*, p. 19.

[17] Hudson and Tingey (eds.), *The Records of the City of Norwich* , vol. 2, pp. xcvii, 159–60.

[18] Stanford (ed.), *The Ordinances of Bristol*, p. 13.

[19] Smith (ed.), *The Maire of Bristowe*, p. 49. In 1520–1 grain prices were also high in Newcastle, Lincoln, and Exeter. At Exeter, the town government also bought grain to sell to the poor. See Welford, *History of Newcastle and Gateshead*, vol. 2, p. 5; Hill, *Tudor and Stuart Lincoln*, pp. 30–1, 222; Beveridge, "A Statistical Crime," 532; Slack, *Poverty and Policy*, p. 117.

[20] Gras, *The Evolution of the English Corn Market*, p. 80.

alderman bequeathed a sum of money to buy grain annually to be stored in new granary. That year grain was bought for the "Common Weale of this Citie."[21] A further supply of grain was bought in 1521 when, according to Hall's chronicle, the price of a quarter of wheat in the city was 20 s.[22] Moreover, after the harvest of 1520, the mayor and aldermen began the practice of borrowing money from the guilds and companies of the city to buy grain to supply city markets with the intention of lowering prices. On this first occasion, the loan was £1,000 and justified as a "good and politique provision" in the face of the "great Derth and Scarcitie of Whete."[23] Such provisions, usually involving purchases of grain from the Baltic region, were to become the norm during future scarcities throughout the sixteenth century, not only in London but also in Norwich, Bristol, Shrewsbury and probably other towns as well.[24]

While there appears to be no obvious surviving response of Henry VIII's government to the scarcity of 1519–22, there is a possibility that a royal proclamation of January 26, 1522 was related to the scarcity. The proclamation was designed to protect the supply lines of London. It stated that all those commissioned to buy, purvey, or ship grain for the king's household or army as well as all justices of the peace, sheriffs, customers, and other officers were prohibited from seizing grain from those who were engaged in buying or shipping it to supply London.[25] This may have been a precautionary measure on the king's part to prevent a disruption in London's food supply when planning for another campaign against France later in the year. On August 24, 1522 the king ordered all those with grain, beer, and other victuals to supply his growing army in France. In return, such shipments would be free of customs and other tolls at both ends of the trip.[26] Later in 1522, the king imposed a prohibition on export of grain and ordered those with grain to sell to bring it to ports to supply his soldiers bound for France.[27] A similar situation had arisen in 1512–13 during an earlier campaign in France. On December 15, 1512 a royal proclamation prohibited the

[21] *Ibid.*, p. 81 nt. 2.   [22] Hall, *Chronicle*, p. 632.

[23] Gras, *The Evolution of the English Corn Market*, p. 82 nt. 3; Leonard, *The Early History of English Poor Relief*, pp. 24–5.

[24] Gras, *The Evolution of the English Corn Market*, pp. 80–5, 421–5; Wriothesley, *A Chronicle of England*, vol. 1, pp. 147, 156, 163; vol. 2, pp. 15, 30, 37, 45–7; Kingsford (ed.), "Two London Chronicles," p. 47; *LP*, vol. 14 pt. 1, 209; Hudson and Tingey (eds.), *The Records of the City of Norwich*, vol. 2, pp. xcvii, ci–cii, 161, 126–7; Pound, "Government and Society," pp. 253, 266–8; Smith (ed.), *The Maire of Bristowe*, pp. 61–3; Owen, *A History of Shrewsbury*, vol. 1, p. 400.

[25] Hughes and Larkin eds., *Tudor Proclamations*, vol. 1, pp. 134–5.

[26] *Ibid.*, p. 139. See also a similar proclamation the following year on August 21, 1523.

[27] *Ibid.*, pp. 140–1.

engrossing, forestalling, or regrating of wheat or other victuals or the shipping of them from one part of England to another or overseas, except by those individuals commissioned to buy victuals for the king's army.[28] Soon thereafter, it must have been realized that such a blanket prohibition on the movement of foodstuffs would disrupt London markets so on March 11, 1513 a proclamation similar to that of January 26, 1522 allowing those who bought grain and other victuals for the supply of London to go about their business without interference from anyone.[29]

The Crown's response to scarcity, 1527–1529

If there was little or no central government response to scarcity in the period 1519–22, matters changed soon after the failure of the harvest of 1527, which appears to have been the result of long periods of heavy rain.[30] Not only was the official response rapid but it was also sustained. For much of the rest of Henry VIII's reign the state of the harvest continued to be of concern to the crown. In the years 1527–9 it is clear that Cardinal Wolsey, the lord chancellor and chief minister of Henry VIII, was in charge of directing crown policy. Slack describes him as "the inventor of Tudor paternalism."[31] The range of Wolsey's paternalist policies included inquiries in 1517–18 into enclosures that were blamed for the decay of tillage, attempts to implement quarantine measures in times of plague, and efforts to control the wandering poor as well as activist policies in response to grain scarcity.[32]

In responding to grain scarcity, Wolsey used the crown's traditional powers to issue proclamations and create commissions to announce and to enforce remedial measures.[33] In November, after the failure of the 1527 harvest, a royal proclamation was issued that prohibited the regrating, forestalling and engrossing of grain.[34] Those who engaged in such activities, which meant in effect withholding grain from the open market, were accused of driving up prices and, as a result, "there is pretended to be more scarcity of wheat and other grain within this realm than (God be Thanked) there is indeed." The king "having tender zeal and

---

[28] *Ibid.*, pp. 99–101.   [29] *Ibid.*, pp. 102–3.
[30] Hall, *Chronicle*, p. 736; Stow, *The Annales of England*, p. 886.
[31] Slack, *Poverty and Policy*, p. 116.
[32] *Ibid.*, pp. 116–17; Slack, *From Reformation to Improvement*, pp. 14–16; Guy, *Tudor England*, pp. 90–5, 171; Scarisbrick, "Cardinal Wolsey and The Common Weal," pp. 45–67; Gwyn, *The King's Cardinal*, pp. 411–63.
[33] For the use of proclamations in Henry VIII's reign in response to scarcity see Heinze, *The Proclamations of the Tudor Kings*.
[34] Hughes and Larkin (eds.), *Tudor Proclamations*, vol. 1, pp. 172–4.

love to the common weal" ordered that all people who had supplies of grain should bring it weekly to sell in local markets "at a reasonable price."[35] Otherwise, they would be punished according to established law. To ensure that grain would be brought to market, the proclamation announced that the king had appointed commissioners in every county to make searches in barns, garners and the like and to compel the owners, after deducting seed and the amount necessary to feed their households until the next harvest, to bring any surplus to the local market to sell. Those who failed to comply were to be punished and their names submitted to the king's council in star chamber.

The proclamation then went on to make a special provision for the needs of London, much like the earlier proclamation of 1513 and 1522 in the city's favor.[36] Given London's grain needs, commissioners, justices of the peace, and other officers were prohibited from interfering with the activities of those who bought grain in every county for the supply of London as long as the counties were left with enough grain for their inhabitants. Finally, the proclamation indicated the king's displeasure with the negligence of justices of the peace and other local officials in their failure to enforce laws against vagabonds, beggars, unlawful games and disorderly taverns and alehouses. It called for swift and vigorous action to remedy the situation. This last provision is one indicator of Wolsey's central role in devising the policies contained in the proclamation.

There survives a second, similar proclamation, undated, but clearly from the same period although probably later than the first. It elaborates upon some of the points contained in the first and appears to reveal growing official anxiety about the deteriorating social situation. In their search for grain, the commissioners were now instructed to call before them all the officials of "every city, borough, town, and village" to discover if they knew of any hidden grain that may have been missed by the commissioners. In addition, local officials were now charged to report to the commissioners the names of all people who refused to bring their surplus grain to market. Such names were then to be forwarded to the king and his council so that the offenders could be summoned to appear. Since many of the commissioners were also justices of the peace, it was also their duty to punish all forestallers, regraters, and engrossers of grain according to the law and then to order them to appear before the king and his council. Finally, regarding the punishment of beggars and vagrants, the commissioners, again as justices of the peace, were

---

[35] *Ibid.*, pp. 172–3.
[36] *Ibid.*, pp. 102–3 and pp. 134–5. See also a similar proclamation of September 25, 1527, pp. 170–1.

commanded to punish them according to the statutes and see that all other local officials fully executed their obligations under the same laws. If the local officials failed in their duty then the justices must "enjoin them, upon pain of £100," to appear before the king and his council in star chamber.[37]

Similar proclamations, with language that indicates growing frustration with the ongoing grain scarcity and high prices, continued to be produced during the years 1528–9. In December 1528, one was issued that covered a number of different topics including archery, handguns, and unlawful games. At the end there was a section condemning forestalling, regrating, and engrossing as the causes of the continuing high prices and scarcity of grain. The king urged every one of his subjects to convey the names of those suspected of committing such offences to local justices of the peace and other officials, who were charged with punishing "the malefactors and offenders." If the magistrates did not act diligently, they would "answer unto the King's highness at their utmost peril."[38]

In August 1529, a brief proclamation was issued that prohibited regrating, which continued to be blamed for the scarcity and high prices of grain.[39] Two months later, in October, a longer proclamation condemned both forestalling and regrating for the scarcity and high prices. Those with surplus grain, beyond seed and household needs, were again urged to bring it to market under the threat of forfeiture of the grain and imprisonment at the king's pleasure, without bail or mainprize. Justice of the peace and other local officials were again charged with putting the proclamation "in effectual and due execution" or else they would answer to the king "at their extreme" peril.[40]

While the proclamations provide some sense of the aim of government policies in response to scarcity, it is difficult to assess their effectiveness. The regular repetition of the same language of condemnation and what can only be called royal bluster creates the impression that little or nothing was achieved. To attempt to assess the effectiveness of Wolsey's policies it is necessary to turn to the grain commissions and the grain surveys that they produced.

It appears that the first grain survey was ordered on September 26, 1527, when commissioners were appointed in Kent to search for grain and to compel those with a surplus to sell it in the market.[41] In the

---

[37] Hughes and Larkin (eds.), *Tudor Proclamations*, vol. 3, pp. 274–5.
[38] Hughes and Larkin (eds.), *Tudor Proclamations*, vol. 1, pp. 177–81. The grain section is on pp. 180–1.
[39] *Ibid.*, p. 188.   [40] *Ibid.*, pp. 190–1.
[41] Heinze, *The Proclamations of the Tudor Kings*, p. 99.

days after the proclamation of November 12, 1527 that announced the nationwide policy of grain searches, commissions were appointed in every county to undertake the searches subdivided into smaller groups to survey different subdivsions of each county and to carry out the other obligations laid upon them in the proclamation.[42] The records of a number of grain searches survive for 1527–8, considerably more than those contained in the list made by Ashley many years ago.[43] He listed surveys for five hundreds in Wiltshire, five wapentakes in Nottinghamshire, nine hundreds in Kent, twelve wapentakes and the town of Scarborough in the north riding of Yorkshire and five parishes in Middlesex. He missed surveys from sixteen hundreds in Northamptonshire, one hundred in Essex, and seven parishes in Middlesex.[44] There is, finally, one brief survey from Staffordshire that Ashley also missed. It lacks any details on the amounts of grain surplus or shortage in local communities that are characteristic of the other surviving surveys.[45]

The surviving surveys are only a small proportion of the number that would have been submitted to the crown if, in fact, the justices in every county actually undertook them. Whether or not they did is an open question. There is evidence that surveys were planned to take place in Norfolk and Suffolk during December 1527.[46] Then, on January 17, 1528, in a letter that the Duke of Suffolk wrote to Wolsey he mentioned that the grain survey undertaken by him and the other commissioners in Norfolk was enclosed.[47] The loss of the Norfolk

---

[42] TNA, SP1/45 ff. 58–9; *LP*, vol. 4 pt. 2, 3587 (4), a standard form for the commission. Commissions sent to the JPs of Berkshire and the JPs of Northamptonshire are in TNA E40/14908 and 14909; *LP*, vol. 4 pt. 2, 3587 (1–2).

[43] William Ashley, *The Bread of Our Forefathers*, pp. 187–8. The originals are: TNA, SP1/45 ff. 199–224 and SP1/46 ff. 149–63 (Wiltshire); SP1/44 ff. 372–5 and SP 1/46 ff. 132–48 (Nottinghamshire); SP1/59, ff. 298–9 (Kent); E 163/10/13 (Yorkshire); E 163/16/19 (Middlesex). All but Middlesex are calendared in *LP*, vol. 4 pt. 2, 3544, 3665 (3), 3819 (1–2), 3822 and vol. 4 *Appendix*, 273.

[44] TNA SP1/45 ff. 60–4, 198, 286–308 (Northamptonshire); SP1/45 ff. 196–7 (Essex); see also Dymond, "The Famine of 1527 in Essex," 29–40. All these grain surveys are calendared in *LP*, vol. 4 pt. 2, 3587 (5), 3665 (1–2), 3712. The survey of seven parishes in Middlesex – Acton, New Brentford, Ealing, Chiswick, Fulham, Kensington and Chelsea – is undated but it is clearly from 1527–8. It is also easy to miss. It is in TNA E 36/257, bound up with four registers of bonds entered into by merchants who were shipping grain either overseas or coastwise to other parts of England in 1530–2. The registers of bonds are briefly calendared in *LP*, vol. 5, 1706 but the survey is not mentioned. Selections from the survey, mainly relating to the parish of Ealing, were published in Pugh "A Grain Shortage of the 1520's," 20–3, 33–7, but the location of the original was not provided.

[45] Leadham (ed.), *Select Cases*, pp. 165–8. It was also printed in Tawney and Power (eds.), *Tudor Economic Documents*, vol. 1, pp. 143–4.

[46] TNA SP 1/45 ff. 194–5; *LP*, vol. 4 pt. 2, 3644.

[47] TNA SP1/46 ff. 122–3; *LP*, vol. 4 pt. 2, 3811.

survey, along with the likely loss of the one for Suffolk, is perhaps indicative of the fate of the others that are missing.[48]

Since the surviving surveys are few in number, it is impossible to offer broad generalizations about the grain supply nationwide. Nonetheless, the existing surveys do reveal marked differences in supply between different counties. The surveys for Nottinghamshire, Northamptonshire, and Kent all reveal large surpluses of grain.[49] Other surveys, especially those for Essex and Wiltshire, reveal shortages of grain but it is difficult to assess their real significance.

Dymond has carefully analyzed the survey of ten parishes in the hundred of Hinckford in northwest Essex begun on December 15, 1527.[50] His analysis is constrained by the kind of information contained in the survey as created by William Clopton who conducted it. Clopton focused on the population of each parish, the existing stock of bread grain (wheat, rye, and maslin lumped together) the stock of barley and malt, the stock of peas, oats, and vetches, the supply of bread grain and drink grain needed until the next harvest, and the shortage or surplus of both. Dymond, following Clopton, found that the total population in the parishes, 1,055 people, had only 179.83 quarters of bread grain in stock but needed 811.85 quarters to get to the next harvest. Similarly they needed 1,124.5 quarters of drink grain but only had 721.25 quarters on hand. With a deficiency of 632.02 quarters of bread grain and 403.25 of drink grain, Dymond concluded that the people of Hinckford were in a dire situation, although there was considerable variation between parishes on the extent of the shortage.[51]

Unfortunately, the Hinckford survey lacks any information on the number of people or households either with a surplus or at least enough grain to last until the next harvest. Nor does it provide information on those whose grain supply was either deficient or nonexistent. The absence of such information makes it hard to assess the severity of the harvest failure's effects on the Hinckford population. Even if such information were provided as it is, for example, in the surviving Wiltshire surveys, it is nonetheless somewhat problematic.[52] The survey for the

[48] The town records of Shrewsbury indicate that a grain survey was undertaken but it does not appear to have survived, Owen, *A History of Shrewsbury*, vol. 1, p. 309.

[49] TNA SP1/44 ff. 372–5; SP1/45 ff. 60–4, 198, 286–308; SP 1/46 ff. 132–48; SP1/59 ff. 298–9; *LP*, vol. 4 pt. 2, 3587 (5), 3665 (2), 3712, 3819 (1); vol. 4 *Appendix*, 273.

[50] TNA SP1/45 ff. 196–7; Dymond, "The Famine of 1527 in Essex," 29–40.

[51] Dymond, "The Famine of 1527 in Essex," 29–33.

[52] I excluded the survey of the Wiltshire hundred of Amesbury from this discussion because of inconsistencies in the kinds of questions asked. In the first five parishes surveyed, the number of people with grain surpluses is listed along with the total population of each parish but it is impossible to determine the number of individuals or households that

hundred of Elstubbe and Everley in Wiltshire shows that there were 133 households with sufficient grain for seed and for sustenance until the next harvest, while some also had a surplus to sell. There were also 116 households with no grain. The survey of the hundreds of Brenche and Dolsend, Underdyche, and Alderbury reveals that there were 110 households with surplus grain, 53 with sufficient grain but no surplus, 86 with insufficient grain for household needs and seed, and 160 with no grain at all. Next to the latter, the commissioners sometimes wrote that such households would need to buy it. Finally, the commissioners also noted that the inhabitants of the parish of Lake in Underdyche hundred would have to buy or borrow grain while, aside from the three households with surplus grain in the parish of Great Wodeforde in the same hundred, the rest of the inhabitants would also have to buy or borrow grain.[53]

One crucial question that none of the grain surveys can answer is in a good year how many of the households that had no grain stored after the failure of the harvest of 1527 would have had grain on hand? In other words, was the harvest failure the cause of their lack of grain or was it their social and economic situation that was to blame, whether the harvest was good or bad? It is reasonable to assume that most of the households that had no grain were headed by men who did not have land beyond, at best, a small holding. Such men probably worked for wages as laborers or artisans and were dependent on the market for food supplemented by what they and their wives could raise on their smallholdings. It is hard to believe that such people would have had a store of grain on hand even at the best of times. It was more likely that they regularly bought bread or small amounts of grain or flour in the market for immediate needs. This also seems to have been the case in the surveyed Middlesex parishes, which also had a high proportion of households with no grain stored, perhaps more understandable because many of those parishes were in the vicinity of London and more urbanized than the surveyed Essex and Wiltshire hundreds.[54]

One other significant limitation of the grain surveys is that each one is a snapshot of a moment in time. As a result, they do not convey any information about what happened during the days and months after the commissioners finished their work. For example, even if the surviving

were short of grain or had none at all. For the next seven parishes it is possible to calculate that 438 people had grain while 635 had none. TNA SP1/45 ff. 199–210; *LP*, vol. 4 pt. 2, 3665 (3).

[53] TNA SP1/45, ff. 211–24; *LP*, vol. 4 pt. 2, 3665 (3).

[54] TNA E163/16/19; E36/257, ff. 45–56. See also Pugh, "A Grain Shortage of the 1520's," 34–7.

grain survey of nine hundreds in Kent from September 1527 show a grain surplus, by June and July 1528 a combination of depression in the cloth industry and growing grain scarcity and high prices drove artisans and laborers in some parts of Kent to protest and insurrection.[55] It is probably safe to assume that the commissioners in those areas, which had grain surpluses, ordered the markets to be supplied weekly as instructed in their commissions. In a few instances the surveys make it clear that such orders had been issued.[56] In one instance, the survey of the hundred of Clayley in Northamptonshire, the commissioner reports that, after the search, the markets were reasonably well supplied.[57] The more difficult question to answer is what was done to supply places that were grain deficient. Their plight is clearly laid out in the brief Staffordshire grain survey. The commissioners report that after searching barns, garners, and the like they concluded that there was insufficient grain in the county to sustain its inhabitants. To meet their needs it would be necessary to buy grain in other counties. They urged that no restraint be put on those counties to prevent them from selling grain to the people of Staffordshire "for their necessary sustynaunce and lyffyng."[58]

There is some evidence that Wolsey understood the kind of problem that Staffordshire faced, even if we do not know what specific relief measures were implemented for that county. The proclamation of November 1527, which was Henry VIII's first response to the harvest failure, contained a section that sought to provide for the safe passage of grain to London from elsewhere in the kingdom to meet the city's needs.[59] Although no grain survey for Norfolk survives, it appears from Wolsey's correspondence that the county's harvest was good, or at least better than that in neighboring Suffolk.[60] There survives a copy of a letter from the Duke of Suffolk to the grain commissioners in Norfolk on shipping grain from that county to other shires in need, which the Duke included in a letter to Wolsey of February 6, 1528. Suffolk instructed the commissioners to allow purchases of grains for other places only insofar as there was enough left to supply London and Norwich as well as the hundreds for which they were responsible. He also ordered a new survey of the surplus of grain before March 1. Finally, anyone who planned to

[55] TNA SP1/48 ff. 28, 47, 51–3, 82–4, 108, 225–6; SP1/49 ff. 60–3; *LP*, vol. 4 pt. 2, 4276, 4298, 4300–1, 4310, 4331, 4414, 4455.
[56] TNA SP1/45 ff. 198, 286–308; E163/10/13; *LP*, vol. 4 pt. 2, 3665 (2), 3712, 3822.
[57] TNA SP1/45 ff. 198; *LP*, vol. 4 pt. 2, 3665 (2).
[58] Leadham (ed.), *Select Cases*, pp. 165–8; Tawney and Power (eds.), *Tudor Economic Documents*, vol. 1, pp. 143–4.
[59] Hughes and Larkin (eds.), *Tudor Proclamations,* vol. 1, p. 173.
[60] TNA SP1/45 ff. 194–5; *LP*, vol. 4 pt. 2, 3664.

ship grain out of the county had to enter a bond that included the name of the port to which it would be shipped.[61]

Some official efforts were made to obtain grain from overseas, although in at least one instance it appears to have been a spectacular failure. On November 2, 1527, the French king approved the export of 200 muids of wheat (1,288.38 quarters) custom free to England for the supply of Wolsey's household. At the same time, the chancellor of France wrote to Wolsey offering up to 800 muids of wheat (5,153.5 quarters), again customs free, to supply English markets.[62] Wolsey must have readily agreed to this because, before November was out, he had offered 200 of the 800 muids to the Duke of Norfolk for distribution to a number of Essex towns and villages in need. Two in particular, Colchester and Bergholt, were "in great necessity." Norfolk wrote to Wolsey on December 1 that the substantial men were grateful and thanked him for this offer, although many of them were reluctant either to put up money for the grain or to send agents to France to bring it back. Nonetheless, Norfolk was confident that after further discussions they would pay by new year's day.[63] By mid-December it appears that Wolsey had made other arrangements for the shipping of the grain to England for Norfolk wrote to remind him of his promise that Essex would get its share of the French grain before it reached London.[64]

Even when proposing to ship wheat to England, the French chancellor made it clear to Wolsey that such shipments were unpopular with many people in France, who wanted a prohibition on export of grain because of their own needs.[65] A year later, in November 1528, English merchants found it difficult to buy grain in France because it was in short supply.[66] This situation appears to be reflected in the statement in Hall's *Chronicle* that during the scarcity of 1527–8 merchants went to France to buy grain on Wolsey's encouragement but came back with none.[67]

Sometime late in 1527, after the failure of the harvest, Joachim Hochstetter, a member of an Augsburg family deeply involved in mining, approached Henry VIII with a proposal.[68] If the king would give him £10,000 he would bring to London 14,000 quarters of wheat bought in Europe and sell it at reasonable prices. Hochstetter also noted that

---

[61] TNA SP1/46 ff. 218–21; *LP*, vol. 4 pt. 2, 3883.

[62] *LP*, vol. 4 pt. 2, 3542–3; Zupko, *French Weights and Measures*, pp. 116–17. As is the case with other traditional measures, there were regional differences in the size of the muid, see pp. 117–20. I used the Paris muid in my calculations.

[63] TNA SP1/45 ff. 97–8; *LP*, vol. 4 pt. 2, 3625.

[64] TNA SP1/45 f. 193; *LP*, vol. 4 pt. 2, 3663.   [65] *LP*, vol. 4 pt. 2, 3543.

[66] *LP*, vol. 4 *Appendix*, 216.   [67] Hall, *Chronicle*, p. 736.

[68] Luu, *Immigrants and the Industries of London*, p. 69.

this would cost the king little because he was sure that the merchants of London would be glad to put up the money for the sustenance of the city's populace. Once that part of the bargain was complete, then Hochstetter would ship another load of wheat valued at £10,000 to be sold at a price to be settled with the king, plus arms and harness worth £5,000.[69]

This was only the opening gambit in a much bigger scheme. Sometime in 1528, Hochstetter persuaded Henry VIII to appoint him as surveyor and master of the gold, silver, copper, and lead mines in England, Wales and Ireland. As part of his proposal he planned to employ 1,000 miners drawn from Germany and elsewhere.[70] It is not clear how Hochstetter and the king planned to divide the profits, but that is of little consequence for it appears that the scheme did not get very far. Although he apparently brought over six experienced German miners to help survey English mines and had also recommended building a smelter at Comb Martin, Devon, sometime in 1529 Hochstetter left England to develop copper mines in Hungary.[71] Before his mining proposal to Henry VIII, Hochstetter and a group of German and Dutch projectors had already received a grant of all the gold and silver mines in Scotland in 1526.[72] Here too, little was achieved.

What then of the promised wheat? That is another tangled tale. It appears that the grain deal with Henry VIII proposed in 1527 was never finalized, since by the end of December 1527 Hochstetter was involved in another deal, to provide grain in return for English cloth, this time with the prominent London merchant, Richard Gresham and his brother John.[73] Early in March 1528, in a letter to Wolsey, Richard Gresham praised Hochstetter as "one of the richest merchants" in Germany and "a great importer of wheat to London" with influence at the imperial court, which he had used to obtain safe conduct for Gresham and two other English merchants, who had been among those arrested along with their ships and goods in retaliation for the arrest of German merchants in England.[74]

Later in 1528, Gresham was singing a different tune in a letter to Wolsey complaining that Hochstetter had not delivered any of the

---

[69] *LP Addenda*, vol. 1, 188–9.   [70] *LP*, vol. 4 pt. 2, 5110; *LP Addenda* vol. 1, p. 564.

[71] *LP*, vol. 4 pt. 2, 5110; Cunningham, *Alien Immigrants to England*, pp. 122–3; Darling, "Non-Ferrous Metals" p. 81.

[72] *Acts of the Parliament of Scotland*, vol. 2, p. 310.

[73] *LP*, vol. 4 pt. 2, 4662, which includes three of four agreements between Hochstetter and Gresham for grain in exchange for cloth. The delivery dates for the grain run from early March to late May 1528.

[74] *LP*, vol. 4 pt. 2, 4018.

11,000 quarters in Baltic grain he had contracted with the Greshams to deliver to London in return for cloth, some, but not all, of which had been shipped in installments to Hochstetter.[75] Hochstetter's response, on May 2, was that when the ships were loaded with grain they were arrested in "Brabant, Bremen and elsewhere."[76] There is some other evidence in an April 6, 1528 report to Wolsey from John Hacket, the English ambassador in the Low Countries, that six ships carrying Hochstetter's grain were arrested at Amsterdam and Antwerp on the orders of the governor of the Low Countries, Margaret of Austria.[77] Hacket asked Margaret to release the ships "saying that Wolsey had written in favor of those who would bring corn or other victuals into England." After some discussion with leading officials in her government, Margaret allowed the two ships at Antwerp to sail for London but the stadtholder of Holland refused to release the four ships at Amsterdam "saying that the Emperor has some actions upon the Hochstetters which my lady and the Council did not know of when they gave this permission."[78] Even if some of that grain reached London, it is unlikely that any of it was intended for the Greshams.

In late August 1528, Hochstetter sent a letter to Henry VIII in which he attempted to vindicate himself. He claimed that the ships with the Greshams' grain were detained at Nieuport in the Low Countries, but made no mention of their release. Then, at some point, he left England for Burgundy. According to Hochstetter, during his absence the Greshams unfairly defamed him as a "bankrupt who had fled from England with other people's money." As a result of this and other false rumors that the Greshams spread in Europe, Hochstetter claimed a business loss of £30,000 and demanded restitution.[79] In the end, according the chronicler Edward Hall, it was merchants of the Steelyard and merchants from Flanders and Holland who provided relief for London by importing large quantities of grain from Danzig, Bremen, Hamburg, and other places in the Baltic.[80]

To strengthen the enforcement of the crown's grain policy in 1527–9 the two proclamations that had announced the establishment of the grain commissions to search for grain also stated that the names of forestallers, regrators, and engrossers should be forwarded to the King's council in star chamber.[81] There survives in the records of that court an undated list

[75] *LP*, vol. 4 pt. 2, 4662. The actual grain total calculated from the statements of deficiencies from Richard and John Gresham was 10, 812 quarters.

[76] *LP Addenda* vol. 1, 583.   [77] *LP*, vol. 4 pt. 2, 4147.   [78] *Ibid.*, 4244.

[79] *Ibid.*, 4662.   [80] Hall, *Chronicle*, pp. 736, 744.

[81] Hughes and Larkin (eds.), *Tudor Proclamations*, vol. 1, p. 173 and vol. 3 p. 275.

of forestallers and regrators of grain markets presented by constables and bailiffs in Bedfordshire and Buckinghamshire that may well date from 1527–8.[82] In addition, there are incomplete records of three cases in star chamber from the 1527–8 period that deal with forestalling or engrossing grain plus one other undated fragment of a similar case that might date from the same period, a few surviving odds and ends of what must have been, at one time, a much larger archive.

On January 8, 1528, a bill was submitted to star chamber by William Bareth gentleman and others on behalf of the inhabitants of Oundell in Northamptonshire accusing James Newby of being a regrator and forestaller "contrary to the kynges lawse" and the king's grain commission proclaimed in the open market of Oundell on December 7, 1527.[83] According to the bill, on three consecutive market days after the commission was proclaimed, Oundle refused to bring grain to market but sold it to strangers, presumably from his own garner.[84] On the third market day, December 28, William Bareth went to buy grain in the market and there "he hard the pore peple make grett lamentacyon for corne." In the market there were ten to twelve buyers for every seller. Bareth persuaded the local bailiff to go to Newby's house to try to make him bring grain to market but he failed in his efforts. Then, in the presence of the grain commissioners, Bareth accused Newby of being a forestaller and regrator. The commissioners ordered him to bring grain to market but he refused.[85] Other counts against Newby included selling malt on December 26 to a known regrator and forestaller, conspiring with three others to enhance the market price of grain, and buying grain in Cambridgeshire and Northampton and keeping it off the market to enhance prices.[86] In his answer to the bill, James Newby proclaimed his innocence on all charges. He only bought grain lawfully and, except for one market day in Christmas week, he sold most of his grain in the market where he also planned to sell what he had left. Finally, Newby claimed that he never bought grain and hoarded it to enhance the market price.[87]

In 1529, the constables of Yaxley and Holme in Huntingdonshire submitted a bill in star chamber that accused Thomas Alward and Christopher Branston, both of Lynn in Norfolk, of forestalling, engrossing and regrating a total of 490 quarters of barley, oats, peas, and beans, bought in an area within seven miles of Yaxley, which they then shipped to Norfolk. As a result, the price of peas and beans in local markets

<hr />

[82] TNA STAC2/26/103.   [83] Leadam (ed.), *Select Cases*, pp. 168–9.
[84] *Ibid.*, pp. 169–73.   [85] *Ibid.*, pp. 173–4.   [86] *Ibid.*, pp. 175–6.
[87] *Ibid.*, pp. 177–8.

rose 2s the quarter.[88] These actions were not only contrary to the king's proclamation of November 1527 but also showed no regard either for "the comon welthe of the Realme nor the necessary and nedefull sustentacion of the kinges pore subgiettes."[89]

Unfortunately, the loss of the star chamber order and decree books means that in these first two cases the court's final judgments do not survive, although the fragmentary records of the next two cases provide evidence of the likely results if the defendants were found guilty. The first is a draft of a bill submitted by Roger Barbour of Bedfordshire. According to that bill, on January 30, 1528 the court had decreed that since Barbour, on a number of occasions, had bought a total of 400 quarters of barley in the markets of Shefford and Bedford in Bedfordshire for 5s 8d a quarter and sold it for 8s a quarter, he must sell 60 quarters of barley in each of three markets in the shire for 6s the quarter. The sales were to be carried out under the supervision of four gentlemen, probably grain commissioners, appointed by the court. In addition, the court voided all the sales of the 400 quarters of barley at 8s the quarter. Now John Wright, who had bought 100 quarters at 8s, was suing Barbour in the court of common pleas to enforce the contract in violation of the star chamber decree. It turns out that, by the date of Barbour's star chamber bill, the price of barley had risen to 9s the quarter so 8s seemed like a bargain to Wright but not to Barbour who would need to buy barley at 9s or more and then sell it at 8s. Barbour asked the court for an injunction that would stop Wright's suit in common pleas going any further.[90]

The record in the next case is an undated and badly faded rejoinder by Robert Brill and Thomas Hert to the replication of William Brew. According to the rejoinder William Brew regrated barley in Reading on a number of occasions, each time buying 300 quarters for 2s 4d the quarter and thereby caused the market price to rise to the "ondoyng of the poore people." Moreover he would only sell at a price that he himself set. Brew also brought 100 quarters of malt to Reading to sell when it was 6s 4d the quarter, but Brill and Hert, who were justices of the peace, aided by the bailiffs of the town, compelled the sale of the malt at 5s 4d the quarter because "the poor people of the country made gret [lam] entacion" to them. Although Brew's bill that started his case has not survived, there is little doubt that it was the forced sale of the malt that drove his star chamber suit.[91]

---

[88] *Ibid.*, pp. 178–82. There is a second bill in the case that will be discussed in Chapter 7 as part of an exploration of the popular response to scarcity, pp. 182–4.
[89] *Ibid.*, p. 179.   [90] TNA STAC2/3 f. 109.   [91] TNA STAC2/25/200.

Regulation after Wolsey's fall

In the years after Cardinal Wolsey's fall, the crown remained active in the regulation of grain marketing. At least through 1535, grain commissions continued to exist. After that date they seem to have disappeared, although in 1544 the search powers of the grain commissioners were transferred directly to the justices of the peace in each county.[92] There was, however, a marked change in focus of official grain policy, perhaps as a result of Thomas Cromwell's growing influence. Export prohibitions became much more frequent, along with a greater emphasis on punishing illegal export. At the same time, major concerns of the crown continued to be providing grain and other victuals to supply Calais and Boulogne and related military activities. Then, towards the end of Henry VIII's reign, the provisioning needs of the war with France began to dominate grain policy. After the poor harvest of 1545, commissions were revived to search for surplus grain, not for the purpose of compelling sale in local markets to help consumers but for meeting the needs of the king's army. At the same time, the king's agents on the continent made considerable effort to buy up as much grain as they could for the same purpose.

In the regulation of grain marketing, the crown continued to express concern about the effects of forestalling, engrossing, and regrating, which were condemned in a proclamation of November 1534. The language was similar in tone and substance to the proclamation of 1527, which had set out the powers of the new grain commissioners. It blamed the rise of grain prices, especially those of wheat and rye, on "the subtle invention and craft of divers covetous persons" and ordered that no one should buy wheat or rye to sell again except to supply London and other towns or to make bread "to be sold to his subjects." Such grain purchasers were to find sureties before a grain commissioner that they would follow through on such sales. Also, those with enough wheat and rye to meet their household and seed needs were prohibited from buying grain. Those engaged in agriculture could only buy wheat and rye for seed, if they proved before a grain commissioner that they needed to make such a purchase or, within eight days of buying such grain, they brought an equivalent amount of their own wheat and rye to sell in the market. All those with surplus grain beyond their household and seed requirements, were to bring it to market in fixed quantities as ordered by the grain commissioners and sell it at reasonable prices. Finally, all local officials and "all other his loving subjects" were urged to inform the grain

---

[92] Hughes and Larkin (eds.), *Tudor Proclamations*, vol. 1, pp. 221–2, 343–5.

commissioners, the chancellor or the king's council of all offenders, who would be punished with fines or possible imprisonment.[93]

From late August to November 1535 after another poor harvest, Cromwell received a number of reports of high prices and scarcity from different parts of the country. In London there were fears that the price of bread would double and force the poor to beg or steal. The prices of all grains were high.[94] From Kent it was reported that after the harvest the price of a quarter of wheat had doubled to 12s and that regrators were buying up large quantities of grain to sell in London, where they could get 14 or 15s per quarter.[95] There were also complaints of regrators buying large amounts of grain in Lincolnshire and Holderness and driving up prices in the city of York.[96] A report was received from Shropshire that the scarcity of grain was increasing and was the cause of more frequent robberies.[97] In a letter dated September 4, 1535, the London merchant Stephen Vaughan told Cromwell that the price of grain had grown to such a high price that the people were in need of his help against regrators.[98] As a consequence of these reports, and others that have not survived, lord chancellor Audley drafted a proclamation along with new commissions to search for grain that were issued by September 30.[99] Unfortunately, nothing appears to have survived of either the proclamation or the commissions.

In November 1544, another proclamation, similar to that of November 1534, blamed the recent rise in the prices of all grains on those who had accumulated great quantities, far beyond their household and seed needs, and kept it off the market in order to drive up prices. Such engrossers were condemned as "having more respect to their own private lucre and advantage than to the commonwealth of this his highness' realm." Grain prices were so high, according to the proclamation, "that his majesty's loving subjects cannot gain, with their great labours and pains, sufficient to pay for their convenient victuals and sustenance." The remedy was, in fact, a revival of the grain commissions with the justices of the peace receiving the authority of commissioners.

Within twenty days of the issue of the proclamation, the justices of the peace in each county or borough were to meet and divide themselves into groups of two, each of which would be assigned a number of hundreds, wapentakes, rapes, commotes, or towns and villages within the county for the purpose of searching "the houses, barns and yards" of those likely to have a grain surplus beyond their needs until the next

---

[93] *Ibid.*, pp. 221–2. See also *LP*, vol. 7, 1417.   [94] *LP*, vol. 9, 152, 274–5, 700.
[95] *Ibid.*, 110, 243, 353, 399.   [96] *Ibid.*, 456.   [97] *Ibid.*, 841.   [98] *Ibid.*, 274.
[99] *Ibid.*, 358, 487.

Feast of All Saints (in effect after the harvest of 1545). When a surplus was discovered, the justices were to compel the owner in the king's name to sell it in the market and to provide each owner with a written schedule of amounts of grain and dates when it was to be sold. Anyone who refused to comply was to be fined 3s 4d for each surplus bushel not brought to market.[100] Unfortunately, there appears to be no surviving evidence to assess the effects of the enforcement of any of the three proclamations of 1534, 1535, and 1544.

The origin of the requirement that exporters of grain and other products must buy a license from the king is unclear but certainly it had been regularly in force from the reign of Edward II onward. There was a change in 1437 during the reign of Henry VI when the king agreed to a temporary statute valid only until the next parliament that allowed the export of grain without a license when the prices of a quarter of wheat and a quarter of barley were below 6s 8d and 3s respectively.[101] By 1439, the time of the next parliament, the bad harvests of 1437 and 1438 had occurred, licensing had been restored and there was little chance of a renewal of the 1437 statute. In 1442 the statute was renewed for ten years and in 1445 it was renewed permanently, a result of the decline in grain prices which remained low for most of the remaining years of the fifteenth century and into the early years of the sixteenth.[102] In May and July 1482, Edward IV reintroduced licensing for all grain exports as did Henry VII in 1492.[103] These were apparently only temporary measures in effect during scarcity.

During much of the reign of Henry VIII, certainly in the periods 1516–31 and 1535–47, licenses or bonds were generally required for the export of grain, although as a result of military provisioning needs there were two short term complete export bans issued in 1544 and 1545. From 1516 until 1531 export licenses were regularly issued but there appears to be no surviving proclamations imposing prohibitions on unlicensed export during those years.[104] The first surviving proclamation prohibiting the export of grain and other victuals dates from September 7, 1531, although there is some evidence that an earlier proclamation was

---

[100] Hughes and Larkin (eds.), *Tudor Proclamations*, vol. 1, pp. 343–5.

[101] *Parl. Rolls*, "Henry VI: January 1437," item 21; *SR*, vol. 2, pp. 295–6, 15 Hen. VI c. 2.

[102] *Parl. Rolls*, "Henry VI: January 1442, item 23; "Henry VI: February 1445," item 33; *SR*, vol. 2, pp. 319–20, 20 Hen. VI c. 6; pp. 331–2, 23 Hen. VI c. 5.

[103] Steele (ed.), *A Bibliography of the Royal Proclamations*, vol. 1, pp. clxxvii–viii; Hughes and Larkin (eds.), *Tudor Proclamations*, vol. 1, p. 27; *CPR, 1476–85*, pp. 264, 320, 329.

[104] Jones, *Inside the Illicit Economy*, p. 210 and nt. 14, which contains references to some of the many licenses to be found in the relevant volumes of *LP Henry VIII*.

issued before July 29 of that year.[105] Although Heinze describes this proclamation as a prohibition on unlicensed exports, there is no mention of licensed shipments in the text. It appears to be a complete ban on export brought on by the fear of the "scarcity and excessive dearth of corn and other victuals."[106] Then in 1534 parliament passed a statute that prohibited export of grain and other victuals without a license from the king, which remained in effect for the rest of the reign and beyond.[107] After the poor harvest of 1535 a number of Cromwell's correspondents, who reported scarcity and high prices in their localities, urged him to prohibit unlicensed export.[108] The result was a prohibition effective sometime in September or October but there is no surviving text.[109] Yet another lost prohibition was issued before February 19, 1539.[110] A final prohibition dates from February 14, 1541, although there is only a partial text extant.[111]

The justification for the long period of export regulation up until the autumn of 1545 is made clear in the proclamations of 1531 and 1541 and the statute of 1534, all of which emphasize the needs of the consumers and condemn the activities of engrossers and regrators. The first proclamation refers to the king's concern with "the commonwealth and commodity of his loving subjects" who might suffer from scarcity and high prices in a "year not being so fruitful as was trusted" because of bad weather. Thus it was necessary to restrain export of grain and other victuals to prevent people, who only looked "to regard their own private lucre and advantage," from taking the foodstuffs out of the country and worsening the situation.[112] The surviving fragment of the second proclamation only refers generally to the king's "special regard and respect to the advancement of the commonwealth of this his realm" and "to the relief and comfort of his loving subjects."[113] The statutory prohibition on unlicensed export was part of a larger statute that was passed in response to a rise in the price of foodstuffs created by "the gredy covetousnes and appitites" of engrossers and regrators.[114]

---

[105] Hughes and Larkin (eds.), *Tudor Proclamations*, vol. 1, pp. 201–3; Heinze, *The Proclamations of the Tudor Kings*, p. 302.

[106] Heinze, *The Proclamations of the Tudor Kings*, p. 148.

[107] *SR*, vol. 3, pp. 438–9, 25 Hen. VIII c. 2.   [108] *LP*, vol. 9, 110, 152, 243, 353.

[109] *Ibid.*, 255, 534; Heinze, *The Proclamations of the Tudor Kings*, p. 302.

[110] *LP*, vol. 14 pt. 1, 319. 426.

[111] Hughes and Larkin (eds.), *Tudor Proclamations*, vol. 3, pp. 280–1; Leadam, *Select Cases* (ed.), pp. 230–3; Heinze, *The Proclamations of the Tudor Kings*, p. 179 and nt. 3.

[112] Hughes and Larkin (eds.), *Tudor Proclamations*, vol. 1, pp. 201–3.

[113] Hughes and Larkin (eds.), *Tudor Proclamations*, vol. 3, pp. 280–1.

[114] *SR*, vol. 3, pp. 438–9, 25 Hen. VIII c. 2.

In the specific case of grain, the purpose of licensing was to limit export in times of scarcity in order to direct more supplies to domestic markets and thereby limit price rises. There was also another purpose behind the licensing of grain and other goods and that was raising revenue. Licenses cost money that could either go directly to the crown from the merchant who bought one or to the government official or courtier who was rewarded with a license in lieu of salary and sold it to the merchant.[115] One of the striking ironies is that a licensing system, designed to control and limit export of grain and other goods, encouraged smuggling, because the cost of any license was not only unpredictable but usually great enough that it added considerably to the merchant's costs.

It is clear that some merchants smuggled unlicensed cargoes of grain. In 1534 Cromwell received a report that keels taking wood from Norwich to Yarmouth also carried hidden wheat and other merchandise, which were surreptitiously loaded onto ships bound for Spain and Portugal.[116] Cromwell received another report in February 1539 from Lowestoft in Suffolk of large quantities of grain being exported, some of it paying customs, some shipped illegally.[117] In a parliamentary statute of 1543, on the preservation of the river Severn, it was noted that a great deal of grain was being brought down river in boats and transferred to ships waiting in the river five miles below Bristol, which then exported the grain without paying customs duties.[118] This may have been a longstanding custom since the same allegation was first made as early as 1348.[119]

In his study of smuggling at Bristol in the sixteenth century, Evan Jones focuses on another form of smuggling by Bristol merchants. For example, in December 1540 John Smyth bought a license to export 100 quarters of wheat to Spain for £25. In addition he had miscellaneous costs of 30s 4d. The wheat cost 8s. per quarter but his other costs added an additional 5s 4d to each quarter.[120] This was the incentive that drove Smyth and others to smuggle. When Smyth's ship sailed in February 1541 he had paid customs duties on the licensed 100 quarters of wheat but his accounts show that he had actually 504 quarters of wheat on board. Smyth's accounts also show that he made payments to four

---

[115] Jones, *Inside the Illicit Economy*, pp. 27–9.   [116] *LP Addenda*, vol. 1, 338–9.

[117] *LP*, vol. 14 pt. 1, 967.

[118] Jones, *Inside the Illicit Economy*, p. 109; *SR*, vol. 3, pp. 906–7, 34, 35 Hen. VIII c. 9. For other accounts of such activity later in the century see Vanes (ed.), *Documents illustrating the Overseas Trade of Bristol*, pp. 39–40, 46, 134.

[119] *CPR, 1348–50*, pp. 67–8.

[120] Jones, *Inside the Illicit Economy*, p. 29. For another account of smuggling later in the sixteenth century see Williams, *The Maritime Trade of the East Anglian Ports*, pp. 15–33, 41–9.

customs officials, no doubt so they would turn a blind eye to the added 404 quarters of wheat.[121] This was only one voyage among many that he undertook in 1539–46.[122]

During periods when exports were either banned or licensed, those who moved grain either coastwise within England and Wales or to Calais and later Boulogne often had to enter bonds that they would ship it to a specified port and return to the port of departure with a certificate signed by an official at the destination that the grain had arrived there so that the bond could be discharged. If a certificate was not returned then the bond was forfeited to the crown.[123] There was always the temptation to enter a bond for shipping to a domestic port and then sail for a foreign port, if grain prices in Europe were high enough to risk it, on the assumption that the failure to return the certificate would not be noticed because of bureaucratic delay or inefficiency.[124]

If the system of export licenses unintentionally created one entrepreneurial group, the smugglers, the effort to stop illegal export created another, the common informers. Since Tudor government lacked police institutions to identify, arrest, and prosecute offenders, it relied on common informers to do the job. Such informers were encouraged to act by the possibility of financial reward, one half of the fine imposed on a convicted smuggler. The other half went to the crown. The amount of the fine was based on the value of the goods smuggled. To begin a legal case the informer could submit a bill either to the court of exchequer or to star chamber.[125] We have scant knowledge about the total number of informations related to smuggling submitted to the exchequer in Henry VIII's reign, but we do know that 253 were entered in 1509–58 for offences allegedly committed by Bristol merchants.[126] Forty-eight were for smuggling grain, and forty-five for other foodstuffs.

---

[121] Jones, *Inside the Illicit Economy*, pp. 100–1. For another example of this practice at Chichester in 1541, see Nicholas (ed.), *Proceedings and Ordinances of the Privy Council*, vol. 7, pp. 170–1.

[122] Jones, *Inside the Illicit Economy*, pp. 106–7.

[123] Hughes and Larkin (eds.), *Tudor Proclamations*, vol. 1, pp. 203, 341, 357, 360. There are a number of surviving registers of such bonds. See TNA SP1/67 ff. 17–28, *LP*, vol. 5, 391; TNA E36/257, ff. 1–43, *LP*, vol. 5, 1706; *LP*, vol. 15, 256.

[124] For examples of such switching of destinations see *LP*, vol. 15, 61, Jones, *Inside the Illicit Economy*, pp. 114–16, and Vanes (ed.), *Documents Illustrating the Overseas Trade of Bristol*, p. 109. For an example of the requisite inefficiency see Heinze, *The Proclamations of the Tudor Kings*, p. 149 and nt. 176. For an example of entering a bond to ship grain to Calais but ending up taking it to London to sell, see *APC 1542–1547*, p. 281.

[125] Hughes and Larkin (eds.), *Tudor Proclamations*, vol. 1, p. 203; *SR*, vol. 3, pp. 438–9, 25 Hen. VIII c. 2.

[126] Vanes (ed.), *Documents illustrating the Overseas Trade of Bristol*, p. 165.

In the period 1541–3, the common informer George Whelplay submitted at least twenty informations in star chamber against a number of merchants who were accused of shipping unlicensed grain contrary to the prohibition of February 16, 1541. As Geoffrey Elton noted in his entertaining account of Whelplay's career, the main interest in the cases "lies in the number and geographical variety." The cases covered thirteen ports in seven counties, leading Elton to conclude that "he must have employed something like a small detective agency."[127] There also survive from 1540–4 records of eight other smuggling cases brought in star chamber by eight different informers.[128] This is probably only a surviving fraction of the informations on smuggling that were originally submitted to the court. Beyond the paucity of cases, there is the problem that the full record has not survived for any of them. As a result, we cannot really judge the effectiveness of prosecution by common informer. Even if we agree with Elton "that Whelplay's informations bear the stamp of truth" and surmise that the others submitted to the court were equally true, we have little knowledge of their outcomes. There also remains a lingering suspicion that much of the smuggling of grain and other goods went undetected.[129]

The provisioning needs of Henry VIII's army 1544–1546

In the years 1544–6 Henry VIII undertook or planned a number of military efforts. Those included campaigns in Scotland and France in 1544, the defence of England against a possible French invasion in the summer of 1545, the defence of Boulogne in 1545, and a planned campaign in France in the spring of 1546. For the French campaign in 1544, an army of 40,000 men had been assembled at Calais by mid-June. After the king arrived on July 14, the army conducted two sieges, one of Boulogne, which fell on September 14, the other of Montreuil, which failed. The king departed for England on September 20, but his army was left behind to defend Calais and Boulogne. In the summer of 1545 the king had mustered at least 30,000 men, in three armies, and 12,000 men at sea for the defense of England against a possible invasion by the French, plus another force on the northern border to guard against any intervention by the Scots on behalf of their French allies. The French

---

[127] Elton, *Star Chamber Stories*, pp. 94–5.
[128] TNA STAC 2/8 ff. 150–1; 2/2/170; 2/2 ff. 210–16; 2/17/195; 2/19/209; 2/20/188; 2/22/17; 2/23/183, 208, 210; 2/29/96; Leadham (ed.), *Select Cases*, pp. 277–84. See also Nicholas (ed.), *Proceedings and Ordinances of the Privy Council*, vol. 7, pp. 264–6.
[129] Elton, *Star Chamber Stories*, p. 97.

siege of Boulogne that began in early summer 1545 was finally broken in late September of that year. For a new campaign against France, an army of 30,000 men was sent to Calais in the spring of 1546. In the end that campaign did not happen because the English and French made peace in June 1546.[130]

Those campaigns were not only expensive, with a total bill of an estimated £ 2,134,784, but also required large amounts of grain and other victuals.[131] As a result, the aims of Henry VIII's regulation of the grain market underwent a major shift. Some regulations that once responded to the needs of consumers were now used to ensure food for the king's sailors, soldiers and horses. On January 7, 1544, a prohibition on the export of grain, beer, butter, and cheese was proclaimed. This was a total prohibition so that even those who already had export licenses could not use them. Any violation of the proclamation would result in forfeiture of the cargo, a fine, and imprisonment at the king's pleasure. The justification for this action, "the necessary affairs of this realm" clearly implies military purposes especially since the proclamation states that without this prohibition there "may be great hindrance, loss, and detriment to such exploits and enterprises as for the defence of the King's majesty's subjects and annoyance of his grace's ancient enemies be thought requisite."[132] The phrase "ancient enemies" undoubtedly refers to the Scots and the French.

It may be the case that the unintentional effect of the export prohibition of January 7 was the reduction of supplies going to Calais. As a result, on October 6, 1544, when Henry VIII had returned to England after the successful siege of Boulogne, a proclamation was issued urging all of those with grain and other victuals to ship them to Boulogne and Calais after entering bonds to deliver the supplies there and nowhere else and return with a certificate signed by officials of either town that the goods had been received.[133] A month later, on November 15, another proclamation blamed the rise in grain prices on those who engrossed grain and held it off the market to drive up prices. It was this proclamation that gave the justices of the peace the power previously given to corn commissioners to search for surplus grain beyond household needs and compel its sale in the market.[134] As matters evolved in the

[130] Wernham, *Before the Armada*, pp. 156–63; Scarisbrick, *Henry VIII*, pp. 443–64.
[131] *LP*, vol. 19 pt. 1, 140, 205 (4), 272 (11); *LP*, vol. 19 pt. 2, 689; *LP*, vol. 20 pt. 2, 202, 502, 976; *APC 1542–47*, pp. 180–1, 189–90, 246, 248; Guy, *Tudor England*, p. 192. For a more detailed discussion of the victualling needs of Henry VIII's armies see Everitt, "The Marketing of Agricultural Produce," pp. 519–23.
[132] Hughes and Larkin (eds.), *Tudor Proclamations*, vol. 1, p. 324.   [133] *Ibid.*, pp. 340–1.
[134] *Ibid.*, pp. 221–2, 343–5.

coming months, however, it is likely that the motive behind this action was not concern for the needs of consumers but rather military provisioning requirements.

On September 5, 1545, the proclamation of the previous year that encouraged the shipment of grain and other victual to Calais and Boulogne was renewed for the purpose of supplying the army under siege in Boulogne.[135] It is likely, however, that such encouragement did not produce the volume of food shipments to Calais and Boulogne that the crown hoped for. The explanation is probably because the harvest of 1545 was poor. In mid September the chancellor, Thomas Wriothesley, noted that everywhere, except Norfolk, wheat was at 20s per quarter and hard to find.[136] The solution was another version of the grain commissions. On October 19 and 25, 1545, privy council letters were sent to two gentlemen, three in one case, in each of the following counties: Norfolk; Suffolk; Wiltshire; Berkshire; Buckinghamshire; Middlesex; Cambridgeshire; and Hertfordshire. They were ordered to search for surplus grain to meet the king's needs. In their searches, they were to pay close attention to regrators and others who had large quantities of grain beyond their needs.[137] Such instructions imply that the earlier proclamation of November 15, 1544 that ordered the justices of the peace to search for surplus grain and compel its sale in the open market produced poor results for the king. Moreover, while privy council letters were sent to the justices of the peace in Norfolk and Suffolk instructing them to help the commissioners, none appear to have been sent to the justices in the other counties.[138] Also, the two commissioners for Norfolk and Suffolk, Sir John Jerningham and Osbert Mountford, were royal purveyors.[139] All of this implies that the crown wanted to control this operation through loyal servants. On December 7, 1545 Sir Roger Townesende, the Chief Justice of Chester, and Robert Holdiche were added as help to the commissions of Jerningham and Mountford.[140] Earlier, on September 28, 1545, the privy council had ordered Townesende and Sir William Paston to deal with fraudulent malt makers in Norfolk and Suffolk.[141]

On December 4, 1545 a prohibition was imposed on any provisioning of cheese and bacon in Essex until February 2, 1546, except for Calais and Boulogne.[142] No doubt provisioning meant buying in large

---

[135] *Ibid.*, pp. 356–67.   [136] *LP*, vol. 20 pt. 2, 366. See also *APC 1542–47*, p. 254.
[137] *APC 1542–47*, pp. 258–9, 261. For evidence of the activities of the Norfolk commissioners against regrators and engrossers, see pp. 283, 290–1.
[138] *Ibid.*, pp. 259.   [139] *Ibid.*, 267, 283.   [140] *Ibid.*, pp. 176, 284.   [141] *Ibid.*, p. 246.
[142] Hughes and Larkin (eds.), *Tudor Proclamations*, vol. 1, pp. 358–9.

quantities beyond immediate household needs. The next day another proclamation was issued imposing a ban until February 2, 1546 on the shipment of grain, butter, and cheese from Norfolk and Suffolk except for the provisioning of Boulogne, Calais, and London. Those with grain were to inform the commissioners how much they had bought since Easter, from whom and in what towns, and the amount remaining in their hands. In addition, shippers of grain and other victuals were required to enter bonds that they would ship only to one of the three permitted destinations and return within four months with signed certificate to prove that the shipment had reached the chosen destination. Those who violated the terms of either proclamation would be punished by forfeiture of their victuals or cargo, imprisonment and a fine to the king.[143] The justification for both proclamations was the defence of the king's subjects and "the annoyance of his grace's enemies."[144]

Through the month of December, the crown continued to be concerned about the butter and cheese supply. On December 29, the privy council sent letters to the mayor of Norwich and the bailiffs of Ipswich and Colchester complaining about butter and cheese being moved into those towns at night from the Norfolk and Suffolk countryside in order to hide those victuals from the king's commissioners and thereby hindering the provisioning of Boulogne and Calais. The leaders of the town governments were instructed to aid the, unnamed, bearers of the letters "to make serche from howse to howse what masse of buttre and chese could be founde."[145]

Then on January 18, 1546 crown grain policy oscillated again in a proclamation requiring licenses for the export of grain, cheese, and butter from Norfolk and Suffolk. This new proclamation admitted that the previous proclamation of December 5, 1545 that had required shippers to enter bonds before shipping such foodstuffs to Calais and Boulogne had failed in its aim. Bonds had been entered but many of the shippers had taken their cargoes elsewhere for "their own private lucres and commodities" and left "Calais and Boulogne unfurnished." The bonds would now be replaced with royal licenses. The usual penalties for non-compliance with such proclamations were restated.[146] Then, on April 7, 1546, the Earl of Hertford, commander of the English forces in France wrote to Sir William Paget, the king's secretary, to complain about the shortage of grain and other victuals at Calais and Boulogne.[147] On receipt of Hertford's letter on April 18, the chancellor was ordered to issue a proclamation, that appeared the next day, to encourage the

---

[143] *Ibid.*, pp. 359–60.   [144] *Ibid.*, pp. 359.   [145] *APC 1542–47*, pp. 300–1.
[146] *Ibid.*, p. 363.   [147] *LP*, vol. 21 pt. 1, 566.

shipment of grain and victuals to the new haven in Boulogne through a prohibition on licensing and a restoration of bonds with all the usual punishments for violators.[148] The only explanation for this oscillation between bonds and licenses is that neither worked well but that the crown had no alternative strategy, so it continually bounced between the two. Finally on June 27, 1546 the fever broke. A proclamation announced that peace had been made with France and that merchants were free to ship grain anywhere, as long as they had a royal license to export or entered a bond to ship coastwise in England, with all the usual penalties for non-compliance.[149]

There is no doubt at all that the king and his military ambitions drove grain policy in the years 1544–6. This is clear in a privy council letter of January 28, 1546 to the duke of Norfolk, written on behalf of the king. It gives the duke a dressing down for his attempt to moderate the king's demands for Norfolk grain to provision his army. At the beginning, the letter refers to the duke's opinion that "the grete scaresetie of grayne in Norfolk" made him doubt that the amount expected from the county could in fact be provided for the king's needs. At first, the king took this "in good parte" but then he discovered that some gentlemen of Norfolk had not only refused to release any of their surplus grain for his use but had set a bad example for others to refuse as well. The letter also observed that it was from such self-serving gentlemen that the duke had received his information about the scarcity in the county. As a result, the king was skeptical about the level of scarcity that had been reported to him and insisted that the duke must help gather the original quantities of grain required from Norfolk. In addition, the duke was to summon the named gentlemen who had refused to contribute grain and order them to make their contributions and to help the grain commissioner, Osbert Mountford, to collect the rest of the county's grain contribution.[150] That same day a letter was sent to Mountford that the reluctant gentlemen and the duke of Norfolk would help him collect the grain.[151]

A further indication of the kings provisioning needs is found in March 1546 when the search for victuals was extended to Kent and Sussex. Anthony Aucher and John Manne were instructed to buy foodstuffs in the two counties and arrange for their shipment to the Earl of Hertford and his army in France.[152] Only once did the crown admit that its search for grain and other victuals might have negative effects on the populace. On January 2, 1546, a proclamation stated that there was soon

---

[148] *APC 1542–47*, p. 390; Hughes and Larkin (eds.), *Tudor Proclamations*, vol. 1, p. 367.
[149] Hughes and Larkin (eds.), *Tudor Proclamations*, vol. 1, pp. 370–1.
[150] *APC 1542–47*, pp. 325–6.   [151] *Ibid.*, p. 326.   [152] *Ibid.*, pp. 353–5.

to be a large provision of grain from Wiltshire "for the furniture of our army upon the sea." Since, however, scarcity of grain would "breed a great lack and danger to our subjects" there would a prohibition on all provisioning in the county until Easter, with the same penalties for violators as found in the earlier prohibitions.[153]

In addition to seeking domestic grain and other victuals to supply Calais and Boulogne, Henry VIII's government in 1544–6 tried to buy them in Europe, mainly for its French outposts but also for London. The best documented of those efforts dates from the first six months of 1546, before the peace with France. In mid-January of that year, because of the scarcity of grain and victuals available in England for the supply of Calais and Boulogne, the king sent William Watson and John Dymock to meet with Stephen Vaughan, now the king's factor or agent in the Low Countries, to discuss the possibility of buying grain and other victuals there and in the Baltic.[154] Their instructions were to buy 6,000 quarters of wheat at 22s or less per quarter and 2,000 quarters of rye and maslin at 20s or less. If the price of grain was higher, Watson and Dymock were to give the merchants a small amount of earnest money to hold the grain until they communicated with the king and received his approval to buy at that price. They were also to discover the prices of 3,000 gammons (hinds or rumps) of bacon, 3,000 flitches (sides) of bacon, 100 martinmas beefs, 200 weighs of cheese, and 100 barrels of salted butter and send the information immediately back to the king.[155]

In late January, Watson and Dymock decided to divide the task with the former going to the Baltic and Dymock to the Low Countries and Westphalia. When they and Stephen Vaughan wrote to the privy council from Antwerp to explain their plan, they noted that grain was scarce in southern Europe and that there were many merchants from Spain and Portugal in the city buying as much grain as they could. As a result of the Iberian competition, Vaughan and the others concluded that offering a small amount of earnest money to hold grain until the king approved of the transaction would never work.[156] Before Watson went to the Baltic, he and Dymock went to Holland to enquire about prices. In Dordrecht, they found grain but, since the price was higher than they were authorized to pay, they moved on to Amsterdam where again grain prices were too high and there was little to buy. A month earlier, Spanish and Portuguese merchants had bought all the available grain. Since then,

---

[153] Hughes and Larkin (eds.), *Tudor Proclamations*, vol. 1, p. 362.
[154] *LP*, vol. 21 pt. 1, 65.   [155] *Ibid.*, 54; *APC 1542–47*, pp. 311, 313.
[156] *LP*, vol. 21 pt. 1, 126.

Amsterdam's waters had iced up and no grain supply ships could reach the city. They believed that once the ice melted more grain would arrive and prices would fall.[157]

In Amsterdam, Watson and Dymock heard that there was no grain available either at Hamburg or Lubbeck in the Baltic. When Watson finally got to Bremen, also in the Baltic, on February 9, he found that there was a prohibition on export until the ice broke up and grain began to come down river to the city.[158] So then Watson moved on to Danzig, which was in the same condition as the other Baltic cities. On February 14, the magistrates of Danzig wrote to Henry VIII that they had no grain to export because of the ice but when grain did arrive they would send him what they could spare.[159] Six days later, Stephen Vaughan made an agreement with Erasmus Schetz, and his son, merchants of Antwerp, to ship 4,000 quarters of wheat and 6,000 quarters of rye from Danzig when the waters were open after the middle of Lent. One quarter of the wheat and half of the rye would be sent to Newcastle, the main provisioning center for the English forces in the north, and the rest to London and Dover. Through the latter port a large volume of supplies for Boulogne and Calais flowed. The agreed price on delivery was 25s per quarter for wheat and 16s for rye but £1,000 was to be paid immediately in advance.[160] Late in March, the privy council notified Vaughan of the king's approval of the agreement.[161]

Also in late March, another agent at Antwerp, William Damsell, entered an agreement with Adrian and Michael Koshler of Danzig to supply a total 3,500 quarters of rye and 500 of wheat to London and Dover on the same terms as Vaughan's agreement with Schetz. As earnest money, the sum of £200 was to be paid immediately to the Koshlers' agent in London.[162] At the same time, the king entered into an agreement with two London merchants, who agreed to supply 2,000 quarters of rye at 16s per quarter, one half to be delivered to Berwick and the other to Newcastle by July 13.[163] While the source of the grain was not mentioned, it was probably the Baltic. Meanwhile, having received permission from the king, Dymock had bought 2,000 quarters of wheat and 500 of rye at Dordrecht and 2,000 quarters

---

[157] *Ibid.*, 170.   [158] *Ibid.*, 170, 195.

[159] *Ibid.*, 218. Henry VIII received similar letters sent by the magistrates of Lubbeck on February 26 and Bremen on March 7, *ibid.*, 287, 352. On March 1, the magistrates of Hamburg had written to the king that a poor grain harvest in their part of Germany meant that they had no grain to spare, *ibid.*, 307.

[160] *Ibid.*, 251, 298.   [161] *APC 1542–47*, p. 357.

[162] *LP*, vol. 21 pt. 1, 359, 376, 428; *APC 1542–47*, pp. 426–7.

[163] *APC 1542–47*, p. 360.

of rye at Amsterdam by March 13. He also purchased 3,000 gammons of bacon, which were to be shipped to Calais and Boulogne.[164]

While Mary of Hungary, the regent of the Low Countries appointed by the emperor Charles V, gave Dymock license, on March 19, to ship any butter and cheese he bought, she refused to grant an export license for the grain bought at Dordrecht because it was grown in Cleves and Julich, both imperial possessions. Since the grain had come down the Rhine in a time of scarcity, the regent believed it should be used to relieve the emperor's own subjects.[165] Despite every effort of Edward Carne, the English ambassador to the Low Countries, to persuade the regent to grant the license she would not change her mind.[166] In one letter to Sir William Paget, Carne observes that the regent "is always in one song, that she cannot give license for any passage thereof."[167] In frustration, Dymock contemplated bribing the customs officials at Dordrecht to allow the grain to be shipped without a license, but apparently he thought better of it.[168] Although he received a letter on May 2 from the privy council ordering him to sell the Dordrecht grain, Dymock made an attempt to ship some of the 500 quarters of wheat from Dordrecht to Amsterdam where he believed he could bribe customs officials to allow it to go on to Calais, but the customer at Dordrecht would not allow it. In the end Dymock sold all the grain, making a profit of 600 Flemish pounds for the king.[169]

The sale of the grain did not end Dymock's travails. Sometime in late May, he was arrested and imprisoned in Antwerp for slanderous speech about the emperor, his placards (probably those against heresy) and the sacraments. Dymock was released in early June and banished from Antwerp on orders of the regent. In her order to release him, she noted that although his crimes deserved the death penalty she acted mercifully for Henry VIII's sake.[170] Dymock also faced some major difficulties in getting grain from Bremen in the Baltic. At some point, before March 23, 1546, William Watson made an agreement to buy 1,000 quarters of wheat at Bremen. On hearing that, Dymock sent money to buy another 2,000 quarters.[171] On April 6, he received news from his servant at Bremen that the 1,000 quarters bought by Watson was shipped for London, Dover and Calais, but that his own purchase of 2,000 would not be sent until after Easter.[172] By April 24 Dymock was sure that the

---

[164] *LP*, vol. 21 pt. 1, 383. In Dymock's later letters the amount of grain bought at Dordrecht rose to 2,600 quarters of wheat and rye. See e.g. *ibid.*, 450.
[165] *Ibid.*, 407, 420–2.
[166] *Ibid.*, 422, 434, 455–6, 463, 511–13, 525, 541, 546, 550, 614, 673.   [167] *Ibid.*, 512.
[168] *Ibid.*, 450, 541.   [169] *Ibid.*, 768, 529.   [170] *Ibid.*, 1062–3.   [171] *Ibid.*, 211.
[172] *Ibid.*, 273.

2,000 quarters were on their way.[173] Unfortunately, the authorities at Bremen imposed a ban on export until Whitsunday so none of the wheat had yet been shipped.

Nonetheless, on May 7 Dymock was optimistic that the wheat would be shipped by mid-May but two days later he was less sanguine when his servant reported that only a part of Watson's 1,000 quarters and only 700 quarters of his 2,000 were going to be shipped.[174] He planned to go to Bremen on May 10 to sort things out but it is likely that he did not go because of his arrest. Eventually, he arrived there on June 15 to discover that local territorial princes had arrested much of the wheat and would not release it until they received letters from Henry VIII, which never came. Although Dymock had already paid for the 2,000 quarters of wheat on the promise that it would be shipped within eight days after Easter, only 1,200 in the end were delivered. In the case of Watson's 1,000 quarters destined for London only 320 arrived.[175] Despite Dymock's problems with the Dordrecht and Bremen grain, he did succeed in shipping 6,706 gammons of bacon from Antwerp, no doubt intended for the English army in France and in sending nine ships from Amsterdam, four to Calais and five to Dover, loaded with 1,520 quarters of rye plus butter, cheese and bacon.[176] He was able to ship the rye because it was Baltic grain unlike the grain at Dordrecht, whose export was forbidden.[177]

A larger question, that is probably impossible to answer completely, is how much grain did Henry VIII actually receive from foreign sources in the first six months of 1546? The agreement with Erasmus Schetz and his son for 4,000 quarters of wheat and 6,000 of rye was probably fulfilled. The total cost of the grain at 25s per quarter for wheat and 16s for rye was £9,600. We know that Schetz received at least £6,000 in payment for grain.[178] It is even more likely that the agreement between William Damsell, Adrian and Michael Koshler for 500 quarters of wheat and 3,500 of rye on the same terms as that with Erasmus Schetz was fulfilled. The full contract cost £3,450. Koshler was paid £200 immediately.[179] Then on June 14, 1546 John Dymock informed the Privy Council that he had delivered 5,000 Flemish pounds to Damsell for grain, which his brother-in-law had bought. That sum is around £3,300 very close to the amount owed to the Koshlers, although it might have varied according to

---

[173] *Ibid.*, 333.   [174] *Ibid.*, 381, 387–8.   [175] *Ibid.*, 540–1, 656–67.
[176] *Ibid.*, 228, 260–1, 266–7, 528, 656.   [177] *Ibid.*, 450, 455.
[178] Schetz received an upfront payment of £1,000 when the agreement was arranged on February 18, 1546 and four payments totaling £5,000 for grain on June 24, July 3, and July 21 *LP*, vol. 21 pt. 1, 251, 298; *APC 1542–47*, pp. 465, 472, 488.
[179] *LP*, vol. 21 pt. 1, 360, 376, 428. *APC 1542–47*, pp. 426–7.

changes in the exchange rate.[180] In the end it, is difficult to determine not only the crown's grain requirements for its planned military endeavors, but also how effective it was in fulfilling them from both domestic and foreign sources. Perhaps Scarisbrick was right in his surmise that "perhaps the desperate shortage of food which bad harvests brought in their train and his failure to raise victuals and enough munitions on the continent drove him [the king] to peace."[181]

For much of Henry VIII's reign his government implemented a largely consistent policy in response to grain scarcity. That policy was a mixture of the old and the new. The old, which can be traced back to at least the reign of Edward II, involved campaigns against forestalling and other traditional market offences plus prohibitions on the export of grain and efforts to import grain from Europe The new was the appointment of grain commissioners in every county with power to search for stocks of grain in the barns and granaries of individual subjects and to compel the sale in local markets of excess grain beyond seed requirements and household needs until the next harvest. While the governments of Edward III, Richard II, and Henry VI did issue commissions to search for grain during scarcities in their reigns, the nationwide reach of the grain commissions of 1527 was novel and so too was their continued use throughout Henry VIII's reign. Moreover, such search powers in the hands of the justices peace, with some modification, remained central features of governmental response to grain scarcity until 1631.[182]

One crucial dimension of grain policy in Henry VIII's reign was that for many years the direction of policy was in the hands of the king's first ministers, first Wolsey and then Cromwell. Both appear to have been committed to efforts that would alleviate scarcity in the interest of consumers. There is some evidence that Wolsey used the court of star chamber to punish those who were charged either with market offences or refusal to bring surplus grain to market. In addition to renewing grain commissions, Cromwell made a forceful attempt to enforce export prohibitions by encouraging prosecution in exchequer or star chamber of those who illegally exported grain. The significance of the two chief ministers is underlined by events after they were no longer in charge. This is particularly obvious in 1545–6, when Henry was in control and apparently there was no one in his government who could restrain his ardor for war. As a result, grain policy was wrenched away from aiding consumers to provisioning the military.

---

[180] *LP*, vol. 1 pt. 1, 1061–2.   [181] Scarisbrick, *Henry VIII*, pp. 462–3.
[182] Slack, "Books of Orders," 1–22; Slack, *Poverty and Policy*, pp. 117, 140–1.

7   The official language of Commonwealth and the popular response to scarcity in the reign of Henry VIII

Henry VIII's government regularly used the language of paternalism and commonwealth in proclamations and other official responses to grain scarcity and high prices in order to convey the king's concern for the welfare of his subjects and to condemn the greed and self-interest of those who undermined that welfare through hoarding grain to drive up prices for their own private gain. There is little doubt that one of the main aims of such language was to keep the populace quiescent and prevent any outbursts of popular anger at scarcity and high prices. These outbursts might take the form of seditious words, riot, or rebellion. When they were likely or actually occurred, then the tone of official language in response quickly changed to one of maintaining order and punishing the disorderly.

The language of Commonwealth

In the proclamation of November 12, 1527, that condemned those who did not bring their grain to market to sell and announced the establishment of the grain commissions to search for hoarded grain, it was made clear that the king was motivated by "tender zeal and love to the common weal of this his realm and subjects."[1] Similar language is to be found in the proclamation of December 4, 1528 that blamed high grain prices on "the inordinate iniquity and covetousness of certain evil disposed persons, more regarding their own particular enriching than the due order of charity and commonwealth of this realm."[2] Some of the grain commissions of late 1527 blamed the scarcity "on sundry persons preferring their singuler lucre before the commune weale of this said realme."[3]

---

[1] Hughes and Larkin (eds.), *Tudor Proclamations*, vol. 1, p. 172. For other examples with similar language see pp. 206–7, 352.
[2] *Ibid.*, p. 180. For other proclamations with similar language see pp. 188, 190, 202, 221–2, 343.
[3] TNA, E 40/14908 and 14909; *LP*, vol. 4 pt. 2, 3587 (1–2).

In another version of the commission, hoarders were blamed for holding grain back from the market "in wretched hope of dearthe and unreasonable gayn." As a result, "the povertie might be brought in daunger to perish for lacke of foode."[4] Further condemnations of the sharp practices and avarice of dealers in grain are to be found in a number of other proclamations, including one of September 1531 that prohibited export of victuals, another of November 1534 against forestalling, engrossing, and regrating, and yet another of November 1544 on the high price of grain.[5] A further example of such condemnatory language is to be found in the statute of 1534 on food prices that included a prohibition on the export of grain without the king's license.[6]

Current historians of early modern England appear to have reached a consensus on the origin of the idea of commonwealth or commonweal. That consensus is based on an argument, made some years ago by Starkey, that the political conflict of Henry VI's reign between the supporters of the Lancastrian king and the followers of Richard, duke of York and his son, who eventually became Edward IV, produced a "new language of politics," namely "the term 'commonweal'."[7] According to Starkey, the term originated as a rallying cry for the Yorkist opponents of Henry VI, who used it to promote a program of reform and revival in contrast to the corrupt, ineffectual, and palsied government that they overthrew.[8]

The central problem with the view that "commonweal" or "commonwealth" represented something new from the mid fifteenth century onward is that it gives short shrift to similar language used widely in official documents from at least the early fourteenth century onward.[9] In fact, the only novelty in the words commonwealth and commonweal may well be that they are in English and represent an Englishing of the Latin *res publica* and *communi utilitate* or the law French *commune bien* and *commune profite*. In William Worcester's *The Boke of Noblesse*, addressed to Edward IV in 1475, but probably drafted or rewritten over a number of years beginning in the 1450s, there are some passages that define

---

[4] TNA, SP1/45, ff. 58–9; *LP*, vol. 4 pt. 2, 3587 (4).

[5] Hughes and Larkin (eds.), *Tudor Proclamations*, vol. 1, pp. 201–3, 221–2, 343–5.

[6] *SR*, vol. 3, pp. 438–9, 25 Hen. VIII c. 2.

[7] Starkey, "Which Age of Reform?" pp. 18–19. For examples of the influence of Starkey's view on the novelty of the word commonweal in the 1450's see Guy, "The King's Council," pp. 124–7 and Early Modern Research Group, "Commonwealth," 663.

[8] Starkey, "Which Age of Reform?" pp. 20–3.

[9] This assertion is based on a word search in the electronic version of *Parl. Rolls* and a reading of the preambles to the medieval statutes printed in *SR*. I have also picked up a few other examples in the Patent Rolls and Close Rolls but I am sure that a more thorough search than I was able to make would turn up many other examples.

res publica or *commune profite*.[10] These include the "naturalle love that a prince shulde have to his peple, as doing his trew diligence to doo that may be to the common wele of his peple, whiche is to be understonde in the executing of justice egallie. And for to keep them in tranquillite and pece within hemsilfe" and "every man after his power and degre shuld principallie put hlm in devoire and laboure for the avaunsment of the comon profit of a region, contre, cite, towne, or housholde."[11] Wakelin observes that Worcester "uses the phrases res publica, commonweal, and common profit apparently interchangeably."[12] Twice in *The Boke*, Worcester makes it clear that *comon profit* or *comyn profit* is the English translation of *res publica*.[13] In one telling reference to Worcester's translation, Starkey describes "common profit" as "the key phrase of the new and still unfinalized English political language," a judgment reiterated in the recent article by the Early Modern Research Group.[14] What these scholars seem to have missed is that common profit expressed as the law French *commune profite* is regularly to be found in medieval statutes and parliament rolls, along with other language that appears to have the same meaning.

In the printed *Statutes of the Realm*, the earliest examples of the language of common profit are to be found in the preambles of a number of statutes between 1235 and 1322. The provision of Merton of 1235–6 contains *de communi utilitate regni*.[15] Later, in the 1275 statute of Westminster, the following occurs *pur le commun profit de Seint Eglise & del reame*.[16] In a 1299 preamble there is an elaborate reference back to the confirmations of the Charters in 1297, *ad honorem Dei & Sancte Matris Ecclesie ac commodum tocius populi regni nostri*.[17] An even more elaborate French version is found in the ordinances of 1311, *al honor de Dieu & al honor & profit de Seint Eglise & al honor de nous & a nostre profit & a profit de nostre poeple*.[18] Variations on this formula are to be found in subsequent statutes of Edward II's reign in 1320, 1321–2 (exile of the Despensers), and 1322 (statute of York repealing the 1311 ordinances).[19] Another Latin version of Edward II's reign is found in the price setting

[10] For the work's authorship and composition see McFarlane, "William Worcester," pp. 212–15.
[11] Worcester, *The Boke of Noblesse*, pp. 21, 56–7.
[12] Wakelin, *Humanism, Reading, and English Literature*, p. 115. Morgan, "The Household Retinue of Henry V," pp. 73–4 and nt. 37.
[13] Worcester, *The Boke of Noblesse*, pp. 55, 68.
[14] Starkey, "Which Age of Reform?" p. 24; Early Modern Research Group, "Commonwealth," 665–6.
[15] *SR*, vol. 1, p. 1. For another version, *pro communi utilitate tocius regni*, see p. 4.
[16] *Ibid.*, p. 26.   [17] *Ibid.*, pp. 126–7.   [18] *Ibid.*, p. 157.   [19] *Ibid.*, pp. 180–1, 189.

ordinance of 1315, which is described as *pro communi utilitate populi dicti regni*.[20] In a telling example of the interchangeability of words, the phrase became *rei publice* when the ordinance was discussed in the *Vita Edwardi Secundi*.[21]

Beginning in 1327 and running through 1489, there is enrolled one or more statutes per parliament, each consisting of a number of different chapters. Many such statutes have a general preamble, often invoking God, the Church, and the common profit in a variety of forms. In the following discussion variations in the references to God and the Church will be ignored in order to focus solely on the language of common profit. In the preambles to many statutes of Edward III there is a wide range of language, which includes *a commune profit du poeple, pur commune profit de lui [the king] & de son people*, and *pur esse & quiete de son poeple*.[22] The most common formula to be found in the preambles of Richard II's statutes is *pur le commune profit du roialme*.[23] Variations include *pur especial commune profit & ease de nostre poeple* and *pur commune profit de ses lieges de son dit roialm*.[24] There are also Latin versions, *pro commune utilitate regni nostri* and *commodumque regni Angli et utilitatem rei publice*.[25] Also in Richard II's reign another formula appears once, *commune profit & universal bien de tout le roialme*.[26] This is reminiscent of the language in the preamble to the statute of York of 1322 during Edward II's reign that repealed the ordinances of 1311, *pur le bien de son roialme*.[27] In the statutes of Henry IV and V the formula becomes *le commune bien & profit de tout le roialme*, although preambles are rare in both reigns[28]

In Henry VI's reign, preambles became much more frequent and the formula changed to *le bien du Roy & de son dit roialme* with variations.[29] One late variation is *pur les commune bien & profit de tout le roialme*.[30] There are also two Latin preambles with similar language, *communi utilitate dicti regni*.[31] The preambles to the statutes of Edward IV's reign contain the same formulas as those of Henry VI, while the preamble to the statute produced by Richard III's sole parliament reverts to *comen profit du roialme* as does the statute of Henry VII first parliament.[32] Henry's second parliament, of 1487, includes the following, *pur le comen bien de cest son realme*. A contemporary English version of the statute

[20] *Foedera*, vol. 2 pt. 1, p. 263; *Parl. Rolls*, "Edward II: January 1315," item 37.

[21] Childs (ed.), *Vita Edwardi Secundi*, pp. 102–3.

[22] *SR*, vol. 1, pp. 257, 281, 295, 345. For other variations in the language of the preambles in Edward III's reign see pp. 255, 265, 270, 319, 332, 355, 371, 385, 390, 396.

[23] *SR*, vol. 2, pp. 6, 12, 17, 23, 32, 36.   [24] *Ibid.*, pp. 39, 61.   [25] *Ibid.*, p. 26.

[26] *Ibid.*, p. 55.   [27] *SR*, vol. 1, p. 189.   [28] *SR*, vol. 2, pp. 132, 191.

[29] *Ibid.*, pp. 216, 227, 229, 232, 272, 278, 289, 295, 301, 315.   [30] *Ibid.*, p. 353.

[31] *Ibid.*, pp. 238, 369.   [32] *Ibid.*, pp. 392, 403, 431, 452, 468, 477, 500.

translates *comen bien* as *comenwele*.[33] Finally, beginning with Henry VII's third parliament, of 1488–9, statutes were enrolled only in English so the full preamble reads "To the Worship of God and of all Holy Chirche and for the comenwele and profit of this his reame."[34] Thereafter the practice of providing a single preamble to multi chapter statutes ends but many individual statutes of Henry VII's reign contain references to the *comen wele* in various spellings.[35] At the same time, the invocation of God and the Church largely disappears, although in one instance, from 1495, unlawful assemblies were described as "to the high displeasure of all myghty god and the greate lette of the comen Weele of this londe."[36] In one other statute, of the same year, the grant of a benevolence produces language that recalls past usage "for the suertie, profite, wele and commoditie of us all youre true liegemen and subgettis."[37]

When we turn to the parliament rolls of 1327–1504, language similar to that in the statutes occurs, but with greater frequency. The phrase containing *pur commune profit* in all its various renditions is undoubtedly the most common at least through the reign of Henry IV but it becomes much less common in subsequent reigns. Beginning in Richard II's reign *pur le bien commune* begins to appear.[38] It was used during the reign of Henry IV in phrases that combines the two, such as *pur le bien et commune profit du roialme* and *pur commune bien et profit du roialme*.[39] While this formula continued to be used in the parliament rolls of Henry V there are quite a number of variations in language. Moreover, for the period 1327–1421 there are also a number of different Latin phrases contained in the parliament rolls. These included *pro utilitate et quiet tocius communitatas regni nostri Anglie* and *pro utilitate populi regni nostri Anglie* in 1344, *pro omni utilitate regnis nostri* in 1380, *rei publice* in 1384, *pro bono et utilitate regni* and *pro commodo et utilitate regni* in 1399, and *dicti regni utilitatem* in 1421.[40]

---

[33] *Ibid.*, p. 509.   [34] *Ibid.*, p. 524.

[35] *Ibid.*, p. 524, 4 Hen. VII, c. 19; p. 549, 7 Hen. VII, c. 1; p. 570, 11 Hen. VII c. 3; p. 575, 11 Hen VII, c. 9; p. 576, 11 Hen. VII, c. 10; p. 636, 12 Hen. VII, c. 1; p. 636, 12 Hen. VII, c. 3; p. 636, 12 Hen. VII, c. 5. It is likely that a more thorough search of the statutes of Henry VII, than I made, would turn up even more examples of the language.

[36] *Ibid.*, p. 570.   [37] *Ibid.*, p. 576.

[38] *Parl. Rolls*, "Richard II: October 1386," item 18; see also "Richard II: April 1384," item 4, *profit au bien de commune* and "Richard II: February 1388," pt. 1, item 40, *pur le bien et profit du nostre dit seignour et tout son roialme*.

[39] *Parl. Rolls*, "Henry IV: October 1399," pt. 1, items 66, 67; "January 1401," item 39; "September 1402," items 4, 10; "October 1407," item 14.

[40] *Parl. Rolls*, "Edward III: June 1344," items 49, 50; "Richard II: January 1380," item 40; "Richard II: November 1384," item 3; "Henry IV: October 1399" pt. 1, items 30, 57, see also item 15, 18; "Henry V: May 1421," item 18.

Although the parliament rolls of Henry VI contain many examples of the French formulas of his predecessors, there are considerably more in Latin than in any previous reign. These include references to *rei publice, regni commodo, pro bono publico,* and *bonum publicam.*[41] While French and Latin remained the dominant languages in the parliament rolls of Henry VI, a few documents in English began to be enrolled. In a commons petition of 1423 there can be found "for the ese of the poeple," "for the more ese of the peple," and "for the commen ese." In another of 1435, there occurs "to the commen gode and the universall wele of his royaume." A third petition, two years later mentions, "the commen prouffit," "for the commen weale of the same [realm]" and "for the wele of you oure sovereign lord and of this youre roialme." In 1445 yet another petition includes "for common wele of this said reaume." Finally, in the parliament 1453–4, the Duke of York, then the king's lieutenant, was described as acting for "the commune welle."[42]

Beginning in 1461, with the coming of Edward IV to the throne, and running through the reign of Henry VII until 1504, when the parliament rolls end, the use of "commyn wele" becomes more frequent, while the instances of French and Latin formulas declined rapidly. This is not surprising since English was rapidly displacing Latin and French as the language of the rolls. One example of that displacement can be seen from two commons petitions, one of 1414 the other of 1463. The first is a petition on behalf of the fletchers of London that pattern makers should be prohibited from using aspen wood favored by the fletchers *pur profit du roi et de roialme.*[43] The second is a petition from the pattern makers of London that they be allowed to use aspen wood "for the commen wele."[44] Despite the growing dominance of English, some Latin documents continued to be enrolled, such as orders to prorogue parliament, letters patent, and the chancellor's speech that opened a new parliament. As a consequence *rei publice, commune bonum,* and *bonum publicum* continue to be found in the rolls.[45]

The idea of the common good and the language associated with it was deeply rooted in the high middle ages. As Susan Reynolds observes:

---

[41] *Parl. Rolls,* "Henry VI: July 1433," item 11; "January 1437," item 5; "November 1439," item 32; "February 1445," items 10–12; "March 1453," item 22; "July 1455," item 19.
[42] *Parl. Rolls,* "Henry VI: October 1423" item 55; "October 1435," item 19; "January, 1437," item 37; "February, 1445," item 45; "March, 1453," item 31.
[43] *Parl. Rolls,* "Henry V: October 1416," item 24.
[44] *Parl. Rolls,* "Edward IV: April 1463," item 57.
[45] *Parl. Rolls,* "Edward IV: November 1461," item 15; "April 1463," items 39, 48; "June 1467," items 16, 18; "October 1472 first roll," item 12; "Henry VII: November 1485," item 1; "January 1489," items 1, 25; "October 1491" items 1, 25; "January 1497," opening speech; "January 1504," opening speech.

"Protection and promotion of the common good, whether it was called "utilitas communis," "utilitas publica," or less often "bonum commune," was therefore supposed to be a primary object of government – along, of course, with the welfare of the church and of the king and kingdom, with which it ought to coincide."[46] The use of the language of the common good was of course not limited to England but it was widespread in medieval Europe, including France, Germany, and the Low Countries.[17] In the Low Countries during the early fifteenth century the language of the common good became closely associated with the ruling Dukes of Burgundy who appropriated it to justify their actions to enhance "economic welfare and prosperity, a stable coinage, and internal concord and peace."[48]

The roots of the idea of the common good lay in the writings of theologians such as Albertus Magnus and Thomas Aquinas, who drew in turn on the much earlier works of Aristotle, Cicero, and Augustine. In his remarkable work on medieval political thought, Kempshall argues that there were "two definitions of common good" in the works of Albertus and Aquinas that were derived from their classical predecessors. One was "bonum commune," meaning "moral goodness and the life of virtue." The other was "communis utilitas," defined as "material advantage and the security of peace."[49] In his ensuing discussion of the ideas of Albertus and Aquinas Kempshall works out the political implications of the common good. One important issue for Albertus was the contrast "between common good and individual self-interest," exemplified by the "distinction between kingship and tyranny."[50] A king governs in the interest of the "res publica" on behalf of "the common good of his people." On the other hand a tyrant pursues only "his own profit and private advantage."[51] Aquinas, following Albertus, argued that the aim of law and justice is "the common benefit and the common good."[52]

Occasionally in the parliament rolls there are fuller echoes of scholastic discourse. In a few commons petitions between 1362 and 1504, concerning mainly economic issues, the activities of selfish individuals who seek only their *singuler profit* are condemned as damaging the "common good." In 1376 a petition on behalf of the commons of Middlesex who once fished in the river Brent *a grant commun profit,*

---

[46] Reynolds, *Before Eminent Domain*, p. 117. For another review of the language of the common good in fourteenth century England see Fletcher, "De La Communauté Du Royaume au Common Weal," 359–72.

[47] Lecuppre-Desjardin and Van Bruaene (eds.), *De Boni Communi.*

[48] Stein, Boele, and Blockmans, "Whose Community?" p. 168.

[49] Kempshall, *The Common Good*, pp. 24–5.   [50] *Ibid.*, p. 44.   [51] *Ibid.*, pp. 44–5.

[52] *Ibid.*, p. 112.

but now find that people who have land along the river have erected weirs *pur lour singuler profit* that greatly reduced their catch. A year later, another petition with similar wording was submitted to regulate fishing on the Thames. In that same parliament there was a petition calling for the regulation of the price of herring *a commune profit de tout le roialme* because some individuals were buying up herring *pur lour singuler profit, a grant meschief de tout la roialme*. In 1504, on two occasions, similar petitions were submitted to parliament. One was against monopolies created by guilds and companies in a number of cities and towns. They were condemned as being "for ther owne singuler profite," "ageynst the commen profite of the people" and "contrarie to the king's prerogatyfe, his laws and the common weyll of his subjects." The other was a petition that opposed the repeal of a statute of 1495 on apprenticeships in the Norwich worsted trade. Supporters of the repeal were characterized as acting "for ther owne singuler profite contrarie to the comen weale of the seide citie."[53]

Other examples of scholastic discourse are to be found in some of the speeches made by fifteenth-century chancellors at the opening of parliament. Not surprising since they were all bishops or archbishops. In November 1415 the Bishop of Winchester noted that *Sine justicia non regitur res publica*, while the Bishop of Bath and Wells quoted Seneca's letter 94 at the opening of the parliament of January 1442, *leges necesssarie sunt ad gubernacionem rei publice*. Later, in November 1485, the Bishop of Worcester opened proceedings with a statement that parliaments are elected *non propter privatum et singulare comodum set propter eis et regno publicum et commune bonum*. In January 1489, the bishop's opening speech stated that under a prince *res publica viget justiciaque floret*.[54]

There can be no doubt that, when Henry VIII issued proclamations announcing his love for the common weal and condemning the iniquity of grain hoarders, who drove up the price of grain and put their own "singuler lucre" before the needs of the commonwealth, he was drawing on a rhetorical tradition that was much older than its supposed mid-fifteenth-century origins. That language of the common good is, of course, found in statutes and parliamentary petitions that touch on wide range of issues, local and national. Nonetheless, in the specific case of the regulation of the food market, and especially in response to scarcity

---

[53] *Parl. Rolls*, "Edward III: April 1376," item 57; "January 1377," items 30, 63; Henry VII, January 1504," items 17, 29. For a petition against Papal provisions that uses the same language, see "Richard II: January 1380," item 37.

[54] *Parl. Rolls*, "Henry V: November 1415," item 1; "Henry VI: January 1439," item 1; "Henry VII: January 1489," item 1. Even more extensive discourses on the common good can be found in the opening speeches to the parliaments of July 1433, January 1437, November 1487, January 1489, October 1495, January 1497 and January 1504.

and high prices, there are a number of examples worth pointing out. In Edward II's reign the food price setting ordinance of 1315 and the king's letter of 1321 to the justices of the London Eyre on regulating food prices were justified as *pro communi utilitate*, while the proclamation imposing a prohibition on the export of grain after the failure of the 1315 harvest was for *commode populi nobis*.[55] In 1351 Edward III's government issued an ordinance regulating the sale of foodstuffs in London *pur commune profit du people*.[56] During the first eight months of 1391, Richard II, in response to scarcity, sent five separate letters to officials in different ports ordering them to allow the import of grain and other foodstuffs free of customs or other duties *pro rei publice et relevatio populi*.[57] In 1438–9, Henry VI issued a number of commissions to enquire into the activities of forestallers, engrossers, and regrators who were buying up large quantities of grain in order to profit from famine conditions. Such people were described as interested only in their *singulari commodo* and without *visceribus pietatis*. Their activities were described as against either *gubernationus politice rei publice* or *gubernatione politicam et bonum publice*.[58]

In reflecting on the language of Henry VIII's proclamations, it is important to note that, despite their condemnation of the greed and iniquity of forestallers and the like who thought only of their own profit and ignored the commonwealth, these were hardly radical ideas. Recently, Wood has argued that the language announcing the social policies of the government of Edward VI either "mimicked the language of popular politics" or "echoed popular political speech." One example given is a 1551 proclamation against forestalling that referred to "the greedy malice of covetouse men."[59] The text of the proclamation contains even stronger language, which is worth quoting: "the greedy malice and insatiable covetous desires of the breeders, broggers, engrossers, graziers, victualers, and forestallers (minding only their own lucre without respect of the commonwealth to the great damage impoverishing and disquieting of his majesty's subjects)"[60] While it is clear that there was a radical popular view of commonwealth, quite different from that

---

[55] *Foedera*, vol. 2 pt. 1, pp. 263, 276, 442; *Parl. Rolls*, "Edward II: January 1315," item 37; *CCR, 1318–23*, pp. 287, 308–9.

[56] *Foedera*, vol. 3 pt. 1, pp. 233–4.

[57] TNA, C54/232 m. 10v; C54/233, mm. 35, 34; *CCR, 1389–92*, pp. 257, 265, 348, 388, 390. See also TNA, C54/232, m. 16v and *CCR, 1389–92*, p. 332 for a similar letter with the same words ordering that no tolls should be levied on foodstuffs being carried between Oxford and Woodstock.

[58] TNA, C66/443, mm. 27v, 23v; C66/445, m. 25v; *CPR, 1436–41*, pp. 266, 268, 369.

[59] Wood, *The 1549* Rebellions, pp. 81, 148.

[60] Hughes and Larkin (eds.), *Tudor Proclamations*, vol. 1, p. 526. For similar words in other Edwardian proclamations imposing prohibitions on export of grain and other victuals see p. 435 (October, 1548), p. 496 (July 1550), p. 499 (September 1550).

held by the political elite, it is more likely, as Shagan has argued, that the rebellious commons of 1548–9 "coopted much the same commonwealth language that the government itself had been using."[61] Certainly, the language in the proclamation of 1551 is neither radical nor popular. It comes, instead, from the long tradition of government pronouncements on the common good or commonwealth into which Henry VIII's language also fits.

The popular response

While Henry VIII's government was adept at using the language of commonweal or common good, it was sometimes accompanied by, or supplanted by, a language that demanded the maintenance of order and the punishment of the disorderly in the name of the commonwealth. In the two versions of the proclamations of late 1527 on searches for hoarded grain there can also be found such language that was specifically aimed at vagabonds and beggars. In the first version, they were blamed for "idleness and vice unpunished" and various crimes "to the great inquietation of the King's true subjects and to the no little grief and displeasure of our said most dread sovereign lord."[62] In the second, there was added a section on the growing numbers of rogues and vagabonds "to the great hindrance and decay of the commonwealth of this realm."[63] The proclamation of 1530 that ordered the punishment of vagabonds and beggars with a whipping, if they were found wandering beyond their place of origin or last abode, also decries their increasing numbers and idleness as the "mother and root of all vices." Idleness is also described as "chief subverter and confounder of commonweals."[64]

Henry VIII's policy of maintaining order and punishing disorder that was aimed at the vagrant poor could be quickly refocused on the respectable among the lower orders, if they engaged in any disorder that those in authority thought might destabilize the commonwealth. In a letter of December 1527 to Wolsey, the Duke of Norfolk listed some of the crown's concerns, such as speaking "secretly or openly any seditious words, secret assemblies, murmurs or any disobedient manner."[65]

---

[61] Shagan, *Popular Politics*, p. 280. For the popular version of the commonwealth see Wood, *The 1549 Rebellions* and Rollison, *A Commonwealth of the People*.

[62] Hughes and Larkin (eds.), *Tudor Proclamations*, vol. 1, p. 174.

[63] Hughes and Larkin (eds.), *Tudor Proclamations*, vol. 3, p. 275.

[64] Hughes and Larkin (eds.), *Tudor Proclamations*, vol. 1, pp. 191–3. For other examples of such language see pp. 206–7, 352.

[65] TNA, SP1/45, ff. 272–3; *LP*, vol. 4 pt. 2, 3703.

The letters of William Warham, Archbishop of Canterbury, contain particularly rich and revealing examples of elite opinion about the lower orders, who were regarded as light headed, irrational, and motivated only by their passions, especially after drinking in an alehouse. In May, 1525, Warham and his fellow commissioners, appointed to collect the Amicable Grant in Kent, explained to Wolsey their difficulties with an indiscrete multitude of "small substaunce" who were difficult to control "bicause multitudes comonly be more ruled after thaire own self wilfulnes than after good reason or discretion and some woll fall in to fumes, and so fallen woll not be ruled by other persons, nether can or woll well rule or ordre thaymselves."[66]

In another letter, of April 1528, Warham informed Wolsey of his actions in response to a crowd that came to his manor in Kent to request his help in obtaining repayment of the forced loan. In the course of the letter he wrote that he had been careful not "to incense the yncertayne and wavering braynes of the said multitude. For comonly in a multitude the more parte lack both wytt and discretion and yet the same mor part woll take upon theym to rule the wisor." When the representatives of the crowd were in the archbishop's presence they were deferential towards him, but after the crowd left he learned "that some lewde persons emonge thaym spake unfytting wordes after they had been in the town and dranke theyr fill."[67]

Disorder in response to the scarcity and high prices of grain could include a number of different kinds of actions such as seditious words, food riot, seizure of food, or insurrection. Two complicating factors in 1528 were unemployment or underemployment in the cloth industry and the failure of the king to pay back the forced loan of 1522–3. This resulted in an explosive mix of lack of money and rising grain prices in a number of counties. Overall, disorder was confined to five years, 1527–32, with one notable exception in Somerset during 1536. Nonetheless, some of the protests of this period provide us with scraps of evidence that provide insights into popular attitudes.

Between November 1527 and July 1532, there were a number food riots and related protests in Norwich and Yarmouth and one in London plus a seizure of grain on the Severn in July 1531. On November 25, 1527, at mile end one mile east of London, a crowd attempted to seize the bread that the bakers of Stratford in Essex were bringing in carts to supply the city. The carts were rescued and brought to the city only

---

[66] "Archbishop Warham's Letters," pp. 25–7; *LP*, vol. 4 pt. 1, 1306.
[67] TNA, SP1/ 47, f. 230; *LP*, vol. 4 pt. 2, 4188. For other examples of "simulated deference," see Hindle, "Exhortation and Entitlement," pp. 116–17.

through the efforts of the mayor and sheriffs of London.[68] A similar episode that had occurred earlier, in 1512, conveys a sense of the desperation of those who were either hungry or feared hunger. When the bread carts from Stratford arrived in the city, "there was such presse about them, that one man was readie to destroy an other, in striving to be served."[69] Later in the century, an even more graphic example comes from Shrewsbury, during the severe dearth of 1596. After the bailiffs and aldermen had bought 3,200 bushels of Baltic rye in London, they sold much of it at cost to the commons of the town. Forty quarters of the rye were sold to the bakers weekly to make bread for the poor. When the bread was being sold to the poor who, for lack of it, "were lycke to perrishe," they were "so unruly and gredie to have it so that the baylyffs , vi men and other officers, had mutche adoe to serve them."[70]

There was considerable discontent in Norwich over high grain prices from late 1527 through July 1532. At Christmas 1527, scarcity made the commons of Norwich "redy to ryse upon the ryche Men." This was followed by an attempted rising led by a man named Young "who would have perswaded the Commons to have taken the Corn by force from the Sellers in the [Market] Cross." The commons, on the other hand, decided that they would starve "if they harmed those who brought grain to market since they would not return."[71] Around Christmas 1529, there was also "an insurrection on Account of Corn" that the Duke of Suffolk put down "before it came to any Head."[72] On August 3, 1532, twelve women were found guilty of participating in another "insurreccion," in Norwich on July 20, of that year. Their crime was forcing the owners of grain to sell it in the market place at less than the price set by the mayor. Six of them were sentenced to be tied to a cart's tail and whipped round the marketplace. One was respited "because infirm." The other five made fines.[73]

The explanation for these protests in Norwich is simple, dire social conditions brought on by grain scarcity, poverty and unemployment. In 1522 and 1527 the aldermen of Norwich were compelled to buy grain to supply the city's market.[74] Later, in July 1532, the city faced another difficult situation because "nowe of late grayn hath here with ben soore and grevously mowntid to high and excesse prises to the grette pennury

[68] Stow, *Annales of England*, p. 904; *LP*, vol. 4, *Appendix*, 127.
[69] Stow, *Survey of London*, vol. 1, p. 156.
[70] Leighton (ed.), "Early Chronicles of Shrewsbury," pp. 335–6; Owen, *History of Shrewsbury*, vol. 1, p. 400.
[71] Blomefield, *An Essay*, vol. 3, p. 198.   [72] *Ibid.*, p. 198.
[73] Hudson and Tingey, (eds.), *The Records of the City of Norwich*, vol. 2, pp. 163–5.
[74] *Ibid.*, pp. 159–61.

and punysshement of the poore people, and many tymes cornes skantly
brought to the market place here withinne this citie to serve the poore
commoners and inhabitauntes of the same whereunto they evermore
must nedely truste."[75] Part of the problem, according to the city government, was that innkeepers, bakers, and brewers were buying up most of
the grain that came to market, leaving little for the poor. The solution was
a local ordinance that innkeepers and other victuallers should not purchase any grain in the market but they had to make other arrangements to
obtain it on penalty of forfeiting the value of any grain bought in violation
of the ordinance. Moreover, the owner of any grain brought to market that
remained unsold after the ringing of the market bell was required to move
it to a granary that the city had built in the market place, in order to store
it until the next market day. Failure to comply with this section of the
ordinance would result in a fine of 6s 8d for every sack not conveyed to
the granary. One wonders about the success of such an ordinance, since
the exclusion of innkeepers and the like from the market would result in
them making private deals with farmers to buy their grain before it came to
market thus continuing the shortage of grain in Norwich market.[76]

In December 1532, the Norwich city council passed another ordinance that reveals the poverty and hunger of female spinners of yarn. The
trade was "nowe moche soore and grevouslye mynysshed of late in
somoche" that many poor people having no other way to make a living
were compelled to beg for their meat and drink "for Cristes sake."[77] One
difficulty for the spinners was lack of access to wool. Butchers normally
sold sheep skins with the wool in large quantities to leather tewers,
parchment makers, glovers and others, leaving little for the spinners.
The solution was an ordinance that instructed the butchers to sell their
sheep fells to poor women only before noon between Christmas and
clipping time for the first year and between November 1 and clipping
time thereafter. After the noon hour, the fells could be sold to anyone
who was a resident of the city.[78]

Unlike Norwich, which was an inland city that was greatly dependent
on textile and other trades to support its population, Yarmouth, twenty
miles to the east, was a port that depended on the sea.[79] Yarmouth's
economic fortunes appear to have declined from a high point in the
first half of the fourteenth century when it was the center of a major
herring industry and its ships traded widely in European salt and wine.[80]

---

[75] *Ibid.*, p. 116.   [76] *Ibid.*, pp. 116–18.   [77] *Ibid.*, p. 119.   [78] *Ibid.*, pp. 119–20.
[79] Pound, "The Social and Trade Structure of Norwich," pp. 49–69.
[80] Saul, A., "English Towns in the Late Middle Ages," pp. 75–88; Saul, A., "Great
Yarmouth," pp. 105–15.

Nonetheless, in the reign of Henry VIII the town was a major shipper of grain. For example, between Michaelmas, 1530 and Michaelmas 1531, 3,300 quarters of wheat and 1,350 quarters of malt were shipped to London and elsewhere in England, while 2,103 quarters of wheat and 9,800 quarters of malt and barley were exported overseas in the same period.[81] While evidence is lacking for grain exports from Yarmouth in earlier years, when a food riot occurred in 1527, the men who participated aimed only to prevent the export of grain. "But it went so far, that divers young men that joined with them were executed for it."[82]

Sometime in mid-1532, before July 24, there was another food riot in Yarmouth, doubtless provoked by high grain prices that were believed to be the result of continued export. The participants were all women whose actions were described in the surviving record as "a great riott and unlawfull assemble of many evill disposed women at ouer town of Yarmouth, which as is thought could not have ben don without the mayntenaunce, supportacione, and abeytyng of their husbandes and other misruled persons."[83] On July 24, a signet letter authorized the keeper of the great seal to issue a commission of oyer and teminer to Sir Robert Norwich, chief justice of the king's bench, and other judges to try the women immediately after the next assizes at Norwich.[84] Unfortunately, we do not know their fate.

In the west of England during the sixteenth and seventeenth century, the river Severn remained a major conduit for the transport of grain from Worcestershire, Wiltshire and Gloucestershire down river to Bristol. The river was the city's lifeline, especially in times of scarcity, That is why, in 1522, when grain prices were very high the mayor had authorized a number of men to travel to Worcestershire to buy grain for the city. When the grain arrived in Bristol it brought down the prices in the market and provided relief and comfort to the inhabitants.[85] In July 1531, when the city was in need of grain once more "in tyme of Scrarsenes and necessitie,"[86] the Mayor hired a mariner, Robert Graunger, and his boat, *The George*, to go up river to Tewkesbury to buy grain. Graunger managed to purchase 2 wey and 16 bushels (roughly twelve quarters) of wheat and 4.5 quarters of beans.[87]

There are two versions of what happened on Graunger's voyage back down river. One is in a bill of complaint that the mayor and commonalty

[81] TNA, SP 1/67, ff. 133–4; *LP*, vol. 5, 451.   [82] Blomefield, *An Essay*, vol. 3, p. 198.
[83] TNA, C82/658, 24 July, 24 Henry VIII; *LP*, vol. 5, 1207 (45).   [84] *Ibid.*
[85] Smith (ed.), *The Maire of Bristowe*, p. 49.
[86] The quotation comes from the star chamber decree in the case in Veale (ed.), *The Great Red Book of Bristol*, pt. 4 p. 17.
[87] TNA, STAC2/6, f. 95, Bill of complaint from the mayor and commonalty of Bristol.

of Bristol submitted to star chamber on behalf of Graunger, the other is in the surviving star chamber decree in the case.[88] In the first account, Graunger's return trip down river ended at Hempstead near Gloucester. There, twenty or more individuals (seven are named in the bill) riotously assembled and with force and against the king's peace, boarded *The George* "lyke pyrettes and robbers." They then put Grainger on the shore and sailed off with the boat and its cargo of grain.[89] In the second account, contained in the final decree of the court, there is no mention of the twenty or more rioters, instead Robert Poole and Thomas Bell sheriffs of the town of Gloucester, who were not mentioned in the original bill of complaint, are blamed for stopping and seizing Graunger's boat and "without any sufficient authorite and lauful meanys" selling the grain. It turns out, as well, that the mayor of Gloucester ordered the sheriffs to take this action.[90] One can only surmise that it was through the depositions of witnesses that the court got to the heart of the issue. Also it is quite probable that the sheriffs seized the grain and sold it because of scarcity and high prices at Gloucester, close to which city *The George* had to travel on its way to Bristol. As punishment for the sheriffs, the court decreed that before Christmas they must supply Bristol with the amount of grain equivalent to that which they sold. Also the mayor and sheriffs of Gloucester were ordered to pay costs in the amount of £6. 13s 4d to the mayor and commonalty of Bristol.[91]

Between March and June 1528 there were indications of unrest or fear of unrest in a number of counties including Wiltshire, Somerset, Hampshire, Berkshire, Suffolk, Essex, and Kent, which peaked with an attempted insurrection in Kent. To the effects of the high prices and scarcity of grain, following the failure of the 1527 harvest, was added disruption in the cloth trade. In January 1528 England, allied with France, declared war on the emperor Charles V. This had dire short-term consequences for the English cloth trade. Antwerp in the Low Countries was the main market for English cloth and it was also part of Charles V's empire. On February 21, 1528, Margaret of Hungary, regent of the Low Countries, ordered the arrest of all English merchants, followed by a stoppage in trade. At the same time, English merchants in Spain were arrested, which disrupted trade and also had a negative effect on the cloth industry, which relied on Spanish olive oil to treat

---

[88] *Ibid.*; Veale (ed.), *The Great Red Book of Bristol*, pt. 4, pp. 17–18. There is also a summary of the decree in Smith (ed.), *The Maire of Bristowe*, p. 52.
[89] TNA, STAC2/6, f. 95.
[90] Veale (ed.), *The Great Red Book of Bristol*, pt. 4, pp. 17–18.   [91] *Ibid.*

wool before it was combed. Normal trade relations with both countries were not fully restored until a truce in June 1528.[92]

The first signs of trouble were in Suffolk in early March 1528, when the Duke of Norfolk reported to Cardinal Wolsey on conditions in that county. According to his letter, Sir Robert Drewry had recently committed to jail "diverse lewde persons of Bury" who planned to stir up "an unlawfull assembley" and he was trying to discover any others who were involved in this "folyshe besynes." Norfolk also noted that he had ordered the prisoners to be taken to the king in London so that they would suffer more severe punishment than they would receive in Suffolk and thereby make other offenders "more fearefull." He then went on to describe the kinds of punishment meted out for similar offences in the past, such as the Duke of Suffolk imprisoning offenders in Norwich or himself imprisoning offenders and then banishing them from the county or setting them in the stocks or the pillory. But he concluded that such punishment was not warning enough for "lyght ill disposed personys." During this discourse, Norfolk wondered if the law would allow the prisoners to be executed, although Sir Robert thought not, because "they dyd never act."[93]

What heinous crime had those "diverse lewde person," five in total, committed to draw the wrath of the Duke of Norfolk? In Sir Richard Drury's examination of John Davy, thatcher, he confessed that sitting at dinner, with others on the last day of February, he said there would be a rising of two or three hundred "poore fellows," himself included on March 3. They planned to go "to the kynges grace and to my lord cardenall besechyng theym of remedy for the lyvyng of poore men which cowde not lyve." In the course of the examination, Davy also implicated four other men, his own servant, a smith, and two pinners.[94] The crime was uttering seditious words, as Sir Richard Drury noted in his letter to Wolsey.[95] What we do not know is how much ale was consumed at the dinner when Davy talked about the rising, but such words were dangerous, especially when they included mention of a march on London, whatever the motive, even if it did not occur. To propose such an action no doubt evoked official memories of the 1381 peasants' revolt and Jack Cade's rebellion in 1450.

The last we hear of Davy and two of his unnamed companions is that, when they were sent to London, they were imprisoned in the Tower and

---

[92] Gunn, "Wolsey's Foreign Policy," pp. 167–8; Wernham, *Before the Armada*, p. 118.
[93] TNA, SP1/47, ff. 61–2; *LP*, vol. 4 pt. 2, 4012 (1).
[94] TNA, SP1/47, f. 64; *LP*, vol. 4 pt. 2, 4012 (2).
[95] TNA, SP1/47, f. 65; *LP*, vol. 4 pt. 2, 4013.

examined. It was found that there were great inconsistencies between the examinations taken by Sir Richard Drury in Bury and those taken in the Tower so they were all sent to Wolsey on May 31, 1528.[96] The fate of the prisoners is unknown. Finally, beyond poverty there is no other clear indication of what drove Davy and the rest to imagine going to appeal to the king and the cardinal. It could have been the high price of food or the economic disruption produced by the loss of markets for cloth, which must have affected other trades as well. Perhaps it was a combination of both.

When Norfolk wrote the letter on the "diverse lewde persons of Bury," he also had another problem on his mind. He was planning to meet soon with some of the "most substanciall clothiers of Suffolk" to persuade them not to shut down cloth making because of rumors from London that "English merchaunts be detained in Flanders."[97] In less than a week, Norfolk met with forty clothiers and told them that the rumors that English merchants had been arrested in the Low Countries were false and managed to persuade them to continue to employ their workers and produce cloth. Norfolk was relieved at his success, for otherwise he would have faced two or three hundred women making "sewte to have the clothiers to set them, their husbandes, and chylderne on worke."[98] There was another fear that Norfolk did not express on this occasion, but was clearly instrumental in driving government policy. That was fear of riot or insurrection by hungry and unemployed cloth workers. In his *Chronicle*, Hall praises Norfolk's actions in appeasing the Suffolk cloth workers who had begun "greatly to murmur." If the duke had not acted as he did, the workers would have "fallen to some riotous act."[99]

What may also have haunted Norfolk and other officials, charged with maintaining order at the local level, was the prospect of another mass popular rising like that of 1525 against the amicable grant. That rising was in opposition to an extortionate attempt by Henry VIII to raise money from his subjects to pay for his grandiose foreign policy. While there was resistance to the grant across Norfolk, Suffolk, Kent, and Essex the epicenter was the cloth making towns of southern Suffolk. A surviving list of 528 men, from Babergh and Cosford Hundreds in Suffolk, indicted for participation in the rising, shows that 188 were textile workers, 163 were laborers, 124 were engaged in a range of trades, and 49 were involved in agriculture.[100] Bernard has argued, persuasively,

---

[96] TNA, SP1/48, f. 81; *LP*, vol. 4 pt. 2, 4309.
[97] TNA, SP1/47 ff. 61–3; *LP*, vol. 4 pt. 2, 4012 (1).
[98] TNA, SP1/ 47, ff. 89–90; *LP*, vol. 4, pt. 2, 4044.   [99] Hall, *Chronicle*, p. 745.
[100] Pound, "Rebellion and Poverty," pp. 317–30.

that the major cause of the resistance to the amicable grant was the heavy taxation that the crown had imposed on its subjects in the period 1522–5. First was the forced loan of 1522–3, which was followed by a subsidy that parliament granted in 1523, which was still being collected when the amicable grant was levied. The amicable grant was the last straw as artisans, laborers, and small holders were faced with the daunting task of finding the money to pay their share. Moreover, in the specific case of cloth workers, there were fears that the levy would disrupt the local economy and produce unemployment. The result was open rebellion that forced the crown to back down.[101]

When Norfolk reported his success with the forty clothiers he also recommended that Wolsey should try to persuade the merchants at Blackwell hall in London to sell the cloths that they had on hand, no doubt to enable them to buy more from the clothiers to keep the industry going and the workers employed.[102] Perhaps following this advice Wolsey met with London merchants later in March to tell them that the king ordered them to buy cloth from the clothiers as they usually did "upon pain of his high displeasure." The merchants replied that they had no market for the cloth and already had more on hand and did not know what to do with them. Then Wolsey began to threaten them with loss of their trading privileges. After that it is not clear from Hall's account if there was any resolution of the issue.[103] One thing is certain, however, the disruption of the cloth industry continued up to early June and the discontents of the workers spread and intensified.

Already the discontent had spread to the cloth making town of Westbury in Wiltshire. It had been reported to the king that clothiers who could not sell their cloth in London had ceased employing their workers. Workers from Westbury, "having no means to get their lyving," planned to go to the king "for remedye therein." William Lord Sandys, who was informed of this action, agreed to go with some men from Hampshire into Wiltshire to pacify the workers.[104] What action Sandys took is unknown, but on March 12 he received letters from the king and Wolsey ordering him to prevent clothiers in Hampshire from putting away their workers "by reason whereof eny unlawfull assemble might arise to the violacion of the peace or provocacion of eny other light persons to doo the semblable." Sandys replied that he had the clothiers

---

[101] Bernard, *War, Taxation and Rebellion*, pp. 110–49; MacCulloch, *Suffolk under the Tudors*, pp. 289–98.

[102] TNA, SP1/ 47, f. 90; *LP*, vol. 4 pt. 2, 4040.   [103] Hall, *Chronicle*, pp. 745–6.

[104] TNA, SP1/ 47, f. 87; *LP*, vol. 4 pt. 2, 4043.

before him and they agreed to keep their men in work. He also hoped that the same would happen in the neighboring counties of Berkshire and Wiltshire.[105]

About a week later, Thomas, Lord Berkeley and others reported to Wolsey that the inhabitants of Gloucestershire were "quyett and conformabull." This was probably the result of the fact, as the letter reports, that the clothiers were willing to keep their workers employed as long as they could. Nonetheless, Lord Berkeley advised that a way needed to be found soon to sell the cloth because it was impossible for the clothiers "to contynue theyr workemen on worke." In neighboring Wiltshire it appears that there had been an assembly of people at Devizes, a cloth making center. No doubt they were cloth workers fearing unemployment. Berkeley, however, denied the report that had reached the king that men of Gloucestershire had gone to the Devizes assembly.[106] Later, in a letter probably addressed to Lord Berkeley, Wolsey praised the actions of the mayor of Devizes and John Erneley, a Wiltshire justice of the peace, in persuading the "light persons" assembled at Devizes to go home.[107]

In early April, there was a report of insurrections at Taunton and Bridgewater but no details were provided.[108] On April 2, Henry, Earl of Essex reported to Wolsey the arrest of John Bosswell, clothier of Colchester in Essex, for "suspicious words," contained in a letter to a Goodman Sammys, who probably sent it to the authorities. Bosswell owed money to Sammys for wool and wrote to him on March 13 that he could not pay him anything at the moment because he and the other clothiers could not sell cloth even at half price and had barely enough money to pay the spinners. Unless things changed the clothiers would be "utterly undonn." Then come the fateful words: "the marchanttes sayth that they wyll not bey a cloth without that we can cause the comyne for to arise for to complayne to the kynge and shew hyme how they be not half set a wourke and tyll that day be come we shall never have remedy."[109]

On April 5, Essex wrote to Wolsey that he had examined Bosswell, who had confessed to writing the letter but no one else had any knowledge of the contents. Clearly, Essex was concerned a larger conspiracy was afoot that might produce a rising. After explaining, in the examination, that he wrote the letter to gain more time to pay his debt, Bosswell

---

[105] TNA, SP1/47, f. 100; *LP*, vol. 4 pt. 2, 4059.
[106] TNA, SP1/47, f. 122; *LP*, vol. 4 pt. 2, 4085.
[107] *LP*, vol. 4 pt. 1, 4191. The original appears to have been mutilated, thereby destroying the name of the addressee.
[108] *LP*, vol. 4 pt. 2, 4141.   [109] TNA, SP1/47, ff. 164–5; *LP*, vol. 4 pt. 2, 4129.

gave an account of the origin of his statement that a rising of the commons would be the solution to the problems in the cloth industry. He had been in London on the Friday after Ash Wednesday to sell a few cloths at Blackwell hall. Bosswell tried to sell his cloths to John Tyndall, merchant of London. Tyndall said if he bought them, he could not sell them. Then Tyndall uttered the words, repeated in Bosswell's letter, that the commons needed to rise and complain to the king. Since Bosswell had implicated a Londoner, he and his examination were sent Wolsey, fate unknown.[110]

Beginning in mid-April the crisis began to intensify and official anxieties became more and more focused on the situation in Kent. Here, the confluence of three issues produced a potentially explosive mix. Those issues were the continuing high prices and scarcity of grain, the ongoing disruption of the cloth industry, and the failure of the king to repay, as promised, the forced loan of 1522–3. The failure of the king to repay the loan in early 1524, as scheduled, was one of the grievances that had caused resistance to the amicable grant of 1525.[111] On April 14, 1528, a crowd estimated at 100 in number, came to the residence of William Warham, Archbishop of Canterbury, at Knoll in Kent to speak to him. He thought it best that they send only five or six of "the discretyst of them" to explain what they wanted. The representatives said that "they and theyr neighbors at home being poore and nedy" wanted him to persuade the king to repay the loan.[112] Warham then asked the representatives who had advised or motivated them to take this action. They replied "povertie only" and said further that they and their neighbors that remained at home "lackyd bothe mete and money." Finally, the representatives claimed that no one advised them "but their own myndes, on complanyng to another of theyr poverties."[113] The Archbishop was skeptical of the truth of these answers but did not say anything because he did not want to anger them. Nonetheless, when the representatives "humbly beseched" him to explain to the king their poverty and desire to have the loan paid, Warham replied that if they abstained from unlawful assemblies and wrote a petition containing their needs, he would give it to the king. The representatives seemed content with that answer but Warham makes it clear in his letter that he did not believe this crisis was over.[114]

[110] TNA, SP1/ 47, ff. 176–7, *LP*, vol. 4 pt. 2, 4145.
[111] Bernard, *War, Taxation and Rebellion*, pp. 118–19.
[112] TNA, SP1/ 47, f. 229; *LP*, vol. 4 pt. 2, 4188.   [113] TNA, SP1/47, f. 229v.
[114] *Ibid.*, ff. 229v–30.

Wolsey was appalled at Warham's actions, news of which had spread into Essex and Suffolk and was "right pleasant to the people." In the Cardinal's opinion that news "should be repressed at once, lest it grow worse."[115] Around April 22, he wrote to the Archbishop that his response to the crowd would embolden others to ask for the repayment of the loan.[116] At the same time, Wolsey was nervous enough about the situation that he wrote, probably to Lord Berkeley in Gloucester, to be ready with 8 or 900 foot and 100 horse to deal with any popular assemblies. Similar letters were sent to others in Wiltshire and Berkshire.[117] At roughly the same time, the king and Wolsey informed Norfolk that he should stay in Suffolk throughout the month of May. Norfolk advised Wolsey that the lords Oxford, Essex, and Fitzwalter should also be instructed to stay in Essex because they had great power there "iff any besynes shuld chaunce." Norfolk also requested a commission for himself, the Duke of Suffolk, and Lord Barnes to assemble the king's people, "iff need shalbe." Finally Norfolk observed that he had heard of the people of Kent coming to Archbishop Warham for help in getting the loan repaid. In his opinion, there should be no more talk of it "for that is more to be Feared then any other thyng, there be so many that would Fayne have agayne their money that it is herd whom men may trust in that case."[118]

There appear to have been no "unlawful assemblies" in the weeks immediately following the flurry of correspondence to and from Wolsey. Nonetheless, sometime before May 1 the inhabitants of a number of communities in Kent submitted their petition to Warham requesting repayment of the loan.[119] On May 2, Warham sent Richard Sisley, who had a draft of the petition in his hand and Thomas Colhurst who copied the petition, to Lord Rochford and Sir Henry Guildford to be examined, no doubt to discover who was actually behind it. It was, however, Warham's opinion that Sisley did not know who wrote the original petition or who gave the orders.[120] Then another suspect, Thomas Merser of Hawkehurst, was identified as the person who composed the petition. He was attached on the order of Sir Edward Guildford and sent

---

[115] *LP*, vol. 4 pt. 2, 4189.   [116] *Ibid.*, 4190.   [117] *Ibid.*, 4191.

[118] TNA, SP1/47, f. 231; *LP*, vol. 4 pt. 2, 4192.

[119] TNA, SP1/ 47 ff. 209–10; *LP*, vol. 4 pt. 2, 4173, misdates the document to April 14. The actual petition states that it was to be delivered to Warham on May 3, but the letter referenced in the next footnote shows that Warham had the petition before May 1 and, moreover, that he had an interlined draft not the finished petition. This may mean that he received earlier information that allowed him to take Sisely and the draft into custody before it was finished.

[120] TNA, SP1/ 47, f. 343; *LP*, vol. 4 pt. 2, 4236.

up to Wolsey on May 8.[121] That appears to have been the end of the search for the "mastermind." Ultimately, the problem was solved, no doubt to the king's satisfaction, when parliament in 1529 passed a statute that wiped out the king's obligation to repay the loan.[122]

Also in May 1528, the problems in the cloth industry resurfaced. On May 4 Norfolk wrote to Wolsey that a number of clothiers in Suffolk were "makyng lamentable complaint" that they could not sell their cloths in London and would only be able to keep their workers employed for another two or three weeks. In addition, they said that lack of oil would shut down production unless some arrived from Spain.[123] In the middle of May, Sir Henry Guildford reported on conditions in Kent. As was the case with the Norfolk clothiers, those of Kent complained that they could not keep all their men employed much longer because of the lack of sale for their cloth. As a result "a greate companie shal be set to ydelnes." Guildford and his brothers talked to the clothiers and he hoped that they would not put away any of their workfolks before harvest time. Nonetheless, Guildford told Wolsey that he would be vigilant and hoped no "evil demeanor shall spring or arise." He concluded by wishing that Wolsey would find a remedy for the situation since the cloth workers would not be in employment for long.[124]

Sir Henry Guildford's hope that no "evil demeanor shall spring or arise" proved to be a false one. On May 24, Guildford's brother, Edward, arrested some "evill disposyd persons," who were planning an insurrection, it turns out, in Cranbrook and the neighboring village of Goudhurst, important centers of the cloth industry. Three were sent to Wolsey to be examined. Henry Guildford advised Wolsey "that lytell pitie may be shewed upon theym but that they maie suffer to the dredfull example of all the shire."[125] Five days later, Lord Rocheford reported to Wolsey that Kent was quiet but he and his friends and servants were ready to suppress disorder and hoped that the offenders would be punished "in example of amendment to all them that be of lyght and evyll disposicion."[126] That same day, Sir Henry Guildford also wrote to Wolsey that all but three of the twenty suspects had been apprehended, while the others had fled. He was sure that the planned rising was crushed.[127]

[121] TNA, SP1/48, f. 6; *LP*, vol. 4 pt. 2, 4243. See also TNA, SP1/234, f. 241; *LP, Addenda*, vol. 1 pt. 1, 456.
[122] *SR*, vol. 3, pp. 315–16, 21 Hen. VIII c. 24.
[123] TNA, SP1/48, f. 2; *LP*, vol. 4 pt. 2, 4239.
[124] TNA, SP1/48, f. 28; *LP*, vol. 4 pt. 2, 4276.
[125] TNA, SP1/48, f. 47; *LP*, vol. 4 pt. 2, 4296.
[126] TNA, SP1/48, ff. 51–2; *LP*, vol. 4 pt. 2, 4300.
[127] TNA, SP1/48, f. 53; *LP*, vol. 4 pt. 2, 4301.

The surviving examinations of the suspects are mutilated. Nonetheless, it is clear that those involved had been engaged in loose talk on a number of occasions from at least May 10 to May 23. On one occasion Nicholas Love, fuller, had asked John Bigg, clothier of Goudhurst, what the men of London planned if they had no sale for their cloths? On another occasion Robert Mylner, in an imaginative outpouring, said to Love than when they rose they would seize Cardinal Wolsey, put in him a boat that had four holes bored in it that were then filled with pins. The cardinal and his boat would then be taken out to sea by another boat, whose crew would pull the pins and sink the cardinal. On May 12, at the house of William Grastroft, shoemaker of Goudhurst, Nicholas Love said to John Ungely, husbandman: "Thou seest we be in much poverty. If I can get company to get corn of the riche men, wilt thou be one of them to help get hit?" Ungeley replied: "Yes , if the company was sufficient." Then on May 17, a Cranbrook fuller told Thomas Nyklyn, minstrel or fiddler, that there were fifty people in Cranbrook ready to rise. Two days later, St Dunstan's day, William Warre, laborer, went to Cranbrook to find out how many men would join. His uncle, a clothworker of Cranbrook, said he would help and 100 men would be ready.

On May 21, Nicholas Love and a dozen others met at Grastroft's house in Goudhurst to drink and plan. They proposed to go to the house of Sir Alexander Culpeper, take his harness and "habilments of war," and force him to go along with them. Then they would go on and do the same at the houses of Sir Edward Guildford and Master Darell. During this meeting, Robert Mylner, in another imaginative outpouring, recalled words that John Freeman of Cranbrook reported about the cry of Robert of Ridsdale [Robin of Redesdale] when he uttered a proclamation "Who made this cry? Robert à Rydesdale, Jack Straw and I."[128] This was a call to bolster courage and link the rising at Cranbrook with leaders of the Peasants, Revolt of 1381 and the Northern Rebellion of 1469.[129] Of course, nothing came of it. Too many people knew about the plan, since the participants talked too much. Inevitably information got to the ears of the authorities and all that was left was a trial and executions.

On June 4, 1528 the trial was held at Rochester Castle in Kent before commissioners of oyer and terminer. Nine men were accused of treason, seven were found guilty and sentenced to death, the other two were indicted but they had fled. Ten others were accused of misprision of

---

[128] TNA, SP1/48, ff. 82–4; *LP*, vol. 4 pt. 2, 4310; the social status of suspects comes either from the examinations or the report of the trial, TNA, SP 1/48, f. 108; *LP*, vol. 4 pt. 2, 4331.

[129] For other examples of rebels using such language, see Wood, *The 1549 Rebellions*, p. 10.

treason (that is having knowledge of treason but not reporting it). They were all found guilty and sentenced to death. However, those who were convicted all agreed in court that Thomas Smyth, blacksmith, was falsely accused and should be pardoned. He had been twice at meetings with the others at William Grastroste's house but never consented to participate in their planned rising. The commissioners agreed to put his name forward to Wolsey to obtain a pardon from the king, which was issued on October 23, 1528.[130]

The occupations of the nineteen accused ranged across a number of occupations: 1 yeoman, 2 weavers, 2 fullers, 1 tailor, 1 cutler, 2 shoe-makers, 2 blacksmiths, 1 miller, 1 minstrel, and 6 laborers.[131] This pattern of social and occupational status appears to confirm a sixteenth-century truism, an early example of which can be found in a letter, dated May 10, 1517, from Richard Fox, Bishop of Winchester, to Wolsey. On reaction to a recent riot at Southampton, Fox observed that if any commotion happens in Hampshire Wiltshire, Berkshire, or Somersetshire "yt shalbe by the meanes of weavers, fullers, sheremen, and other journeymen artificers."[132]

In reflecting on what drove these men of Kent to plan an insurrection in May 1528, it is difficult to weigh the various possibilities, discontent over the king's failure to repay the loan, the disruption of the cloth trade, or the high prices and scarcity of grain. Perhaps it was a combination of all three. While the loan was not mentioned in the examinations of the suspects, certainly in late April, after Warham's meeting with the crowd of protestors at his manor, the government was anticipating some kind of disorder. There was mention of the cloth industry's problems in the examinations, when it was reported that Nicholas Love had wondered what the men of London would do if they had no sale for their cloth. Moreover, in mid- May Sir Henry Guilford was hoping there would be no disorder as a result of disruption in the cloth industry, but he was ready for it happening.

In the end, it is likely that high prices and scarcity of grain played the largest role in moving the participants to insurrection. In the examinations, Nicholas Love is reported as saying we are in poverty and should go and take rich men's grain. Moreover, the petition for the repayment of the loan that Warham finally obtained reveals that the impoverishing effects of the high price of grain motivated the petitioners. Finally, there are two letters of Sir Edward Guildford to Wolsey that describe the

---

[130] TNA, SP1/48, f. 108; *LP*, vol. 4 pt. 2, 4331, 4896 (23).
[131] TNA, SP1/48, f. 108; *LP*, vol. 4 pt. 2, 4331.
[132] TNA, SP1/ 232 f. 23; *LP, Addenda*, vol. 1 pt. 1, 185.

upward spiral of grain prices in Kent in June and July 1528. On June 24, Guildford reported that, within the space of a month, wheat prices in Cranbrook market had risen from 12s per quarter to 20s, a famine price. As a result "the kinges poure subiectes in these parties doo make great mone and lamentation for that there cometh so little corn to the markettes and that is broght in at unreasonable price." He also anticipated correctly that prices would continue to rise probably until the next harvest.[133] Nine days later, the price of wheat had risen to 23.3s per quarter, "to the great sorrowe and lamentation of the Kinges poure subiects."[134]

What makes the planned Cranbrook insurrection of great interest is the survival of the examinations of the suspects that record the language of the rebels. Two other incidents provide further examples of such language, one at Yaxley, Huntingdonshire in 1528–9 and the other at Taunton, Somerset, in 1536. The events in the first incident are described in a Star Chamber Bill of 1529 submitted on behalf of the inhabitants against Thomas Aylward and Christopher Branston alias Glover, both of Lynn, for forestalling, regrating, and engrossing. This is in fact the second bill of complaint in the case.[135] Its particular interest lies in the language used in the conversations that it reports, for it provides insights into the conflicts and intemperate disputes that grain scarcity produced.

On November 30, 1528, Aylward was loading his barge with peas to ship to Lynn when a poor man of Yaxley came by and asked him where he was taking the peas. Aylward replied: "haist thowe any thyng to doo therwith, For I am not there to gyve the accompt." The poor man replied that the previous year the men of Lynn had carried all the peas to Scotland leaving the people pining from hunger. Then he said to Aylward that if he planned to carry the peas away to Scotland this time, "we wold stey theym untill we knewe futher of the kynges pleasour therin, For as we do thynk, that yoo do against the kynges commandement in that behalf." This reply infuriated Aylward, who threw down his glove in defiance against all of those in the town that would attempt to stop him declaring "he wold have the pees, or he wold reyse an C of as good Fytynge men as the kynge hath any." It is possible that Aylward's words to the poor man could have been construed as seditious or even treasonable words directed at the king, of the kind that led to severe

---

[133] TNA, SP1/48, ff. 225–6; *LP*, vol. 4 pt. 2, 4414.

[134] TNA, SP1/49, f. 60; *LP*, vol. 4 pt. 1, 1952.

[135] Leadham (ed.), *Select Cases*, pp. 178–82 is the first bill, which is discussed earlier in Chapter 6.

punishment of others. But Aylward was not yet finished. On January 1, 1529, another poor man of Yaxley, Richard Shryve, was walking between that town and Stilton when he met Aylward. Shryve asked him "have ye nott bought pees Inowgh yete?" Aylward became infuriated again, jumped off his horse, drew his sword, and came at Shryve "vyolently." Shryve only escaped with his life by shifting "the better for hym self." No doubt this meant he ran away.[136]

Finally, there is an episode in Taunton, Somerset of late March 1536 that Elton found confusing or difficult to understand because it "sprang up without any substantial cause" and "had nothing to do with either the political or the religious changes of the time."[137] In fact, the issue that provoked a crowd to disorder was certainly a substantial one for ordinary folk. In early April, a report from the justice of the peace of Somerset to Cromwell provides a clue as to the motives of the crowd in a reference to the fact "the power people doith myche complayne them of the skaresnes and deirth of grayne."[138] What may have set off the crowd is a commission that was sent into Somerset "to take upp corne," according to Wriothesley's chronicle.[139] Such a commission was probably authorized to bury grain for the king and might have been blamed for driving up prices in Taunton market.

There appears to be no surviving evidence of what protest action the crowd first took at Taunton, but a number of them had been imprisoned at the order of the Somerset JPs by March 28. Then, on that day, a crowd assaulted three Somerset JPs sitting at Quarter Sessions and proclaimed "We wyll have Thomas Plomer and his fellowes out of prison or ellys we wyll dye for hit" and then "we wyll have Plomer and his fellowes out of prison or ells hit shall cost a thowsand mens lyves."[140] A few days later, Henry Longe, JP of Wiltshire, informed Cromwell that he had heard from his colleagues in Somerset that the crowd from Taunton had gone to Frome, a cloth making center in the northeast of the county, in hopes of raising more support. Instead, many of them were apprehended and imprisoned. A search for other suspects was conducted in Devizes and Trowbridge, clothmaking towns in neighboring Wiltshire, but none were found.[141] In discussing the disorder, Longe's letter placed particular

[136] *Ibid.*, 182–4; Tawney and Power (eds.), *Tudor Economic Documents*, vol. 1, pp. 144–5.
[137] Elton, *Policy and Police*, p. 108. Elton did not appear to care much about popular attitudes or behavior.
[138] TNA, SP1/239, f. 288; *LP, Addenda*, vol. 1 pt. 1, 1058.
[139] Wriothesley, *A Chronicle of England*, vol. 1, p. 61.
[140] TNA, KB27/1102, Rex, rot. 9.
[141] TNA, SP1/239, f. 287; *LP, Addenda*, vol. 1 pt. 1, 1056.

emphasis on towns that "be stondyng upon craftsmen on whois wylful-
ness we have moste thought daunger to setle."[142]

The language used in the king's bench record that describes the assault
on the JPs indicates the seriousness with which the government regarded
the incident. It was an action that represented a war against the king
and aimed to deprive him of his majesty and power.[143] This meant that
when a trial was held at Taunton in late April, before a commission of
oyer and terminer, the charge would be treason. Eighty-five people were
found guilty. Twelve were executed while seventy-three were pardoned.
Another fifty-seven were still at large when the trial took place.[144] In fact
most of the accused came from Cannington, Bridgwater, and Taunton,
which appear to have been the centers of the rising.[145] No doubt that is
why the executions were evenly spread among the three.[146] We know the
occupational status of 123 of the accused. Seventy-four of them were
from a wide range of trades with the largest concentrations being fourteen shoemakers and ten tailors. In addition there were eight spinsters.
The other forty-nine included two yeomen, eight laborers and thirty-nine
husbandmen, thirty-seven of them from Cannington.[147]

The popular protests discussed here, which were the products of both
the scarcity and high prices of grain and the disruption in the cloth trade,
did not represent a major threat to the Tudor state unlike rebellions such
as the Lincolnshire Rising and the Pilgrimage of Grace in Henry VIII's
reign and the Rebellions of 1547–9 in the reign of his son, Edward VI.[148]
Nonetheless, the punitive response of Henry VIII's government to seditious words, food riots or the possibility of insurrection, even if it did not
always go beyond words, reflects not merely the official fears that even
the most minor protest or disorder might develop into something much
worse but also an insistence on obedience above all. While the king in his
proclamations projected sympathy and concern for the poor in time of
need as well as anger at those who sought to profit from grain scarcity
such sentiments demanded obedience and restraint from disorder in
return. If disorder did occur then punishment would follow so that order
could be restored.

---

[142] TNA, SP1/239, f. 288; *LP*, *Addenda*, vol. 1 pt. 1, 1058.
[143] TNA, KB27/1102, Rex, rot. 9.
[144] TNA, SP1/239, f. 292; *LP*, *Addenda*, vol. 1 pt. 1, 1063; TNA, C82/712, May 26,
   28 Hen. VIII; *LP*, vol. 10, 1015 (26).
[145] TNA, C82/712, May 26, 28 Hen. VIII; *LP*, vol. 10, 1015 (26).
[146] TNA, SP1/239, f. 292; *LP*, *Addenda*, vol. 1 pt. 1, 1063.
[147] TNA, C82/712, May 28 Hen. VIII; *LP*, vol. 10, 1015 (26).
[148] For these rebellions see Fletcher and MacCulloch, *Tudor Rebellions* and Wood,
   The 1549 Rebellions.

Perhaps the clearest expression of the official attitude towards popular disorder is to be found in the homily *An Exhortacion concernyng Good Ordre and Obedience to Rulers and Magistrates* of 1547, one of a number designed to be read in churches on Sunday. The maintenance of hierarchy, obedience, and good order are central to the homily. "For where there is no right ordre, there reigneth all abuse, carnall liberttie, enormitie, syn and babilonicall confusion."[149] Without kings, magistrates, judges and the like "no man shal ride or go by the high waie unrobbed; no man shall slepe in his awne house or bed unkilled, no man shall kepe his wife, children and possessions in quietnes: all thing shal be in common and there must nedes folow all mischief and utter destruction, both of soules, bodies, goodes and common wealthes."[150]

Later, in vivid language, the homily condemns any kind of resistance to the king: "it is an intollerable ignoraunce, madnesse and wickednesse for subjects to make any murmuryng, rebellion, resistence, commocion, or insurrection agaynst their moste dear and most dread sovereigne lorde and kyng, ordeined and appoynted of God's goodnesse for their commoditie, peace, and quietnes."[151] This passage reflects some of the crown's concerns with popular unrest that the Duke of Norfolk expressed in a letter to Cardinal Wolsey in December 1527, which included speaking "secretly or openly any seditious words, secret assemblies, murmurs or any disobedient manner."[152] There can be little doubt that the ideas in the homily and Norfolk's letter were commonplace among the governing elite, particularly since *Certain Sermons or Homilies* was frequently enough used that it was published in thirty-four editions between 1547 and 1687.[153]

---

[149] Bond (ed.), *Certain Sermons or Homilies*, p. 161.   [150] *Ibid.*, pp. 161–2.
[151] *Ibid.*, p. 167.   [152] TNA, SP1/45, ff. 272–3; *LP*, vol. 4, pt. 1, 1659.
[153] Bond (ed.), *Certain Sermons or Homilies*, p. 46.

8   The moral economy, 1547–1631 and beyond

The long tradition of the English monarchy's commitment to regulating the grain market in the interest of consumers, especially the poorer among them, continued well after 1547. The innovations associated with Cardinal Wolsey's response to the failure of the 1527 harvest, particularly the establishment of commissions to undertake searches for grain with the added power to compel the owners to bring it to market, provided the model for future official responses to scarcity up until 1631. While it is clear that Wolsey's creation of the grain commissions nationwide was a substantial administrative expansion of the earlier efforts in the reigns of Edward III, Richard II, and Henry VI during periods of scarcity, nonetheless in other respects Wolsey's policies were much like those of his medieval predecessors. These included prohibitions on export of grain, enforcement of laws against forestalling, regrating and engrossing, and encouraging the import of grain from overseas to supply English markets. Such medieval precedents also continued to be significant elements in the English crown's response to dearth in the years after 1547.

Searches for grain to be undertaken by justices of the peace were ordered after the failures of the harvests of 1549, 1550, and 1556.[1] In 1552, Edward VI's parliament passed the first statute against market crimes that added regrating and engrossing to forestalling. It opens with an observation that in the past there were statutes against forestalling but none against regrating and engrossing.[2] It remained on the statute book until repealed in 1772.[3] After a poor harvest in 1586, the Elizabethan privy council, in January 1587, ordered the distribution of a book of orders to the justices of the peace in every county that contained instructions on how they were to respond to scarcity.[4] The book was reissued, with some revisions, in response to scarcity in 1594, 1595, 1600, 1608,

---

[1] Slack, "Social Policy," pp. 105–6.   [2] *SR*, vol. 4, pp. 148–50, 5 &6 Ed. VI, c.14.
[3] Hay, "Moral Economy, Political Economy and Law," pp. 96–8; Hay, "The State and the Market in 1800," pp. 102–3; Randall, *Riotous Assemblies,* pp. 234–5.
[4] *Book of Orders,* 1587.

1622, and for the last time in 1630.[5] Moreover, in August 1596 the privy council instructed the sheriffs and justices of peace of every county to continue enforcement of the 1595 edition.[6]

The aim of the book of orders was the regulation of the market in order to meet the subsistence needs of consumers. To that end, emergency regulations compelled the transfer of grain from private hands to the open market place. Justices of the peace, with the help of juries, were empowered to make inventories of grain held by individuals and to order owners, with a surplus beyond their household and seed requirements, to sell it regularly in the market in specified portions. It was hoped that such sales would help depress the market price. The justices were also enjoined to supervise closely the operation of the markets within their jurisdictions. After the opening bell, only the poor were to be served for the first hour, in the 1587 edition, and for the first two hours, in the 1595 and subsequent editions, except that of 1600 which specified the first two hours in summer and the first in winter.[7] The justices were also instructed to make an effort to persuade sellers of grain "that the poore may bee served of Corne at convenient and charitable prices." Finally, the persuasions of the magistrates were to be accompanied by exhortations in sermons in churches that "the richer sort bee earnestly mooved by Christian charitie, to cause their Graine to be solde under the common prices of the Market to the poorer sort. A deede of mercie, that wil doubtlesse be rewarded of Almightie God."[8]

Other provisions of the book included the regulation of the activities of purchasers of large quantities of grain such as badgers, carriers, bakers, brewers, and maltsters. The justices were given the power to issue licenses that showed how much grain large purchasers could buy and the destination of the grain. Such licenses had to be shown at the time of purchases in the market. To prevent profiteering, millers were prohibited from buying grain on their own account and were limited to grinding only the grain that others brought to the mill. The justices were also expected "to take order with the common Bakers for the baking of Rye, Barley, Pease, and Beanes for the use of the poore." They were also to control the amount of barley that was converted into malt for brewing, while oats were to be substituted where feasible. At the same time, the justices were urged to reduce the number of alehouses, again to reduce the conversion of barley to drink. As part of their supervision of bakers and brewers, the justices were to appoint "special and fit people" to ensure that the poor were well dealt with "in their Weightes and Assizes."

[5] *Book of Orders*, 1594, 1595, 1600, 1608, 1622, and 1630.   [6] *APC, 1596–7*, pp. 80–3.
[7] *Book of Orders*, 1594, 1595, 1600, 1608, 1622, and 1630.   [8] *Book of Orders*, 1587.

Finally, the names of engrossers who hoarded grain were to be forwarded to the attorney-general for future legal action, probably in star chamber.[9]

At the heart of the book of orders were principles central to the moral economy: 1) grain ought to be bought and sold only in open public markets held at known times and places; 2) the public market appropriately regulated ought to have as a primary aim the provision of a subsistence to the poor at affordable prices; 3) open marketing, reinforced by public or community opinion, would put moral pressure on sellers to moderate the prices they charged to the poor. The only exception to the regulation that all grain should be bought and sold in open market was sales directly "to poor handicrafts men or day labourers" in their home parishes.[10]

Other dearth measures included control of coastal grain shipments and prohibition on the export of grain overseas. Although separate commissioners were appointed to enforce prohibitions on grain export, the 1587 book of orders urged justices of the peace in maritime counties to act to prevent illegal export if the commissioners were negligent.[11] In the 1595 and subsequent editions, this section on shipping was considerably expanded. It states that the only shipping of grain by sea allowed was that from one English port to another and for "the provisions of London, shipping or such like." This was to be enforced by customs officers, port officials and commissioners (many of whom were also justices of the peace). Each shipper of grain had to enter a bond with sufficient sureties to guarantee that the cargo reached its named destination and return with a certificate testifying to that fact signed by the chief magistrate of that port.[12]

From the first issue in 1587, the book of orders recognized the problems of poverty, low wages, and unemployment that deprived many of enough money to buy food. It urged the enforcement of wage regulations and poor laws, including the raising of higher rates to sustain the poor and the provision of stocks of raw material to set them on work. In particular, the book urged that "the Clothiers, that have in former times gained by that trade, not nowe in this time of dearth to leave off his trade, whereby the poore may bee set on worke." If the existing poor rate in any parish did not provide enough money to sustain its unemployed poor, "it may be nowe for this time of dearth be charitably increased."

---

[9] Hawarde, *Les Reportes*, pp. 71, 75–6, 77–9, 91; Gardiner (ed.), *Reports of Cases*, pp. 43–9, 82–9; Barnes, "Star Chamber and the English Attempt at Absolutism," p. 17.

[10] *Book of Orders*, 1587. For examples of such direct sales of small amounts to the laboring poor see Walter, "The Social Economy of Dearth," pp. 100–1.

[11] *Book of Orders*, 1587.   [12] *Book of Orders*, 1594, 1595, 1600, 1608, 1622, and 1630.

If a parish was unable to provide such an increase because of its large population of poor people, then neighboring parishes with fewer poor should help provide relief.[13]

Another significant relief measure, beyond the book of orders, consisted of the central government's encouragement of the import of foreign grain and the effort of local town officials to raise money to buy grain elsewhere in the country or from overseas, especially the Baltic, to be sold at less than the market price to the poor. In London during the dearths of 1594–7, the city gilds and companies provided loans to buy grain, about 1,000 quarters a year, to be sold to the poor at less than the market price.[14] Even more impressive, was the large volume of grain imports from the Baltic that reached London in those years. In a letter to the mayor of London on October 31, 1596, the privy council noted that twenty ships carrying Baltic grain had arrived in the Thames. The council urged, in the queen's name, that the grain be sold to relieve her poor subjects "out of her princely care" and not sold to those who engrossed large quantities to sell at high prices and obtain "an unlawefull gaine to the oppression of the poore people."[15] Between October 1596 and March 1597, 110,000 quarters of imported grain reached London.[16]

Some of the Baltic grain shipped to London was sold to supply other towns. In 1596, the aldermen of Shrewsbury bought 3,300 bushels of rye in London at 8s per bushel and sold it at the same price in Shrewsbury market where the going price for rye was 12s and 14–15s for wheat. In March 1597, a merchant bought 200 quarters of rye at 5s 8d per bushel in Tewkesbury that had come up river from Bristol and carried it to Shrewsbury where he sold it at the same price.[17] A Bristol alderman bought £1,200 worth of wheat and rye (source unknown, although probably the Baltic or the Low Countries) and supplied the market regularly with a quantity of grain between Christmas 1594 and Michaelmas 1595. The following year another merchant bought 3,000 quarters of Baltic rye in London to provision Bristol.[18] These are only selections of such actions in the 1590s, which were numerous enough to persuade Peter Clark that imported grain "helped provincial towns, as well as

---

[13] For more detailed discussions of the crown's mixed success in alleviating low wages and unemployment in the cloth industry see Sharp, *In Contempt of all Authority*, pp. 53–81 and Walter and Wrightson "Dearth and the Social Order," 35–8.

[14] Gras, *The Evolution of the English Corn Market*, pp. 82–6, 421–5; Power, "London and the Control of the 'Crisis' of the 1590's," 373; Clark, "A Crisis Contained?" p. 57.

[15] *APC, 1596–7*, p. 281.   [16] Clark, "A Crisis Contained?" p. 58.

[17] Leighton (ed.), "Early Chronicles of Shrewsbury," pp. 335–6; Owen, *A History of Shrewsbury* vol. 1, p. 400 and nt. 1.

[18] Smith (ed.), *The Maire of Bristowe* , pp. 62–3.

London, to ride out the worst of the crisis."[19] It also appears to be the case that the arrival of Baltic grain in London in May 1631 was a major factor in overcoming the ongoing scarcity that resulted from the poor harvest of 1630. So much grain arrived, with more on the way, that the importing merchants found it difficult to sell it at a price that would cover their costs.[20] During that same scarcity Charles I sought to obtain sixteen shiploads of rye from Russia and the city of London contracted for 10,000 quarters of grain from Ireland.[21]

Some years ago Walter and Wrightson made the persuasive argument that the official dearth responses in the book of orders and other measure were in harmony with popular views of scarcity and high prices. In their opinion, "popular explanations were derived from customary views of the ideal ordering of economic transactions, firmly centred on the marketplace, informed by the notions of the just price and the conscionable course of dealing and governed by the imperative of maintaining neighbourly harmony and well-being." Such views were legitimated by the crown's announced policies that confirmed "traditional economic presuppositions permeated by moral and religious overtones."[22]

The government's condemnation of the activities of middlemen, engrossers and forestallers fitted well with the popular views of the causes of dearth as did the official moral outrage, expressed in letters and proclamations, about the avarice of the evil men who hoarded grain and made the poor suffer.[23] For example, a privy council letter of August 1596, circulated to the sheriffs and justices of the peace nationwide, states that the engrossing of corn and forestalling of markets "by covetuous men in buying out of the markett at farmors' howses great quantities of corne hathe bene the cause of the dearthe lately growne." The letter then goes on to suggest remedial action "rather then to have her Majesty's poore loving subjects to be in this cruell sorte forced to famine."[24]

The religious duty of monarchs to act on behalf of their subjects in times of dearth is clearly expressed in a privy council letter of August 1596 addressed to the archbishop of Canterbury and in a royal proclamation of June 1600 that condemned the hoarding of grain. The letter

---

[19] Clark, "A Crisis Contained ?" p. 59. For further examples of town magistrates and some rural ones buying grain to supply local markets, see pp. 58–9 and Walter, "The Social Economy of Dearth," pp. 118–20. Also see pp. 120–8 for a perceptive discussion of the significance of informal relief or charity in times of dearth.

[20] *APC, 1630–1*, pp. 325, 345, 378–9, 400; *Analytical Index*, p. 388.

[21] *APC, 1630–1*, pp. 74–5, 89, 146,152,167–8, 279; *Analytical Index*, pp. 388–9.

[22] Walter and Wrightson, "Dearth and the Social Order," 31.

[23] *Ibid.*, 30–1. For a similar discussion of the relationship between royal paternalism and the moral economy of the poor see Thompson, "The Moral Economy," 83, 95, 98.

[24] *APC, 1596–7*, pp. 81–2.

urged the archbishop to instruct the preachers in his province to exhort the owners of grain to aid the poor and reject the "dishonest and unchristian kinde of seeking gaine by oppression of theire poore neighbours." The letter also railed against "the covetous disposicion of the farmers and ingrossers of corne that seeke all excessive and ungodly lucar by whording up of corne and making more scarcety then there is." Finally, the letter emphasized the "princely care she [the Queen] hathe of the poorer sorte of her people"[25] The proclamation noted the Queen's concern for regulation of the food market in times of dearth, "perceiving well how bitter a thing the scarcity of victuals is to the poorer sort of her people (of whom her majesty is no less tender than of the richest, seeing Almighty God doth expect from her an account of all those over whom He hath chosen her to be the ruler here on earth)."[26]

Examples of the language of royal paternalism, based on the ruler's Christian duty to see to the welfare of his or her subjects, especially the poor are legion for the sixteenth and early seventeenth century, but they were hardly novel. This book has argued that royal concern for the poor can be traced back to the thirteenth century in such legislation as the assize of bread and the first regulation of forestalling. From then onward there is a continuous history of royal market regulations and responses to dearth in the interest of all consumers but with special concern for the poorer among them. The Tudor and early Stuart monarchs built their ideas of the commonwealth and the common good on medieval foundations.

While one might conclude that the work of Walter and Wrightson on the book of orders and other dearth measures in the sixteenth and seventeenth centuries brought royal paternalism and the moral economy of the poor together, they were not the same. Thompson observed that the moral economy of the poor was more particular in outlook than paternalism. "The economy of the poor was still local and regional, derivative from a subsistence–economy. Corn should be consumed in the region in which it was grown, especially in times of scarcity."[27] In contrast, paternalist interests were national, or at least extra regional, in scope. This meant difficult choices and, sometimes, contradictory policies in times of dearth, best illustrated in the management of the grain supply of two cities, London and Bristol.

The book of orders was grounded on the principle of open, public marketing, while private, out of market dealing, was suspect.

[25] *APC, 1596–7*, pp. 94–6.
[26] Hughes and Larkin, (eds.), *Tudor Proclamations*, vol. 3, p. 215.
[27] Thompson, "The Moral Economy," 98.

The purchase of foodstuffs before they reached market was technically forestalling and the practice could lead to prosecution, especially in times of scarcity. At the same time, private dealing was clearly on the increase during the sixteenth century. London, which with its suburbs had grown to a population of roughly 200,000 in 1600, was supplied in good part through private marketing that drew on a wide area of southern England including the home counties, the Thames valley, the southern midlands and East Anglia. The agents of London buyers had the financial means to make long term, out of market arrangements with producers, including the extension of credit and the purchase of crops while still in the ground, thereby cornering the market.

The effects of London's demands on local markets are well illustrated in a letter from Henry Cocke, a Hertfordshire justice of the peace, sent to the privy council after the poor harvest of 1594. According to Cocke, in the past the bakers and brewers of London had depended on Hertfordshire middlemen to supply them but now they and their agents actively scoured local markets buying and transporting grain on their own accounts, thereby cutting out and impoverishing provincial loaders. For Cocke, concerned with food supply and order in Hertfordshire, one advantage of the local loader, who bought grain and then moved it to London, was that he "dothe usuallye buye by lycense in the open markettes." Presumably therefore his activities could be monitored. The disadvantages of London brewers and bakers entering directly into local grain deals was that they "withoute lycense doe for the most parte buye verie great quantities of corne as well in markettes as allsoe at mens' howses." Finally, Cocke offered a general observation on the effects of London buyers on local markets: "The Cytie is growne to be exceadinge populous, therefore the expenses therof must neades be great, which principallye they have from some few sheares [shires] neare adioyninge unto them, which therbye generallye are verie muche annoyed for by the daielye carryinge awaye of the commodities therof, the prices of thos which remayne are much raysed to the hinderaunce of the greattest number of the inhabitauntes of the same."[28]

In responding to complaints about the activities of London buyers in provincial markets, the crown was faced with difficulties that made a simple prohibition impossible. In fact, significant new language was added to the 1595 reissue of the book of orders and subsequent reissues, which created the possibility that the privy council could take whatever actions necessary, including presumably the authorizing of large scale out

---

[28] TNA, SP12/254/10.

of market purchases, in order to provision urban areas. The whole paragraph containing the wording is new. It opens as if it were a direct and positive response to the complaints of Henry Cocke. Buyers from London and other cities were "not to be permitted to buy Corne or other victuall but in open market" and only two hours after the market was opened and the poor had been served. This section is then followed by a qualifying sentence, which radically alters the apparent limitation on the activities of urban buyers. "Neverthelesse, for the better furnishing of your sayd Cities with necessarie provisions and in convenient maner, it is ordered that further provisions shall be from time to time made for them in such sort as the Lords of her Maiesties Counsell shal further direct in that behalfe."[29]

In the minds of privy councilors, the supply of foodstuffs to London and other large towns was evidently too complex a business to be left to the small scale, face to face transactions typical of the traditional methods of the open market that underlay the central message of the book of orders. What Thompson said about the supply of towns in the eighteenth century was equally true about their supply in the earlier period: "urban markets simply could not be supplied without the operation of factors [i.e. dealers] whose activities would have been nullified if legislation against forestallers had been strictly enforced."[30] In times of dearth, London continued to be provisioned, with official permission, through the kind of large scale purchases in local markets and private out of market deals, which Henry Cocke deplored and which both publically stated official policy and community standards condemned as contrary to the commonweal.

Take one example: on August 27, 1597, the privy council wrote to the sheriffs and justices of the peace nationwide strongly condemning forestallers "as wycked people in condicions more lyke to wolves or cormerants then to naturall men." The council instructed local officials to identify those individuals who engaged in grain transactions for private grain and then take legal action against them, including sending the most notorious to London for punishment. The letter also emphasized that, since the main aim of official policy was to bring down the price of food and relieve the poor, it was of special concern to the council that men of substance and standing were involved in such transactions. They had to be restrained "to avoyde the just offence of the inferyour sort, which cannot be but greeved to see soche corrupcions in the better sorte suffered without restraint."[31] Nonetheless, two months later

---

[29] *Book of Orders*, 1595.   [30] Thompson, "The Moral Economy," 87.
[31] *APC, 1597*, pp. 359–61.

the privy council, clearly acting in accord with the 1595 modifications of the book of orders, sent warrants to officials in eight counties ordering them to allow buyers, licensed by the mayor and aldermen of London, to purchase a total of 15,200 quarters of grain to supply the city. The warrants provided authorization that the purchases were to take place out of market, despite official proclamations and orders prohibiting such practices.[32]

There are other indications of the importance that the government attached to the supply of the capital. On a number of occasions, magistrates in producing counties held up shipments of grain to London because they feared that large shipments from their localities would produce scarcity, high prices, and possibly riot. The privy council, on receipt of notification of such actions, just as regularly ordered release of the shipments, even at the cost of raising prices and provoking riot in producing areas, since the capital's needs were so pressing. In this regard, there survives an illuminating exchange between a Cambridgeshire justice of the peace, Robert Beaumont, and William Cecil in an earlier scarcity year, 1565, when there was an official prohibition on the export of grain. On June 18, Beaumont informed Cecil that in the previous two weeks 3,000 quarters of grain had been shipped from Cambridgeshire to the Norfolk port of Lynn thereby driving up prices in local markets. Beaumont requested that some sort of official restraint be imposed on the "insatiable goulfe [gulf] of Lynne" which deprived Cambridgeshire of needed grain. At the same time, officials at Cambridge University also wrote to the privy council with a similar request because the shipping of grain was "pinching poor scholars bellies." The joint reply from Cecil and the earl of Leicester makes it quite clear that London's needs had priority. Beaumont was informed that Cambridgeshire and neighboring counties were "accustomed" to supply London with grain shipped through Lynn; the continuance of such shipments was necessary not only to supply the city but also to encourage the husbandman with "the comfort of gayne." The only crumb of comfort offered to Beaumont was the suggestion that, if prices continued to rise, he could impose a temporary halt on the transportation of grain from Cambridgeshire until he satisfied himself that it was not being fraudulently exported overseas but only being lawfully transported to London or other parts of England.[33]

---

[32] *APC, 1597–8*, pp. 42–4. The counties were Kent, Essex, Sussex, Suffolk, Norfolk, Berkshire, Buckinghamshire, and Oxfordshire.

[33] TNA, SP12/36/67 and 69, the latter is a draft of the reply from Cecil and Leicester; Lee, "Feeding the Colleges," 260.

In early February 1587, about a month after the first book of orders was issued, the privy council was forced to deal with the threat of grain scarcity in London. The sheriffs and justices of the peace in seven counties had restrained London buyers from purchasing grain in their markets. While admitting that such an action was "by occasion of the late orders," the council made it clear that, since London's grain needs were so great, the badgers and other suppliers of London must have access to the grain in the named counties.[34] In late February, other letters were sent to the same seven counties ordering that provision for London and Middlesex should not be restrained.[35] Despite these letters, the shipment of grain to London from its usual sources of supply continued to be restrained by local authorities thus making grain scarcer and more expensive in the city. As a consequence, William Cecil, lord treasurer, and four other privy councillors were instructed to meet with some of the aldermen of London plus knights and gentlemen from the counties in question, who happened to be in the city for the current session of parliament, and work out an agreement on supplying London with grain.[36] By the end of February, an agreement had been reached specifying how much licensed grain buyers from London could purchase every week in the markets of each county. In return for the lifting of the restraint, the aldermen of London agreed that the licensed buyers would enter bonds that they would not exceed the weekly amount and would not attempt to engross more.[37]

Problems related to London's grain supply recurred in the dearth years 1595–8. The privy council had to send letters to a number of local officials ordering them to lift restraints on grain shipments to London: from Kent in October, 1595 and February, 1596; from Norfolk, Suffolk, Essex in October, 1596; from Kent again in March 1597; and from Norfolk again in January 1598.[38] As a consequence of the lifting of restraints, there were riots in Kent in 1595 and 1597 and in Norfolk in 1597 that aimed to prevent such shipments to London.[39] No doubt it was the official government view that distress and disorder in the provinces were more tolerable and less disruptive to political stability than if they had occurred in the capital. As one historian has

---

[34] *APC, 1586–7*, pp. 319–20. The counties were Hampshire, Oxfordshire, Kent, Essex, Berkshire, Hertfordshire, and Surrey.
[35] *Ibid.*, pp. 338–9.   [36] *Ibid.*, pp. 342–3.
[37] *Ibid.*, pp. 359–60. By the time the agreement was made the list of seven counties was somewhat different from the original list. The counties were Kent, Berkshire, Buckinghamshire, Bedfordshire, Norfolk, Cambridgeshire, and Oxfordshire.
[38] *APC, 1595–6*, pp. 19–20, 221; *APC, 1596–7*, pp. 269–70, 534; *APC, 1597–8*, p. 237.
[39] Sharp, *In Contempt of All Authority*, pp. 19–20; Clark, "Popular Protest," 368, 373–4.

noted about London's food needs, "short of desperation elsewhere, the City enjoyed a privileged status."[40]

During the scarcity year 1630–1, the privy council had to press local officials in London's neighboring counties, such as Kent, Sussex and Hampshire, to give buyers, licensed by the mayor, access to their markets in order to meet the city's needs.[41] The council also regularly authorized shipments of grain to London as well, 1,500 quarters of wheat and 500 of barley from Cornwall in November 1630, 3,000 quarters of grain from Norfolk to be shared with Westminster, Essex and Suffolk, 2,000 from Kent and 155 from Sussex, in December 1630, plus a further 500 from Sussex in April, 1631.[42]

From 1347 to 1547, the movement of grain along the river Severn between Tewkesbury and Bristol had been a major concern of the central government, especially in times of scarcity. Such concern was focused not only on the free movement of grain along the river but overland from neighboring counties as well. In addition to ensuring that grain got to towns such as Gloucester and Bristol, there was an additional concern to prevent the smuggling of grain from Bristol to foreign destinations.

In the scarcity years 1586–7 and 1595–7 the privy council made considerable efforts to enforce the traditional policy of encouraging the free movement of grain overland and down the Severn. At the same time, the council encountered problems in balancing the grain needs of the different communities along the river with its commitment to keep grain moving as freely as possible. As early as April 1586, the council wrote to the commissioners for restraint of grain (in effect justices of the peace) in Wiltshire, Somerset, and Gloucestershire to allow properly licensed buyers from Bristol to buy a reasonable amount of grain to supply the city, which was experiencing scarcity and high prices because less grain than normal was being brought to its market.[43] A few days later, the council wrote to the magistrates of the city Gloucester and of Gloucestershire expressing its concern about the rising prices of grain in both the city and the county, which in its opinion was caused by the failure of grain owners to supply the markets. The council recommended grain searches and orders to those with a surplus to bring a set amount weekly to market.[44] One consequence of these rising prices was food riots along the Severn south of Gloucester. Twice in late April, cloth workers, who

[40] Power, "London and the 'Crisis' of the 1590s," 372.

[41] *APC, 1630–1*, pp. 116–18, 121, 152, 156, 167, 169–70.

[42] *Ibid.*, pp. 126, 143, 170–2, 304–5.   [43] *APC, 1586–7*, pp. 69–70.

[44] *Ibid.*, pp. 71–2. This order was issued roughly eight months before the first *Book of Orders*.

were either unemployed or could not afford to feed their families on the wages they earned, stopped boats shipping grain down river and carried the cargoes away. For at least a week after the second riot, large crowds gathered on both sides of the river, no doubt with intention of preventing further movements of grain.[45]

Later, in September 1596, the privy council received a report from Gloucestershire of grain scarcity and high prices in the county that were the result of the making of an excessive amount of malt and the transportation of that malt and other grain down the Severn to Bristol. In reply, the council wrote to the lord lieutenant, sheriff, and justices of the peace of the county that they should suppress excessive malt making and restrain the shipping of grain down river "until the want of that countrie be in good sort releeved."[46] At the same time, another council letter was sent to the magistrates of Gloucester to reduce the amount of malt making within the city.[47] These letters, however, resulted in more problems than the council anticipated. Within a month, the privy council had received information on Bristol's need for grain. As a result, the council wrote to the justices of Gloucestershire that brewers, bakers, and others authorized by the mayor of Bristol should be allowed "to buy a moderate quantity of graine" in the county's markets for the supply of the city and ship it down river.[48] Similar letters were sent to justices of Worcestershire and to the magistrates of Gloucester and Worcester to allow authorized buyers from Bristol to buy grain and ship it overland or by river.[49]

In November, it was Gloucester's turn to complain about the council letter sent in September on the suppression of excessive malt making. As a result of the letter, the justices of Gloucestershire had restrained farmers and badgers from bringing grain, especially barley to the city, but this meant that grain became scarce and expensive in the city's market. The privy council responded in a letter to the justices of Gloucestershire to allow the city "to be sufficiently served with corne."[50] Despite this order, it is clear that many in the city of Gloucester were unhappy with the continued transport of grain down river. Sometime in 1597, the mayor of Gloucester ordered the pulling of the chains across the Severn to prevent vessels with grain and other victuals from moving down stream. Despite complaints from the town of Tewkesbury, the brewers of Bristol, and the Severn boatmen, and a ruling by the assize judges that the chains should be removed, they were still up in June, 1598 when the privy council ordered their removal.[51]

---

[45] Sharp, *In Contempt of All Authority*, p. 15.   [46] *APC, 1596–7*, pp. 152–3.
[47] *Ibid.*, p. 154.   [48] *Ibid.*, pp. 226–7.   [49] *Ibid.*, pp. 227–8.   [50] *Ibid.*, pp. 335–6.
[51] Bennett, *The History of Tewkesbury*, p. 308; *APC, 1597–8*, pp. 488–9.

During the scarcity of 1630–1, the council was forced, once again, to write to the magistrates of counties that normally supplied Bristol to allow the movement of grain by boat to the city and allow buyers licensed by the city to purchase grain in their markets.[52] Despite this letter, it does not appear that Bristol was in nearly as difficult a situation as it had been in the scarcity years of the 1590s. There are also numerous other examples, during the scarcity years of 1586–7, the 1590s, and 1630–1, of the privy council ordering local justices in a number of counties, who had prohibited the movement of grain out of their county, to allow badgers and other dealers, mainly from towns, to purchase grain and transport it to their home communities suffering from scarcity.[53]

Scholarly assessments of the book of orders and related dearth measures have ranged from the negative judgments of Fletcher to the more balanced views of Slack. Fletcher's view is that the book of orders was "an inflexible instrument."[54] It was only through the activities of local justices of the peace, who ignored or modified the book that real relief was provided to the poor and needy. In fact, significant local initiatives that Fletcher points to, such as increasing the poor rates so that those without work could buy food and selling grain directly to the poor in their home parishes so they did not have to come to market were contained in the 1587 book of orders and subsequent reissues, except that of 1600 did not refer to raising the poor rates.[55]

Fletcher is also highly critical of the "Council's failure to lift restraints on transport of grain from one county to another."[56] In fact, as discussed above, on receiving notice of local justices preventing movement of grain to other communities that were in need, the privy council regularly ordered the lifting of prohibitions. Such orders often include criticisms of local magistrates for imposing them in the first place. Two of Fletcher's examples of the council's failures relate to restraints that prevented Rye and Hastings in Sussex being supplied with grain during the scarcity

---

[52] *APC, 1630–1*, pp. 125–6. See also pp. 233–4 a letter of February 16, 1631 authorizing the shipment of 1,500 quarters of grain from Cornwall to Bristol.

[53] In 1586–7: *APC, 1586–7*, p. 362, *APC, 1587–8*, pp. 40–2, 78, from Hampshire to West Surrey; pp. 369–70 from Hertfordshire to Uxbridge, Middlesex; p. 382, from Cambridgeshire to Walden, Essex. In the 1590s: *APC, 1597*, pp. 84–5, from Southampton to Salisbury; *APC, 1597–8*, pp. 144–5 from the neighboring rapes in Sussex to Rye; pp. 314–17, from Worcestershire and Gloucestershire to Warwickshire. In 1630–1: *APC, 1630–1*, p. 126, from Cornwall to Exeter; pp. 175–6, from Isle of Thanet to Maidstone; pp. 206–7, from Norfolk to Aldborough; p. 210 from Sussex and Kent to Maidstone; p. 240, from Suffolk to Nayland; pp. 242, 330, from Sussex to Hastings; pp. 309, from Sussex to Rye.

[54] Fletcher, *Reform in the Provinces*, p. 193.

[55] *Ibid.*, pp. 194–5, 197–8; *Book of Orders*, 1587, 1594, 1595, 1600, 1608, 1622, and 1630.

[56] Fletcher, *Reform in the Provinces*, p. 195.

of 1630–1. He asserts that the council was slow on lifting its ban on the movement of grain to the two towns.[57] In fact, it was a ban imposed by the local justices of Sussex not the council. The council's letters ordering the justices to allow grain to get to both towns in April and May 1631 make it clear that information on the needs of Rye and Hastings had only recently reached London.[58] Another example of what Fletcher calls a lack of "bureaucratic flexibility" concerns an attempt to supply grain to the city of Gloucester in 1630. According to Fletcher, a badger petitioned the council for permission to buy grain in South Wales and ship it to Gloucester but the "Council reacted stubbornly."[59] The meaning of that reaction is quite unclear, since on November 24, 1630 the privy council approved a proposal from John Keyme to ship 200 bushels of barley and 100 of oats from the counties of Pembroke and Carmarthen to the city of Gloucester.[60]

Slack recognizes that local magistrates were the ones responsible for using the book of orders to restrain the shipment of grain from their counties, despite the urging of the privy council that grain must be shipped to towns or other counties in need.[61] In effect, he believes that in imposing prohibitions on the movement of grain justices of the peace were more in tune with the popular view that local grain should be consumed locally than was the central government. In good part this was because such a commitment to localism reduced the chances of riot and other disorder by the needy poor.[62] At the same time Slack, like Fletcher, appears to be unaware of the fact that the first book of orders of 1587 and every subsequent reissue encouraged the direct sale of grain to the poor in their home parishes; it was not an innovation of 1630–1.[63] It may only be a matter of emphasis but Slack appears to minimize the significance of the section in the original 1587 book of orders and subsequent reissues that emphasize wages and employment and increasing poor rates to help the poor and over emphasizes the novelty of similar sections in the new Caroline book of orders on poor relief issued in 1631.[64]

---

[57] *Ibid.*   [58] *APC, 1630–1*, 309, 330, 337.

[59] Fletcher, *Reform in the Provinces*, p. 195.   [60] *APC, 1630–1*, p. 126.

[61] Slack, "Dearth and Social Policy,"10–11; Slack, *Poverty and Policy*, pp. 145–6; Slack, "Books of Orders," 12.

[62] Slack, *Poverty and Policy*, pp. 145–6. The argument that a major reason for the commitment of local justices to the enforcement of the book of orders was the belief, correct as it turned out, that it would reduce the incidence of food riots was first made by Walter and Wrightson, "Dearth and the Social Order," 32–4.

[63] Slack, *From Reformation to Improvement*, p. 65.

[64] *Book of Orders*, 1587; Slack, "Books of Orders," 13.

There certainly were, as Slack indicates, complaints about the book of orders and sometimes opposition to the book or other dearth regulations.[65] This was particularly true of Norfolk where the justices of the peace were reluctant to regulate the export of grain, a reflection of the fact that landowners and shippers in this major grain producing area regularly pressured the justices and the privy council to be allowed to sell grain wherever they could get the best price.[66] It is not surprising then that grain smuggling was rife from Norfolk and other East Anglian communities when official prohibitions were imposed on export.[67] In the scarcity year 1630–1, a number of grain owners in different counties were punished, mainly by the privy council, for failing to bring grain to market or for engrossing. After admitting their offences they were ordered to bring their grain to market and sell it, usually to the poor, at sixpence per bushel below the market price.[68]

Earlier, during the scarcity years 1594–8 a number of men who engrossed grain contrary to the book of orders were charged and found guilty in the court of star chamber and were sentenced to a range of punishments including the pillory, fines, and imprisonment.[69] By far the most interesting case that star chamber dealt with in those years was that of a man called Mison, whose Christian name and county of residence are not reported. He had clearly refused to bring grain to market and was charged with seditious words in contempt of the justices of peace, the book of orders, the queen, and the privy council. His seditious words were: "they [the poor] are knaves, I will keepe none of there bastardes, my goodes are myn owne, they, nor the queene, nor the Councelle have to doe with my goodes, I will doe what I liste with them." He was fined £100, sentenced to the pillory, and bound over for his good behavior.[70]

It is difficult to know how many others would have agreed with Mison's assertion that his grain was his own and he could do with it what he wished. One could imagine, however, that in Norfolk, among farmers who sought freedom to export grain even in times of dearth, that such a view might be common. They also seem to have been common among commercially oriented farmers and landowners in Kent.[71] At the

---

[65] Slack, "Books of Orders," 12–13.

[66] Hassell Smith, *County and Court*, pp. 18–19, 99–102.

[67] Williams, *The Maritime Trade of the East Anglian Ports*, pp. 18–19, 25–33, 35–49, 72.

[68] *APC, 1630–1*, pp. 148, 168–9, 175, 182, 222, 245, 310–11, 338, 371–2.

[69] Hawarde, *Les Reportes*, pp. 71, 75–6, 78–9, 91. These reported cases may only represent a small fraction of those heard in star chamber. Only a systematic search in the records of the Elizabethan court would provide an answer to any question about their numbers.

[70] *Ibid.*, p. 104.

[71] Hipkin, "The Structure, Development, and Politics of the Kent Grain Trade," pp. 125–8.

same time, given the widely held views that those in authority had a moral obligation to aid the poor in time of scarcity, including protecting them from the covetous and sinful nature of those who sought to profit from scarcity through forestalling, engrossing, and regrating, it is difficult to imagine that Mison's views were so widespread they could have resulted in the actual creation and implementation of a free market policy in the period 1587–1631, which some modern historians appear to believe would have been the better response to scarcity.[72] Nonetheless, such views had a future and would, in the end, gut both paternalism and the moral economy.

The main problem facing government in its attempts to enforce the book of orders and related dearth measures in the period 1587–1631 was not the rise of free market views, although such views may have lain behind grumbling against the dearth orders in Norfolk and elsewhere, but it was the localism of popular moral economy ideas.[73] There was not a single nationwide moral economy of the poor but a multiplicity of local, community based moral economies, which made competing claims on available grain.[74] Such competing claims are especially clear on the river Severn from 1347 up through 1631. The city of Gloucester including its magistrates, the inhabitants of the Forest of Dean, and the rural cloth workers of Gloucestershire and Wiltshire, made repeated claims on the grain coming down river to supply Bristol, while the people of Bristol made their own claims on grain outward bound from that city. Popular actions similar to that along the Severn can be found in many other places where grain movement was stopped by the actions of either the local populace or local magistrates.

One particularly illuminating series of competing claims on grain, during the scarcity years between 1586 and 1631, is explored in the work of Hipkin on Kent.[75] Kent was a major supplier of grain to London during the whole period but in scarcity years its grain was of crucial importance for feeding the city's population. That meant the privy council acted regularly to ensure that grain moved freely from Kent to London during scarcities.[76] In May 1630 for instance, the Earl of Suffolk, warden of the Cinque Ports, issued a prohibition on the shipping of grain from

---

[72] Slack, "Dearth and Social Policy," 13 and n. 57. For the continuing vitality of medieval views of marketing, especially of foodstuffs, in the early modern period, see Davis, *Market Morality*, pp. 413–47.

[73] For examples of such grumbling see Slack, "Book of Orders," 14 and "Dearth and Social Policy," 10.

[74] Slack calls this phenomenon "local chauvinism" in "Dearth and Social Policy," 11.

[75] Hipkin, "The Structure, Development, and Politics of the Kent Grain Trade," 99–139.

[76] *Ibid.*, 132.

the ports of east Kent but by January 1631 the privy council had cancelled that prohibition in order to allow the movement of grain to London, where it was in increasingly short supply. One result of the lifting of the prohibition and the free movement of grain to London was a series of disorders in Kent that included seizure of grain either in ports or in towns through which it passed on the way to be shipped.[77] Most of the grain was grown in east Kent by farmers, great and small, who looked to London as a major market. Some of the larger farmers were directly involved in the grain trade but much of that trade was in the hands of well-off merchants in the ports of east Kent, although in times of scarcity numerous London bakers and other metropolitan buyers sought to buy grain directly from the farmers.[78]

The grain merchants of Faversham, one of the leading ports sending east Kent grain to London, controlled the town's magistracy and were perceptive enough to realize that the sight of grain being shipped to London during scarcity could easily provoke the town's poor to protest and attempt to stop the shipments. As a consequence, in hard times, Faversham's magistrates and farmers bringing grain to the port for shipment to London, supplied the poor with grain at less than the market price.[79] In Hipkin's words the magistrates of Faversham were only interested in helping "our poor" who were members of a "little commonwealth."[80] In effect, their moral economy extended only as far as the town limits.

There were other little commonwealths in Kent, particularly in grain deficient areas in west and southern Kent governed largely by justices of the peace. It was from such justices like William Lambarde, who were deeply committed to the enforcement of the book of orders, that came calls for prohibitions on the export of grain and the redirection of grain towards helping their poor. But, as Hipkin makes clear, such justices were only concerned with the needs of the poor in their own communities.[81] They did not consider the needs of the London poor, who would face hunger if grain shipments from Kent were prohibited, just as the merchants and magistrates of Faversham and other ports did not consider the needs of the poor of west and southern Kent when they insisted on their freedom to ship grain to London. Finally, Hipkin points out that those poor who were driven by necessity to attempt to prevent the shipment of grain out of Kent also did not consider the needs of the London populace.[82] For every level of Kent society it was the bounded local community with its own moral economy that mattered. In times of

---

[77] *Ibid.*, 118, 131–2.   [78] *Ibid.*, 119–25, 133–4.   [79] *Ibid.*, 122, 128–9.
[80] *Ibid.*, 128–9.   [81] *Ibid.*, 124–8.   [82] *Ibid.*, 129.

scarcity, the only institution that made an effort to look at the broader national picture was the privy council, which attempted the near impossible task of balancing and satisfying the competing moral economy claims on grain that different communities made.

In subsequent scarcity years after 1630–1, the localism of the moral economy became even more obvious as the commitment of the central government to paternalism began to waver. In 1647–50 there was a series of poor harvests that produced dearth and scarcity nation wide.[83] In the past, central government response to such a crisis would have included the issue of a prohibition on export, the reissue of the book of orders, and the enforcement of related dearth measures against market manipulation as soon as it was known that the harvest of 1647 was poor. In addition, those remedial measures would have continued to be enforced through the subsequent harvest failures of 1648 and 1649. In contrast, the governmental response in 1647–50 was feeble and late. It was not until March 1649 that the parliamentary government took any action. It issued a prohibition on the export of grain. In addition, the attorney-general was instructed to prosecute engrossers of grain, what Hindle calls "a star chamber strategy" but it was one without the requisite court.[84] Finally, local justices of the peace were ordered to relieve the poor with grain and punish engrossers.[85]

The book of orders, on the other hand, was never reissued. This was no doubt a result of the growing unpopularity of the activist fiscal and religious policies of Charles I that involved extensive use of the royal prerogative in the 1630s, which tainted the prerogative based social policy of the book of orders.[86] That social policy depended for enforcement, in part, on the use of the star chamber, which also grew in unpopularity in the 1630s when used to punish the king's political and religious critics. Not only was the star chamber swept away by the long parliament but there was an earlier indicator of the likely unpopularity of Charles I's prerogative based social policy in the scarcity year 1637–8 when the privy council failed to reissue the book of orders.[87]

Despite the failure of the central government to act decisively in response to the crisis of 1647–50, local magistrates in a number of counties, especially Wiltshire, acted on their own authority to punish engrossers and enforce market regulations similar to those in the book of orders so that grain would be brought to the market to sell to the poor, sometimes at less than the market price. Also there were local attempts

---

[83] Hindle, "Dearth and the English Revolution," 64–98.   [84] *Ibid.*, 73.
[85] *Ibid.*, 74; R. B. Outhwaite, "Dearth and Government Intervention," 395.
[86] Hindle, "Dearth and the English Revolution," 72–3.   [87] *Ibid.*, 73.

to limit the conversion of barley into malt in order to direct more of the barley crop towards bread making. Related to this were traditional campaigns against alehouses.[88] As Hindle shows, behind the actions of the local magistrates, many of whom appear to have been reluctant to act, lay pressure from petitioning campaigns by the unemployed and hungry who complained of their plight and called on the magistrates, usually at quarter sessions or meetings of the assizes, to act to enforce the traditional market regulations. Occasionally the distress of the poor resulted in riot.[89] Hindle concludes by observing that the harvest crisis of 1647–50 saw "the transmission of responsibility for the regulation of the markets from the 'political economy of absolutism' to 'the moral economy of the poor'."[90] This point becomes even clearer in the late seventeenth and the eighteenth centuries.

During the eighteenth century there were a number of periods of dearth and scarcity that resulted in widespread food riots. These included 1727–9, 1739–40, 1756–7, 1766–8, 1772–3, 1783, 1795–6, and 1799–1801.[91] Not only were there many more riots in this century compared to earlier periods, but they were also larger and more intense. The historian who shaped the study of the eighteenth-century food riots and still commands the respect and admiration of later historians who work in this field is Thompson. His long article on the moral economy of the English crowd has become a classic of social history.[92]

More recently, Bohstedt published a book that surveys the food riots of the period 1586–1801 in great detail.[93] While there is much to admire in the book, including its chronological range and the thoroughness of his research, he does seem, at times, to make too much of the difference between his work and Thompson's, especially in his dismissal of the moral economy's significance. This is particularly obvious in Bohstedt treatment of the book of orders and the laws against forestalling, regrating, and engrossing. He claims that there is a disconnect between Thompson's argument that memories of the policies associated with these sixteenth-century creations of the Tudor monarchy provided the basis of the moral economy of the eighteenth-century crowd and the actual behavior of the crowd during food riots.[94] Since, for instance, there is no direct evidence that eighteenth-century rioters mentioned the book of orders or the statute against forestalling and other market

---

[88] *Ibid.*, 74–8.   [89] *Ibid.*, 78–91.   [90] *Ibid.*, 95.
[91] Randall, *Riotous Assemblies*, p. 98. For a similar situation in the 1690s and 1709–10 see Beloff, *Public Order*, pp. 56–75.
[92] Thompson, "The Moral Economy," 76–136.   [93] Bohstedt, *The Politics of Provisions*.
[94] Thompson, "The Moral Economy," 83, 87–8, 107–15.

offences when in action, then the moral economy was, in Bohstedt's view, at best only a lubricant (whatever that means) of their actions. In one passage describing the actions of eighteenth-century rioters he claims that they "did not justify their actions in the language of old regulations and paternalistic texts about forestallers, regrators and engrossers." Leaving aside any question that might be raised about what we know about the ability of eighteenth-century rioters to read such regulations and texts, Bohstedt contradicts himself in the next sentence when he states that rioters "did suspect, denounce and attack engrossers or hoarders of grain."[95] In a later section Bohstedt notes that rioters "plundered granaries suspected of engrossing (hoarding) for the export and wholesale trades."[96] He also admits that rioters were "angry at millers and dealers whom they believed to raise prices as hoarders (engrossers), or monopolizers or jobbers."[97] To argue as Bohstedt does that unless the rioters quoted chapter and verse of the book of orders or the statute such official pronouncements must have had no influence on the rioters' behavior, misses the point that the actions of the rioters in attacking engrossers and the like reveal the likely influence of the old regulations on their behavior, rather than any words they may have uttered.[98]

Also, Bohstedt misses another obvious point when denying the influence of the memory of the book of orders on eighteenth-century food rioters. Among the book's major regulations are instructions to the justices of the peace to appoint juries to search for surplus stocks of grain so that it could be sold weekly in local markets to keep prices down.[99] Since the book of orders was not issued after 1630, it could be argued that later riotous crowds took the law into their hands and acted out their own radical version of the dearth orders. They took on the responsibility that the central and local governments had abandoned and conducted searches of their own for grain stocks in barns, mills, or granaries. These stocks were either seized outright and distributed among the rioters or taken to the market place where they were sold at a lower price that poorer consumers could afford. Such actions constituted the majority of eighteenth-century food riots.[100] The other major form of food rioting in the opinion of both Bohstedt and Thompson was stopping shipments of grain either by land or water to other parts of England or overseas.[101]

---

[95] Bohstedt, *Politics of Provision*, p. 105. For more lubrication see pp. 130–1, 146.
[96] *Ibid.*, p. 116.   [97] *Ibid.*, pp. 118–19.   [98] *Ibid.*, p. 119.   [99] *Ibid.*, p. 70.
[100] *Ibid.*, pp. 122, 192.
[101] *Ibid.*, pp. 122, 192; Thompson, "The Moral Economy," 99–100.

One final point is that in 1347, two hundred and forty years before the first issue of the book of orders, food rioters in Bristol, Lynn and Boston acted very much like their early modern successors in stopping the export of grain, unloading ships and either taking the grain away or forcing its sale at lower prices[102] While the ideas of the moral economy and paternalism died in the early nineteenth century as a result of increasing rapid social and economic change, they still remain fruitful and provide significant insight into the behavior of the crowd and the crown in the late medieval–early modern periods.

[102] See Chapter 3.

Bibliography

MANUSCRIPT SOURCES

THE NATIONAL ARCHIVES

C54	Close Rolls
C66	Patent Rolls
C82	Warrants for the Great Seal
C145	Miscellaneous Inquisitions
E36	Exchequer Books
E40	Original Deeds Series A
E163	Miscellanea of the Exchequer
JUST1	Eyre Rolls, Assize Rolls, etc.
KB27	Coram Rege Rolls
SP1	State Papers Henry VIII
SP12	State Papers Domestic Elizabeth I
STAC2	Star Chamber Henry VIII

PRINTED PRIMARY SOURCES

Acts of the Parliament of Scotland, 12 vols. (London: Record Commission, 1814–75).

"Archbishop Warham's Letters," *Archaeologia Cantiana* 1 (1858), 9–41.

Acts of the Privy Council of England, 46 vols. (London: HMSO, 1890–1964).

Analytical Index to the Records known as the Rembrancia Preserved among the Archives of the City of London 1579–1664 (London: Francis, 1878).

A New Charge given by the Queenes commandement, to all Justices of Peace, and all Maiors, Shiriffes, and all principall Officers of Cities, Boroughs, and Townes corporate, for execution of sundry orders published the last yeere for staie of dearth of Graine, 1595.

Bateson, M. (ed.), *Records of the Borough of Leicester, 1509–1603* (Cambridge: Cambridge University Press, 1905).

Bond, R. B. (ed.), *Certain Sermons or Homilies (1547) and a Homily against Disobedience and Wilful Rebellion (1570): A Critical Edition* (Toronto: University of Toronto Press, 1987).

Brie, F. W. D. (ed.), *The Brut* (London: Early English Text Society, 1908).

Byerly, B., and Byerly, C. (eds.), *Records of the Wardrobe and Household 1285–1286* (London: HMSO, 1977).

Calendar of Close Rolls, 46 vols. (London: HMSO, 1892–1963).

Calendar of Fine Rolls, 22 vols. (London: HMSO, 1911–63).

Calendar of Inquisitions Miscellaneous, 8 vols. (London: HMSO, 1916–68 and Woodbridge: Boydell, 2003).

Calendar of Patent Rolls, 54 vols. (London: HMSO, 1891–1916).

Cam, H. M. (ed.), *The Eyre of London, 14 Edward II 1321* (London: Selden Society, 1968).

Campbell, B. M. S., "Three centuries of English crop yields, 1211–1491" (2007), www.cropyields.ac.uk.

Childs, W. R. (ed.), *Vita Edwardi Secundi* (Oxford: Clarendon Press, 2005).

Clark, G., "The Price History of English Agriculture, 1209–1914" in A. J. Field, G. Clark, and W. S. Sundstrom (eds.), *Research in Economic History*, vol. 22 (Amsterdam: Elsevier, 2004), pp. 41–75.

Delpit, J. (ed.), *Collection Generale Des Documents Francais Qui Se Trouvent En Angleterre* (Paris: Dumoulin, 1847).

Dobson, R. B. (ed.), *The Peasants' Revolt of 1381* (London, Macmillan, 1986).

Foedera, Conventiones, Litterae, etc. 4 vols. (London: Record Commission, 1816–69).

Gairdner, J. (ed.), *The Historical Collections of a Citizen of London in the Fifteenth Century* (London: Camden Society, 1876).

Gardiner, S. R. (ed.), *Reports of Cases in the Courts of Star Chamber and High Commission* (London: Camden Society, 1886).

Given-Wilson, C., Brand, P., Phillips, S., Ormrod, M., Martin, G., Curry, A., and Horrox, R. (eds.), *Parliament Rolls of Medieval England*, www.british-history.ac.uk/report.aspx?pubid=1241.

Hall, E., *Chronicle* (New York: AMS Press, 1965).

Harding, A. (ed.), *The Roll of the Shropshire Eyre of 1256* (London: Selden Society, 1981).

Hardy, T. D. (ed.), *Register of Richard de Kellawe, Lord palatine and Bishop of Durham, 1314–1316*, 4 vols. (London: Rolls series, 1874–8).

Harris, M. D. (ed.), *The Coventry Leet Book or Mayor's Register* (London: Early English Text Society, 1909).

Hawarde, J. *Les Reportes del Cases in Camera Stellata 1593–1609*, W. P. Baildon (ed.), (Privately Printed, 1894).

Hector, L. C. and Harvey, B.F. (eds.), *The Westminster Chronicle 1381–1394* (Oxford: Clarendon Press, 1982).

Horrox, R. (ed.), *The Black Death* (Manchester: Manchester University Press, 1993).

Horwood, A. J. (ed.), *Year Books of the Reign of Edward I*, 5 vols. (London: HMSO, 1866–74).

Hudson W. and Tingey, J. C. (eds.), *The Records of the City of Norwich*, 2 vols. (Norwich: Jarrold and Sons, 1911).

Hughes, P. L. and Larkin, J. F. (eds.), *Tudor Royal Proclamations*, 3 vols. (New Haven: Yale University Press, 1964–69).

Jones, P. E., (ed.), *Calendar of Plea and Memoranda Rolls of the City of London, Preserved among the Archives of the Corporation of the City of London at the Guildhall 1437–1457* (Cambridge: Cambridge University Press, 1954).

Kingsford, C. L. (ed.), "Two London Chronicles from the Collections of John Stow" in *The Camden Miscellany*, vol. 12 (London: Camden Society, 1910).

Leadham, I. S. (ed.), *Select Cases before the King's Council in the Star Chamber 1509–1544* (London: Selden Society, 1911).

Leighton, W. A. (ed.), "Early Chronicles of Shrewsbury 1372–1603," *Transactions of the Shropshire Archaeological and Natural History Society* 3 (1880), 239–352.

Letters and Papers, Foreign and Domestic, of the Reign of Henry VIII, 23 vols. (London: HMSO, 1862–1932).

Luard, H. R. (ed.), *Matthaei Parisiensis, monachi sancti Albani, chronica majora*, 7 vols. (London: Rolls series, 1872–83).

Maitland, F. W., Harcourt, L. W. V., and Craddock, W. (eds.), *The Eyre of Kent 6 and 7 Edward II, 1313–1314* (London: Selden Society, 1910).

Martin, G. H. (ed.), *Knighton's Chronicle 1337–1396* (Oxford: Clarendon Press, 1995).

Meekings, C. A. F. and Crook, D. (eds.), *The 1235 Surrey Eyre* (Guilford: Surrey Record Society, 1979).

Musson, A. with Powell, E. (eds.), *Crime, Law and Society in the Later Middle Ages* (Manchester: Manchester University Press, 2009).

Munro, J. H., "Revisions of the Phelps Brown and Hopkins 'basket of consumables' commodity price series 1264–1700" (n.d.) www.economics.utoronto.ca/munro5.

Nicholas, H. (ed.), *Proceedings and Ordinances of the Privy Council of England*, 7 vols. (London: Record Commission, 1834–37).

Nichols, F. M. (ed.), *Britton*, 2 vols. (Oxford: Clarendon Press, 1865).

Nicolas, H. N. (ed.), *A Chronicle of London from 1089 to 1483* (London: Longman, 1827).

Orders Appointed by his Maiestie to be straightly observed for the preventing and remedying of the dearth of Graine and other Victuall, 1608.

Orders Appointed by his Maiestie to be straightly observed, for the preventing and remedying of the dearth of Graine and other Victuall, 1622.

Orders Appointed by his Maiestie to be straightly observed, for the preventing and remedying of the dearth of Graine and Victuall, 1630.

Orders devised by the especiall commandement of the Queenes Maiestie for the reliefe and stay of the present dearth of Graine within the Realme, 1586/87.

Owen, D. (ed.), *The Making of King's Lynn: A Documentary Survey* (London: The British Academy, 1984).

Palgrave, Francis (ed.), *Parliamentary Writs* 2 vols. (London: Record Commission, 1827–34).

Prestwich, M. (ed.), *York Civic Ordinances, 1301* (York: Borthwick Institute of Historical Research, 1976).

Reynolds, S. (ed.), *Registers of Roger Martival, Bishop of Salisbury 1315–1330*, vol. 3 (Torquay: Canterbury and York Society, 1965).

Richardson, H. G. and Sayles, G. O. (eds.), *Select Cases of Procedure without Writ under Henry III* (London: Selden Society, 1941).

(eds.), *Fleta* (London: Selden Society 1955).

Riley, H. T. (ed.), *Chronicles of the Mayors and Sheriffs 1188–1274* (1863) www.british-history.ac.uk/report.aspx?pubid=560.

(ed.), *Memorials of London and London Life 1276–1419* (London: Longman, 1868).

Rotuli Parliamentorum, 6 vols. (Record Commission, 1783).

Rymer, T. (ed.), *Foedera*, vol. 5 (Farnborough: Gregg, 1967).

Sharpe, R. R. (ed.), *Calendar of the Letters from the Mayor and Corporation of the City of London, 1350–1370* (London: Francis, 1885).

(ed.), *Calendar of the Letter-Books of the City of London 1275–1509*, 12 vols (London: Francis, 1899–1912).

Smit, H. J. (ed.), *Bronnen tot de Geschiedenis van den handel met Engeland, Schotland en Ierland 1150–1485*, 2 vols. ('S-Gravenhage: Martinus Nijhof, 1928).

Smith, L. T. (ed.), *The Maire of Bristowe is Kalendar*, (London: Camden Society, 1872).

Speciall Orders and directions by the Queenes Maiesties commandement, to all Justices of Peace, and all Maiors, Shiriffes, and all principall Officers of Cities, Boroughs, and Townes corporate, for stay and redresse of dearthe of Graine, 1600.

Stanford, M. (ed.), *The Ordinances of Bristol 1506–1598* (Bristol: Bristol Record Society, 1990).

Statutes of the Realm, 11 vols. (London: Record Commission, 1810–28).

Steele, R. (ed.), *A Bibliography of the Royal Proclamations of the Tudor and Stuart Sovereigns 1485–1714*, vol. 1 (New York: Burt Franklin, 1967).

Stow, J., *The Annales of England* (London: Ralfe Newbery, 1600).

Survey of London, 2 vols. C. L. Kingsford (ed.), (Oxford: Clarendon Press, 1908).

Sutherland, D. W. (ed.), *The Eyre of Northamptonshire 3–4 Edward III, 1329–1330* (London: Selden Society, 1983).

Tawney, R. H. and Power E. (eds.), *Tudor Economic Documents*, 3 vols. (New York: Barnes and Noble, 1962).

Taylor, J., Childs, W. R. and Watkiss, L. (eds.), *St. Albans Chronicle*, vol. 1 (Oxford: Clarendon Press, 2003).

The renewing of certaine Orders devised by the speciall commandement of the Queenes Maiestie, for the reliefe and stay of the present dearth of Graine within the Realme: in the yeere of our Lord 1586, 1594.

Thomas, A. H. (ed.), *Calendar of early Mayor's Court Rolls, Preserved among the Archives of the Corporation of the City of London at the Guildhall, 1298–1307* (Cambridge: Cambridge University Press, 1924).

(ed.), *Calendar of Plea and Memoranda Rolls Preserved among the Archives of the Corporation of the City of London at the Guildhall 1323–1412*, 3 vols. (Cambridge: Cambridge University Press, 1926–32).

Thomas, A. H. and Thornley, I. D. (eds.), *The Great Chronicle of London* (Gloucester: Alan Sutton, 1983).

Vanes, J. (ed.), *Documents Illustrating the Overseas Trade of Bristol in the Sixteenth Century* (Bristol: Bristol Record Society, 1979).

Veale, E. W. W. (ed.), *The Great Red Book of Bristol*, pt. 4 (Bristol: Bristol Record Society, 1953).

Von Runstedt, H-G. (ed.), *Hansisches Urkundenbuch*, vol. 7 (Weimar: Hermann Bölaus, 1939).

Worcester, W., *The Boke of Noblesse Addressed to King Edward the Fourth on His Invasion of France*, J. G. Nichols (ed.), (New York: Burt Franklin, 1972).

Wriothesley, C. *A Chronicle of England during the Reigns of the Tudors, from A. D. 1485–1559*, W. D. Hamilton (ed.), 2 vols. (London: Camden Society, 1875).

SECONDARY SOURCES

Allen, M., "Silver Production and the Money Supply in England and Wales, 1086-c.1600," *Econ. Hist. Rev.* 64 (2011), 114–31.

  Mints and Money in Medieval England (Cambridge: Cambridge University Press, 2012).

Alsford, S., "*The Men behind the Masque: Office-Holding in East Anglian boroughs, 1272–1460,*" www.trytel.com/~tristan/towns/mcontent.html.

Appleby, A., *Famine in Tudor and Stuart England* (Stanford: Stanford University Press, 1978).

Ashley, W., *The Bread of Our Forefathers* (Oxford: Clarendon Press, 1928).

Astill, A. and Grant, A. (eds.), *The Countryside of Medieval England* (Oxford: Blackwell, 1988).

Aston, T. H., Cross, P. R. Dyer, C. and Thirsk, J. (eds.), *Social Relations and Ideas: Essays in Honour of R. H. Hilton* (Cambridge: Cambridge University Press, 1983).

Aston, T. H. (ed.), *Landlords, Peasants and Politics in Medieval England* (Cambridge: Cambridge University Press, 1987).

Aston, M., "A Kent Approver of 1440," *Bulletin of the Institute of Historical Research* 36 (1963), 82–90.

  "Corpus Christi and Corpus Regni: Heresy and the Peasants' Revolt," *Past and Present* 143 (1994), 3–47.

Bailey, M., "The Commercialisation of the English Economy 1086–1500," *Journal of Medieval History* 24 (1998), 297–311.

Bailey, M. and Rigby, S. (eds.), *Town and Countryside in the Age of the Black Death: Essays in Honour of John Hatcher* (Turnhout: Brepols, 2012).

Baker, J. H., *An Introduction to English Legal History*, 3rd ed. (London: Butterworths, 1990).

Baldwin, J., "The Medieval Theories of the Just Price: Romanists, Canonists, and Theologians in the Twelfth and Thirteenth Centuries," *Transactions of the American Philosophical Society* 49 (1959), 1–92.

Barnes, T. G., "Star Chamber and the English Attempt at Absolutism" (unpublished paper delivered at a legal history workshop, University of Chicago Law School, May 8, 1980), pp. 1–21.

Béaur, G., Schofield, P.R., Chevet, J-M. and Pérez Pícazo, M. T. (eds.), *Property Rights, Land Markets and Economic Growth in the European Countryside, Thirteenth-Twentieth Centuries* (Turnhout: Brepols, 2013).

Beloff, M, *Public Order and Popular Disturbances 1660–1714* (London: Frank Cass, 1963).

Bennett, J., *The History of Tewkesbury* (Privately Printed, 1830).

Bellamy, J. G., *The Law of Treason in England in the Later Middle Ages* (Cambridge: Cambridge University Press, 1970).

Criminal Law and Society in Later Medieval and Tudor England (Gloucester: Sutton, 1984).

Bennett, J. M., *Ale Beer, and Brewsters in England: Women's Work in a Changing World 1300–1600* (New York: Oxford University Press, 1996).

Berggren, L., Hybel, N. and Landen, A. (eds.), *Cogs, Cargoes, and Commerce: Maritime Bulk Trade in Northern Europe, 1150–1400* (Toronto: Pontifical Institute of Mediaeval Studies, 2002).

Bernard, G. W., *War, Taxation and Rebellion in Early Tudor England: Henry VIII, Wolsey and the Amicable Grant of 1525* (Sussex: Harvester Press, 1986).

Beveridge, W. H., "A Statistical Crime of the Seventeenth Century," *Journal of Economic and Business History* 1 (1929), 503–33.

Blomefield, F., *An Essay towards a Topographical History of the County of Norfolk*, vol. 3 (London: William Miller, 1806).

Bohstedt, J., *The Politics of Provisions: Food Riots, Moral Economy and Market Transition in England c.1550–1850* (Farnham: Ashgate, 2010).

Bolton, J. L., *Money in the Medieval English Economy, 973–1489* (Manchester: Manchester University Press, 2012).

Braddick, M. J. and Walter, J. (eds.), *Negotiating Power in Early Modern Society: Order, Hierarchy and Subordination in Britain and Ireland* (Cambridge: Cambridge University Press, 2001).

Braid, R., "Economic Behavior, Markets and Crises: the English Economy in the Wake of Plague and Famine in the 14th century" in S. Cavaciocchi (ed.), *Le interazioni fra economia e ambiente biologico nell' Europa preindustriale, secc. XIII-XVIII*, (Firenze: Firenze University Press, 2010), pp. 335–72.

Brewer, J. and Styles, J (eds.), *An Ungovernable People: The English and their Law in the Seventeenth and Eighteenth Centuries* (New Brunswick: Rutgers University Press, 1980).

Britnell, R.H., "The Proliferation of Markets in England 1200–1349," *Econ. Hist. Rev.* 34 (1981), 209–21.

"Forstall, Forestalling and the Statute of Forestallers," *English Historical Review* 102 (1987), 89–102.

The Commercialisation of English Society 1000–1500 (Cambridge: Cambridge University Press, 1993).

Britnell, R. H. and Campbell, B. M. S. (eds.), *A Commercializing Economy: England 1086 to c.1300* (Manchester: Manchester University Press, 1995).

Britnell, R. H., "Commercialisation and Economic Development in England, 1000–1300" in R. H. Britnell and B.M.S. Campbell (eds.), *A Commercializing Economy: England 1086 to c.1300* (Manchester: Manchester University Press, 1995), pp. 7–26.

Britnell, R. H. and Hatcher, J. (eds.), *Progress and Problems in Medieval England: Essays in Honour of Edward Miller* (Cambridge: Cambridge University Press, 1996).

Britnell, R. H., *Britain and Ireland 1050–1530: Economy and Society* (Oxford: Oxford University Press, 2004).

Brooks, N., "The Organization and Achievements of the Peasants of Kent and Essex in 1381" in H. Mayr-Harting and R. I. Moore (eds.), *Studies in Medieval History presented to R. H. C. Davis* (London: Hambledon Press, 1985), pp. 247–70.

Burley, S. J., "The Victualing of Calais, 1347–65," *Bulletin of the Institute of Historical Research* 31 (1958), 49–57.

Bush, M. L. (ed.), *Serfdom and Slavery: Studies in Legal Bondage* (London: Longman, 1996).

Cam, H. M., "Studies in the Hundred Rolls: Some Aspects of Thirteenth Century Administration" in P. Vinogradoff (ed.), *Oxford Studies in Social and Legal History* (Oxford: Clarendon Press, 1921).

"Some Early Inquests before 'Custodes Pacis'" in H. M. Cam, *Liberties and Communities in Medieval England* (London: Merlin Press, 1963), pp.168–72.

Camden, W., *Britannia or a Chorographical Description of Great Britain, Ireland and Adjacent Islands*, E. Gibson (ed.), (London, 1695).

Campbell, B. M. S., "Population Pressure, Inheritance and the Land Market in a Fourteenth-Century Peasant Community" in R. M. Smith (ed.), *Land, Kinship and Life-Cycle* (Cambridge: Cambridge University Press, 1984), pp. 87–134.

(ed.), *Before the Black Death: Studies in the 'Crisis' of the Early Fourteenth Century* (Manchester: Manchester University Press, 1991).

Campbell, B. M. S., Galloway, J. A., Keene, D. and Murphy, M., *A Medieval Capital and Its Grain Supply: Agrarian Production and Distribution in the London Region c.1300* (Belfast and London: Historical Geography Research Series no. 39, 1993).

Campbell, B. M. S., "Ecology versus Economics in Late Thirteenth and Fourteenth Century English Agriculture" in D. Sweeney (ed.), *Agriculture in the Middle Ages; Technology, Practice, and Representation* (Philadelphia: University of Pennsylvania Press, 1995), pp. 76–108.

English Seigniorial Agriculture 1250–1450 (Cambridge: Cambridge University Press, 2000).

"The Sources of Tradable Surpluses: English Agricultural Exports 1250–1350" in L. Berggren, N. Hybel, and A. Landen (eds.), *Cogs, Cargoes, and Commerce: Maritime Bulk Trade in Northern Europe, 1150–1400* (Toronto: Pontifical Institute of Mediaeval Studies, 2002), pp. 1–30.

"The Agrarian Problem in the Early Fourteenth Century," *Past and Present* 188 (2005), 3–70.

"The Land" in R. Horrox and W. M. Ormrod (eds.), *A Social History of England, 1200–1500* (New York: Cambridge University Press, 2006), pp. 179–237.

"Four Famines and a Pestilence: Harvest, Price, and Wage Variation in England, 13th to 19th Centuries" in B. Liljewall, I. A. Flygare, U. Lange, L. Ljunggren, and J. Söderberg (eds.), *Agrarhistoria på många sätt 28 studier om människan och jorden: festskrift till Janken Myrdal på hans 60-årsdag* (Stockholm: Kungl. Skogs- Och Lanntbruksakademien, 2009), pp. 23–56.

"Nature as Historical Protagonist: Environment and Society in Pre-Industrial England," *Econ. Hist. Rev.* 63 (2010), 281–314.

"Physical Shocks, Biological Hazards, and Human Impacts: The Crisis of the Fourteenth Century Revisited" in S. Cavaciocchi (ed.), *Le Interazioni Fra Economia E Ambiente Biologico Nell'Europa Preindustriale Secc. XIII-XVIII* (Firenze: Firenze University Press, 2010), pp. 13–32.

"Agriculture in Kent in the High Middle Ages" in S. Sweetinburgh (ed.), *Later Medieval Kent 1220–1540* (Woodbridge: Boydell, 2010), pp. 25–54.

Campbell, B. M. S. and Ó Gráda, C., "Harvest Shortfalls, Grain Prices and Famines in Preindustrial England," *Journal of Economic History* 71 (2011), 859–86.

Campbell, B. M. S., "Grain Yields on English Demesnes after the Black Death" in M. Bailey and S. Rigby (eds.), *Town and Countryside in the Age of the Black Death: Essays in Honour of John Hatcher* (Turnhout: Brepols, 2012), pp. 121–74.

"Land Markets and the Morcellation of Holdings in Pre-Plague England and Pre-Famine Ireland" in G. Béaur, P. R. Schofield, J-M. Chevet and M. T. Pérez Pícazo (eds.), *Property Rights, Land Markets and Economic Growth in the European Countryside, Thirteenth-Twentieth Centuries* (Turnhout: Brepols, 2013), pp. 197–218.

Carlin, M. and Rosenthal, J. (eds.), *Food and Eating in Medieval Europe* (London: Hambledon, 1998).

Carus - Wilson, E. M. (ed.), *Essays in Economic History*, 3 vols. (London: Arnold, 1966).

Carus-Wilson, E. M., "The Overseas Trade of Bristol" in E. Power and M. M. Postan (eds.), *Studies in English Trade in the Fifteenth Century* (London : Routledge, 1951), pp. 146–83.

Cavaciocchi, S. (ed.), *Le Interazioni Fra Economia E Ambiente Biologico Nell'Europa Preindustriale Secc. XIII-XVIII* (Firenze: Firenze University Press, 2010).

Childs, W. R.,"Moving Around" in R. Horrox and W. M. Omrod (eds.), *A Social History of England, 1200–1500* (New York: Cambridge University Press, 2006), pp. 260–75.

Clark, G., "The Long March of History: Farm Wages, Population, and Economic Growth, England 1209–1869," *Econ. Hist. Rev.* 60 (2007), 97–135.

Clark, P., "Popular Protest and Disturbance in Kent, 1558–1640," *Econ. Hist. Rev.* 29 (1976), 365–82.

"A Crisis Contained? The Condition of English Towns in the 1590s," in P. Clark (ed.), *The European Crisis of the 1590s: Essays in Comparative History* (London: Allen and Unwin, 1985), pp. 44–60.

(ed.), *The European Crisis of the 1590s: Essays in Comparative History* (London: Allen and Unwin, 1985).

Cohn, S., *Popular Protest in Late Medieval English Towns* (Cambridge: Cambridge University Press, 2013).

Coleman, C. and Starkey, D. (eds.), *Revolution Reassessed: Revisions in the History of Tudor Government and Administration* (Oxford: Clarendon Press, 1986).

Crook, D., *Records of the General Eyre* (London: HMSO, 1982).

"Derbyshire and the English Rising of 1381," *Historical Research* 60 (1987), 9–13.

Cunningham, W., *Alien Immigrants to England* (London: Swan Sonnenschein, 1897).

Curry, A. and Matthew, E. (eds.), *Concepts and Patterns of Service in the Later Middle Ages* (Woodbridge: Boydell, 2006).

Darby, H. C., *The Medieval Fenland* (Newton Abbot: David and Charles, 1974).

Darling, A. S., "Non-Ferrous Metals" in I. McNeil (ed.), *An Encyclopedia of the History of Technology* (Routledge: London, 1990), pp. 47–144.

Davis, J., "Baking for the Common Good: A Reassessment of the Assize of Bread in Medieval England," *Econ. Hist. Rev.* 57 (2004), 465–502.

"The Cross and the Pillory: Symbolic Structures of Commercial Space in Medieval English Towns" in S. Ehrich and J. Oberste (eds.), *Städtische Räume im Mittelalter* (Regensberg: Schnell and Steiner, 2009), pp. 241–59.

Medieval Market Morality: Life, Law and Ethics in the English Marketplace, 1200–1500 (Cambridge: Cambridge University Press, 2012).

"Market Regulation in Fifteenth-Century England," in B. Dodds and C. D. Liddy (eds.), *Commercial Activity, Markets and Entrepreneurs in the Middle Ages: Essays in Honour of Richard Britnell* (Woodbridge: Boydell, 2011), pp. 81–106.

De Roover, R., "The Concept of the Just Price: Theory and Economic Policy," *Journal of Economic History* 18 (1958), 418–34.

Dodds, B. and Liddy, C. D. (eds.), *Commercial Activity, Markets and Entrepreneurs in the Middle Ages: Essays in Honour of Richard Britnell* (Woodbridge: Boydell, 2011).

Doig, J., "Political Propaganda and Royal Proclamations in Late Medieval England," *Historical Research* 71 (1998), 253–80.

Dyer, C., "The English Diet in the Later Middle Ages" in T. H. Aston, P. R. Cross, C. Dyer, and J. Thirsk (eds.), *Social Relations and Ideas: Essays in Honour of R. H. Hilton* (Cambridge: Cambridge University Press, 1983), pp. 191–216.

"The Social and Economic Background to the Rural Revolt of 1381" in R. H. Hilton and T. H. Aston (eds.), *The English Rising of 1381* (Cambridge: Cambridge University Press, 1987), pp. 9–42.

"The Rising of 1381 in Suffolk: Its Origins and Participants," *Proceedings of the Suffolk Institute of Archaeology and History* 36 (1988), 274–87.

"The Consumer and the Market in the Later Middle Ages," *Econ. Hist. Rev.* 42 (1989), 305–27.

Standards of Living in the Later Middle Ages: Social Change in England c.1200–1520 (Cambridge: Cambridge University Press, 1990).

"Changes in Diet in the Late Middle Ages: The Case of Harvest Workers" in C. Dyer, *Everyday Life in Medieval England* (London: Hambledon Press, 1994), pp. 77–99.

Everyday Life in Medieval England (London: Hambledon Press, 1994).

"Attitudes towards Serfdom in England 1200–1350" in M. L. Bush (ed.), *Serfdom and Slavery: Studies in Legal Bondage* (London: Longman, 1996), pp. 277–95.

"Trade, Urban Hinterlands and Market Integration 1300–1600: A summing up" in J. A. Galloway (ed.), *Trade, Urban Hinterlands and Market Integration c. 1300–1600* (London: Centre for Metropolitan History Working Paper no. 3, 2000), pp. 103–9.

Dyer, C., Coss, P. and Wickham, C. (eds.), *Rodney Hilton's Middle Ages: An Exploration of Historical Themes* (Oxford: Oxford University Press, 2007).

Dymond, D., "The Famine of 1527 in Essex," *Local Population Studies* 26 (1981), 29–40.

Duffy, E., "Religious Belief" in R. Horrox and W. M. Ormrod (eds.), *A Social History of England, 1200–1500*, pp. 293–339.

Early Modern Research Group, "Commonwealth: The Social, Cultural, and Conceptual Context of an Early Modern Keyword," *The Historical Journal* 54 (2011), 659–87.

Ehrich, H. and Oberste, J., eds., *Städtische Räume im Mittelalter* (Regensberg: Schnell and Steiner, 2009).

Eiden, H., "Joint Action against 'Bad' Lordship: The Peasants' Revolt in Essex and Norfolk," *History* 83 (1998), 5–30

Elton, G. R., *Star Chamber Stories* (London: Methuen, 1958).

Policy and Police: The Enforcement of the Reformation in the Age of Thomas Cromwell (Cambridge: Cambridge University Press, 1972).

Everitt, A., "The Marketing of Agricultural Produce" in J. Thirsk (ed.), *The Agrarian History of England and Wales 1500–1640* (Cambridge: Cambridge University Press, 1967), pp. 466–592.

Faith, R., "The 'Great Rumour' of 1377 and Peasant Ideology" in R. H. Hilton and T. H. Aston (eds.), *The English Rising of 1381*(Cambridge: Cambridge University Press, 1987), pp. 43–73.

"The Class Struggle in Fourteenth Century England" in R. Samuel (ed.), *People's History and Socialist Theory* (London: Routledge, 1981), pp. 50–60.

Farmer, D. L. "Marketing the Produce of the Countryside" in E. Miller (ed.), *The Agrarian History of England and Wales 1348–1500* (Cambridge: Cambridge University Press, 1991), pp. 324–430.

Field, A. J., Clark, G. and Sundstrom, W. A. (eds.), *Research in Economic History*, vol. 22 (Amsterdam: Elsevier, 2004).

Fletcher, A., *Reform in the Provinces: The Government of Stuart England* (New Haven: Yale University Press, 1986).

Fletcher, A. and MacCulloch, D., *Tudor Rebellions*, rev. 5th ed. (Harlow: Pearson, 2008).

Fletcher, D., "De La Communauté Du Royaume au Common Weal: Les requêtes anglaises et leur strategies au XIVe siècle," *Revue française dhistoire des idées politiques* 32 (2010), 359–72.

Fox, A. and Guy, J. (eds.), *Reassessing the Henrician Age: Humanism, Politics and Reform 1500–1550* (Oxford: Blackwell, 1986).

Fox, H. S. A., "Exploitation of the Landless by Lords and Tenants in Early Medieval England" in Z. Razi and R. Smith (eds.), *Medieval Society and the Manor Court* (Oxford: Clarendon Press, 1996), pp. 518–39.

Fryde, E. B., "The English Farmers of the Customs 1343–51," *Transactions of the Royal Historical Society* 5th ser., 9 (1959), 1–17.

Peasants and Landlords in Later Medieval England c. 1380–c.1525 (Stroud: Sutton, 1996).

"Economic Depression in England in the Second and Third Quarter of the Fifteenth Century" in R. W. Kaeuper (ed.), *Violence in Medieval Society* (Woodbridge: Boydell, 2000), pp. 215–26.

Fryde, N., "Antonio Pessagno of Genoa, King's Merchant of Edward II of England" in *Studi in memoria di Frederigo Melis*, vol. 2 (Naples: Giannini, 1978), pp. 159–78.

Galloway, J. A., "One Market or Many? London and the Grain Trade of England" in J. A. Galloway (ed.), *Trade, Urban Hinterlands and Market*

Integration, c. 1300–1600 (London: Centre for Metropolitan History Working Paper no. 3, 2000), pp. 23–42.

(ed, *Trade, Urban Hinterlands and Market Integration c. 1300–1600* (London: Centre for Metropolitan History Working Paper no. 3, 2000).

Gast, M., Sigaut, F. and Beutler, C. (eds,), *Les techniques de conservation des grains à long terme: leur role dans la dynamique des systèmes de cultures et des sociétés* (Paris: Centre National de la Recherche Scientifique, 1985).

Gilchrist, J., *The Church and Economic Activity in the Middle Ages* (London: Macmillan, 1969).

Given-Wilson, C., *The Royal Household and the King's Affinity: Service, Politics and Finance in England 1360–1413* (New Haven: Yale University Press, 1986).

Goldberg, P. J. P., "Mortality and Economic Change in the Diocese of York," *Northern History* 24 (1988), 38–55.

Gras, N. S. G., *The Evolution of the English Corn Market from the Twelfth to the Eighteenth Century* (Cambridge Mass: Harvard University Press, 1915).

Griffiths, R. A., *The Reign of King Henry VI* (Berkeley: University of California Press, 1981).

Gunn, S. J., "Wolsey's Foreign Policy and the Domestic Crisis of 1527–8" in S. J. Gunn and P. G. Lindley (eds.), *Cardinal Wolsey: Church, State and Art* (Cambridge: Cambridge University Press, 1991), pp. 149–77.

Gunn, S. J. and Lindley, P. G. (eds.), *Cardinal Wolsey: Church, State and Art* (Cambridge: Cambridge University Press, 1991).

Guy, J., "The King's Council and Political Participation" in A. Fox and J. Guy (eds.), *Reassessing the Henrician Age: Humanism, Politics and Reform 1500–1550* (Oxford: Blackwell, 1986), pp. 121–47.

Tudor England (Oxford: Oxford University Press, 1990).

Gwyn, P., *The King's Cardinal: The Rise and Fall of Thomas Wolsey* (London: Barrie and Jenkins, 1990).

Hammel-Kiesow, R., "Lubeck and the Baltic Trade in Bulk Goods" in L. Berggren, N. Hybel, and A. Landen (eds.), *Cogs, Cargoes, and Commerce: Maritime Bulk Trade in Northern Europe, 1150–1400* (Toronto: Pontifical Institute of Mediaeval Studies, 2002), pp. 53–91.

Hanawalt, B., *Crime and Conflict in English Communities 1300–48* (Cambridge Mass.: Harvard University Press, 1996).

Hassell Smith, A., *County and Court: Government and Politics in Norfolk 1558–1603* (Oxford: Oxford University Press, 1974).

Hatcher, J., *Plague, Population and the English Economy 1348–1530* (London: Macmillan, 1977).

"England in the Aftermath of the Black Death," *Past and Present* 144 (1994), 3–35.

"The Great Slump Of The Mid-Fifteenth Century," in R. H. Britnell and J. Hatcher (eds.), *Progress and Problems in Medieval England: Essays in Honour of Edward Miller* (Cambridge: Cambridge University Press, 1996), pp. 237–72.

Hay, D., Linebaugh, P., Rule, J. G., Thompson, E. P. and Winslow, C. (eds.), *Albion's Fatal Tree: Crime and Society in Eighteenth Century England* (New York: Pantheon, 1975).

Hay, D., "The State and the Market in 1800: Lord Kenyon and Mr Waddington," *Past and Present* 162 (1999), 101–62.

"Moral Economy, Political Economy and Law" in A. Randall and
A. Charlesworth (eds.), *Moral and Economy and Popular Protest: Crowds,
Conflict and Authority* (Basingstoke: Macmillan, 2000), pp. 93–122.

Heinze, R. R., *The Proclamations of the Tudor Kings* (Cambridge: Cambridge
University Press, 1977).

Hewitt, H. J., *The Organization of War under Edward III 1338–1362* (Manchester:
Manchester University Press, 1966).

Hill, J. W. F., *Tudor and Stuart Lincoln* (Cambridge: Cambridge University Press,
1956).

Hilton, R. H., "Peasant Movements in England before 1381" in E. M. Carus –
Wilson (ed.), *Essays in Economic History* vol. 2 (London: Arnold, 1966),
pp. 73–90.

A Medieval Society: The West Midlands at the End of the Thirteenth Century
(New York: Wiley, 1966).

Hilton, R. H. and Aston, T. H. (eds.), *The English Rising of 1381* (Cambridge:
Cambridge University Press, 1987).

Hindle, S., "Exhortation and Entitlement: Negotiating Inequality in Rural
Communities" in M. J. Braddick and J. Walter (eds.), *Negotiating Power
in Early Modern Society: Order, Hierarchy and Subordination in Britain and
Ireland* (Cambridge: Cambridge University Press, 2001), pp. 102–22.

"Dearth and the English Revolution: The Harvest Crisis of 1647–50," *Econ.
Hist. Rev.* 61 no. SI (2008), 64–98.

Hipkin, S., "The Structure, Development, and Politics of the Kent Grain Trade,
1552–1647," *Econ. Hist. Rev.* 61 no. SI (2008), 99–139.

Holt, J. C., *Magna Carta*, 2nd ed. (Cambridge: Cambridge University Press,
1992).

Horrox, R., *Richard III: A Study of Service* (Cambridge: Cambridge University
Press, 1989).

Horrox, R. and Ormrod, W. M. (eds.), *A Social History of England, 1200–1500*
(New York: Cambridge University Press, 2006).

Hoskins, W. G., "Harvest Fluctuations in English Economic History,
1480–1619," *Agricultural History Review* 12 (1964), 25–46.

Hybel, N., "The Foreign Grain Trade in England, 1250–1350" in L. Berggren,
N. Hybel, and A. Landen (eds.), *Cogs, Cargoes, and Commerce: Maritime Bulk
Trade in Northern Europe, 1150–1400* (Toronto: Pontifical Institute of
Mediaeval Studies, 2002), pp. 212–41.

Ives, E. W., Knecht, R. J. and Scarisbrick, J. J. (eds.), *Wealth and Power in Tudor
England: Essays Presented to S. T. Bindoff* (London: The Athlone Press,
1978).

Jenks, S., "The English Grain Trade 1377–1461" in M. Gast, F. Sigaut and
C. Beutler (eds,), *Les techniques de conservation des grains à long terme: leur
role dans la dynamique des systèmes de cultures et des sociétés* (Paris: Centre
National de la Recherche Scientifique, 1985) vol. 3 fasc. 2, pp. 501–26.

Jones, E. T., "Illicit Business: Accounting for Smuggling in Mid-Sixteenth
Century Bristol," *Econ. Hist. Rev.* 54 (2001), 17–38.

*Inside the Illicit Economy: Reconstructing the Smugglers' Trade of Sixteenth Century
Bristol* (Farnham: Ashgate, 2012).

Jordan, W. C., *The Great Famine: Northern Europe In The Early Fourteen Century*
(Princeton: Princeton University Press, 1996).

Justice, S., *Writing and Rebellion: England in 1381* (Berkeley: University of California Press, 1994).

"Religious Dissent, Social Revolt and 'Ideology'," in C. Dyer, P. Coss, and C. Wickham (eds.), *Rodney Hilton's Middle Ages: An Exploration of Historical Themes* (Oxford: Oxford University Press, 2007), pp. 205–16.

Kaeuper, R. W., "Law and Order in Fourteenth Century England: The Evidence of Special Commissions of Oyer and Terminer," *Speculum* 54 (1979), 734–84.

(ed.), *Violence in Medieval Society* (Woodbridge: Boydell, 2000).

Keene, D., "Crisis Management in London's Food Supply, 1250–1500" in B. Dodds and C.D. Liddy (eds.), *Commercial Activity, Markets and Entrepreneurs in the Middle Ages: Essays in Honour of Richard Britnell* (Woodbridge: Boydell, 2011), pp. 45–62.

Kempshall, M. S., *The Common Good in Late Medieval Political Thought* (Oxford: Clarendon Press, 1999).

Kermode, J., *Medieval Merchants: York, Beverley, and Hull in the Later Middle Ages* (Cambridge: Cambridge University Press, 1998).

Kershaw, I., "The Great Famine and Agrarian Crisis in England 1315–1322," *Past and Present* 59 (1973), 3–50.

Kowalski, M, "A Consumer Economy" in R. Horrox and W. M. Ormrod (eds.), *A Social History of England, 1200–1500* (New York: Cambridge University Press, 2006), pp. 238–59.

Lecuppre-Desjardin, E. and Van Bruaene, A-L. (eds.), *De Boni Communi: The Discourse and Practice of the Common Good in the European City (13ᵗʰ – 16ᵗʰ c.)* (Turnhout: Brepols, 2010).

Lee, J. S., "Feeding the Colleges: Cambridge's Food and Fuel Supplies 1450–1560," *Econ. Hist. Rev.* 56 (2003), 305–27.

"Grain Shortages in Late Medieval Towns," in B. Dodds and C. D. Liddy (eds.), *Commercial Activity, Markets and Entrepreneurs in the Middle Ages: Essays in Honour of Richard Britnell* (Woodbridge: Boydell, 2011), pp. 63–80.

Little, L. K., *Religious Poverty and the Profit Economy in Medieval Europe* (Ithaca: Cornell University Press, 1983).

Liljewall, B., Flygare, I. A., Lange, U., Ljunggren, L. and Söderberg, J. (eds.), *Agrarhistoria på många sätt 28 studier om människan och jorden: festskrift till Janken Myrdal på hans 60-årsdag* (Stockholm: Kungl. Skogs-Och Lanntbruksakademien, 2009).

Lloyd, T. H., *Alien Merchants in England in the High Middle Ages* (Brighton: Harvester, 1982).

England and the German Hanse, 1157–1611: A Study of their Trade and Commercial Diplomacy (Cambridge: Cambridge University Press, 1992).

Lucas, H. S., "The Great European Famine of 1315, 1316 and 1317" in E. M. Carus-Wilson (ed.), *Essays in Economic History*, vol. 2 (London: Arnold, 1966), pp. 49–52.

Loach, J. and Tittler, R. (eds.), *The Mid-Tudor Polity c. 1540–1560* (Basingstoke: Macmillan, 1980).

Luu, L. B., *Immigrants and the Industries of London 1500–1700*, (Aldershot: Ashgate, 2005).

MacCulloch, D., *Suffolk under the Tudors: Politics and Religion in an English County 1500–1600* (Oxford: Clarendon Press, 1986).

Maddicott, J. R., "The English Peasantry and the Demands of the Crown 1294–1341" in T. H. Aston (ed.), *Landlords, Peasants and Politics in Medieval England* (Cambridge: Cambridge University Press, 1987), pp. 285–359.

Marvin, J, "Cannibalism as an Aspect of Famine in Two English Chronicles" in M. Carlin and J. Rosenthal (eds.), *Food and Eating in Medieval Europe* (London: Hambledon, 1998), pp. 73–86.

Masschaele, J., "Transport Costs in Medieval England," *Econ. Hist. Rev.* 46 (1993), 266–79.

"The Multiplicity of Medieval Markets Reconsidered," *Journal of Historical Geography* 20 (1994), 255–71.

Peasants, Merchants, and Markets: Inland Trade in Medieval England, 1150–1350 (New York: St. Martin's, 1997).

"The Public Space of the Marketplace in Medieval England," *Speculum* 77 (2002), 383–421.

Mate, M., "Monetary Policies in England, 1272–1307," *The British Numismatic Journal* 41 (1972), 34–79.

"High Prices in Early Fourteenth-Century England: Causes and Consequences," *Econ. Hist. Rev.* 28 (1975), 1–16.

Mayhew, N. J. and Walker, D. A., "Crockards and Pollards: Imitation and the Problem of Fineness in a Silver Coinage" in N. J. Mayhew (ed.), *Edwardian Monetary Affairs 1279–1344: A Symposium held in Oxford, August 1976*, (Oxford: British Archaeological Reports, 36, 1977), pp. 125–46.

Mayhew, N. J. (ed.), *Edwardian Monetary Affairs 1279–1344: A Symposium held in Oxford, August 1976*, (Oxford: British Archaeological Reports, 36, 1977).

Mayr-Harting, H. and Moore, R. I., (eds.), *Studies in Medieval History Presented to R. H. C. Davis* (London: Hambledon Press, 1985).

McFarlane, K. B., "William Worcester: A Preliminary Survey" in K. B. McFarlane, *England in the Fifteenth Century* (London: Hambledon, 1981), pp. 199–224.

England in the Fifteenth Century (London: Hambledon, 1981).

McKisack, M., *The Fourteenth Century 1307–1399* (Oxford: Clarendon Press, 1959).

McNamee, C., *The Wars of the Bruces: Scotland, England and Ireland 1306–1328* (East Linton: Tuckwell, 1997).

McNeil, I. (ed.), *An Encyclopedia of the History of Technology* (Routledge: London, 1990).

Miller, E., *The Abbey and Bishopric of Ely* (Cambridge: Cambridge University Press, 1951).

(ed.), *The Agrarian History of England and Wales 1348–1500* (Cambridge: Cambridge University Press, 1991).

Miller, E. and Hatcher J., *Medieval England: Rural Society and Economic Change 1066–1348* (London: Longman, 1978).

Medieval England: Towns, Commerce and Crafts (London: Longman, 1995).

Morgan, D., "The Household Retinue of Henry V and the Ethos of English Public Life" in A. Curry and E. Matthew (eds.), *Concepts and Patterns of Service in the Later Middle Ages* (Woodbridge: Boydell, 2006), pp. 64–79.

Müller, M., "The Aims and Organization of a Peasant Revolt in Early Fourteenth Century Wiltshire," *Rural History* 14 (2003), 1–20.

"Conflict and Revolt: The Bishop of Ely and His Peasants at the Manor of Brandon in Suffolk c. 1300–81," *Rural History* 23 (2012), 1–19.

Musson, A., *Public Order and Law Enforcement: The Local Administration of Criminal Justice: 1294–1350* (Woodbridge: Boydell, 1996).

Musson, A. and Ormrod, W. M., *The Evolution of English Justice: Law, Politics and Society in the Fourteenth Century* (Basingstoke: Macmillan, 1999).

Musson, A., *Medieval Law in Context: The Growth in Legal Consciousness from Magna Carta to the Peasants' Revolt* (Manchester: Manchester University Press, 2001).

Neville, C. J., "Common Knowledge of the Common Law in Later Medieval England," *Canadian Journal of History* 29 (1994), 461–78.

Newfield, T., "A Cattle Panzootic in Early Fourteenth-Century Europe: Causes and Consequences," *Agricultural History Review* 57 (2009), 155–90.

Nicholas, D., *Medieval Flanders* (London: Longman, 1992).

Nightingale, P., "The Growth of London in the Medieval English Economy" in R. H. Britnell and J. Hatcher (eds.), *Progress and Problems in Medieval England: Essays in Honour of Edward Miller* (Cambridge: Cambridge University Press, 1996), pp. 89–106.

Ormrod, W. M., *The Reign of Edward III: Crown and Political Society in England 1327–1377* (New Haven: Yale University Press, 1990).

"Agenda for Legislation, 1322-c1340," *English Historical Review* 105 (1990), 1–33.

"The Peasants' Revolt and the Government of England," *Journal of British Studies* 29 (1990), 1–30.

"The Crown and the English Economy 1290–1348" in B. M. S. Campbell (ed.), *Before the Black Death: Studies in the "Crisis" of the Early Fourteenth Century* (Manchester: Manchester University Press, 1991), pp. 149–83.

Outhwaite, R. B., "Dearth and Government Intervention in English Grain Markets, 1590–1700" *Econ. Hist. Rev.* 34 (1981), 389–406.

Owen, H., *A History of Shrewsbury*, vol. 1 (London: Harding Lepard, 1825).

Owst, G. R., *Literature and Pulpit in Medieval England* (New York: Barnes and Noble, 1961).

Preaching in Medieval England (New York, Russell and Russell, 1965).

Pam, D. O., *The Hungry Years: The Struggle for Survival in Edmonton and Enfield before 1400* (Edmonton Historical Society: Occasional Paper no. 40, 1980).

Parker, P., *The Making of King's Lynn: Secular Buildings from the 11th to the 17th Century* (London: Phillimore, 1971).

Pelham, R. A., "The Provisioning of the Lincoln Parliament of 1301," *University of Birmingham Historical Journal* 3 (1951–52), 16–32.

Phythian-Adams, C., *Desolation of a City: Coventry and the Urban Crisis of the Late Middle Ages* (Cambridge: Cambridge University Press, 1979).

Pollard, A. J., "The North-Eastern Economy and the Agrarian Crisis of 1438–1440, *Northern History* 25 (1989), 88–105.

Pound, J. P., "The Social and Trade Structure of Norwich 1525–1575," *Past and Present* 34 (1966), 49–69.

Pound, J. F., "*Government and Society in Tudor and Stuart Norwich 1525–1675*" (PhD dissertation: University of Leicester, 1974).

"Rebellion and Poverty in Sixteenth Century Suffolk: The 1525 Uprising against the Amicable Grant," *Proceedings of the Suffolk Institute of Archaeology and History* 39 (1999), 317–30.

Powell, E., "Special Oyer and Terminer Proceedings 1262–1443," (Typescript list in TNA)

Power, E. and Postan, M. M. (eds.), *Studies in English Trade in the Fifteenth Century* (London : Routledge, 1951).

Power, M. J., "London and the Control of the 'Crisis' of the 1590's," *History* 70 (1985), 371–85.

Prescott, A., "Writing about Rebellion: Using the Records of the Peasants' Revolt of 1381," *History Workshop Journal* 45 (1998), 1–27.

Prestwich, M., "Edward I's Monetary Policies and Their Consequences," *Econ. Hist. Rev.* 22 (1969), 106–16.

The Three Edwards: War and State in England 1272–1377 (London: Weidenfield and Nicolson, 1980).

Edward I (Berkeley: University of California Press, 1989).

Pugh, E. P. H., "A Grain Shortage of the 1520's," *Local Historian* (Ealing Local History Society), 2 and 3(1962), 20–3, 33–7.

Randall, A. and Charlesworth, A. (eds.), *Markets, Market Culture and Popular Protest in Eighteenth-Century Britain and Ireland* (Liverpool: Liverpool University Press, 1996).

Moral Economy and Popular Protest: Crowds, Conflict and Authority (Basingstoke: Macmillan, 2000).

Randall, A., *Riotous Assemblies: Popular Protest in Hanoverian England* (Oxford: Oxford University Press, 2006).

Razi, Z., *Life, Marriage and Death in a Medieval Parish: Economy, Society and Demography in Halesowen 1270–1400* (Cambridge: Cambridge University Press, 1980).

"The Struggles between the Abbots of Halesowen and Their Tenants in the Thirteenth and Fourteenth Centuries" in T. H. Aston, P. R. Cross, C, Dyer, and J. Thirsk (eds.), *Social Relations and Ideas: Essays in Honour of R. H. Hilton* (Cambridge: Cambridge University Press, 1983), pp. 151–67.

Razi, Z. and Smith R. (eds.), *Medieval Society and the Manor Court* (Oxford: Clarendon Press, 1996).

Reay, B. (ed.), *Popular Culture in Seventeenth-Century England* (London: Croom Helm, 1985).

Reynolds, S., *Before Eminent Domain: Towards a History of Expropriation of Land for the Common Good* (Chapel Hill: University of North Carolina Press, 2010).

Rigby, S. H., *English Society in the Later Middle Ages: Class, Status and Gender* (New York: St. Martin's, 1995).

"Introduction: Social Structure and Economic Change in Late Medieval England" in R. Horrox and W. M. Omrod (eds.), *A Social History of England, 1200–1500* (New York: Cambridge University Press, 2006), pp. 1–30.

Rollison, D., *A Commonwealth of the People: Popular Politics and England's Long Social Revolution, 1066–1649* (Cambridge: Cambridge University Press, 2010).

Rosser, G., "Going to the Fraternity Feast: Commensality and Social Relations in Late Medieval England," *Journal of British Studies* 33 (1994), 430–46.

Samuel, R., (ed.), *People's History and Socialist Theory* (London: Routledge, 1981).

Saul, A., "English Towns in the Late Middle Ages: The Case of Great Yarmouth," *Journal of Medieval History* 8 (1982), 75–88.

"Great Yarmouth and the Hundred Years War in the Fourteenth Century," *Historical Research* 52 (1979), 105–15.

Scarisbrick, J. J., *Henry VIII* (Berkeley: University of California Press, 1968).

"Cardinal Wolsey and the Common Weal," in E. W. Ives, R. J. Knecht and J. J. Scarisbrick, (eds.), *Wealth and Power in Tudor England: Essays Presented to S. T. Bindoff* (London: The Athlone Press, 1978), pp. 45–67.

Schofield, P. R., "Dearth, Debt and the Local Land Market in a Late Thirteenth-Century Village Community," *Agricultural History Review* 45 (1997), 1–17.

"The Social Economy of the Medieval Village in the Early Fourteenth Century," *Econ. Hist. Rev.* 61 no. SI (2008), 38–63.

Seaborne, G., *Royal Regulation of Loans and Sales in Medieval England: "Monkish Superstition and Civil Tyranny"* (Woodbridge: Boydell, 2003).

"Assize Matters: Regulation of the Price of Bread in Medieval London," *Journal of Legal History* 27 (2006), 29–52.

Shagan, E. H., *Popular Politics and the English Reformation* (Cambridge: Cambridge University Press, 2003).

Sharp, B., *In Contempt of All Authority: Rural Artisans and Riot in the West of England* (Berkeley: University of California Press, 1980).

"Popular Protest in Seventeenth-Century England" in B. Reay (ed.), *Popular Culture in Seventeenth-Century England* (London: Croom Helm, 1985), pp. 271–308.

"The Food Riots of 1347 and the Medieval Moral Economy" in A. Randall and A. Charlesworth (eds.), *Moral Economy and Popular Protest: Crowds, Conflict and Authority* (Basingstoke: Macmillan, 2000), pp. 33–54.

Sheldon, R., Randall, A., Charlesworth, A. and Walsh, D., "Popular Protest and the Persistence of Customary Corn Measures: Resistance to the Winchester Bushel in the English West" in A. Randall and A. Charlesworth, (eds.), *Markets, Market Culture and Popular Protest in Eighteenth-Century Britain and Ireland* (Liverpool: Liverpool University Press, 1996), pp. 25–45.

Slack, P., "Social Policy and the Constraints of Government, 1547–58" in J. Loach and R. Tittler (eds.), *The Mid-Tudor Polity c. 1540–1560* (Basingstoke: Macmillan, 1980), pp. 94–115.

"Books of Orders: The Making of English Social Policy, 1577–1631," *Transactions of the Royal Historical Society* 5th ser., 30 (1980), 1–22.

Poverty and Policy in Tudor and Stuart England (London: Longman, 1988).

"Dearth and Social Policy in Early Modern England," *Social History of Medicine* 5 (1992), 1–17.

From Reformation to Improvement: Public Welfare in Early Modern England (Oxford: Clarendon Press, 1998).

Slavin, P., "The Great Bovine Pestilence and its Economic and Environmental Consequence in England and Wales 1318–50," *Econ. Hist. Rev.* 65 (2012), 1239–66.

Smith, R. M. (ed.), *Land, Kinship and Life-Cycle* (Cambridge: Cambridge University Press, 1984).

Smith, R. M., "Families and Their Land in an Area of Partible Inheritance: Redgrave, Suffolk" in R M Smith (ed.), *Land, Kinship and Life-Cycle* (Cambridge: Cambridge University Press, 1984), pp. 135–95.

"Human Resources" in G. Astill and A. Grant (eds.), *The Countryside of Medieval England* (Oxford: Blackwell, 1988), pp. 182–212.

"A Periodic Market and Its Impact on a Manorial Community: Botesday, Suffolk, and the Manor of Redgrave, 1280–1300" in Z. Razi and R. Smith (eds.), *Medieval Society and the Manor Court* (Oxford: Clarendon Press, 1996), pp. 450–81.

Starkey, D., "Which Age of Reform?" in C. Coleman and D. Starkey (eds.), *Revolution Reassessed: Revisions in the History of Tudor Government and Administration* (Oxford: Clarendon Press, 1986), pp. 13–27.

Stein, R., Boele, A., and Blockmans, W., "Whose Community? The Origin and Development of the Concept of Bonum Commune in Flanders, Brabant and Holland (twelfth-fifteenth century)" in E. Lecuppre-Desjardin and A-L. Van Bruaene (eds.), *De Boni Communi: The Discourse and Practice of the Common Good in the European City (13th – 16th c.)* (Turnhout: Brepols, 2010), pp. 149–69.

Stone, D., *Decision Making in English Agriculture* (New York: Oxford University Press, 2005).

"The Consumption of Field Crops in Late Medieval England" in C. M. Woolgar, D. Serjeantson and T. Waldron (eds.), *Food in Medieval England: Diet and Nutrition* (New York: Oxford University Press, 2006), pp. 11–26.

"The Black Death and Is Immediate Aftermath: Crisis and Change in the Fenland Economy, 1346–1353" in M. Bailey and S. Rigby (eds.), *Town and Countryside in the Age of the Black Death: Essays in Honour of John Hatcher* (Turnhout: Brepols, 2012), pp. 121–74.

Stevenson, J., *Popular Disturbances in England 1700–1870* (London: Longman, 1979).

Storey, R. L., *The End of the House of Lancaster* (New York: Stein and Day, 1967).

Sutherland, D. W., *Quo Warranto Proceedings in the Reign of Edward I 1278–1294* (Oxford: Clarendon Press, 1963).

Sweeney, D. (ed.), *Agriculture in the Middle Ages; Technology, Practice, and Representation* (Philadelphia: University of Pennsylvania Press, 1995).

Sweetinburgh (ed.), *Later Medieval Kent 1220–1540* (Woodbridge: Boydell, 2010).

Thirsk, J. (ed.), *The Agrarian History of England and Wales 1500–1640* (Cambridge: Cambridge University Press, 1967).

Thomas, A. H., "Notes on the History of the Leadenhall, A. D. 1195–1488," *London Topographical Record* 13 (1923), 1–22.

Thompson, E. P., "The Moral Economy of the English Crowd in the Eighteenth Century," *Past and Present* 50 (1971), 76–136.

"The Crime of Anonymity" in D. Hay, P. Linebaugh, J. G. Rule,
E. P. Thompson, and C. Winslow (eds.), *Albion's Fatal Tree: Crime
and Society in Eighteenth Century England* (New York: Pantheon, 1975),
pp. 255–308.

Vinogradoff, P. (ed.), *Oxford Studies in Social and Legal History* (Oxford:
Clarendon Press, 1921).

Wakelin, D., *Humanism, Reading, and English Literature 1430–1530* (Oxford:
Oxford University Press, 2013).

Walker, S., "Rumour, Sedition and Popular Protest in the Reign of Henry IV,"
Past and Present 166 (2000), 31–65.

Walter, J. and Wrightson, K., "Dearth and the Social Order in Early Modern
England," *Past and Present* 71 (1976), 22–42.

Walter, J., "Grain Riots and Popular Attitudes to the Law: Maldon and the Crisis
of 1629" in J. Brewer and J. Styles (eds.), *An Ungovernable People: The English
and their Law in the Seventeenth and Eighteenth Centuries* (New Brunswick:
Rutgers University Press, 1980), pp. 85–129.

"The Social Economy of Dearth" in J. Walter and R. Schofield (eds.), *Famine,
Disease and the Social Order in Early Modern Society* (Cambridge: Cambridge
University Press, 1989), pp. 75–128.

Walter, J. and Schofield, R. (eds.), *Famine, Disease and the Social Order in Early
Modern Society* (Cambridge: Cambridge University Press, 1989).

Welford, R., *History of Newcastle and Gateshead*, 2 vols. (London: Walter Scott,
1885).

Wernham, R. B., *Before the Armada: The Emergence of the English Nation
1485–1603* (New York: Harcourt Brace, 1966).

Willan, T. S., *The Inland Trade: Studies in English Internal Trade in the Sixteenth
and Seventeenth Centuries* (Manchester: Manchester University Press, 1976).

Willard, J. F., *Parliamentary Taxes on Personal Property, 1290 to 1334: a study in
Medieval English Financial Administration* (Cambridge Mass.: Harvard
University Press, 1934).

Williams, N. J., *The Maritime Trade of the East Anglian Ports 1550–1590* (Oxford:
Clarendon Press, 1988.

Wood, A., *The 1549 Rebellions and the Making of Early Modern England*
(Cambridge: Cambridge University Press, 2007).

Wood, D., *Medieval Economic Thought* (Cambridge: Cambridge University Press,
2002).

Woolgar, C. M., Serjeantson, D. and Waldron, T, (eds.), *Food in Medieval
England: Diet and Nutrition* (New York: Oxford University Press, 2006).

Wrigley, E. A. and Schofield, R. S., *The Population History of England 1541–1871:
A Reconstruction* (London: Arnold, 1981).

Zupko, R. E., *A Dictionary of English Weights and Measures from Anglo-Saxon
Times to the Nineteenth Century* (Madison: University of Wisconsin Press,
1968).

*French Weights and Measures before the Revolution: A Dictionary of Provincial and
Local Units* (Bloomington: Indiana University Press, 1978).

Index